Criminal-States and Criminal-Soldiers

The United States and her allies have found themselves plunged into 'a war over [humanity's] future social and political organization' with criminal challengers to the nation-state form. These new wars are currently being fought globally with al Qaeda; in Iraq with shifting coalitions of criminal gangs; insurgents; and Jihadi groups; and throughout the Americas with the Maras - the first group of 3rd GEN Gangs to emerge. More new wars are poised to develop, whilst the ongoing ones are far from over, and more attacks are expected upon the homelands of the US and her allies.

This cutting-edge book considers the theoretical and legal side of criminal-state and criminal-soldier emergence and growth; the criminal-states and criminal-soldiers themselves, with particular attention paid to al Qaeda, Hizballah, Mara Salvatrucha (MS 13), Caliphate and Mahdi concerns, Islamic Fundamentalist Use of Beheadings, Criminalisation of Russian State Security, Nuclear Materials Trafficking, and Outlaw Private Security Firms.

With the contributions from international experts, this book makes for critical reading for political scientists and criminal justice students and researchers, policymakers, and military and law enforcement practitioners.

This book was previously published as a special double issue of *Global Crime*.

Robert J Bunker is CEO of the Counter-OPFOR Corporation. He is an applied theorist and futurist with counter-terrorism, less-than-lethal & directed energy weapons, suicide bomber operations, and crime/war operational environment knowledge and expertise. He was the 2006-2007 Futurist in Residence (FIR), FBI Academy, Quantico, VA. He has served as a consultant to US law enforcement, military, governmental, and private industry groups and has lectured at the University level. He is the editor of a series of law enforcement booklets, *Non-State Threats and Future Wars* (Frank Cass, 2003) and *Networks, Terrorism and Global Insurgency* (Routledge, 2005). He can be reached at bunker@law-west.org

Cover Image: A masked Iraqi resistance fighter carries a police flak jacket and rocket propelled grenade launcher after a police station was attacked in Mosul November 11, 2004. Iraqi fighters then set police stations ablaze, captured weapons and brazenly roamed the streets of Mosul on Thursday as Iraq's third largest city appeared to be sliding out of control, residents said. The photographer was shot in the leg and wounded after the picture was taken. (11 Nov 2004 REUTERS/Namir Noor-eldeen).

Criminal-States and Criminal-Soldiers

Edited by
Robert J Bunker

Routledge
Taylor & Francis Group
LONDON AND NEW YORK

First published 2008 by Routledge
2 Park Square, Milton Park, Abingdon, Oxon, OX14 4RN

Simultaneously published in the USA and Canada
by Routledge
711 Third Avenue, New York, NY 10017, USA

Routledge is an imprint of the Taylor & Francis Group, an informa business

Typeset in Trebuchet 10/13pt by Knowledgeworks Global Ltd,
Chennai, India

British Library Cataloguing in Publication Data
A catalogue record for this book is available from the British Library

ISBN 10: 0-415-45765-3 (hbk)
ISBN 10: 0-415-46206-1 (pbk)

ISBN 13: 978-0-415-45765-1 (hbk)
ISBN 13: 978-0-415-46206-8 (pbk)

CONTENTS

Editor's Note

I would like to thank Dr. Mark Galeotti for supporting me on the guest editorship of this special double issue of the journal *Global Crime* and, in fact, for being an important contributor to this work and to the two earlier works leading up to it. Financial support by the Counter-OPFOR Program, National Law Enforcement and Corrections Technology Center-West for the initial phase of this undertaking is also appreciated with the understanding that this work in no way reflects any official policies of the NLECTC-West or the National Institute of Justice. Final funding for this project came from the Counter-OPFOR Corporation, of which I am a cofounder, which believes projects such as this one are too important to be allowed to wither and die. In fact, it is hoped that projects like this one will help to serve as a policy rallying point concerning the recognition that we are engaged in a 'war over social and political organization' with criminal-entities over the future fate of how humanity will live and organize itself.

The keen editing skills of my wife, mother of our four sons, and corporate partner, Pamela L. Bunker must also be acknowledged in making this work a success along with the many other contributors to this special issue. These practitioners and theorists, warriors and scholars are, by name, Dave Grossman, Robert Klitgaard, Matt Begert, Martin van Creveld, John Robb, Brian Levin, Mark T. Clark, Hakim Hazim, Youseff Aboul-Enein, Michael P. Arena, John P. Sullivan, Max G. Manwaring, Louise I. Shelley, Graham Hall Turbiville, Jr., Lisa J. Campbell, and Keith Weston. For those of you who have supported me on this and many other endeavors in defense of our great nation and her allies, a hearty thank you.

Dr. Robert J. Bunker
CEO
Counter-OPFOR Corporation
Los Angeles, CA
October 2006

Preface: Hunting Wolves*

Dave Grossman

> Honor never grows old, and honor rejoices the heart of age. It does so because honor is, finally, about defending those noble and worthy things that deserve defending, even if it comes at a high cost. In our time, that may mean social disapproval, public scorn, hardship, persecution, or as always, even death itself. The question remains: What is worth defending? What is worth dying for? What is worth living for?[1]

One Vietnam veteran, an old retired colonel, once said this to me: "Most of the people in our society are sheep. They are kind, gentle, productive creatures who can only hurt one another by accident." This is true. Remember, the murder rate is six per 100,000 per year, and the aggravated assault rate is four per 1,000 per year. What this means is that the vast majority of Americans are not inclined to hurt one another.

Some estimates say that two million Americans are victims of violent crimes every year, a tragic, staggering number, perhaps an all-time record rate of violent

This essay is partially derived from sections of the work, 'On Combat' (PPCT Research Publications, 2004), written by Lt. Col. Dave Grossman with Loren W. Christensen.

Dave Grossman, Lt. Col. US Army (Ret.), is an internationally recognized scholar, author, soldier, and speaker who is one of the world's foremost experts in the field of human aggression, violence, and violent crime. He was a sergeant, paratrooper, Army Ranger, West Point psychology professor and Professor of Military Science. In 1998, Lt. Col. Grossman retired with over 23 years' experience in leading U.S. soldiers worldwide. Since retirement he has devoted himself full time to teaching, writing, speaking and research. He has combined his experiences to become the founder of a new field of scientific endeavor which he has termed "killology." In this new field Lt. Col. Grossman has made revolutionary new contributions to our understanding of killing in war, the psychological costs of war, the root causes of the current "virus" of violent crime that is raging around the world, and the process of healing the victims of violence in war and peace. Lt. Col. Grossman is the author of On Killing which was nominated for a Pulitzer Prize. He co-authored Stop Teaching Our Kids to Kill: A Call to Action Against TV, Movie and Video Game Violence, which have received international acclaim. On Combat is Lt. Col. Grossman's most recent book and the long-awaited sequel to On Killing. Today he is the director of the Killology Research Group and is on the road almost 300 days a year training elite military and law enforcement organizations worldwide about the reality of combat.

1. William J. Bennett, 'In a lecture to the United States Naval Academy', November 24, 1997.

crime. But there are almost 300 million Americans, which means that the odds of being a victim of violent crime is considerably less than one in a hundred in any given year. Furthermore, since many violent crimes are committed by repeat offenders, the actual number of violent citizens is considerably less than two million.

Thus, there is a paradox and we must grasp both ends of the situation: We may well be in the most violent times in history but violence is still remarkably rare. This is because most citizens are kind, decent people who are not capable of hurting each other, except by accident or under extreme provocation. They are sheep.

I mean nothing negative by calling them sheep. To me it is like the pretty, blue robin's egg. Inside it is soft and gooey but someday it will grow into something wonderful. But the egg cannot survive without its hard blue shell. Police officers, soldiers, and other warriors are like that shell and, someday, the civilization they protect will grow into something wonderful. For now, though, they need warriors to protect them from the predators.

"Then there are the wolves," the old war veteran said, "and the wolves feed on the sheep without mercy." Do you believe there are wolves out there who will feed on the flock without mercy? You better believe it. There are evil men in this world and they are capable of evil deeds. The moment you forget that or pretend it is not so, you become a sheep. There is no safety in denial.

"Then there are sheepdogs," he went on, "and I'm a sheepdog. I live to protect the flock and confront the wolf." Or, as a sign in one California law enforcement agency put it, "We intimidate those who intimidate others."

If you have no capacity for violence then you are a healthy productive citizen: a sheep. If you have a capacity for violence and no empathy for your fellow citizens, then you are defined as an aggressive sociopath—a wolf. But what if you have a capacity for violence and a deep love for your fellow citizens? Then you are a sheepdog, a warrior, someone who is walking the hero's path. Someone who can walk into the heart of darkness, into the universal human phobia, and walk out unscathed.

The Gift of Aggression

> What goes on around you... compares little with what goes on inside you.[2]

Everyone has been given a gift in life. Some people have a gift for science and some have a flair for art. And warriors have been given the gift of aggression. They would no more misuse this gift than a doctor would misuse his healing arts but they yearn for the opportunity to use their gift to help others. These people, the

2. Ralph Waldo Emerson.

ones who have been blessed with the gift of aggression and a love for others, are our sheepdogs. These are our warriors.

One career police officer wrote to me about this after attending one of my Bulletproof Mind training sessions:

> I want to say thank you for finally shedding some light on why it is that I can do what I do. I always knew why I did it. I love my [citizens], even the bad ones, and had a talent that I could return to my community. I just couldn't put my finger on why I could wade through the chaos, the gore, the sadness, if given a chance try to make it all better, and walk right out the other side.

Let me expand on the old soldier's excellent model of the sheep, wolves, and sheepdogs. We know that the sheep live in denial; that is what makes them sheep. They do not want to believe that there is evil in the world. They can accept the fact that fires can happen, which is why they want fire extinguishers, fire sprinklers, fire alarms and fire exits throughout their kids' schools. But many of them are outraged at the idea of putting an armed police officer in their kid's school. Our children are dozens of times more likely to be killed, and *thousands* of times more likely to be seriously injured, by school violence than by school fires but the sheep's only response to the possibility of violence is denial. The idea of someone coming to kill or harm their children is just *too hard*, so they choose the path of denial.

The sheep generally do not like the sheepdog. He looks a lot like the wolf. He has fangs and the capacity for violence. The difference, though, is that the sheepdog must not, cannot and will not *ever* harm the sheep. Any sheepdog who intentionally harms the lowliest little lamb *will* be punished and removed because, in fact, they have gone mad and turned into a wolf. The world cannot work any other way, at least not in a representative democracy or a republic such as ours.

Still, the sheepdog disturbs the sheep. He is a constant reminder that there are wolves in the land. They would prefer that he didn't tell them where to go, or give them traffic tickets, or stand at the ready in our airports in camouflage fatigues holding an M-16. The sheep would much rather have the sheepdog cash in his fangs, spray paint himself white, and go "Baa."

Until the wolf shows up. Then the entire flock tries desperately to hide behind one lonely sheepdog. As Kipling said in his poem about "Tommy" the British soldier:

> While it's Tommy this, an' Tommy that, a' "Tommy, fall be'ind,"
> But it's "Please to walk in front, sir," when there's trouble in the wind,
> There's trouble in the wind, my boys, there's trouble in the wind,
> O it's "Please to walk in front, sir," when there's trouble in the wind.[3]

The students, the victims, at Columbine High School were big, tough high school students and, under ordinary circumstances, they would not have had the time of day for a police officer. They were not bad kids; they just had nothing to say to a cop. When the school was under attack, however, and SWAT teams were clearing

3. Kipling, R. (1892) 'Tommy', *Barrack-Room Ballads.*

the rooms and hallways, the officers had to physically peel those clinging, sobbing kids off of them. *This* is how the little lambs feel about their sheepdog when the wolf is at the door. Look at what happened after September 11, 2001, when the wolf pounded hard on the door. Remember how America, more than ever before, felt differently about their law enforcement officers and military personnel? Remember how many times you heard the word *hero*?

Understand that there is nothing morally superior about being a sheepdog; it is just what you choose and are called to be. Also understand that a sheepdog is a funny critter: He is always sniffing around out on the perimeter, checking the breeze, barking at things that go bump in the night, and yearning for a righteous battle. That is, the young sheepdogs yearn for a righteous battle. The old sheepdogs are a little older and wiser but they move to the sound of the guns when needed right along with the young ones.

Here is how the sheep and the sheepdog think differently. The sheep pretend the wolf will never come, but the sheepdog lives for that day. After the attacks on September 11, 2001, most of the sheep, that is, most citizens in America said, "Thank God I wasn't on one of those planes." The sheepdogs, the warriors, said, "Dear God, I wish I could have been on one of those planes. Maybe I could have made a difference." When you are truly transformed into a warrior and have truly invested yourself into warriorhood, you *want* to be there. You *want* to be able to make a difference.

While there is nothing morally superior about the sheepdog, the warrior, he *does* have one real advantage. Only one. *He* is able to survive and thrive in an environment that destroys 98 percent of the population.

There was research conducted a few years ago with individuals convicted of violent crimes. These cons were in prison for serious, predatory acts of violence: assaults, murders, and killing law enforcement officers. The vast majority said that they specifically targeted victims by body language: slumped walk, passive behavior, and lack of awareness. They chose their victims like big cats do in Africa when they select the one out of the herd that is least able to protect itself.

However, when there were cues given by potential victims that indicated they would not go easily, the cons said that they would walk away. If the cons sensed that the target was a "counter-predator," that is, a sheepdog, they would leave him alone unless there was no other choice but to engage.

One police officer told me that he rode a commuter train to work each day. One day, as was his usual, he was standing in the crowded car, dressed in blue jeans, T-shirt and jacket, holding onto a pole and reading a paperback. At one of the stops, two street toughs boarded, shouting and cursing and doing every obnoxious thing possible to intimidate the other riders. The officer continued to read his book, though he kept a watchful eye on the two punks as they strolled along the aisle making comments to female passengers, and banging shoulders with men as they passed.

As they approached the officer, he lowered his novel and made eye contact with them. "You got a problem, man?" one of the IQ-challenged punks asked.

"You think you're tough, or somethin'?" the other asked, obviously offended that this one was not shirking away from them.

"As a matter of fact, I am tough," the officer said, calmly and with a steady gaze.

The two looked at him for a long moment and then, without saying a word, turned and moved back down the aisle to continue their taunting of the other passengers, the sheep.

Some people may be destined to be sheep and others might be genetically primed to be wolves or sheepdogs. But I believe that most people can choose which one they want to be, and I'm proud to say that more and more Americans are choosing to become sheepdogs.

Seven months after the attack on September 11, 2001, Todd Beamer was honored in his hometown of Cranbury, New Jersey. Todd, as you recall, was the man on Flight 93 over Pennsylvania who called on his cell phone to alert an operator from United Airlines about the hijacking. When he learned of the other three passenger planes that had been used as weapons, Todd dropped his phone and uttered the words, "Let's roll," which authorities believe was a signal to the other passengers to confront the terrorist hijackers. In one hour, a transformation occurred among the passengers—athletes, business people, and parents—from sheep to sheepdogs and together they fought the wolves, ultimately saving an unknown number of lives on the ground.

> "Do you have any idea how hard it would be to live with yourself after that?"

> There is no safety for honest men except by believing all possible evil of evil men.[4]

Here is the point I like to emphasize, especially to the thousands of police officers and soldiers I speak to each year. In nature, the sheep, real sheep, are born as sheep. Sheepdogs are born that way and so are wolves. They didn't have a choice. But you are not a critter. As a human being, you can be whatever you want to be. It is a conscious, moral decision.

If you want to be a sheep, then you can be a sheep and that is okay but you must understand the price you pay. When the wolf comes, you and your loved ones are going to *die* if there is not a sheepdog there to protect you. If you want to be a wolf, you can be one, but the sheepdogs are going to hunt you down and you will never have rest, safety, trust or love. But if you want to be a sheepdog and walk the warrior's path, then you must make a conscious and moral decision every day to dedicate, equip, and prepare yourself to thrive in that toxic, corrosive moment when the wolf comes knocking at the door.

For example, many officers carry their weapons in church. They are well concealed in ankle holsters, shoulder holsters, or inside-the-belt holsters tucked into the small of their backs. Anytime you go to some form of religious service, there is a very good chance that a police officer in your congregation is carrying.

4. Burke, E. (1791) *Reflections on the Revolution in France.*

You will never know if there is such an individual in your place of worship until the wolf appears to slaughter you and your loved ones.

I was training a group of police officers in Texas and, during the break, one officer asked his friend if he carried his weapon in church. The other cop replied, "I will *never* be caught without my gun in church." I asked why he felt so strongly about this, and he told me about a police officer he knew who was at a church massacre in Ft. Worth, Texas, in 1999. In that incident, a mentally deranged individual came into the church and opened fire, gunning down 14 people. He said that officer believed he could have saved every life that day if he had been carrying his gun. His own son was shot and all he could do was throw himself on the boy's body and wait to die. That cop looked me in the eye and said, "Do you have any idea how hard it would be to live with yourself after that?"

Some individuals would be horrified if they knew this police officer was carrying a weapon in church. They might call him paranoid and would probably scorn him. Yet these same individuals would be enraged and would call for "heads to roll" if they found out that the airbags in their cars were defective or that the fire extinguisher and fire sprinklers in their kids' school did not work. They can accept the fact that fires and traffic accidents can happen and that there must be safeguards against them. Their only response to the wolf, though, is denial, and all too often their response to the sheepdog is scorn and disdain. But the sheepdog quietly asks himself, *"Do you have any idea* how *hard* it would be to live with yourself if your loved ones were attacked and killed, and you had to stand there helplessly because you were unprepared for that day?"

The warrior must cleanse denial from his thinking. Coach Bob Lindsey, a renowned law enforcement trainer, says that warriors must practice "when/then" thinking, not "if/then." Instead of saying, "If it happens then I will take action," the warrior says, "*When* it happens then I *will* be ready."

It is denial that turns people into sheep. Sheep are psychologically destroyed by combat because their only defense is denial, which is counterproductive and destructive, resulting in fear, helplessness, and horror when the wolf shows up.

Denial kills you twice. It kills you once, at your moment of truth when you are not physically prepared: You didn't bring your gun; you didn't train. Your only defense was wishful thinking. Hope is *not* a strategy. Denial kills you a second time because even if you *do* physically survive, you are psychologically shattered by fear, helplessness, horror, and shame at your moment of truth.

Chuck Yeager, the famous test pilot and first man to fly faster than the speed of sound, says that he *knew* he could die. There was no denial for him. He did not allow himself the luxury of denial. This acceptance of reality *can* cause fear, but it is a healthy, *controlled* fear that will keep you alive:

> I was always afraid of dying. Always. It was my fear that made me learn everything I could about my airplane and my emergency equipment, and kept me flying respectful of my machine and always alert in the cockpit.[5]

5. Yeager, C. & Janos, L. (1985) *Chuck Yeager, An Autobiography*, Bantam Books, New York.

Gavin de Becker puts it like this in *Fear Less,* his superb post-9/11 book, which should be required reading for anyone trying to come to terms with our current world situation:

> ...denial can be seductive, but it has an insidious side effect. For all the peace of mind deniers think they get by saying it isn't so, the fall they take when faced with new violence is all the more unsettling. Denial is a save-now-pay-later scheme, a contract written entirely in small print, for in the long run, the denying person knows the truth on some level.[6]

And so the warrior must strive to confront denial in all aspects of his life and prepare himself for the day when evil comes.

If you are a warrior who is legally authorized to carry a weapon and you step outside without that weapon, then you become a sheep, pretending that the bad man will not come today. No one can be "on" 24/7 for a lifetime. Everyone needs down time. But *if* you are authorized to carry a weapon and you walk outside without it, just take a deep breath, and say this to yourself... "Baa."

This business of being a sheep or a sheepdog is not a yes-no dichotomy. It is not an all-or-nothing, either-or choice. It is a matter of degrees, a continuum. On one end is an abject, head-in-the-grass, sheep and on the other end is the ultimate warrior. Few people exist completely on one end or the other. Most of us live somewhere in between. Since 9/11 almost everyone in America took a step up that continuum, away from denial. The sheep took a few steps toward accepting and appreciating their warriors and the warriors started taking their job more seriously. The degree to which you move up that continuum, away from sheephood and denial, is the degree to which you *and* your loved ones will survive, physically *and* psychologically, at your moment of truth.

Hunting Wolves

The reality of the post-Cold War era is that, while the Soviet Union and Warsaw Pact are now gone, new threats have emerged to threaten our nation. These threats are developing in an operational environment found in many places of the world, characterized by the blurring of crime and war. This operational environment is also emerging in small enclaves within major American and European cities. The recent rioting in France by gang members, extremists, and disenfranchised residents is but one example of this trend.

This blurring of crime and war results in a capability gap for our sheepdogs, our anti-predators, in their solemn mission of protecting our citizens from the pre-existing and new breeds of wolves now developing. In response to this, today the peacekeepers and the peace officers are moving toward each other. Around the world, warriors in blue (police and other peace officers) and warriors in green

6. de Becker, G. (2002) *Fear Less: Real Truth About Risk, Safety, and Security in a Time of Terrorism*, Little, Brown, New York.

(soldiers, marines and other peacekeepers) find themselves facing the same kinds of missions.

Increasingly, the police must face organized opponents armed with assault rifles and bombs. Indeed, they may very well face deliberate acts of war from international terrorists. In response, police have begun to carry assault rifles and call upon Special Weapons and Tactics (SWAT) teams.

Meanwhile, the military is finding that the use of artillery and air strikes in peacekeeping and counterterrorism missions can be counterproductive and that it can be more effective to use small teams on a "beat" or checkpoint. In Bosnia and New York, Iraq and Los Angeles, and Afghanistan and Littleton, Colorado, the police are becoming more like the military in equipment, structure, and tactics, while the military is becoming more like the police in equipment, mission, and tactics.

What of these wolves that we now face? Yes, indeed the older predators still exist and will not go away. Petty criminals, street thugs, and serial murderers will remain. It is the new and emerging wolves, however, that represent the even greater threat. These predators belong to terrorist and insurgent groups, drug cartels, 3rd generation street gangs, warlords, pirate groups, and criminal-states. While individual rape, murder, and other atrocities may be on their minds, as tragically experienced by the young schoolgirls at Beslan, we now face predators happily willing to slaughter the population of entire cities, given the means.

The warriors, scholars, and warrior-scholars writing in this work on "Criminal-States and Criminal-Soldiers" have much to say on this topic. In many cases, not only do they succinctly discuss and analyze the threats that we face, but also provide suggestions and solutions on how to counter them.

Such thinking becomes more critical by the day. Already our older warriors, and the younger ones that have taken the oath since 9/11, are being increasingly called upon to hunt down this new breed of wolves on American streets and overseas. Many of these criminal-soldiers will be destroyed like rabid dogs with a bullet straight to the brain—the preferred method to take down a suicide bomber. Others, like Zacarias Moussaoui (the Al Qaeda terrorist), will be locked away in a solitary cell for 23 hours a day, with little to no human interaction and no hope of ever achieving the twisted dreams of martyrdom.

The specific demise of these criminal-soldiers matters little in the end to us. What does matter is that the sheep and their precious lambs, our beloved masses of law abiding citizens and their children, are not harmed in the process of hunting down the new and still evolving form of predator known as the criminal-soldier.

Introduction: Subverting Corruption

Robert Klitgaard

The process of corruption—both physical and moral—is a dominant theme in this work on "Criminal-States and Criminal-Soldiers" edited by Robert J. Bunker. Concerns over states and corruption have a long legacy. Four decades ago, the political scientist Colin Leys asked "what is the problem about corruption?"[1] Following a line that might remind one of the sociologist Robert Merton, or the political philosopher Niccolò Machiavelli, Leys argued that corruption has its functions, even its benefits. Under awful conditions, bribery and its close relatives may be socially and not just privately beneficial. The political scientist Samuel Huntington chimed in: "In terms of economic growth the only thing worse than a society with a rigid, overcentralized, dishonest bureaucracy is one with a rigid, overcentralized, honest bureaucracy."[2]

These scholars had a point. But nowadays, it is easier for us, sensitized by both passionate denunciations and econometric estimates, to reel off some of the costs. Systemic corruption distorts incentives, undermines institutions, and redistributes wealth and power to the undeserving. When corruption undermines property rights, the rule of law, incentives to invest, then economic and political development are crippled. In extreme cases, state institutions may become vulnerable to criminalization or capture by illegitimate groups seeking to expand their influence

Robert Klitgaard is the President of Claremont Graduate University, where he is also a University Professor. He formerly was a professor at Harvard, Yale, the University of Natal, and the University of Karachi, and has been on the faculty of the World Economic Forum and the World Bank Institute. His eight books include High-Performance Government: Structure, Leadership, Incentives (edited with Paul Light, RAND, 2005) and Corrupt Cities (with Ronald MacLean-Abaroa and H. Lindsey Parris, ICS Press and World Bank Institute, 2000).

1. Leys, C. (1965) 'What is the Problem about Corruption?', *The Journal of Modern African Studies*, vol. 3, no. 2, pp. 215–230.
2. Huntington, S. P. (1968) *Political Order in Changing Societies*, Yale University Press, New Haven.

and power. Even Huntington pointed out that "a society in which corruption is already pervasive, however, is unlikely to be improved by more corruption."[3]

Since Huntington wrote those words in 1968, the fight against corruption has progressed. In the 1990s we experienced a first stage of anticorruption efforts, where consciousness is raised about the existence and harms of corruption. In many countries, such as Indonesia, India, and Colombia, there seems to be a sea change in public opinion, as elections are increasingly fought in terms of what to do about corruption.

The second stage considers anticorruption measures, in effect adding systems analysis to consciousness raising. Many civil service reforms are moving beyond "capacity building" to emphasize information, incentives, and competition. Research is moving beyond perceptions of corruption to studies of where in government and markets the vulnerabilities to corruption lie.

I believe the next phase, a third stage in the fight against corruption, will address what to do when corruption has become systematic. What can be done if consciousness raising and prevention have failed, if corruption has become the norm, and if political will cannot be counted on? In other words, how can systemic corruption be subverted?

"Normal" to Systemic Corruption

Consider a real example, stripped down and renamed to protect its identity. PHS is the part of a country's health ministry that distributes pharmaceuticals and health services to the poor. There are eligibility cards and subsidies, supply chains and special health posts, and lots of contracting and procurement. Corruption has always existed in PHS. But suddenly, things get worse.

The country's president is involved in a scandal unrelated to PHS. He may be impeached. Parliament forms a committee to investigate. The president and his party try to influence the committee. A relative of the committee chairman is named the director of PHS. Other new appointments in PHS are from the same region as the committee chairman.

Procurement becomes deeply corrupted. Competitive bidding, once the norm in 90 percent of procurement contracts, is used in less than half. The other half are declared "emergencies" and are let without competition through PHS's regional offices. In the words of one official, "Many of these people decide which firms will get the contract and then both manage the project and are responsible for auditing it."[4]

Even when procurement is competitive, abuses spread. Contract specifications are tailored to enhance the chances of favored suppliers. Cost overruns are approved in exchange for bribes.

3. Huntington, *op. cit*.
4. Citation not provided because of the sensitivity of this real world example.

Politicization undercuts external controls. The president's party installs a compliant individual as the new director of the supreme audit agency. The attorney general, the president's old friend, is unwilling to pursue sensitive cases.

As the corruption in PHS grows, organizational chaos ensues. The manual of procedures is abandoned. Eligibility cards are allocated through extortion and fraud. Theft becomes widespread, and medicines disappear. Some files disappear, then many more, so that, even if investigations or audits are started, there are often no records. No one is sure if contracts have been let or if funds are available. As a result, some contractors are not paid. Delays and further rounds of corruption follow. Eventually, suppliers charge higher prices or retire from this market, leading to less competition and further opportunities for corruption and inefficiency. An honest auditor finds a PHS warehouse full of televisions, champagne glasses, and so forth.

PHS free-falls into financial collapse. Health care for the poor disintegrates.

Action in Normal Circumstances

What can be done? At the second stage of fighting corruption, a variety of measures can be taken to prevent corruption.

- *Agents* (that is, public officials) are selected on the basis of competence and honesty.
- *Incentives* are structured to reward projects and purchases with excellent results. Penalties are exacted from those who give or receive bribes.
- A variety of mechanisms are used to *gather information* about the possibilities of corrupt behavior at each stage of its development—information ranging from bidding patterns to comparative costs to the lifestyles of the individuals involved.
- *Competition* is encouraged.
- Official *discretion* is circumscribed—for example, by conducting objective studies of, and specifying clear criteria for, government procurement and other administrative practices.
- The *moral* costs of corrupt behavior are sometimes emphasized through codes of conduct, publicity campaigns, and the encouragement of reputations for probity by the firms involved.

But because corruption has become systemic, PHS has suffered breakdowns in all these areas.

- Suddenly, key *agents* are selected through a political process whose purpose is to give them access to public wealth. Their *incentives* are to make money for their political masters, and these agents are protected by those masters and by the president. Less dramatically, for most officials in PHS, pay has fallen far below the private sector, leading to a loss of qualified personnel. Careers in PHS are not advanced through a record of economical purchases and successful projects. Contracting firms are not punished for poor results.

There are few official incentives to discover and prosecute corruption and, increasingly, there are strong political pressures not to do so. The penalties for corruption are weak—ranging from black marks in the personal record to suspension—and are applied only rarely.

- The many possible mechanisms used to *gather information* about performance and about possible corruption are now underemployed or abandoned. Administrative chaos has gutted record keeping and accounting, so that information useful for investigating and controlling corruption is often missing.
- *Competition* has been undercut in many ways. Instead of using a well-organized process for contracting based on technical criteria to judge bids and firms, it is decentralized and is subject to monopoly power *plus* discretion *minus* accountability.
- Some political appointees have the *discretion* to let contracts without competition or technical reviews.
- The social sanction on being corrupt diminishes as systemic corruption takes hold. Honest firms find it harder to do honest business. Reputation matters less and less, and, indeed, phantom firms are created for corrupt purposes.

When systems are so thoroughly corrupted, there may be little, if any, political will to reform them. Calling for better agents, improved incentives, better information, more competition, less official discretion, and higher economic and social costs is well and good. But who is going to listen? Who is going to act? The usual anticorruption remedies may not work. Now what?

Analogy of Disease

Consider an imperfect but suggestive analogy. Corruption is like HIV/AIDS. It is a problem in every country, and especially prevalent and damaging in a few—the interested reader need only consult the bottom of the list of corrupt countries created every year by Transparency International. The social consequences are at many levels, including economic. Finally, the contagious disease is difficult to combat, and it may adapt itself, much like an insurgent group or narco-cartel, to efforts to defeat it.

What might be called the first stage of reacting to either corruption or HIV/AIDS is a raising of consciousness. In a number of books—such as *Los Fabricantes de Miseria* by Plinio Apuleyo Mendoza, Carlos Alberto Montaner, and Alvaro Vargas Llosa—corruption is attributed to bad attitudes regarding authority and probity.[5] The political culture is a pernicious sort of "privatization of the State," the informal and illicit private use of government by the political class and its allies.

The cure for corruption? Moral renovation, cultural change, an elevation of consciousness. (Incidentally, this is where Colin Leys sought a remedy forty

5. Barcelona: Plaza, 1999.

years ago. The "line of escape," he wrote, is "a nucleus of 'puritans' applying pressure for a code of ethics.")[6] The problem with this advice is practical. We know little about how to engineer a moral renovation so we must also work at other levels.

A second stage of reacting to HIV/AIDS or corruption emphasizes prevention: keep healthy bodies free of contagion. The anticorruption measures described above, from selecting better agents to raising the economic and social costs of corruption, are derived from this approach.

Analyzing and Attacking Corrupt Systems

But what if corruption has already become embedded? When prevention has failed, a third stage of fighting corruption is also needed, one that goes after the disease. New questions arise, as Table 1 suggests.

In addition to strengthening government institutions, the task is now to weaken corrupt institutions. This is difficult but not impossible. "To engage in corruption," law professor Philip Heymann notes, "a government official and a private party have to identify each other as potential corrupt partners, and find a way to reach an agreement, and then deliver what each has promised without being detected. Each of these steps can be extremely difficult, for in each there are vulnerabilities to detection."[7]

The corrupt system itself should be analyzed from beginning to end. For example, how are corrupt buyers and sellers found and matched? How do they make and enforce their implicit contracts? What footprints do their illicit transaction create, and what steps do they take to cover them up?

Then, countermeasures should be designed. For example, how might undercover agents be introduced to the system in order to disrupt it? Who are the disaffected in the corrupt system, and how may they be induced to defect? How might corrupt contracts be exposed, undercut, or destabilized? How might disinformation be injected into the corrupt system to create false impressions, schisms, distrust, and risk?

With these questions in mind, let us return to the case of PHS. How might the corrupt coalition of the president, the congressional committee, the contractors, the political appointees, and PHS be subverted? Here are a few ideas.

- Disseminate information that the corrupt system would like to keep hidden. For example, our research in PHS easily documented the switch from 90 percent competitive bidding to 50 percent. The "emergency" contracts had been recorded, and it could readily be shown that most had been awarded to cronies of political appointees. Inserting this information into the public

6. Leys, *op. cit.*
7. Heymann, P. (1995) 'Dealing with Corruption: The United States as an Example', unpublished paper, Harvard Law School, Cambridge.

Table 1 Stages two and three in the fight against corruption

	Stage two: fighting "ordinary" corruption	*Stage three: fighting systemic corruption*
Key metaphor	Controlling corruption	Subverting corruption
Medical analogy	Strengthen the body to prevent the disease from taking hold. Examples: exercise, nutrition, lifestyle	Attack the disease itself. Examples: antibiotics, chemotheraphy, surgery
Use analysis to find out	Where healthy systems are vulnerable and how to strengthen them	Where organized corruption is itself vulnerable and how to weaken it
Some key analytical questions	How are agents selected? How is the principal-agent-client relationship structured? What are the incentives? How can discretion be clarified and circumscribed? How can accountability be enhanced? How can the moral costs of corruption be increased?	How are corrupt deals made and kept secret? How are corrupt goods and services delivered? How are members recruited and disciplined? What "foot-prints" are there from corrupt activities? How can risks and penalties be created or enhanced? How can corrupt activities be carried out with impunity, and where are they vulnerable?
Draw inspiration from	Best practices in business management; public health programs	Best practices in fighting organized crime, pathology and medicine
Key functions in the fight against corruption	Audit, systems design, incentive and personnel systems, control, citizen oversight	All of these, *plus* undercover agents, infiltrators, turncoats and key witnesses, "dirty tricks"
Key actors in the fight against corruption	People who run the system. The "principal" (metaphorically, the people in practice, the people in charge)	People who can influence and, if necessary, subvert the corrupt system. Citizens, professional associations, the press, business groups, some government agencies or levels of government

dialogue will not automatically lead to change. But exposure creates new tensions for the corrupt system and may generate antibodies.

- Some corrupt appointees have grown rich. Purchases of houses and cars and other forms of conspicuous consumption can be documented and then shared with the press. In the 1970s, for example, a courageous leader of the Philippines' Bureau of Internal Revenue used such measures to subvert a virulent form of organized corruption.
- The prices of various goods and services can be compared with prices before the erosion of PHS, with prices in the private sector, and with prices in neighboring countries. All these comparisons reveal PHS's current corruption. They can provide a focal point for public outrage and the monitoring of improvements. A similar idea—the benchmarking of the prices of rural works—was successfully applied during the 1980s to combat corruption in Bolivia's Social Emergency Fund; and Argentina recently undermined corruption through national dissemination of local prices of school lunches and of hospital supplies.
- One can give information to, and then work with, the firms that could potentially compete for PHS's business, as well as with associations of industry leaders, auditors, and lawyers. Pressure points can thereby be found and exploited to push for change.
- Organized extortion for PHS eligibility cards can be undermined by using undercover agents, confidential exit interviews, and video cameras.
- In both Italy and New York, successful efforts against organized crime have subverted the Mafia's culture of secrecy. Crucial have been such measures as using undercover agents, planting electronic surveillance devices, and inducing key insiders to become state witnesses. Also, misinformation and "dirty tricks" have been used to create distrust among the Mafiosi—for example, planting false rumors that someone was a turncoat or catalyzing animosity among various factions. Could similar steps be imagined in PHS or, more broadly, in the national government?

These are interesting possibilities—but who might undertake them? The list of potential actors is long: citizens' groups, including Transparency International; the press; religious groups; business groups, which realize that, viewed as a whole, business loses from systemic corruption; and international organizations. Sometimes a congressional committee can be the catalyst, at other times a supreme audit authority or a ministry of justice or a police department. Even within a corrupted agency, the infection is never complete, and given the opportunity, people ranging from secretaries to technicians to long-term civil servants may be valuable sources of information about exactly how the corrupt system functions.

Ideally, third-stage anticorruption efforts will bring together all of these actors in informal and formal networks to subvert systemic corruption and aid in the suppression of the criminalization of public and private institutions.

Where is Systemic Corruption Most Severe?

Systemic corruption can worsen as various forms of central government control break down or recede. One example is when a state collapses in the face of unrest or postcommunist trauma, being replaced in part by organized crime and corruption. Another example—less dramatic but perhaps more widespread—is what happens when federal functions devolve upon localities and municipalities. In extreme cases, the result can be post-modern form of feudalism/warlordism and state failure.

In our book, *Corrupt Cities,*[8] Ronald MacLean-Abaroa, Lindsey Parris, and I note that around the world, local governments are susceptible to systemic corruption. Compared with national governments, municipal administrative systems are usually weaker. Pay scales for professionals are lower, leading on average to lower-quality personnel. The risks of co-optation by élites or populists are higher. In the hands of unscrupulous opportunists or idealists unable to manage, city governments can easily become the sites of petty tyrannies, systemic corruption, or both.

Even in rich countries, the threats are real. The substance and style of city management are changing in ways that promise better governance but simultaneously offer more opportunities for corruption. "Many of the recent changes in local government," the Audit Commission of the United Kingdom asserts, "have been away from centralized controls and tight financial regimes and have increased the risks of fraud and corruption occurring."[9] According to one estimate, provincial governments in Japan have 3 times more officials than the national government but produce 15 times the reported number of corruption cases and 4 times the number of arrested officials. In New York City, the cost of past corruption in school construction alone is measured in the hundreds of millions of dollars. Public-private partnerships, correctly considered the wave of the future, can mutate into systemic corruption.

No wonder local corruption is a topic of increasing concern. The Chilean policy analyst Claudio Orrego points out that "all the objectives that have been established for the reform of the municipal sector (increasing their legitimacy and democratization, increasing the efficiency and effectiveness of their services, and increasing citizen participation), can be summarized as part of this broader goal: strengthening accountability."[10]

When corruption does become systemic, as it did in PHS, the usual anticorruption measures are insufficient. Not obsolete, to be sure: there will always be a need to

8. Klitgaard, R., MacLean-Abaroa, R. & Lindsey Parris, Jr., H. (2000) *Corrupt Cities: A PracticalGuide to Cure and* Prevention, ICS Press and World Bank Institute, Oakland.

9. Audit Commission (1993) *Protecting the Public Purse, Probity in the Public Sector: Combating Fraud and Corruption in Local Government*, HMSO, London, p. 3.

10. Orrego, C. (1995) 'Citizen Participation and the Strengthening of Accountability in Chile's Municipal Governments', Unpublished manuscript, April, p. 5.

raise consciousness about corruption's costs and to make the institutions of state and market less vulnerable to corruption. But we also need new thinking about new modes of action by new sorts of actors that can facilitate joint efforts to subvert corruption. This will allow us to counter one of the processes that is resulting in the criminalization of private and public institutions of states on a global level.

Overview: Defending Against Enemies of the State

Robert J. Bunker & Matt Begert

> I, _____, do solemnly swear (or affirm) that I will support and defend the Constitution of the United States against all enemies, foreign and domestic; that I will bear true faith and allegiance to the same; and that I will obey the orders of the President of the United States and the orders of the officers appointed over me, according to regulations and the Uniform Code of Military Justice. So help me God.
>
> Oath of Enlistment[1]

Robert J. Bunker, Ph.D., is CEO of the Counter-OPFOR Corporation. He has been a member of the Los Angeles County Terrorism Early Warning Group since 1996 and has counter-terrorism operational planning experience. He is a past Counter-OPFOR consultant, National Law Enforcement and Corrections Technology Center-West (NLECTC-West), a program of the National Institute of Justice (NIJ). He is also a former Adjunct Professor, National Security Studies Program, California State University San Bernardino; past Fellow, Institute of Land Warfare, Association of the United States Army; and former Professor, Unconventional Warfare, American Military University, Manassas Park, Virginia. Professional LE related training includes Intelligence Support to Force Protection, Anti-Terrorism Course & Force Protection Operations Course, and Mirror Image (Jihadi) Course. Dr. Bunker has provided 150 briefings and presentations on terrorism, future warfare & conflict, suicide bombers, less lethal weapons and directed energy weapons. He has written over 100 essays in publications such as *The Police Chief*, *The Tactical Edge*, *California Journal of Law Enforcement*, *Parameters*, *Military Review*, *Marine Corps Gazette*, *Special Warfare*, *Airpower Journal*, *Naval Institute Proceedings*, and numerous military encyclopedias. He is the editor of a series of law enforcement booklets, *Non-State Threats and Future Wars* (Frank Cass: 2003), and *Networks, Terrorism and Global Insurgency* (Routledge: 2005). **Matt Begert** is currently assigned as the operations officer of the Los Angeles based National Law Enforcement and Corrections Technology Center-West, which is a grant-funded field activity of the National Institute of Justice, Department of Justice. His focus is the identification of emerging threats to public safety, concept development and implementation of countermeasures to those threats, and the technical and operational development of less lethal, non-lethal, or medium force option technology as well as general operational support to public safety agencies. He is an officer in the Marine Corps, not currently serving, with experience in a variety of ground and aviation assignments. Operational ground assignments include being commander of a recruit training company and team leader of a Marine element assigned to infantry units of the US Army, the Republic of Korea Marine Corps, the Royal Thai Marine Corps and to the 5th Brigade, Special Forces, Republic of Korea Army. Aviation assignments include flying experience with a Marine Attack Squadron aboard the carrier USS Ranger and as an instructor in a Navy aircrew training/replacement squadron. He has degrees in anthropology and journalism from the University of Kansas and has completed the Naval War College Senior Officers Course. His personal awards include the Defense Superior Service Medal, the Air Medal with Combat "V", the Army Commendation Medal, the Navy Commendation Medal and the Sea Service Deployment Ribbon with 4 stars. He was born and raised on a farm in Kansas and is the son of a Marine who served in World War II.

1. US Army Center for Military History (n.d.) 'Oath of Enlistment' [online]. Available at: www.army.mil/cmh-pg/.

Sworn military and law enforcement personnel take oaths of allegiance to defend the Constitution and 'to protect and to serve' the people of their communities. These solemn duties are not taken lightly and are integral to the functioning of a free and democratic nation based on the rule of law. The emergence of the criminal-soldier and the organizations created by this enemy of the people, such as criminal-states and virtual networks, will present many new challenges for and burdens on our nation's defenders.

Ultimately, we are facing a 'war over [humanity's] social and political organization'. The nation-state's place as the dominant human organizational form will be decided as an outcome of this struggle against varied and multiple opponents.[2] Even more importantly, accepted norms and modes of behavior – the very values guiding how humans live and raise their families – represent the stakes on the table. The potentials of a world in which criminal forms of behavior dominate should, at the very least, be unsettling. Such a world would see its values conceivably derived from norms based on slave holding, illicit drug use, sexual activity with minors and their exploitation in prostitution, torture and beheadings, the farming of humans for body parts, the killing of innocents for political gain and personal gratification (as sport), and the desecration of the dead. Concepts such as due process, right to a jury trial, individual privacy concerns, the right to vote, women's rights to literacy, and self-determination, and the personal freedoms that so many Americans take for granted (life, liberty and the pursuit of happiness) do not even exist. In many failed regions, lawless zones, and criminal enclaves, this world – what could be considered an age of 'Post-Modern Barbarism' or the historical equivalent of a 'Dark Renaissance' (imagine the domination of Europe by the forces of the Spanish Inquisition) – has already come about and is spreading.

One of the biggest challenges our nation's protectors will face is how to contend with the morphing of criminals into criminal-soldiers within the borders of the United States. The emergence of such indigenous 'enemies of the state' would undoubtedly pose a host of legal and societal issues for the American public and its government.[3] This trend has already begun with Jihadi groups in Western Europe and Canada. A recent case in Florida with a disrupted plot to blow up the Sears Tower in Chicago and sporadic cases in other states may signal that this trend is well underway domestically.[4]

2. Or that of its legitimate successor form – possibly the Market-State articulated by Phillip Bobbitt or a geographically expansive Regional-State (such as a NAFTA based entity derived from Canada, the United States and Mexico) – should it come to be.

3. The first steps towards the creation of 'enemies of the state' status have already taken place with a) gang injunctions– taking away Constitutional rights to free assembly of gang members, b) the designation of career criminals as 'three-strikers' who are given life prison terms, and c) pedophiles and sexual predators who are banned from living in certain areas and must wearing 24 hour anklet monitoring devices.

4. US Department of Justice, 'Seven Florida Men Charged with Conspiring to Support al Qaeda, Attack Targets in the United States', Friday, June 23, 2006, [online]. Available at: www.usdoj.gov; Other Jihadi cases have also sprung up in California, Ohio, Virginia, and New York; Tyrangiel, J. (2006) 'The Jihadi Next Door?', *Time*, July 3, pp. 26–28.

US Homeland Security Perspectives

The post-9/11 world, especially the one that exists in the United States in its Washington corridors of power and along the beltway, has witnessed the creation of a confusing jumble of programs and initiatives to contend with non-state and criminal-state threats. All of this disjointed planning and activity is beginning to unfortunately resemble yesterday's response in terms of how we engaged our opponents in modern state-on-state warfare, that is, to create a monumental governmental bureaucracy and wage an industrial war of attrition against a peer competitor. The 'sledgehammer approach' to taking out opposing states and their coalitions stood us well in the First and Second World Wars, as did its modified use during the Cold War, but in this new struggle our relapse to such a military strategy is blatantly insufficient as a means to protect our people and the American values that we so cherish.[5]

To better understand how times and, in fact, warfare have changed, we need to rethink how US homeland security should be viewed and approached. The modern paradigm of the government obligation to protect US citizens and other persons is a Constitutional interpretation that divides the threat into crime and war. Crime is an internal social problem and the criminal justice system is the mechanism used for its suppression. It is reactive in that the system allows crime to occur and criminals are pursued and punished after-the-fact. The set of rules are based on laws of a civil society inside a nation. There are rights of individual freedom but that does not include the right to commit crime. Existing parallel to, but distinctly separate from, the criminal justice system is an additional public safety capacity that includes fire suppression and public health. Fire and health safety have a limited capacity to deal with the aftermath of crime, such as responding to an arson fire or dealing with the intentional spread of disease. The umbrella of management of these assets is often called emergency management. This is a bureaucratic function, not an operational function. These separate functional areas coordinate but do not institutionally cooperate and, for simplicity, law enforcement, firefighting, and public health can be labeled *Public Safety*.

War is an external threat based on the political system among nation-states and the rule set includes the right of nations to use force in defense. Unlike crime, war is conditionally legal, but only between or among nation states. Figure 1 depicts this concept with one exception. That exception is the overlap in the Venn diagram between crime and war. The interaction of crime and war is not explainable using the modern paradigm. In this post-modern, increasingly globalized world, the complete separation of crime and war fails to describe the current threat.

5. During the Cold War our attrition strategy was focused economically, ideologically and to a lesser extent militarily on the Soviet Union. We ultimately drove the Soviets into the ground via military spending—not through the actual application of military force as was the case in the First and Second World Wars. In the Global War on Terrorism (GWOT) the US is increasingly relying on the 'sledgehammer approach' to combating terrorism and insurgency. In some ways this is analogous to trying to kill roaches with a mallet.

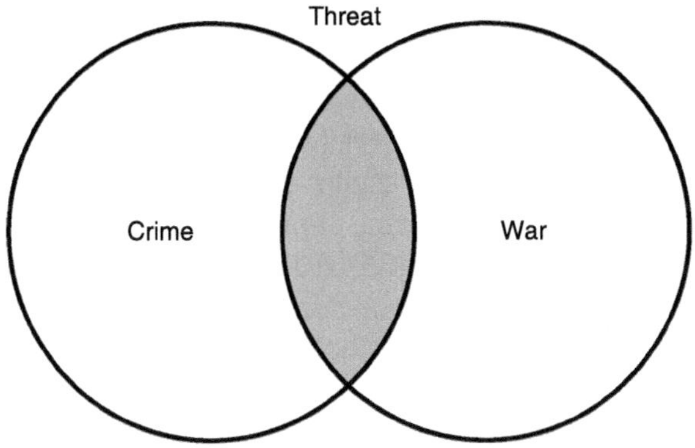

Figure 1 Threat environment. This represents the threat of crime and war. The area of convergence is the source of terrorism-based activity, as well as any other threat that has the characteristics of both crime and war. Source: Courtesy of Counter-OPFOR Corporation©

Figure 2 portrays the new security environment of the more complex post-modern world. It does not depict the *threat*, which is the purpose of Figure 1, but rather the *threat response* to a dynamic and changing threat that is not yet well defined.

This new threat involves the illegitimacy of crime coupled with the use of force against nations by groups that are not nations. These new challengers to the modern status quo perform as criminals with the defacto status of nations and are able to do so by operating within the overlap of crime and war. Neither the criminal justice system nor the National Security structure of nation states is oriented to meet this challenge.

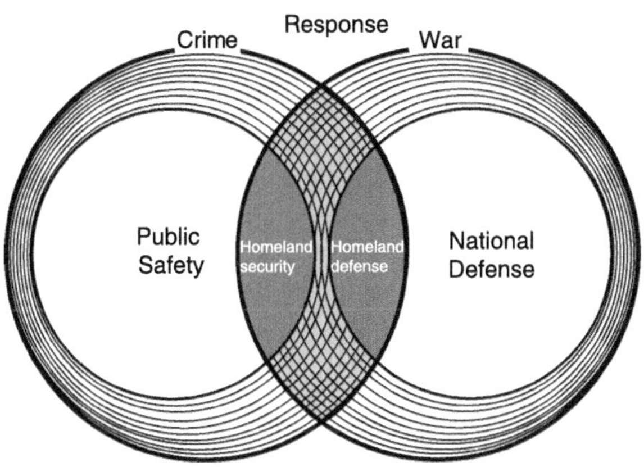

Figure 2 New Security (Response) Environment. This represents the response to crime, war, and the overlap of crime and war. The public safety system response, Homeland Security, views it as a crime threat and the National Security system identifies it as a war threat. The conceptual and capability gap in the center of the diagram (crosshatched) exists because the two systems do not connect, coordinate, or cooperate. Source: Courtesy of Counter-OPFOR Corporation©

The bombing of the USS Cole, for example, can be viewed as both a crime and an act of war. The Cole was a US warship in a foreign port. An attack on a US vessel is usually considered an act of war. However, the FBI investigated the incident, took the crime scene back to the lab for forensic analysis, and called the sailors victims. That is a traditional crime response.

The 1993 bombing of the World Trade Center was labeled crime and handled as such. The September 2001 attack and destruction of the Twin Towers was treated as war. Both events were performed by criminal, non-state organizations. These events occurred in the unexplained, undefined overlap of crime and war in Figure 1. The Public Safety system and the National Security system have responded separately to this challenge based on the perception of the problem from Figure 1, without factoring in the very different security environment influenced by the combination of crime and war. In the modern world, these events were aberrations. In the post-Modern world of the 21st century, such may be the norm.

The Department of Homeland Security is a bureaucratic re-organization with the intent to create better efficiency to an inside-the-border response capability. In other words, an expansion of current functions with an attempt to add existing capabilities of emergency response and public health to a crime enforcement and punishment system in a coherent way based on the existing system of separated functional areas. There have been several departmental reorganizations and revisions, suggesting that it is difficult to reorient a system of functional capability based on an inaccurate threat response model.

The Department of Defense and the National Security system exhibit an institutional reluctance to acknowledge a mission change for national security involving any operations within the national borders. The reworked concept of military support to civilian authority still remains a basic logistics support function with parameters and restrictions that are, essentially, unchanged. War is still viewed as only happening outside national borders. The first best step to address this challenge may be to define the concept of a new, and different, threat. The criminal organization with a war-making capability is virtually invisible to the legacy bureaucracies of a nation that defines all threats in separate crime-war scenarios. The current challenge is found within the overlap of crime and war, between the institutional response of the Department of Homeland Security and the Military Support to Civilian Authority function of the Department of Defense. The appropriate response is an active defense and interdiction capability not currently in practice, supported by an intelligence gathering and production capability organized in an operational network rather than a politically-derived bureaucratic hierarchy based on geographical jurisdiction.

New Wars of the 21st Century

The world is now a far different place than that experienced during the Cold War. The honeymoon period after that conflict lasted a little over a decade. We find ourselves in increasing numbers of new wars and engagements with criminal-entities and criminal-states (see Table 1). These conflicts span bewildering combinations of the global, regional, and individual state level and are being waged not only in physical (four dimensional space) 'humanspace' but also in non-physical 'cyberspace' (fifth dimensional space). Currently, three of these new wars are ongoing, one has been concluded with a US and Coalition victory, and two more have the potential to flare up.

The First War; al Qaeda (Global)

Since 9/11/01, the US and her allies have been in open and sustained warfare with al Qaeda and her affiliates and allies. This first new war of the 21st century is with an elusive and often stealth-masked transnational Jihadi insurgency (a virtual rather than territorial criminal-entity). This war is being fought across many regions of the world with major ongoing engagements against insurgents in Afghanistan and along the lawless Pakistani border. Insurgencies in other regions of the world, such as Chechnya, Somalia, and South Asia are also taking place along with sporadic terrorist attacks being directed at Europe and North America. Al Qaeda is thought to have network nodes in some 60 countries throughout the globe. The invasion of Afghanistan is considered a theater of operations within the larger war with al Qaeda. The military operation was directed against al Qaeda's Taliban allies and the al Qaeda training camps and leadership that existed within that criminal-state.

The Second War; Saddam Hussein and Sons (Iraq)

The invasion of Iraq in 2003, on the other hand, was initially directed against the now defunct oligarchic regime under Saddam Hussein and his tribal group manifest in his Ba'athist Party. Saddam's regime had no links to the 9/11 al Qaeda attack and, in retrospect, much US congressional debate rages over the wisdom of launching this war.

This debate aside, the invasion of Iraq represents the second war of the 21st century with a criminal-state, even though it was also a continuation of the earlier Gulf War from 1991. This war was quickly over and won since a territorial state devoid of nuclear weapons, even one that had been criminalized, stood no chance against the US and her allies on the conventional battlefield.

The Third War; The Iraqi Insurgents (Iraq)

After the fall of Hussein and the Ba'athist party, a non-state insurgency began that was directed against Western occupation forces. The roots of this insurgency can

Table 1 Criminal entities/states and the new wars of the 21st century

New War	OPFOR	Type	Locations	Begun	Status
First	· Al Qaeda & Network Affiliates (Sunni)	· Global Jihadi Insurgency · Virtual-Entity	· Global with nodes in 60 countries	· 9/11/2001 Attacks Initial al Qaeda Declaration of War in 1996	· Ongoing; network decentralizing/ sporadic attacks
Second	· Iraq under Saddam Hussein & Sons	· Oligarchic Regime	· Iraq	· 3/17/2003 US Demand for Saddam to Surrender	· Over; US & Coalition Victory
Third	· Iraqi Insurgent Groups (Sunni, Shia, Ba'athist Party, Foreign Jihad)	· Jihadi Insurgency	· Iraq	· 5/2003 Iraqi Army Disbanded Resistance Cells Activated/Groups Form · Attacks and Bombings Commence	· Ongoing; State fragmenting across ethnic & religious lines/civil war
Fourth	· 3rd GEN Gangs (MS 13, MS 18, et al.)	· State (Community) Failure & Lawless Zones · Virtual-Entities	· The Americas; United States (Parts) Central America South America	· Unknown; *Maras* waging 'societal warfare' but viewed as gang violence (crime) · No US national security threat recognition	· Ongoing; gang numbers, reach, and sophistication increasing
Fifth *(Potential)*	· North Korea under Kim Jong Il	· Oligarchic Regime	· North Korea ·Threat of attack on South Korea	· *No hostilities have broken out*	· Mounting tensions over nuclear weapons and ICBM programs
Sixth *(Potential)*	· Iran under the Ayatollahs (Shia) · Hizballah in Southern Lebanon (Shia)	· State Capture by Ayatollahs · Jihadi Insurgency	· Iran ·Southern Lebanon ·Suicide Bomber 'deterrence threat' to the United States	· Past incidents include US Embassy takeover (1979) and Beirut bombings (1983) · No hostilities have broken out	· Mounting tensions over nuclear weapons program

be traced to the May 2003 disbanding of the Iraqi Army and the activation of former regime resistance cells created prior to the US and Coalition invasion. The time period after the destruction of the ruling Oligarchic regime also witnessed the formation of Shia militia groups and an influx of foreign jihadi fighters. This insurgency – basically a new third war with diverse groupings of criminal entities – is composed of ever-shifting coalitions of former regime loyalists, Shia militiamen loyal to local clerics, criminal gangs, Iranian agents, and foreign jihadi fighters that swear alliance to al Qaeda. Iraq is very much heading down the path to civil war as ethnic and religious cleansing increasingly separates the dominant population groupings into distinct fortified enclaves and areas of influence. Iraq is also viewed at the same time, to the extent al Qaeda forces are concerned, as another theater of operations within the global war with al Qaeda.

The Fourth War; 3rd Gen Gangs (The Americas)

A fourth war with criminal-entities yet distinct from the one with al Qaeda and the insurgents in Iraq, has also recently begun. This war is derived from the recent emergence of the first group of third generation street gangs – the *Maras* in the Americas. These gangs trace their origins to a convergence of over 40 years of street gang and 20 years of drug cartel evolution and growth in the Americas, coupled with insurgency influences from Central America and Colombia. The *Maras* are emerging as a network of tribal confederations with direct linkages to Mexican drug cartels and former El Salvadorian, Nicaraguan, and Colombian insurgents.

No statistics exist on injuries and deaths caused by gang members within the Americas or even within the United States itself. Collection of data is not taking place because no strategic perception concerning the need for this data currently exists. In addition, lack of inter-agency coordination from the local through the federal level and differing definitions of "street gangs" would make the collection of such data, once the need was recognized, initially very difficult until proper reporting procedures were established. Statistics provided by noted authority Sgt. Wes McBride, Los Angeles Sheriffs (Ret) to one of the authors show that, between 1987 and 2005, over 11,000 gang related homicides took place in Los Angeles County alone. The vast majority of these killings were conducted by the less evolved first and second generation gangs. Extrapolation of this data easily suggests, that, in the last 20 years in the United States alone, gang homicides must surely be at least 100,000 in number. That is about twice the battlefield deaths that the United States suffered during the entire Vietnam War and magnitudes greater than the casualties suffered during the 9/11 attack. It can be seen, therefore, that the violence potential of the *Maras*, as they continue to spread and evolve within the Americas, is staggering. At the same time, we must also be cognizant of the domestic potentials for further *Mara* recruitment within the United States from a large and ever growing pool of recent Latin American immigrants.

The Potential Fifth War; Kim Jong Il (North Korea)

Two other distinct new wars with criminal-entities also have the potential of developing in the near term. The on-again off-again tensions with North Korea, a criminal oligarchy under Jong Il, would not be of major concern except for the fact that this criminal-state has nuclear weapons and is in the process of creating ICBM capability with the intent of being able to strike targets within the United States. Jong Il is a true wildcard in international affairs and North Korea a cash-starved nation deriving much of its revenue by means of illicit smuggling, money counterfeiting, and military weapons sales to anyone that can afford to buy the hardware. Nuclear technology and eventual outright nuclear weapons sales to other criminal-states and non-state entities are not beyond the realm of possibility.

The Potential Sixth War; The Ayatollahs and Hizballah (Iran and Southern Lebanon)

Ongoing tension with Iran, not yet fully a criminal-state because of its ongoing democracy movement in the face of Islamic fundamentalism also has great potential for conflict. Concern over a Middle East conflict arising from a pre-emptive American or Israeli attack on Iran's nuclear weapons program is well recognized. With such an attack comes the very real potential for the terrorist group Hizballah, a proxy of Iran and ruler of a criminal enclave in Southern Lebanon, to engage in a campaign of retaliatory suicide bombing attacks within the United States. If such open strife were to take place between the United States and Iran and/or Hizballah, the United States would be drawn deeper into the Israeli-Palestinian conflict. Such an outcome would serve to further polarize US and global Islamic relations and likely result in even greater levels of global strife.

US Grand Strategic Perspectives

US homeland security perspectives, while vitally important, are in themselves not comprehensive enough of a national response to fully counter the rise and type of threats posed by criminal-states and criminal-soldiers (i.e. global criminality). Since homeland security is solely focused on the defense of the homeland, if that is our only response to the new wars and threats that are breaking out, we will be doomed to forever be on the defensive. What is ultimately required, in addition to our duty of protecting the homeland, is the development of an overriding grand strategic imperative. That imperative should be to:

> Ensure that Nation-States (and Ultimately Their Successor Form) Provide the Basis For Post-Modern Social and Political Organization.

The lessons of history are harsh; older state forms have been unable to survive periods of epochal change, or what Lindsay Moore terms "Wars of Destiny".[6] The process of deinstitutionalization of state political, economic, and military structures is too powerful a force to overcome. With this breakdown of the older state form comes societal upheaval and a direct loss of power, influence, and wealth for once dominant peoples with the fate of the citizens of the Western Roman Empire as but one case in point.[7]

The American state and its people are now standing at a rare historic crossroads as we transition from the Modern (Third) to Post-Modern (Fourth) Epoch in human civilization. In order to implement this grand strategic imperative, some changes to the character and nature of American society will be required since, in a war over [humanity's] social and political organization, victorious new state forms and their peoples dominate. The full extent of the changes required is at this point unknown. Our intent should be to preserve as much of the America that we know and love as we can while at the same time recognizing that we have entered a monumental struggle from which any outcome other than victory against drug cartels, virtual states, criminal enclaves and free-states, an emergent Caliphate, Third Generation Gangs, and other criminal-challengers to the nation-state (and its successor form) is unacceptable.

We need to balance our democratic freedoms and responsibilities against suggested components of the above grand strategic imperative tailored for American needs. Ultimately, we should consult the organizing principles of the American state for guidance in this regard. With this in mind, suggested components of the grand strategic imperative – categorized into social and economic, security, and policy groupings – follow.[8]

Social and Economic Components

American values must not be compromised

Much has been reported on in the media concerning the use of secret prisons overseas and the torture of captured non-state 'enemy combatants' i.e. insurgents and terrorists. Such a foreign policy endangers our going down the path of a "Global Dirty War." The well known proverb "The road to hell is paved with good intentions" should not be forsaken. Morally wrong actions cannot be used to justify morally correct or right outcomes. Our end state in this conflict is not to become

6. See Moore, T. L. (2003) 'The Structure of War: Early Fourth Epoch War Research', in *Non-State Threats and Future Wars*, ed. R. J. Bunker, Frank Cass, London, pp. 159–170.
7. Peter F. Drucker is more optimistic about America's future place in the world, see Drucker, P. F. (2005) 'Trading Places', *The National Interest*, no. 79, pp. 101–107. Still his analysis is focused on economics and does not taken in consideration the emergence of new warmaking entities.
8. This listing is not meant to be exhaustive and no doubt considerable debate will be generated by these suggested components. We have tried to focus on what the American nation-state (and its successor form) will need to specifically do to seize the future in the war over social and political organization versus criminal-entities (e.g. their states and soldiers) we now find ourselves. Some obvious suggestions like reigning in the national debt were not listed because they represent obvious things that a nation-state should do even in normal times.

what we are fighting against, that is, not to become intolerant of other cultures and religions and morally corrupted ourselves. Failure to stay the moral course can easily result in the degeneration of the Global War on Terrorism (GWOT) into open societal warfare between diverse religious and ethnic blocs that otherwise should be united in the face of global criminality.

American citizenship must be valued

One of the eroding institutions of statehood, as nation states enter their twilight, is that of the value of being one of its citizens. Too many obligations and duties can accrue over time to members of a state, much like negative amortization on a loan. At some point, these obligations and duties become overly burdensome in relationship to the benefits of citizenship and a person is, in fact, better off not being the citizen of a given state while at the same time residing within its sovereign borders. Some concern already exists over the economic and political benefits foreign nationals gain inside the United States while simultaneously not bearing the full responsibilities and burdens shouldered by US citizens. Immigration itself is not the issue rather measures must be taken to ensure that citizenship (which implies allegiance to the state and a stake in its future) yields more rewards and benefits than simply legal or illegal residency. When just the act of carrying an American passport can now get you killed outright in some regions of the world, the value of holding that citizenship is called into question. The loss in tangible value and prestige of being a US citizen, both actual and perceived, needs to be curtailed.

Maintain the middle-class

Early agrarian American society was primarily based on upper and lower classes and a very small middle class of craftsmen and traders. With the advent of industrialization, a large middle class developed over the course of the last two centuries. That middle class was functional for both economic production and state-on-state warfare derived from the fielding of mass industrial armies. That middle class provided a buffer zone between the haves and have nots in American society and allowed high levels of social mobility to take place. Much of the American mythos is derived from Horatio Alger-like stories that promote the perception that each successive generation is richer, and thus better off, than the last. With qualitative changes in economic production and warfare, the middle class is in decline and no longer functional as a contributing social class to these endeavors.[9] Globalization, the rise of an informational economy, the decline of state-on-state wars, the use of debt to maintain family living standards, and the emergence of a denationalized American elite (a meritocracy based on individual talents) have all contributed to this process.[10] Failure to stem the culling out of the

9. Los Angeles County is an extreme example of this with almost three-fourths of families with children struggling economically. It also tends to be the first to first experience new trends taking place in the US. See Rosenblatt, S. (2006) 'More Youngsters in L.A. County Living in Poverty', *Los Angeles Times*, Thursday, October 19, p. B2.

10. The term 'denationalized American elite' attributed to the political scientist Samuel Huntington, see (2006) 'Meritocracy and its discontents', *The Economist*, October 7, pp. 23–24. See also (2006) 'The revenge of the bell curve', *The Economist*, October 7, pp. 20, 22.

middle class will, in itself, potentially become an internal security issue. Former middle class families will still need to be fed and, when push comes to shove, criminal activities, on both the individual and organized group level, may be resorted to in order to silence the cries of hungry children or purchase warm clothing and adequate shelter. We have seen this time and time again in Russia where a middle class has never really taken hold. The erosion of the American middle class will be an extremely difficult trend to reverse and will require some sort of long-term US government policy intervention.[11]

Our citizens must not be allowed to become soft

One of the maladies of being an overly civilized and affluent people is the age-old dilemma of becoming 'fat and happy' i.e. succumbing to decadence of the mind and body. Ours has become a sedentary and overweight society besieged with hypertension, diabetes, and a laundry list of other physical, emotional, and psychological maladies. Despite this trend, our life expectancies have continued to increase – access to miracle drugs and first rate healthcare keeps us around longer to burden the younger members of our society. General recognition of the lackluster physical state of our population has been around since President Kennedy established the President's Council on Physical Fitness and Sports during his administration; unfortunately, we are still addressing these very same issues. At the same time, our understanding of the hard sciences and foreign languages is dismal. We simply do not graduate enough engineers and scientists. We are possibly even worse in our foreign language skills. A recent report on proficiency in Arabic for the FBI finds that only 33 agents out of 12,000 have even a limited proficiency in that language.[12] Given that the FBI's lead domestic counter-terrorism mandate is now five years old, these figures are more than troubling.[13]

Implement new energy and environmental programs

As global civilization enters the Fourth Epoch, our relationship to energy sources and the environment will change. Increasingly, post-mechanical energy sources will be relied upon for warmaking (e.g. to fully unleash the military potentials offered by directed energy weapons [DEW]) and for the increasing power needs of American society. In turn, old ways of doing business based on 'smoke stack' technologies that result in the wholesale degradation of the environment (strip mining,

11. Interestingly enough while the US middle-class is constricting middle-classes are emerging in China and India derived from the building up of their industrial and informational economies. Does this mean in fifty-years time or so that all three countries may blend towards each other with similar class structures that have been optimized for that future global economy?

12. Eggen, D. (2006) 'FBI Agents Still Lacking Arabic Skills: 33 of 12,000 Have Some Proficiency' *Washington Post*, Wednesday, October 12, p. A01. Of note is a juxtaposition of al Qaeda members and their language skills—because of the global nature of this criminal-entity many are fluent in two or more languages (or dialects) with Arabic being the mother tongue and the language that the prophet spoke.

13. The mandate went into effect on October 26, 2001 when the Patriot Act was signed into law by President George W. Bush. See 'History of the FBI: Change of Mandate: 2001 - Present' (n.d.) [online]. Available at: http://www.fbi.gov/libref/historic/history/changeman.htm.

deforestation, and pollution) can no longer be tolerated. Passive forms of energy collection derived from solar, wind, and tidal power need to be exploited in addition to better battery storage, fuel cell technologies, and more efficient forms of electrical distribution (with lessened energy loss during transmission). Beyond their value as a more sustainable approach to living based on the premise 'do no harm to the environment,' American dependence on foreign oil can thereby begin to be turned around so that foreign regimes, especially those criminalized to greater or lesser extents such as Iran and Russia, lose their economic leverage.

Security Components

Ensure that our soldiers are always feared

The Counter-OPFOR motto "Insque Pradatorious, Inocciduus Praedae"(Always Predators, Never Prey) was meant to convey the fact that American soldiers and Marines always need to be the hunters of the enemy's forces and not the hunted. To a large extent, this motto also applies to law enforcement 's relationship to garden variety criminals with the caveat that the end state is to capture them and bring them to justice rather than closing with and destroying the enemy. Besides being feared, the soldiers (and LE officers) of our state must also be considered just, that is, they have to operate with legitimacy and integrity and have the backing of our people. The emergence of the criminal-soldier makes the above motto especially relevant because the American soldier, Marine, and law enforcement officer represent defenders of the state and enforcers of domestic peace and the rule of law. Our defenders and enforcers have in the past enjoyed a psychological battlefield and street advantage over their opponents and this edge must be retained. The perception of the invincibility of the Roman legionnaire was lost at the Battle of Adrianople in 378 and, for the Knight, it was lost at the Battle of Crecy in 1346.After these battles, the defenders of the Classical and Medieval orders increasingly became the prey of the non-state opponents that had emerged and were eventually swept off the battlefield. Recent events relating to the insurgency in Fallouja and the Israeli invasion of Lebanon give some pause for concern. Radical Shia insurgents in Fallouja used drugs such as adrenaline, amphetamines, and crack so that they would continue fighting even after being severely wounded.[14] Hizballah has also enjoyed a recent elevation in status with its surprise 'victory' over the Israeli Defense Forces (IDF). Some Russian born Israeli soldiers have gone on record saying that Hizballah soldiers are even better trained, equipped, and tougher than Chechen rebels.[15] Another area of consternation has been the

14. Some US Marines have even gone so far as to equate the urban combat taking place in Fallouja as much like that found in a *Dawn of the Dead* horror movie. See Perry, T. (2005) 'Fallouja Insurgents Fought under Influence of Drugs, Marines Say', *Los Angeles Times*, Thursday, January 13, p. A6.

15. 'Hizbullah tougher than Chechens, Russian-born Israeli soldiers say' (2006) *World Tribune*, Wednesday, August 15, 2006, [online] Available at: http://www.worldtribune.com/worldtribune/06/front2453963.0395833333.html. See also Peraino, K., et al. (2006) 'Eye For An Eye', *Newsweek*, August 14, pp. 21–26; 'Nasrallah wins the war' (2006) *The Economist*, August 19, p. 9; King, L. (2006) 'Much Soul-Searching Ahead for Israeli Army', *Los Angeles Times*, Sunday, August 27, p. A9; and Rafei, R. (2006) 'Hezbollah Holds Beirut Rally', *Los Angeles Times*, Saturday, September 23, p. A10.

contracting out of foreign operations and missions to private security and mercenary forces. If this trend is left unchecked, the quality of our state forces will continue to suffer as veteran troops leave for the more lucrative pay of private military corporations. Such a trend could very well hasten the loss of predator status for the defenders of our state who are now facing Shia insurgents fighting high on drugs and far tougher criminal-soldier groups than had before existed.

Gain mastery over the new form of warfare that has developed

The United States is the undisputed master of modern conventional state-on-state warfare. Such mastery does not apply to the new form of 'crime-war' or asymmetric warfare that is emerging. This new, more advanced form of warfare, is derived from 5th dimensional battlespace dynamics, directed energy weaponry, and disruptive network targeting capabilities. Further, given the Epochal nature of the global change now occurring, military force is being increasingly de-institutionalized and vested with private security and mercenary corporations. Full-scale military debates are required to determine the value, or not, of Clausewitzian principals and other staples of the Western conduct of warfare. Further, strategic defensive protection against this new form of warfare need to be planned out for the homeland. Does a national recovery plan exist for the disruptive societal effects of an al Qaeda tactical nuke attack on the Washington, DC area? Will people go back to work and school in the major metropolitan areas of the nation the next day or weeks that follow? Or will the nation suffer national economic crisis and disruption over the ensuing months?

Codify legal protocols for the crime and war operational environment

International and domestic law has been in a perpetual reactionary mode to the emergence of criminal-states and criminal-soldiers for many years now. The very existence of such 'entities' and 'combatants' still confound the organizational and bureaucratic sensibilities of our modern world's institutions and structures. The US and her allies need to clearly identify just exactly what the enemy is (not who it is) at both the individual and organizational levels and recognize that the that enemy is not just in traditional nation-state forms. After satisfying this definitional criteria, derived from bi-partisan research into this new threat, attributes of domestic and international laws pertaining to both criminals and soldiers should be drawn upon to codify legal protocols to address it. One of the best policy terms for criminal-soldiers may currently be the newer term 'unlawful enemy combatants'. If this is the case, what specific search and seizure laws (CONUS) and rules of engagement (OCONUS) can be developed, at the same time as part of a strategic overall policy, for our law enforcement agencies and military services to effectively conduct their missions in the crime-war operational environment?

Follow a containment strategy for Jihadists and third generation gangs

The Soviet Union was contained over a roughly fifty-year period and allowed to ultimately implode due to its own bureaucratic inefficiencies, lack of ideological purpose, and failed attempts at economically attempting to outspend the United States in a global arms race. Currently the United States is engaged in a GWOT, or Long War, against Jihadist groups such as al Qaeda and its many affiliates. The United States is also engaged in another war – this one with 3 GEN Gangs (and to a lesser or greater extent with drug cartels whose organizational structure has become blurred with that of the Maras) throughout the Americas – however, our government and people have not recognized this conflict yet because it is too subtle. Endemic crime, broken families, failed communities and predatory youth groups are viewed simply as another social malaise of our times and not as the vast networks of warring tribal groups that have evolved, and will continue to evolve, into something far more ominous right under our collective noses. Both Jihadists and 3 GEN Gangs cannot be defeated wholesale or decisively with traditional arms – entire armies of eager young recruits can be easily birthed and ready to join the ranks in 8–10 years time. Rather, these OPFORs need to be contained over the long term and somehow re-indoctrinated into the global mainstream – not an easy task given fast social mutation patterns based on the fact that children start giving birth in slums and other failed-communities by the time they are 16, if not younger. Such containment requires a master plan, like the one derived from George Kennan's famous "long telegram" sent from Moscow at the start of the Cold War. This new containment strategy needs to be based on the realities of 21st century conflict against virtual-state opponents and no such strategy has as of yet been developed.

Policy Components

Implement a more nuanced foreign policy

Hand-in-hand with the above containment strategy, US foreign policy needs to become more nuanced. The bulk of the world's population cannot be allowed to perceive the US as a global bully and criminal-soldiers as underdogs to be cheered on, or worse, viewed as valiant warriors with God fully on their side and worthy of direct material support. Far too much of the world, especially those in the world's slums and other no-go areas, cheered and jeered when the Trade Towers came crashing down because they felt America had it coming. Part of the issue is our heavy-handed attempts at spreading the ideology of democracy across the globe. The concept is a noble one, however, you can't shove democracy down people's throats, especially those who yesterday were living in oligarchies (family business or ethnic clan ruled police states) or failed-states that are basically tribal in nature, have little to no basic infrastructure, and are composed of a technically backwards and illiterate population. More constrained and realistic foreign policy goals, and ones that do not overmatch our economic, diplomatic, and military resources, need to be explored for sustained foreign policy operations. In sum, democracy should actively be spread to other peoples of the world but in a more circumspect and less threatening manner.

Openly debate a political accord with Mexico [cooperate closely with Canada]

Full scale Mexican state failure would result in even greater levels of criminalization and lawlessness than are already evident in that state. Simply put, if Mexico dies, we will be trapped in a room with a rotting corpse. Illegal border migrations would increase, as would the flow of illicit products, and corruption levels among American officials along the border. Like it, or not, NAFTA (the North America Free Trade Agreement), implemented in 1994, was an early step towards the economic unification of North America. Economic unification is typically a precursor to eventual political and military unification of state bodies – the same type of integration process is much farther underway under the auspices of the European Union. The debate over the dual voting rights of former Mexican nationals made citizens of the United States and the increasing Mexican-American population of the US Sunbelt suggests that a growing segment of the populations of these two countries have already merged together. Open and candid talks about some sort of long term political accord with Mexico by the United States needs to be addressed. The alternative is turning our backs on Mexico's probable future fate and erecting a reverse Berlin style wall across the southern US border in hopes that it will keep masses of illegal immigrants and festering social ills, such as the influence of drug cartels and corruption, out of our homeland. Some thoughts of a greater 'North America Security Sphere' should also be considered as we continue to cooperate closely with our Canadian neighbors to the North. A unified North American continent spanning Canada, the United States, and Mexico may at some point form the basis of the nation-state successor form in our region of the globe.[16]

Gain 'influence' in cyberspace (5th dimensional space)

Nation-states initially exerted a condition of absolute sovereignty over their territories. This level of sovereignty has been greatly reduced over the last half of the 20th century with new interpretations of international law (such as crimes against humanity), supranational free trade agreements (NAFTA), the inability to control human and illicit product smuggling across porous borders (US and Mexico), and lack of advanced defenses to stop stealth masked terrorist assault teams (9/11). Cyberspace (e.g. the internet, emails, and the world wide web) represents the emergence of a new non-physical dimension that further shreds nation-state pretensions of sovereignty. Some states, such as China, believe that they can contain or exert control over cyberspace in their sovereign lands and are

16. For an interesting perspective on regional states and network commonwealths see Bennett, J. C. (2003/2004) 'Networking Nation-States: The Coming Info-National Order', *The National Interest*, no. 74, Winter, pp. 17–30.

attempting to do so via access control measures. The reality is that gaining high-levels of 'influence' over cyberspace, not attempting to exert sovereignty or control, should be the desired end state. This policy component is derived from the observation that dominant nodes within a network can exert great influence on the overall behavior of the network itself.

Formulate a comprehensive policy concerning illicit (and addictive) substances

One's personal position on the use of illicit and addictive substances is by far one of the most morally charged issues of our times. As we venture further into the post-Modern Epoch, the question of what are 'criminal' and what are 'legitimate' substances will intensify. With regard to legalizing certain substances, this is a 'damned if we do and damned if we don't' issue for America's future vis-à-vis global criminality. It has been recognized that illicit flows provide the economic backbone or logistical foundation of virtual-states and other criminal-entities. By legalizing some illicit substances, the nation-state form could break part of the economic-backbone of those entities and in turn, realize much needed revenue streams, placate masses of American adults that see nothing wrong with occasionally using recreational drugs, and clear out our correctional and court system of numerous illicit substance uses and sellers. The immediate downside is to lose some of our American values as we edge closer to criminal elements, along with the potential increase in illicit substance use that this might generate with our nation's youth. Eventually this issue may come to the forefront over 'direct neural implants for pleasure' or 'happy dermal patches' (drugs have been evolving some time from natural through hybrid and now into highly addictive synthetic forms) or a situation where the majority of the adult American public votes for some sort of national decriminalization of soft illicit substances. Inconsistencies over the fact that other addictive substances such as nicotine, alcohol, and caffeine are not classified as illicit substances further muddles this issue. No policy position is advocated for this issue other than the fact that some sort of national debate pointing towards a consensus is reached and the ensuing policies that develop are implemented.

Create a global network in support of the post-modern state

The nation-state is evolving into the market-state or some other successor form of social and political organization, assuming that it is not defeated or co-opted over the long term by the virtual-state or some other new and more advanced criminal-state form. To ensure that the nation-state and its successor form achieves victory in the global war over humanity's future now underway, global networks in support of our vision of the post-Modern State need to be established. One, initially experimental, but now operational network form that we and other contributors in this work have been involved with intimately is the Terrorism Early Warning (TEW) Group model. It was established in 1996 in the Los Angeles County operational area with the intent of providing a network intelligence early warning capability against criminal-soldiers (e.g. terrorists and other OPFORs). That model has also shown itself to possess many unique direct operational response capability potentials. For more on developing the Global Network support capability, refer to Sullivan and Weston's 'Afterward' which pertains to 'Law Enforcement Response Strategies' in the concluding essay section of this work.

Special Issue Overview

When defending against enemies of the state, both the individual and organizational level of analysis must be taken into consideration. In addition, perspectives on how we arrived at this point in our history – a time when non-state criminal entities increasingly challenge the warmaking monopoly and legitimacy of nation-states – need to be discussed. These concerns and others like them have been the driving force behind this work and those earlier works that it is conceptually linked, *Non-State Threats and Future Wars* and *Networks, Terrorism and Global Insurgency.*[17]

The work is divided into three major thematic sections which address Theory and Law, Criminal-states, and Criminal-soldiers. The work promotes a newer perspective on global crime – one that views evolving forms of global criminality as a direct threat to the very basis of the modern international system (c. 1648) enacted by nation-states over the last three and one-half centuries. Prior to the start of the thematic sections, three front piece essays exist. The first essay provides insights into the psychology of those brave men and women who protect our society and the need for them to shield us from the predators – the wolves – that threaten our families and way of life. The second work identifies the three stages of corruption that exist in the world today and how the last stage – systemic corruption – may be countered. The ideas discussed in this introduction have great applicability for both foreign and domestic US applications now that the border region with Mexico is becoming increasingly compromised by corruption.[18] The third piece provides an overview of some of the criminal threats faced, US homeland security and grand strategic perspectives, and an introduction to the contributions contained in the special issue.

The initial section focuses upon theory and legal issues pertaining to current and emergent internal and external challengers to the nation-state. The first contribution is an update to the important 1996 essay "The Fate of the State" which postulated that the nation-state was coming to its evolutionary end and

17. These earlier works were published by Frank Cass in 2003 (originally appeared as a special issue of *Small Wars & Insurgencies*, vol. 13, no. 3, Summer 2003); and Routledge in 2005 (originally appeared as a special issue of *Low Intensity Conflict and Law Enforcement*, vol. 11, no. 2/3, Winter 2002 respectively).

18. See Vartabedian, R., et al. (2006) 'Rise in Bribery Tests Integrity of U.S. Border', *Los Angeles Times*, Monday, October 23, pp. A1, A16–A17.

would eventually be replaced with another state form of some type in the future. The second work compares and contrasts emergent market-states (nation-state successors) with the virtual-state (criminal-challenger) that has arisen. Much of the market-state discussion and analysis is derived from Philip Bobbitt's seminal work *The Shield of Achilles*. Still, new insights into the nature of virtual-states are presented along with a new futures scenario that is better thought to reflect the domination of the future global economy by virtual-states. The third essay concerns the need to define a new threat to the nation-state – 'Criminal-states'. Past US views on dangerous states are discussed in this essay and four forms of criminal-states are identified. Some initial observations concerning the moral considerations of defining a new threat and its potential impact on US foreign and domestic policies are also provided.

The final contribution in this section looks toward American history for guidance in contending with the new threat of nonaligned terrorist combatants who blur the line between two distinct traditions of military and civilian criminal law. These unlawful enemy combatants pose a dilemma for our legal system and will undoubtedly strike the US homeland again with a significant attack sometime in the future.

The second section spotlights criminal-states. The first contribution examines the work *Vom Kriege* (On War), written by Carl von Clausewitz with underpinnings derived from the ideas of Aristotle, and analyzes its applicability to criminal-states and gangs. This essay directly links with the earlier contribution on defining criminal-states by analyzing the four categories of criminal-states that were articulated. The second work is Jihadist focused and views the world through their lenses of eschatology. Many radical Sunni and Shiite groups embrace a view of the five prophetic stages of Islam. These stages span the rise of the initial caliphate through the projected return of the Mahdi. In order to bring about the fifth and final end of days stage, al Qaeda and other radical Islamic networks are actively promoting jihad activity. The third contribution discusses and analyzes Bin Laden's January 2006 tape that was released after a 13-month hiatus. Works such as these are extremely important because they allow us to better understand the leadership of 'thine enemy' in order to disrupt, dismantle, and, ultimately, defeat them. The fourth work provides a glimpse into Hizballah's global criminal operations. The operations highlighted are intellectual property crime (IPC), drug trafficking, cigarette smuggling, and the African diamond trade. Of concern is the fact that those participating in these worldwide illicit enterprises may someday be tasked to engage in acts of terrorism for Hizballah or at the behest of Iran. The final essay in this section provides insight into the parameters and extent of the criminalization of Russian state security. The systemic nature of the criminalization and corruption of Russian police and military forces is distressing, however, some small glint of hope may now exist in that President Putin is starting to recognize the dangers that this criminal threat poses to the Russian state.

The third section concerns perspectives on the emergence, manifestation, and evolution of the criminal-soldier. Some blurring between the second and third sections are evident with the issue of street gangs in the first two contributions. While some of these groups, the more violent Maras in particular, have crossed over to criminal-soldier status, their half-political and half-social (tribal) networks are very much akin to what could be considered a transnational or virtual criminal-state. The first contribution, by the originator of the Third Generation Gang (3 GEN Gangs) construct, provides an overview of the work that has been produced on this topic and then discusses further evidence to support the model. He then finishes with newer research concerning three GEN Gangs and prison recruitment and linkages to broader conflict, child soldiers, and the 'New Feudalism' that is developing.

The second contribution looks at street gangs as protean insurgents in Post-Modern War. This 'double size' essay is a major effort in both size and scope and not only discusses the threats posed by third generation gangs but goes into detail concerning how they should be countered, drawing upon the Italian state's experiences dismantling the Red Brigades. Because of the major threat these gangs now represent to the Americas and the keen insights developed by this contributor in order to combat them, this major research undertaking was well justified.

The third contribution provides new research and insight into criminal network trafficking in nuclear materials in the former Soviet Union. The author analyzes 'the role of prisons in criminal operations, the interaction of criminals and terrorists, and the character of new organized crime groups' and determines 'that some of the most serious nuclear smuggling is not random or opportunistic'. Further, the author concludes that the professionals behind this trafficking and their developed networks make this trafficking rarely detectable. The fourth contribution provides a totally new and unnerving perspective on the subject of private security firms. While the vast majority of works focus on the pros and cons of these firms in service to Western states and their allies, this approach looks at examples throughout the world where criminal and terrorist groups have either formed or co-opted private security firms to the benefit of their activities and goals. The stated Jihadist intent to infiltrate such companies brings about a whole new dimension not usually recognized in the overall GWOT.

The fifth and final contribution in this section focuses on the use of beheadings by fundamentalist Islam. It provides an historical overview, a discussion of contemporary beheadings, perspectives on state and non-state (criminal) use of beheadings, an analysis of Islamist beheading tactics, and instances of the spread of the tactic. Of interest is the increasing use of the tactic by drug cartels and gangs in Mexico and Central America, as a retaliation tactic by Christian mobs in Nigeria, and the likelihood of its spreading to the United States.

The final afterward contribution provides guidance for police and enforcement agencies when facing criminal-states and criminal-soldiers. In this essay, the operational space, maintenance of stability and order, restoring order in transitional states, constabulary and gendarmerie capabilities (EXPOL), and networking intelligence and law enforcement are explored and discussed.

Acknowledgements

Special thanks to John P. Sullivan, Lisa J. Campbell, Mark Clark, Jim Kuga, and Pamela L. Bunker for comments and insights concerning suggested components of the grand strategic imperative tailored to US needs.

The Fate of the State Revisited

Martin van Creveld

In this article, the state of the state will be discussed under five headings. Part I looks at the state's declining ability to fight other states. Part II examines the effects of modern technology, economics and the media, and briefly the process known as "globalization". Part III outlines the rise, and ongoing fall, of the welfare state. Part IV focuses on the state's ability to maintain public order in the face of various disruptive forces seeking to disrupt or overthrow it. Finally, Part V is an attempt to tie all the threads together and see where we are heading.

Martin van Creveld is one of the leading world-wide experts on military history and strategy, He was born in the Netherlands and has lived in Israel since 1950. He holds a degree from the London School of Economics and has been a faculty member at the History Department, the Hebrew University, since 1971. His eighteen books, which have been translated into fifteen languages, include Supplying War (1978), Command in War (1985), The Transformation of War (1991), The Rise and Decline of the State (1999), and From Sarajevo to Baghdad (2007). Prof. van Creveld has consulted to the defense establishments of several countries, and taught or lectured at practically every institute of higher defense learning from Canada to New Zealand and from Norway to South Africa.

The Waning of Major War

The principal function of the state, like that of all previous forms of government, has always been to fight other states, whether defensively, in an attempt to protect its interests, or offensively, in order to extend them. Usually a state that was unable to do this was doomed to disappear. The best it could hope for was to lead a sort of shadowy existence under the protection of some other, more powerful, state. For example, "Congress Poland" did so during most of the nineteenth century and Afghanistan and Iraq, occupied by foreign troops, do so even as these lines are being written.

Conversely, right from the beginning, the need to fight other states has always played a critical role in the development of the state's most important institutions.[1] This includes the government bureaucracy, originally created in order to levy taxes for the purpose of waging war; the note-issuing state bank, an early 18th-century invention specifically designed to help pay for Britain's military efforts during the wars against Louis XIV; and of course the regular armed forces themselves. In most states, the latter continued to take up the lion's share of expenditure until well into the 19th century.[2]

Driven largely by the need to fight other states, the power of the state expanded from 1700 on. The number of bureaucrats—the term is an 18th-century neologism—increased as did the amount of statistical information they gathered and generated. These "improvements" allowed the most advanced governments to greatly augment the share of GDP they extracted. Meanwhile, developing technology drove war, and war, the development of technology. International competition intensified until, during the last decades of the 19th century, it reached the point where much the world had been turned into an armed camp. Each of the so-called great powers of the time was looking anxiously over its shoulder at all the rest to see which one was the most threatening and which one, being less so for the moment, could be drawn into an alliance.

Most of all, the reforms instituted by the French Revolution led to the nationalization of the masses. With that, there took place a drastic change of the state in the popular consciousness. Thomas Hobbes, John Locke, and many of their 18th-century successors saw the state simply as an instrument for maintaining public order and permitting a civilized life. To quote a rhyme by Alexander Pope: "Over government fools contest/What is best administered is best". Now it became an end unto itself, an earthly god in whose honors monuments were erected, festivals celebrated, and monuments composed and sung.[3] It was a vengeful God who, according to his greatest prophet Georg

1. Porter, B. D. (1994) *War and the Rise of the State*, Free Press, New York.

2. For some figures see Flora, P. et al. (eds) (1983) *State, Economy and Society in Western Europe, 1875-1975*, St. James Press, London, vol. 1, part iv, p. 441; also Kennedy, P. (1987) *The Rise and Fall of the Great Powers*, Vintage, New York, p. 153.

3. See Mosse, G. L. (1975) *The Nationalization of the Masses*, Howard Fertig, New York; also Weber, E. (1976) *Peasants into Frenchmen*, Stanford University Press, Stanford.

Friedrich Hegel,[4] fed on blood and periodically demanded the sacrifice of hundreds of thousands if not millions—for their own highest good, needless to say. Seen from the perspective of our own "post heroic" period,[5] nothing in the history of the modern state is more astonishing than the willingness, occasionally even eagerness, of people to fight for it and lay down their lives for it.

The climax of these developments was reached during the years of total warfare between 1914 and 1945. Acting in the name of the need to protect or extend something known as the national interest, the most important states of the time conscripted their populations and fought each other on an unprecedented scale and with an unprecedented ferocity. Nor was it merely a question of soldiers killing each other in the field. At the grand strategic level, both 1914–18 and 1939–45 were conducted by attrition. This gave the belligerents time to mobilize not only troops but civilians (including women and children) as well as put them to work in the fields and factories behind the front. Under the direction of such figures as Walter Rathenau in Germany, David Lloyd George in Britain, Georges Clemenceau in France, and Bernard Baruch in the United States, the state assumed control over finance, raw materials, production, transportation, labor (including professional qualifications and wages), and even daily calorie intake of their citizens. Though most of these controls were demolished after 1918, the blueprints remained in the drawers. This, in turn, enabled them to be re-instituted even more effectively, and much more quickly, in World War II.

Thanks to the unprecedented mobilization of demographic, economic, industrial, technological, and scientific resources, the two world wars together, and each one separately, dwarfed the conflicts that had taken place in the past. More important to our purpose, mobilization warfare accelerated—if it did not create—technological progress.[6] All through World War II in particular, tens of thousands of scientists and technicians engaged in research and development, producing devices that ranged from radar to computers and from jet engines to ballistic missiles. The climax, reached after years of labor and at enormous expense, arrived on 6 August 1945 when the first atomic bomb exploded over Hiroshima, killing an estimated 75,000 people.

At first, nuclear weapons seemed to put unprecedented military power in the hands of the state; after a few years, though, it began to be realized that this was not exactly the case. So powerful were the weapons in question that, instead of serving war as all their predecessors had done, they threatened to put an end to it.[7] As the number of weapons available world-wide increased and their power

4. See Smith, S. B. (1983) 'Hegel's Views on War, the State and International Relations', *American Political Science Review*, vol. 77, pp. 624–632.

5. See Luttwak, E. N. (1995) 'Towards Post-heroic Warfare', *Foreign Affairs*, May/June.

6. See, for an account by one of the men in charge, Bush, V. (1949) *Modern Arms and Free Men*, Simon and Schuster, New York.

7. Among the first to perceive that nuclear weapons would limit war was Brodie, B. (1946) *The Absolute Weapon*, Ayer Company Publishers, New Haven. The best discussion of nuclear doctrine from 1945 to the Reagan years remains Friedman, L. (1981) *The Evolution of Nuclear Strategy*, St. Martin's Press, New York.

grew from 20,000 kilotons in 1945 to as much as 58 megatons in 1961, wherever they made their appearance large-scale interstate war came to a halt. The first to feel the impact were the two Superpowers, i.e. the US and the USSR. Then it was the turn of their close allies in NATO and the Warsaw Pact, respectively; then of the USSR and China; then of China and India; then of India and Pakistan; then of Israel and its Arab neighbors; and now, it seems, of the two Koreas as well. One by one they acquired the most powerful weapons of all. One by one, they found themselves with their horns locked and unable to fight each other as many of them used to and, perhaps, would have liked to.[8]

This does not mean there have been no attempts to make the world safe for war by breaking the nuclear deadlock. Focusing on the largest, richest, and technologically most advanced state of all, American attempts to find a way to defend against nuclear weapons have been ongoing at least since the mid 1950s. They led through the Nike Zeus missile—planned to achieve its purpose by exploding a megaton-size warhead high above the asset it was intended to "defend"—through the Spartan and Sentinel of the 1960s all the way to President Reagan's "Star Wars" speech of 1983; and from then on to the present Bush administration's National Missile Defense, or NMD.[9] Over the years, the sum spent on these programs has probably exceeded $100 billion and is still growing. Yet even a partial defense against nuclear-tipped ballistic missiles, let alone the cheaper and easier to build cruise missiles, is as far away today as it was fifty years ago; the situation of other countries is much worse still.

As a result, without a single exception, what large-scale interstate wars have taken place since 1945 have been waged either between or against third- and fourth rate military powers. The Korean War, which originally was simply a civil war between the two parts of a country split in half; the five (or six, depending on the way one counts) Arab-Israeli Wars; the three Indian-Pakistani Wars; the Chinese-Indian War; the Chinese-Vietnamese War; the Falklands War, so small that it is often referred to as a mere campaign; the Iran-Iraq War; the First Gulf War, the Afghanistan War, and the Second Gulf War—all these and many others served to illustrate the point. To put it in another way, since 1945 no two powerful states, meaning such as were armed with nuclear weapons or even strongly suspected of having them, have fought each other. By some accounts, they did not even get close to doing so.[10]

Even more striking than the marginalization of the belligerents was the declining scale on which war was waged. Though the world's population has more than tripled since 1945, and though its ability to produce goods and services has increased many times over, both the size of the armed forces and the number of

8. For the way nuclear weapons limited interstate war, first between major powers and then, increasingly, among the rest, see van Creveld, M. (1993) *Nuclear Proliferation and the Future of Conflict*, Free Press, New York.

9. See Mantle, P. J. (2004) *The Missile Defense Equation*, AIAA, Washington, DC.

10. Bundy, M. (1988) *Danger and Survival; The Political History of Nuclear Weapons*, Random House, New York, p. 616.

the major weapon systems that they produce now amount to only a small fraction of what they were sixty years ago. For example, the forces mobilized by the coalition for the First Gulf War were just one fifth the size of those deployed by Germany for its invasion of Russia in 1941, and those used against Saddam in 2003 were only one fifth of those. In most places around the world the shrinking process is still under way. Nor, in the face of the potential for a nuclear holocaust, is there much chance of the mass forces of World Wars I and II being rebuilt in any kind of future that may be foreseen.

The Rise and Fall of the Welfare State

As the state, that power-hungry beast *par excellence*, lost its ability to fight its neighbors, it turned its attention inward. It lies in the nature of a bureaucratic construct that it should seek to control and regulate everything. Doing so, it created the welfare state.

The beginning of this story may be found in the period between 1789 and 1830. First came the French Revolution, which, exported by force of arms across the width and breadth of Europe, broke up the ancient feudal, ecclesiastical, and professional institutions; by atomizing society, it put the state in a much stronger position than ever before.[11] Next came the industrial revolution. Having started in Britain during the 1760s, it brought with it economic freedom, unbridled capitalism (including its worst manifestations—a total lack of planning, widespread poverty, and inhumane exploitation of man by man), and the invisible hand. The influence of figures such as Adam Smith and Friedrich List caused one nation after another to dismantle internal and external economic controls and switch to free trade. With the Manchester School firmly in control, during the first half of the century the motto was *laissez faire*.

After 1850 or so the prevailing mood began to change, at first very slowly and then faster and faster. One reason for this was a number of inquiries, some of them official, others by well known persons of the time, into the often shocking conditions in which working people lived.[12] Another was the military competition mentioned in the previous section; as the most important states became increasingly dependent on mass armies consisting of conscripts and reservists, their rulers felt they could not longer afford to neglect the population that provided those armies to quite the same extent as they had done before. Finally there was the steady, if often stormy, movement towards democratization and the rise in many countries of left-wing, socialist, parties. The former made it necessary, in the words of one British parliamentarian, "to educate our masters". The latter attracted a growing number of voters and threatened violent revolution unless something was done to improve the masses' lot.

11. See Gellner, E. (1983) *Nations and Nationalism*, Cornell University Press, Ithaca.

12. The most famous inquiry of all was Engels, F. (1991) *The Condition of the Working Class in England* [1844], Electric Book Company, London.

Be the exact reasons what they may, the first Factory Acts were passed in Britain during the 1840s over howls of protest by the owners and their spokesmen. The laws' purpose was to put limits on working hours—initially those of women and children, later those of men as well—and institute at least some health and safety controls. Imitated by many countries, originally the new laws only applied to a few industries considered particularly dangerous, such as metal-working and mining. Later in the century they were extended to others such as textile and metalworking plants. Among the last sectors to be reached were agriculture, domestic service—which, until World War II, continued to employ large numbers of people—and small-scale light industry, particularly in the form of sweatshops. These started to be affected, to the extent that they were affected at all, only during the early years of the 20th century.

Once the state had begun to supervise the conditions of labor—including the establishment of labor exchanges, another early twentieth-century development—it soon sought to do the same for education and public health. The pioneer in the former field was Prussia. Following beginnings made during the reign of Frederick the Great, something like universal, although as yet not free, elementary education was achieved in the years after 1815. This feat turned Prussia into a much-imitated model and caused educators from all over the world to flock to see how it was done.[13] In the rest of Europe the real push was provided by the war of 1870–71.[14] The French in particular looked for an explanation for their defeat; unable to agree on one, in the end they pointed a finger at the schoolmaster and his students. By the early 20th century the "utopian vision", to speak with the British Fabian socialist writer Beatrice Webb, of universal elementary education had been achieved in all the most advanced countries.

Advances in public health were made necessary by urban growth and were initially decentralized. In Britain, Germany, and to a growing extent the United States as well, laws were enacted that entrusted the task of providing better sanitation and better disease control to local authorities and municipalities. Taking over from the church and private charitable organizations, these bodies also began providing at least some hospitals for the indigenous ill, the mentally disturbed, and the like. In the most advanced countries, ministries of health were established during the first two decades after 1900 with the task of supervising those countries' entire health systems, including both medical practice and training, In addition, many of them also provided various programs, such as inoculation and pre-natal care, which were compulsory, free, of both.

13. For the rise of the public education system in Germany see Schluenes, K. A. (1989) *Schooling and Society; The Politics of Education in Prussia and Bavaria, 1750–1900*, Berg Publishers, Oxford. For an international perspective on its role in building the modern state, Flora, P. (1972) 'Die Bildungsenwicklung im Prozess der Staaten und Nationsbildung', in *Soziologie und Sozialgeschichte*, ed. P. C. Ludz, Westdeutscher Verlag, Opladen.

14. Kazmias, A. M. (1966) *Politics, Society and Secondary Education in England*, University of Pennsylvania Press, Philadelphia, p. 107 ff.

Like state-run education, state-run welfare was originally a German invention.[15] The 1880s found Bismarck worried about the progress of the Social Democratic Party. Even as he passed laws against them through the Reichstag, he also instituted something known as "The Revolution from Above", including the world's first state-run schemes for unemployment, accident, sickness and old age insurance. Between 1890 and 1914 his example was followed by others through much of Western Europe and Scandinavia. Neither reform or repression, however, were able to stop the march of socialism which appeared to increase its strength year by year. Seen from this point of view, the Bolshevik Revolution of 1917 was anything but an anomaly. Instead, it was an attempt to grab one particularly backward country by the neck, force it to march in the direction others were moving as well, institute universal welfare at a single stroke, and doing so, extend state control to the point where civil society itself almost ceased to exist. Only the United States, with its strong traditions of free enterprise and rugged individualism, resisted the trend and, as a result, found itself trailing far behind. In the land of the dollar it took the Great Depression and 13 million unemployed to make first the New Deal and then social security possible during the 1930s.[16]

Still, what really made the modern welfare state was World War II. As they had already done during World War I, governments took responsibility for running countless aspects of their citizens' lives, including, in theory, the number of inches of hot water they were allowed to put in their tubs. This time, though, they did so with no intention of giving up their power after the conflict had ended. In one developed country after another, extensive health programs covering the entire population—as under the British National Health System which served as the model for many others—were established. To this were added a vast variety of ancillary programs, such as free meals for schoolchildren and the elderly, assistance for the handicapped, cheap public housing, vocational training and retraining, and of course education. The latter often led to free education up to, and in some instances including, the university level.

Accelerating a development that had started during the last years of the 16th century, these developments led to a further huge increase in the number of bureaucrats per head of population and per square mile of territory. For example, in the United States in 1972, one in thirteen people worked for the government; in other developed countries, they were more numerous still. By the end of the 1950s, the number of ministries, which during the state's formative years in the 18th centuries had usually stood at four, had risen to something nearer 20 in most countries. To the minister of justice, the minister of foreign affairs, the minister of war, and the minister of the treasury were added, not necessarily in this order, ministers for interior affairs, police, agriculture, transportation, communications,

15. See Flora, P. and Heidenheimer, A. J. (eds) (1981) *The Development of Welfare States in Europe and America*, Transaction Publishers, New Brunswick; Bruce, M. (1974) *The coming of the welfare state*, Schocken, London; and Berkowitz, E. & McQuaid, K. (1988) *Creating the Welfare State: The Political Economy of Twentieth-Century Reform*, Praeger Publishers, Lawrence.

16. See Badger, A. J. (2002) *The New Deal: The Depression Years*, Ivan R. Dee, Chicago.

education, health, labor, welfare, trade and industry, aviation, energy, and tourism. Some countries believed they absolutely had to have a ministry for the infrastructure, whatever that meant. Others claimed they could not do without one for sport and leisure, whereas during the 1980s many cabinets also came to include portfolios for ecological matters, youth, and women's affairs.

To pay for these programs and these ministries, it was necessary to raise taxes—especially direct ones—until, in countries such as Britain and Sweden, marginal rates of income tax could reach 90 percent and more. Yet taxation was but part of the solution. The nationalization of industry, particularly large-scale industry, had been a key demand made by socialist parties ever since Karl Marx and Fredrick Engels published the *Communist Manifesto* in 1848. The way ahead had been shown by the USSR, which following the Revolution of 1917 took over all important means of production. Elsewhere, Britain in 1926 created the Electricity Board; next, France during the premiership of Leon Blum (1936–37) nationalized its arms industry. Though socialists and communists have filled libraries in an attempt to show that Nazi Germany was the creation of capitalism, in fact its commitment to free enterprise and a market economy was ambivalent at best. By the end of World War II, the German State controlled about 60 percent of the entire economy or, at any rate, what was left of it.

Outside the USSR, the exact identity of the nationalized industries varied considerably. Often they included mass transportation, such as sea, air, and rail; telecommunications, such as telephone and telegraph; energy in the form of electricity and gas, banking, insurance, mining (particularly for coal and, later, oil), and critical branches of manufacturing such as steel, shipbuilding, aviation, and military equipment. Side by side with this went the creation of more and more welfare programs—until almost everybody was receiving some kind of indirect government subsidy (such as free education) and a great many were receiving direct subsidies (e.g. for bringing children into the world) as well. Even in the United States, always a latecomer in such matters, "big government" made its debut during the 1950s. In the 1960s, the Kennedy and Johnson administrations declared "war on poverty", which enabled them to set up, and preside over, a vast expansion of various government programs.[17]

Initially it was hoped to finance the services out of the profits of industry which, having been nationalized, would be made to work for the community at large rather than for their shareholders alone. These hopes, however, were disappointed. In democratic countries, and also in quite a number of non-democratic ones in the "developing" parts of the world, the more government gave, the more people expected from it. Often the success of the welfare state, as in creating conditions that permitted life expectancy to increase by leaps and bounds from the 1960s on and enabling single mothers to survive, also led to even more expenditure; for

17. For the creation of the American welfare state see Freeman, R. A. (1975) *The Growth of American Government; A Morphology of the Welfare State*, Hoover Institute Press, Stanford; also Gilbert, N. & Gilbert, B. (1989) *The Enabling State; Modern Welfare Capitalism in America*, Oxford University Press, New York.

example, in the form of funds targeting old people (who need far more than their share of medical care) and by causing the number of divorces to skyrocket.[18] Nor did the nationalized industries themselves fulfill the hopes that were hung on them. Having been created, before long many of them, run by political appointees on electoral principles rather than following business lines, had become grossly under-capitalized and overstaffed, incurred enormous losses, demanded vast subsidies, and hung like chains round the state's neck.[19] Since politicians were reluctant to meet the deficit by taxation, the outcome was inflation.[20] Finally, by that time, any naïve Weberian belief in the virtues of civil servants[21] had been lost by those who were forced to come into daily contact with them. Instead, they were seen as capricious, secretive, arbitrary, and, as often as not, incompetent too.

By the late 1970s, politicians such as Ronald Reagan ("get government off our backs") in the US and Margaret Thatcher in Britain ("stand on your own feet") were shouting at the top of their lungs, demanding that the welfare state be cut. They found backers in the form of supply-side (the so-called "Monetarist") school of economics whose headquarters was in Chicago and whose prophet, second only to the great Adam Smith himself, was Milton Friedman.[22] All through the 1980s the movement back to 19th-century economics gathered momentum. At the end of the decade it was given a tremendous boost by the collapse of the USSR. For seventy years, Communism had provided an alternative model in which the state, for all its manifold and perceived shortcomings, claimed to have eliminated the worst forms of poverty and promised security from the cradle to the grave. Now the system's sudden demise left the former East Block almost literally naked and their respective civil societies poorer than they had ever been. Not only did *laissez faire* capitalism re-emerge as the only way towards the future, but it no longer felt obliged to apologize for its seamier sides, such as gross inequality, ever-present insecurity for both employers and employees, and the colossal waste resulting from unbridled competition, unplanned development, and the business cycle. To the contrary, many of the advocates of the new economics regarded those features as useful tools towards the all important goals, low inflation and steady economic growth. One author even gained fame by claiming that, since the best possible relationship between states and their citizens had now been discovered in the form of some kind of liberal democracy, history itself was at an end.[23]

18. See, for the crisis of the welfare state, Logue, J. (1985) 'Will Success Spoil the Welfare State?', *Dissent*, Winter; and Leaman, C. (1980) *The Collapse of Welfare Reform; Political Institutions, Policy and the Poor in Britain and the US*, MIT Press, Cambridge.

19. For one country's experience with this kind of thing see Cohen, K. R. (1973) *British Nationalization 1945-1973*, Macmillan, London.

20. See, for some figures, Scammell, W. M. (1983) *The International Economy Since 1945*, Macmillan, London, p. 216.

21. Weber, M. (ed) (1976) *Economy and Society* [1923], G. Roth, New York, p. 481ff.

22. See Hammond, J. D. (ed) (1999) *The Legacy of Milton Friedman*, Edward Elgar Publishing, Cheltenham.

23. Fukuyama, F. (1991) *The End of History*, Avon Books, New York.

As of the early years of the twenty-first century, not even those countries that were loudest in their praise of capitalism had made significant progress in reducing their bureaucracies, much less in cutting taxes as a percentage of GDP. On the other hand, in virtually all countries some of the juicier morsels of the economy—air transport (almost all West European countries), telecommunications (ditto, plus Australia), postal services (Germany, New Zealand), coal (to the extent that there were buyers), oil, gas, banking, and insurance (to the extent that they had been nationalized in the first place) had been sold off. Nor did privatization stop at the sectors which, depending on the country in question, had been nationalized between about 1920 and 1975. In many cases privatization was even being applied to roads—as may yet become the case in Germany[24]—to prisons, and to every kind of service needed by the military from transport to laundry and from maintenance to cooking. Other parts of the economy were deregulated, enabling "healthy competition" to resume in theory but, in practice, often leading to bad maintenance as well as higher consumer prices.

Needless to say, these processes did not advance *pari passu* in all parts of the world. Here and there it was even possible to find countries trying to go in the opposite direction, as Bolivia, nationalizing its oil industry, did. In any case, compared to the socialist or semi-socialist economies of the early 1970s, there has taken place sea-change so vast as to constitute a revolutionary departure. Whether, in the long run, it will also better serve the needs of society remains to be seen.

The State and Globalization

Meanwhile, and often going almost unnoticed, technology had also performed an about-face. The rise of the state is inseparable from that of modern technology.[25] Print, roads, railroads, telecommunications and typewriters—to say nothing of weapons and weapon systems—were among the most important means that enabled the state to increase its power. Separately and in combination, they made possible the establishment and operations of the armed forces, the collection of revenue, the transmission of laws and decrees, and the gathering of information; all in amounts, at speeds, and over distances that had previously been undreamed-of. Conversely, those areas which for one reason or another have failed to establish powerful states are also usually the ones which lag behind in the generation and application of technology of every kind.

From the beginning, though, much post-1800 technology generated by the industrial revolution bore a Janus face. On the one hand, it enabled governments to cast the net of sovereignty farther, and more tightly, than before, helping them control everything within their borders. On the other, it tended to transcend those

24. See *Frankfurter Algemeine Zeitung*, January 26, 2006, p. 41.

25. See, above all, Tilly, C. (1992) *Coercion, Capital and European States, AD 990-1992*, Blackwell, Oxford.

borders, crossing them and turning them into obstacles to dominance. This was because, unlike its predecessors, much modern technology can only operate when, and to the extent that, it is grouped into systems. A plow, a hammer, a musket, even a steam engine or a ship, can do its job even in the absence of others of its kind; if numerous plows are used side by side, or many ships joined into a fleet, each one can still perform its function independently of the rest. Not so an individual railway train, or telegraph apparatus, or a telephone, or a fax machine, or a computer, each of which on its own is useless. The number of such technologies is growing day by day. With them, what matters is above all the *network* of tracks, or wires, or switchboards, which connects each unit with countless others of its kind. Even more critical is the central directing hand that, laying down schedules and sorting out routes and priorities, enables them to communicate with each other at will, in an orderly manner, and without mutual interference.

In theory, each state was, and still is, free to exercise its sovereignty and build its own networks to its own standards while ignoring those of its neighbors and refusing to integrate with them—something which, as the history of railways shows, actually did happen in the beginning. In practice, they could only do so at tremendous cost. The plight of North Korea is a perfect case in point. There, a xenophobic government has imposed isolation on its citizens, forcing them to become self sufficient in all important respects; by so doing, it prevented them from making use of whatever comparative advantages they may have. The price was inability to maximize the benefits of precisely those technologies that have developed most rapidly since 1945, i.e. communication (including data-processing) and transportation. The precise cost of isolation varies with circumstances and the size of the country in question. However, even in the case of the largest ones, it is still substantial—not for nothing has the US, as the country with the largest economy of all, been switching over to the metric system.

To avoid this cost, states had to gain access to international networks, which in turn forced them to grant foreigners access to their own. Furthermore, they also found it necessary to join the international bodies whose task was to regulate the technologies in question on behalf of all. The first such bodies made their appearance around the middle of the nineteenth century. Previously there had often been bilateral and multilateral alliances, some of which were intended to be permanent; however, the International Telegraph Union represented something else entirely. Its foundation, which took place in 1865, marked the first time when states created an organization in which they themselves were members but which at the same time had a legal personality of its own as well as a permanent staff and a permanent headquarters at which it could be reached. Within its own limited field, the organization was authorized to make decisions that were binding on states. It is true that no mechanism for enforcing those decisions was provided either at the time or later. But then one reason for this is precisely that, as experience has shown, in view of the very considerable disadvantages that resulted from remaining aloof, this organization as well as many similar ones could function tolerably well even without such a mechanism.

Serving as a model for others to come, the ITU was followed by the International Postal Union (1874)[26] and the International Bureau of Weights and Standards (1875). A landmark of sorts was reached in 1884 when geographical space was standardized by making Greenwich into the prime meridian; previously Krakow, Uraniborg, Copenhagen, Ter-Goes, Pisa, Augsburg, Isla del Fuego (in the Cape Verde Islands), Rome, Ulm, Tuebingen, Bologna, Rouen, St. Petersburg, Washington D.C., Philadelphia, Munich, Brussels, Rio de Janeiro, Amsterdam, Christiana, Lisbon Pultowa, Cadiz, Madrid, Warsaw, Paris and Stockholm had all competed for the honor.[27] The number of inter-governmental organizations reached 123 in 1951, 280 in 1972, and 395 in 1984.[28] They cover almost every conceivable field of human activity, from the regulation of air transport—the International Air Transport Association, IATA, was probably the only organization which counts more member-states than did the United Nations itself—through the conservation of wildlife all the way to the establishment of measures and standards and the disposal of hazardous materials.

By origin, the UN was simply a coalition of states established in order to fight Germany and Japan in World War II. Since then, becoming permanent, it has tended to take over many other international organizations and put them under a single roof. Like other international organizations it has developed its own legal personality, well-established identity, and bureaucratic mechanism. The latter is by no means identical with that of individual member states whose interests it serves, if at all, only to a very limited extent; witness the constant bickering between the UN and the US as the strongest single member. In many ways, its position resembles that of the medieval papacy; *vox populi, vox dei* (the voice of the people is like the voice of God), as the saying goes.

If only because the UN is capable of offering a forum for a state's opponents to voice its grievances, to oppose it usually means incurring substantial costs in terms of public opinion. Being subject to UN sanctions can also be expensive—as is shown by the fact that, within a year of the ones against South Africa being lifted, the country's foreign trade leaped by no less than thirty eight percent.[29] Furthermore, the Security Council, acting as a sort of global executive, has become increasingly willing to invoke Chapter VII of the U.N Charter and use force to police such states as either upset the international order or engaged in "intolerable" acts against their own populations; points in case being, besides Iraq, Somalia, Bosnia, and, most recently, Afghanistan.

Equally important, states have begun to join together into blocks whose territory is lager than that of individual members. To date, the best known and most successful of these blocks is the European Union; an organization which like no

26. For its history see Zacher, M. W. (1995) *Governing Global Networks: International Regimes for Transportation and Communication*, Cambridge University Press, London, 1995, p. 182 ff.

27. Schaeffer, R. K. (1982) 'The Standardization of Time and Place', *Ascent and Decline in the World System*, ed. Edward Friedman, Sage, London, pp. 71, 79.

28. Held, D. (1988) 'Farewell Nation State', *Marxism Today*, December, p. 15.

29. *World Link*, March-April 1994, p. 99.

other provides a tangible expression of the fact that the economic relationships generated by modern technology are on too large a scale to be effectively dealt with by individual countries. As originally conceived in 1953, the European Common Market had just six members and constituted no more than a free trade zone for coal and steel. Later the agreements were extended to other products as well, and common tariffs *vis a vis* the rest of the world were established.[30] Driven partly by the need to achieve economies of scale and partly by other factors, the Union expanded, until it has become the unit with the third largest number of people (after China and India) and the largest GNP on earth. Over the years it has developed its own legislative, its own High Court, and its own Executive.

Whether the Union will ever become a unified state is doubtful. Yet since 1963, when Community Law was declared to be directly binding on the member states,[31] it certainly made its influence felt on day to day life. Often this happens in entirely unexpected ways: as when the European Court ruled that the Government of Ireland could not prevent its citizens from traveling abroad to have an abortion or when the European Commission fined the British steel industry to the tune of 100,000,000 pounds sterling (1994). By allowing the citizens of member states to move, live and work freely—in some cases, also to have equal access to the social services offered by fellow members—the Union has gone a considerable way towards creating a common citizenship. In 1979, it was provided with a permanent source of revenue in the form of one percent of value-added tax receipts that is paid to it by each of the member states. Since then the Union has become the first non-state organization in modern history to issue a currency of its own, one which has taken the place of those of most member states.

The Union's economic success has encouraged states in other parts of the world to create similar organizations. Though none of them has progressed nearly as far as their model in creating common institutions and imposing a common law, multilateral arrangements aimed at encouraging trade, setting up a common economic front *vis a vis* the rest of the world, and dealing with ecological problems now number in the dozen. To list some of the most important ones only, 1959 saw the establishment of EFTA (European Free Trade Association) all of whose members later joined the European Union. In 1960, this was followed by LAFTA (the Latin American Free Trade Association, which incorporates Mexico and all Latin American countries except Guyana) as well as CACM (the Central American Common Market). UDEAC (Union Douaniere et Economique de l'Afrique Centrale, with Cameroon, the Central African Republic, Congo, and Gabon as its members) was founded in 1966, ASEAN (Association of South East Asian Nations, made up of Indonesia, Malaysia, the Philippines, Thailand and Singapore) in the next year. An Andean Common Market, (ACM), with Bolivia, Chile, Colombia, Ecuador, Peru and Venezuela as its members has existed since 1969 and was later

30. For the early history of the EEC see Milward, A. S. (1984) *The Reconstruction of Western Europe, 1945-1951*, Methuen, London; also Haas, E. B. (1968) *The Uniting of Europe: Political, Social and Economic Forces*, 1950-1957, Stanford University Press, Stanford.

31. See Stirk, P. M. R. (1996) *A History of European Integration since 1914*, Pinter, London, p. 169.

followed by MERCOSUR which includes Brazil, Bolivia, Paraguay, Uruguay, Argentina, and Chile. In 1975, the Economic Community of West African States (ECOWACS) was founded by Benin, Gambia, Ghana, Guinea, Guinea-Bissau, Ivory Coast, Liberia, Mali, Mauritania, Niger, Nigeria, Senegal, Sierra Leone, Togo and Upper Volta. In 1994, the ratification of the North American Free Trade Agreement (NAFTA) by the US, Canada, and Mexico showed that not even the largest and most productive economy in history can exist in isolation.

As the doubling, between 1965 and 1990, of the percentage of world product which was exported suggests,[32] often manufacturing and trading organizations represented in different states were better positioned to use the opportunities provided than were states themselves. Unlike the latter, multinational corporations did not have citizens to protect, welfare payments to make, frontiers to cover, or sovereign territory to worry about. Free of these responsibilities and limitations, they were able to seize economic opportunities wherever they presented themselves, as soon as they presented themselves, and for no longer as they presented themselves. They could do so either on their own, by setting up branch offices, or else by forging alliances with their foreign counterparts. The methods used included common research and development; a division of labor in manufacturing; shared access to distribution and service networks; the acquisition of each other's stock; as well as mergers of the kind that took place in May 1998 when German-based Daimler Benz married American-based Chrysler.

Finally, the unprecedented development of electronic information services seems to mark another step in the retreat of the state.[33] Probably at no time in history has any state been able to exercise complete control over the thoughts of all its citizens; to the credit of the more liberally-minded among them, it must be added that they did not even try. While the invention of print in the fifteenth century greatly increased the amount of information and reduced the cost at which it could be disseminated, the ability to move that information across international frontiers remained limited by the need to physically transport paper (or set up printing presses) as well as language barriers. The latter in particular were important. Their existence meant that, small diplomatic and commercial elites only excepted, information of every kind tended to be distributed very much on a country by country, people by people, basis.

In any event, the first of these problems was solved by the introduction of public radio broadcasting during the 1920s. The advent of television, which relies on pictures instead of words, to a large extent eliminated the second. During the 1980s, cable and satellite TV, as well as videotape, became widely available. Soon it began providing near-instant coverage of events on a global scale; a decade later the advent of internet, which enabled individuals to communicate with each other instantaneously, at all places, at all times, and regardless of distance and

32. World Bank (1992) *World Development*, World Bank, Baltimore, p. 235.

33. See Wriston, W. (1992) The *Twilight of Sovereignty: How the Information Revolution is Transforming our World*, Scribner, New York.

time of day, presented an even greater revolution. Individual states were forced to relax their control over information in favor of people and organizations everywhere which were not sovereign, did not have territory, and were not states. As a result, even the most powerful governments now tend to make policy very much with the so-called "CNN factor" in mind.[34] Others are doing what they can to keep the media out—an effort which, as the fate of the former USSR suggests, will almost certainly fail in the long run.

As of the last years of the twentieth century, the obstacles to "globalization" remain formidable. They include not just the kind of nationalism and xenophobia found in many parts of the developing world in particular; but also the type of regional organization which, so far from opening countries up to world trade, tends to build blocks of them that are relatively closed to it. Still, the impact of globalism and regionalism on individual states is similar.[35] The more important any state, the more likely it is to participate in a very large number of international organizations, be they global, regional, or merely technical. By so doing, it gives up parts of its sovereignty in return for a say in its neighbors' affairs; meanwhile, compared to the period 1945–75, the state's control over both their economies and their citizens' thoughts has undoubtedly declined. Other things being equal, states which join the process and make the best of it are likely to prosper. Whereas those which, whether for religious or ideological or other reasons, refuse to do so have fallen behind and, to all appearances, are doomed to continue falling behind.

The Threat to Internal Order

As governments surrender or lose their hold over many aspects of the media, the economy, and technology, and as public ownership as well as welfare programs stagnate or retreat in almost every country from Sweden to New Zealand, one of the principal functions still remaining to the state is to protect its integrity against terrorism and similar forms of violence in- and outside its borders. Thus the question to be asked is, to what extent it has been successful in this task; is it being mastered, or is it not?

Perhaps the best way to approach the problem is this. From the middle of the seventeenth century until 1914, the armed forces of "civilized" governments—primarily those of Europe, but later joined by North American and Japanese ones—proved themselves more than a match for other political entities and their societies. Over time, this advantage tended to grow: until, at Omdurman in 1896, a handful of British Maxim Guns wiped out entire columns of dervishes as if by magic. These victories permitted the "civilized" states to expand until they

34. See Wriston, W. (1993) 'The Twilight of Sovereignty', *The Flethcer Forum of World Affairs*, vol. 17, no. 2, pp. 117–130; Hodge, Jr., J. F. (1994) 'Media Pervasiveness', *Foreign Affairs*, vol. 73, no. 4, pp. 136–145.

35. Cf. Svetlicic, M. (1996) 'Challenges of Globalization and Regionalisation in the World Economy', *Global Society*, vol. 10, no. 2, pp. 207–223.

controlled almost the entire world. At peak, only three or four non-occidental countries escaped the domination which was often imposed on them by very small parties of foreigners from across the sea.

Since then, the change that has taken place is momentous. Starting in 1941, the year in which the Germans invaded Yugoslavia but, for all their ruthlessness, were unable to control it, countless "advanced" states have seen their armed forces suffer defeat at the hands of under-equipped, ill-trained, ill-organized, often even ill-clad and underfed and illiterate, freedom fighters or guerrillas or terrorists; briefly, by men—and, not seldom, women—who were short on everything except high courage and the determination to endure and persist in the face of police operations, counterinsurgency operations, peacekeeping operations, and whatever other types of operations that were dreamt up by their masters. The list of those who tried, and failed, in the face of such opponents is a long and dishonorable one. The British in Palestine, Malaysia, Kenya, Cyprus and Aden; the French in Indo-China and Algeria; the Americans in Vietnam and Iraq, the Soviets in Afghanistan and Chechnya, the Israelis in Lebanon and the Gaza Strip are some notable examples.

As these examples show, from 1945 on the vast majority of the larger guerrilla and terrorist campaigns in particular were waged in Third World countries; in other words, places where people were either trying to form states of their own or, on the contrary, where existing states had failed to assert their own monopoly over violence. Still it would not be true to say that the developed countries have remained immune to terrorism or that, in them, the problem does not exist. From Germany through France and Italy to Spain and Britain all the way to Japan and Spain, many of them have witnessed at least some terrorist acts take place on their national territories. Not seldom the attacks were deadly as dozens and even hundreds were killed or wounded; in the attacks on the Twin Towers and the Pentagon, almost 3,000 lost their lives in a single day.

How, in the face of these attacks, have the armed forces at the disposal of the state fared? That the most powerful weapons available to them, including specifically the heavy ones which account for the bulk of their budgets, are entirely useless against these and similar movements scarcely requires pointing out. What is needed are intelligence services, police forces, and riot-control forces, all of them operating both in- and out of uniform.[36] And in fact, since the onset of modern terrorism during the late sixties and early seventies, there is scarcely any advanced country which has not attempted to strengthen the "forces of order". Among the most common measures are the expansion of intelligence organizations and their coordination with each other; the establishment of special anti-terrorist squads trained in hostage-rescue operations and the like; the development and acquisition of a vast array of improved radio communications, foolproof identity cards, closed circuit television cameras, metal detectors, X-ray machines, night vision devices, listening devices, automatic bomb-disposal devices, and, most recently, machines

36. See Daeniker, G. (1995) *The Guardian Soldier: on the Nature and Use of Future Armed Conflict*, United Nations Institute for Disarmament Research, New York.

for detecting radioactive, chemical, and biological materials;[37] all backed up by computers where data from these and other sources is stored, collated, processed, and sent to wherever it is needed, instantaneously and sometimes across borders as states try to coordinate their responses to the threat. Should the security forces in certain countries have their way, then it is only a question of time before each and every one of us will be ordered to have his body implanted with a chip that will enable his or her movements to be tracked twenty-four hours a day, seven days a week; and even that is only the tip of the iceberg.

As various groups concerned with the preservation of privacy are telling us,[38] these developments are certainly disturbing. Perhaps even more disturbing, in face of the potential dangers—including, besides the ordinary bomb or guerrilla attack, chemical terrorism, biological terrorism, and nuclear terrorism—is the apparent inability of the various police forces to maintain the monopoly over violence in the hands of the state. Even in developed countries, the most that the majority of them can boast of is to have kept terrorism within "acceptable" boundaries. However, as people get used to watching terrorist actions unfold on TV the definition of what constitutes "acceptable" seems to be stretched year by year. To some extent the change has been recognized by formal international law. In 1977, the Fourth Geneva Convention was signed, affording some protection to combatants who are not recognizable from a distance and do not wear uniforms while participating in military operations.[39]

Meanwhile, from Washington's White House to London's Downing Street, the change that has taken place is obvious even to the casual tourist. Entire city-blocks in which presidents and prime ministers live and work, and which until not so long ago were open to traffic, are being sealed off and turned into fortresses; if only because nobody is willing to assume the responsibility, once closed it is unlikely that they will ever open again. Their protection is entrusted to uniformed and, especially, non-uniformed personnel with every imaginable technological device ready to hand. From Sweden to Israel, leaders who used to walk the streets freely and without an escort have long ceased doing so. They are now seen by the public, if at all, only when they are whisked from one place to another in their curtained, heavily armored, cars; to mislead potential terrorists, there are often several identical cars in a convoy or even several convoys moving in different directions. The places in which they are expected to appear are routinely sealed off and searched, sometimes for days or weeks before the event, as are the surrounding areas. It is the kind of security a Cesare Borgia, constantly assassinating others and constantly fearing assassination himself, might have been proud of and which, just a generation or two ago, was only considered necessary to protect some of the world's worst dictators such as Hitler and Stalin.

37. CNN, 16 March 1998.

38. See e.g. Davies, S. (1996) *Big Brother; Britain's Web of Surveillance and the New Technological Order*, Pan Books, London.

39. See, out of the vast literature, Watkin, K. (2005) *Warriors without Rights? Combatants, Unprivileged Belligerents, and the Struggle over Legitimacy*, Program on Humanitarian Policy and Conflict Research, no. 2, Harvard University, Cambridge, MA.

If only because security is one of the most manpower-intensive fields of human endeavor, providing it can be extremely expensive. To secure a military base or turn a block of government buildings into a fortress is one thing; to offer the same kind of protection to an entire country, another. Even supposing it could be made affordable and effective, it would render ordinary life next to impossible by leading to an intolerable slowing-down of the most ordinary activities. For these and other reasons—including, not least, the likelihood of being criticized in case of failure—many states are reluctant to engage their own forces on the task. At best, they will train anti-terrorist units and keep them in reserve in case they are called upon to deal with high-profile emergencies such as bombings, kidnappings, and the like. The financial and organizational burden represented by day to day security, however, is something which, as experience shows, they are quite ready to shift to private industry and individuals.

Whether because the government has ordered them to, as in the case of civil aviation in many countries, or because they simply do not trust the state to provide them with reasonable security, individuals and private industry have, in fact, been looking after themselves to a growing extent and on a constantly increasing scale. Depending on the nature of the perceived threat, the citizens of many countries have become accustomed to have their belongings checked, and/or their persons searched, each time they enter a department store, movie house, football stadium, rock concert, or similar places where crowds gather and where a terrorist act is therefore both more probable and, should it in fact take place, likely to result in heavy casualties. Individuals, neighborhoods, and corporations have tried to protect themselves against terrorism and crime by hiring private guards, erecting security fences, installing alarm systems and closed circuit TV, demanding proof of identity from employees and visitors who enter and leave buildings and installations, requiring badges, and much more.

While not all countries are affected to the same extent, so far those measures seem to have done little to win the war on terrorism. What they have done is to turn private security into a growth industry *par excellence*, world-wide.[40] In the U.S alone there are currently more people employed by private security firms than there are uniformed personnel in the armed forces; still the expansion is going on as, day by day, more and more targets are perceived as needing protection. Like so many others, the security industry is heavily centralized at the top. Some of the leading firms in the field are presently in command of private armies numbering in the thousands and more.

In many developing countries, notably New Guinea and Sierra Leone and Liberia, mercenaries have already been used to stage coups and countercoups.

40. See, for Germany, Jean d'Heur, B. (1994) 'Von der Gefahrenabwehr als staatlicher Angelegenheit zum Einszatz privater Sicherheitskraefte—einige Rechtpolitische und Verfassungsrechtliche Anmerkungen', *Archiv des Offentlichen Rechts*, vol. 119, no. 1, pp. 107–136; for France, Coqeteau, F. (1990) 'L'etat Face au commerce de la securite', *L'Annee Sociologique*, vol. 40, pp. 97–124; and for Italy, Ogliati-Vittorio, A. M. (1988) 'La Defesa Armata Privata in Italia', *Sociologia del Diritto*, vol. 15, no. 3, pp. 47–71.

While mercenaries do not yet threaten the political stability of developed countries, the range of services they offer is astonishing. They include research and development, both of weapons and of scenarios; recruiting, training, and testing personnel of every sort, from simple guards to the kind who specialize in fortifying entire compounds and conducting sophisticated investigations; selling, renting or leasing equipment that ranges from ten-cent plastic badges and crowd-control equipment all the way to million dollar explosive detectors; vetting personnel, detecting fraud, conducting polygraph tests, and wiretapping; planning, building, and operating security systems of every kind; as well as probing those defenses, also by means of specially designated "red" teams. Perhaps most surprising of all, their clients include not just private individuals, neighborhoods, and corporations, but, in some cases, government itself.

From the men in the boardroom to the guards at the gate, the personnel employed by the private security industry are often ex-military, intelligence and police in search of greener pastures. Sometimes prior service in one of those bodies is a condition for being taken on by the industry in question. In other cases, it is the policemen themselves who moonlight during their free time; they offer their services to everybody from the owners of football teams to shopkeepers.[41] Their training, which is equivalent to that given to the members of the state's own security apparatus, is thus put at the disposal of purely private objectives. As the American occupation of Iraq illustrates very well, with every passing day the members of the security industry and the state's security establishment appear to be growing more and more interchangeable.

Clearly the impact of these developments differs sharply from one place to another. Still, should present trends continue then the outcome is in sight, and indeed already now it is the subject of much science fiction[42] as well as the kind of games that may be run on one's personal computer. The provision of security—which since at least Thomas Hobbes has been recognized as *the* most important function of the corporation known as the state—will again be shared out among other entities.[43] Some will be territorial but not sovereign, i.e. communities larger than states; others, perhaps more numerous, neither sovereign nor territorial. Some will operate in the name of political or ideological or religious or ethnic objectives, others with an eye purely to private gain. Whatever their goals, all will need money to survive. They will get it by contracting with states to do their dirty business for them, or by selling their services to other organizations, or by blackmailing the population;[44] e.g. during

41. See Vardalis, J. J. (1992) 'Privatization of Public Police', *Security Journal*, vol. 3, no. 4, pp. 210–214.

42. E.g. Stephenson, N. (1992) *Snow Crash*, Bantam Books, New York.

43. See Mansbach, R. W., Ferguson, Y. H. & Lampert, D. E. ((1976) *The Web of World Politics, Nonstate Actors in the Global System*, Prentice Hall, Englewood Cliffs, p. 297.

44. On these methods see, in general, Naylor, R. T. (1993) 'The Insurgent Economy: Black Market Operations of Guerrilla Organizations', *Crime, Law and Social Change*, vol. 20, no. 1, pp. 13–51; and, for a case study, Maguire, K. (1993) 'Fraud, Extortion and Racketeering: the Black Economy in Northern Ireland', *Ibid*, vol. 20, no. 4, pp. 273–292.

the PLO's uprising against Israel all three methods were used, whether by different factions or simultaneously by the same ones. Conversely, and as is already the case in some places, it is likely that states will adopt the principle of "user pays". They will start charging fees for at least some kinds of security, such as providing assistance in case of a burglary, which used to be provided—to the extent that they were provided—for free.

Thus the likelihood grows that the state will lose its monopoly over those forms of organized violence which still remain viable in the nuclear age, becoming one actor among many. Spreading from the bottom up, the conduct of that violence may revert to what it was as late as the first half of the seventeenth century: namely a capitalist enterprise little different from, and intimately linked with, so many others. Where princes and other military entrepreneurs used to contract with each other in order to make a profit—an Amsterdam capitalist, Louis de Geer, once provided the Swedish Government with a complete navy, sailors and commanders up to the vice admiral included—in the future various public, semi-public and private corporations will do the same. With some of them security will form their main line of business, whereas with others it will be ancillary. Some will be legal, others criminal; although as time goes on and the various organizations and people interact with each other—if only in order to learn how to provide security better—the differences between them are likely to diminish.

In many so-called developing countries, the situation just described already exists and has, indeed, never ceased to exist. Whether acting on their own—mounting private guards, even setting up entire armies—or by forming agreements with local insurgents, people and corporations are trying to safeguard their property and their operations; a situation often known as neocolonialism.[45] It is true that most citizens of most advanced countries are still able to sleep safely in their beds, albeit that more of those beds are coming to be protected by weapons and surrounded by walls. As of 1999, an estimated three million U.S citizens were living in tens of thousands of gated communities, and the numbers were growing every day.[46] Both for them and for their less fortunate countrymen, future life will likely become less secure, or at any rate more obsessed with security, than the one which was provided by the most powerful states of the past.

Through a Glass, Darkly

Whereas, during the sixty years since 1945, the number of states has tripled, this does not necessarily mean that states, qua organizations, are becoming stronger. Numerical growth may, in fact, be a sign of decay; what everybody has is worth

45. See Clapham, C. (1996) *Africa and the International System, the Politics of State Survival*, Cambridge University Press, Cambridge. Particularly part 3.

46. Blakely, E. J. & Snyder, M. G. (1999) *Fortress America: Gated Communities in the United States*, Brookings Institution Press, Washington, DC, p. 3.

little or nothing. Furthermore, almost all newly-created states are subject to the same forces as the old ones. They are able to fight each other only when they are weak to begin with; their financial, fiscal, and welfare systems are weak; feeling the power of globalization, they hasten to become members of every kind of international organization that will take them; plus, in many cases, they are unable to maintain law and order within their borders.

Will states win the war against terrorism or will terrorism continue to spread, threatening and disrupting the lives of ordinary people not only in developing countries but in developed ones as well? Will the growth of the private security industry strengthen the states that employ it or encourage their citizens to employ it, or will the day come when, like some Frankenstein monster, it turns its guns on those who created it? Will the various measures now being put into place to combat terrorism, from the Patriot Act down, achieve their purpose, or will they merely create a situation where more and more people, losing their faith in the state's essential fairness as well as its ability to protect them, will either start looking after themselves or take up arms against it? At the time of writing, the jury concerning these questions is still out.

Be the answers to these questions as they may, the remaining three processes outlined in this paper seem to be advancing relentlessly. Whatever presidents, prime ministers, ministers of defense, chiefs of staff, and other "strategists" may say, in practice the ability of states to wage war on other states has, largely thanks to nuclear proliferation, been steadily declining over the last sixty years. Whatever socialists (in the US, liberals), may say, in practice almost every state around the world has been cutting its welfare services and privatizing its assets; the latter process has now reached the point where even port-operations and national electricity grids are for sale to domestic and foreign investors. Whatever proponents of national sovereignty may say, in practice advancing technology, particularly transportation and communication, has created a situation where hardly any state can survive, let alone prosper, without becoming involved with, hence in part restricted by, international organizations of every sort.

What the future may bring is anybody's guess. It is, however, likely that, should the four factors described in the present paper continue to operate, the state will gradually find itself replaced, in part at least, by other organizations. Some, such as the European Union and the United Nations, will stand above the state and will be able to demand compliance as a price of further membership. Others, such as the multinational organizations, the media, and various terrorist organizations will be of a completely different kind. What they all have in common is that they either assume some of the functions of the state, such as providing welfare and security, or else use various means to escape its control, or both. What they also have in common is that, thanks largely to the fact that they do not have either sovereign territory or borders, they are better able to take advantage of modern, systems-based, technology than states are.

To sum up, the three hundred something year period that opened at Westphalia in 1648 during which the state was the most powerful and most important organization in which people lived—first in Europe, then in other places too—is coming to an end. The full significance of the transition cannot be foreseen. It is likely to be eventful; and, as is already the case in many "failed" states across Asia and Africa, bloody. Still, given that the last full-scale conflict between the world's most powerful states (World War II) left some sixty million people dead, the future cannot be much worse than the past. To quote a verse by Mao, written in response to the question, what the world would look like in the wake of a nuclear war:

> The sun will keep rising
>
> Trees will keep growing
>
> And women
>
> Will keep having children.

Nation-states, Market-states, and Virtual-states

John Robb

Conventional wisdom looks at the current global conflicts merely through the lens of nation-state conflict. This historical approach sees today's terrorism as proxy conflict. It also assumes that many of our current international security systems can be transformed to accommodate the rise of the current threat.

John Robb is a highly regarded analyst/futurist, with a focus on the intersection of terrorism, infrastructure, technology, and markets. His new book on next generation terrorism, called the Brave New War, is expected in the Spring of 2007. He also wrote an Op-Ed for the New York Times on "Open-Source Warfare" (2005) and an article for Fast Company magazine's tenth anniversary issue called "Power to the People" (a rethink of the future of US security in 2016). He is also known for his ability to identify and aid in the development of trends years before they become global. For example: he was the first professional analyst to cover the Internet in 1995–97, a key player in the launch of online financial services in 1997–2001, and a critical participant in the development of weblogs and RSS in 2001–2003. He is currently working on a global just-in-time/place manufacturing platform that will revolutionize the world's 4th largest industry. Mr. Robb has been quoted as an expert analytical source on technology topics hundreds of times in newspapers such as the New York Times and the Wall Street Journal and has been interviewed on the BBC and CNBC. He has lived, worked, and traveled extensively in Central/South America, Africa, Asia, and Europe. His previous experience includes service in a tier one counter-terrorist unit that worked closely with Delta and Seal Team 6. In this role, he participated in global operations as a mission commander, pilot, and mission planner (El Salvador, Panama, Colombia, Egypt, etc.).

However, this traditionalist framework is simplistic in that it is neither fully explanatory of the current conflict's complexity and dynamism, nor useful as a means to envision future successful scenarios. The reason is due to a failure to accommodate the emergence of a new meta-environment for conflict, that is, a globally integrated economic and societal superinfrastructure. This new environment is in the process of transforming how states operate and cooperate. It has also transformed the nature of the non-state threat by allowing it to gain economic independence, easily mount global operations, and adopt new innovative organizational structures.

Philip Bobbitt, a constitutional legal scholar, provides a more useful framework for analyzing the current situation. Based on the emergence of this super-infrastructure, his book *The Shield of Achilles* makes a historically detailed case that the bureaucratic nation-state is in an inevitable transition to a more competitive form called the "market-state." All of the major nation-states, from China to the US to the countries comprising the EU, are in varying phases of this transition.

The Market-state

The impetus for the creation of the market-state is the loss of the core legitimacy of the nation-state - its ability to provide for the welfare of its people. This welfare is both too expensive and too cumbersome to administer within a hyper-competitive global economic system. As a replacement, according to the framework provided by Bobbitt, nation-states are in the midst of shifting their legitimacy to a new basis: one that will deliver maximal 'opportunity' through the use of market mechanisms.

> Obviously, there will be differences in how to accomplish this:
>
> Because the market-state secures political legitimacy through the active pursuit of opportunity for its citizens but declines to specify the goals for which that opportunity is used, there will be different models whose advocates can plausibly maintain that their constitutional strategy best maximizes opportunity.[1]
>
> From this competition, Philip posits that three dominant methods have emerged,

- *The Entrepreneurial market-state*. This market-state characterizes the US approach. This model minimizes regulation to increase flexibility of approach and consumer choice. It is characterized by privatized health care/pension-s/education/housing, open immigration, and low taxes.[2]

1. Bobbitt, P. (2003), *The Shield of Achilles: War, Peace and the Course of History*, First Anchor Books, New York, p. 669.
2. Ibid. pp. 670–671.

- *The Mercantile market-state*. This is exemplified by Taiwan, Korea, Japan, and Singapore. This approach maximizes employment. To do this, it dictates high savings rates, heavily subsidizes R&D/critical industries, and engineers exchange rates.[3]
- *The Managerial market-state*. This describes the European Union. This model maximizes social cohesion. To accomplish this, it uses cooperative relationships between labor /corporations, broad-based social safety nets, and income normalization through taxation.[4]

Each of these protean market-states [see Table 1] is in the midst of reworking their constitutional structures to maximize the opportunity of their respective populations. We can expect that during this phase transition there will be mistakes, reversals, and revisions in each of the respective approaches as a dispassionate global marketplace adjudicates their efficacy. Although, the competition between market-states is primarily economic, it can, at times, descend into military conflict.

Conflict Between Market-states

The primary source of conflict between market-states, as we have already discussed, will not be ideological but economic. This stands to reason, given that all of them have adopted the same system driven by economic competition. Despite this similarity, the differences in style can result in conflict or an inability to work together to resolve common problems. Bobbitt details three examples of complaints that could lead to this result:[5]

- Mercantile: "exploiting foreign markets while closing their own (not open enough)"
- Entrepreneurial: "failure to get control of consumption and thus exporting inflation (too chaotic)"
- Managerial: "keeping interest rates high (not growing fast enough)"

While it is possible that these complaints could lead to conflict, as trade conflict helped bring the US and Japan to war in World War II, it's unlikely in the current context that these factors would be sufficient for warfare. What Bobbitt doesn't fully address in his book is the most likely factor that could lead to warfare: residual nationalism and nation-state defense spending.

In all three systems, defensive military forces are still the recipients of substantial funding, despite its negative impact on economic competitiveness. Spending at these levels is entirely an artifact of previous nation-state conflict. The penultimate example of this is the US which, according to the author's

3. Ibid. pp. 671-672.
4. Ibid. pp. 672-674.
5. Ibid. P. 675.

Table 1 Market-state and virtual-state typology

	Entrepreneurial	*Mercantile*	*Managerial*	*Virtual*
Ethos	Libertarian	Social Stability	Social Equality	Group preservation
Opportunity Maximized	Set individuals free to make their own decisions	Long-term opportunities of society	We are all equal (Class divisions suppressed)	Group rights Survival
Labor Unions	Weak	Strong (National Industries)	Broad and Participatory Strong National Unions "Stakeholder Company"	None
Savings	Low	High	Medium	Ad hoc
Income Disparity	High	Suppressed	Suppressed	Varies
Interest Rates	High	Low	High	N/A
Immigration	Robust	Shuns It Cultural Homogeneity	Open to "Guest Works" Hostile to new citizens	No territory
Military	All Volunteer Mercenary	Conscription	Conscription	Universal Volunteer
Warfare	Frequent	Avoided	Reluctant but present	Constant
Media Control	None	Varying Degrees	Varying Degrees	Tight
Cohesiveness of Society	Problematic	Dictated	Socially Cohesive Society	Tight
Health Care, Housing, Pensions Education	Privatized Sparse	Frugal	Generous Ubiquitous	Varies Philanthropy
Alienation Type	Working Poor	Young from the Old	No Job Prospects	Criminal
Source of Tension	"Lowest paid workers vastly worse off than high wave earners" Class system	"Productivity and efficiency problems exist because of artificially high employment rates"	"Can get by on welfare benefits alone" Lack of Dignity/Boredom	"Illegitimate use of warfare and criminal economic means."
Incidents	Debt	Financial crisis	Riots	Fragmentation Arrest
Examples	United States	Hong Kong, Japan, Taiwan, Singapore, South Korea	Europe, India Turkey, and Egypt	Al Qaeda, MEND, etc.

estimates, spends as much on defense as the rest of the world combined. While spending by itself isn't a problem, the fact that these large militaries exist makes them a threat since it radically increases the chances that accidents, mistakes, and ill-advised usage could occur. Also, many of the mindsets (sophisticated, but legacy) employed by the military are heavily nationalistic, it can be expected that occasionally there will be agitation to use it in times of tension.

The more worrisome problem is the tendency to use legacy nationalism in times of stress to improve national cohesion. We have seen this in China in its relations with Taiwan and Japan. In the US, we have seen it in relations with Mexico, China, Japan, and Iraq/Iran/Syria. With the EU, it has been directed towards Turkey, Russia, and the US. Since the phase transition to market-states is destined to be rough, since it is attempting a complex judo move that changes out sources of legitimacy, we can expect both those in power and demagogues on the outside to use nationalism at regular intervals in the near future. However, despite these legacy threats, it is reasonable to assume that the mutual interconnectedness made possible by the global superinfrastructure will guard against any major interstate conflict in the future.

This interconnected counter pressure will take the form of corporations and individuals that span both market and state environments. With interests and voices in both spheres, they can be expected to force compromise to most conflicts under the argument that there is "too much to risk." Further, given the dominance of global markets as the platform upon which these market-states exist, we can expect market reaction to become a major factor in any future considerations of conflict. Global credit, equity, and currency markets would be expected to deal with any talk of war between major market participants harshly. The impact of these devaluations would be immediately felt across the entire population of the belligerent states, to the detriment of the critical form of legitimacy, that is, opportunity.

Scenarios

The real security issues within the context of mutually interdependent but competitive market-states isn't deliberate warfare between these states but rather comes from two external sources: unexpected shocks and non-state threats. Bobbitt provides some guidance here. He constructed three scenarios which detail the trade-offs associated with each system (entrepreneurial, managerial, and mercantile) gaining global acceptance as the preferred model. Let's examine the tradeoffs made for each scenario in turn.[6]

The rise of the Entrepreneurial market-state model in Bobbitt's *The Meadow* scenario was made possible by the leadership of the US. Not only did the US succeed on numerous occasions on the battlefield against rogue regimes, it also was able to successfully shepherd the international community through numerous

6. Ibid. pp. 729–744.

rounds of trade liberalization. This combination of successes, led to the global acceptance of the entrepreneurial US market-state model. The community of nations that emerged, i.e. the G-9 (including China), became activist in their approach to security. Spurred by common interest, these nations intervened in those nations that breached established norms of behavior, such as support for terrorism and genocide. Eventually, due to limits on military participation in the developed world, the G-9 adopted private military forces as its main mechanism of enforcement. In many ways, this vision of the future is similar to Thomas Barnett's approach to the future:[7] US-centric, activist, participatory (between the members of the new core), and technically competent (where security is commoditized).

The tradeoff of the US entrepreneurial system was a vast increase in income inequality. Quality of life suffered as violent crime swept increasingly feral global cities. Further, market reforms and regulation were completely ignored. As a result, financial shocks were common and eventually resulted in a severe backlash among developing states. As a result, these states fell back on nation-state bureaucracies to provide for the welfare of their citizens.

The rise of the managerial market-state, *The Park* scenario, points to a rapid deterioration of confidence in the US, leading to global nuclear proliferation. The successor to *pax Americana* was a large number of relatively weak regional security groups that shared nuclear protection (much more common since proliferation began), cultural roots, and trading interests. These new blocs focused exclusively on a narrow set of regional concerns and had the power to block global initiatives (from both the UN or the US) that addressed global problems.

While conflict within these blocs was lessened, their inability to work with the larger global community allowed crisis after crisis to spin out of control. These system shocks and moral disasters increased the tendency of these blocs to turn inward and increased the barriers to external access across economic and social lines. These barriers, in turn, increased unemployment and slowed growth within the blocs. For those states not included in prosperous blocs, such as those in the developing world, it led to major economic disasters.

The final scenario, *The Garden*, is the result of the rise of the mercantile market-state. This scenario begins with the US plunging into isolation and a focus on mercantile economic policy (tariffs, etc.). The impact of this reversal forces the world to adopt the same approach, with each state taking on the burdens of its own defense and economic policy. All of the major institutions of global cooperation were starved of funding and support.

The result of this return to classic modes of sovereignty forced several near misses in inter-state warfare but eventually resulted in a new type of security

7. Barnett, T. P. M. (2004), *The Pentagon's New Map: War and Peace in the Twenty-First Century*, G.P. Putnam's Sons, New York; *Blueprint for Action: A Future Worth Creating*, Putnam Adult, New York, 2005.

system that enshrined state sovereignty as the core value. Due to this inwardly focused system, crises and panics that arose (particularly in the developed world) were left to solve themselves. In order to address the adverse consequences of these system shocks, states launched massive programs in concert with higher taxes to produce technologies and solutions that addressed their domestic impacts.

All three of these scenarios demonstrate the complicated set of tradeoffs that each system provides. In all of these scenarios, large-scale inter-state warfare is avoided. They are messy but they ultimately work to provide economic progress and advancement. Unfortunately, these scenarios studiously avoid the prospect of a new organizational system emerging from the new global superinfrastructure—in the form of the rise of the virtual-state. Bobbitt initially dismisses this threat in a concluding paragraph:

> To shape, if not permanently forestall, this war to come, the society of states must organize in ways that enable it to prevent the proliferation of weapons of mass destruction, to treat expeditionary expeditions as opportunities for consensus building coalitions, and to share information as a means of defense against disguised attacks. By these means, the next epochal war can be converted into a series of interventions and crises, instead of a world-shattering cataclysm or a stultifying and repressive world order.[8]

However, after 9/11 he revised his prognosis:

> Only a state could raise the revenues, muster the armies and organize the logistics required to threaten the survival of another state. Soon this will no longer be true, owing to advances in computer technology, communications and weapons of mass destruction. We are entering a period in which a small number of people, operating without overt state sponsorship but using the enormous power of modern computers, biogenetic pathogens, air transport and even small nuclear weapons, will be able to exploit the tremendous vulnerabilities of contemporary open societies. Because the origin of these attacks can be effectively disguised, fundamental tenets of the nation-state will change.[9]

Virtual-states

The transformative effect of the emerging global superinfrastructure isn't limited to the role of states. It is also going to have a major impact on the role of non-state groups. In contrast to the decline in power experienced by the world's largest states during the transition to market-states, non-state groups will gain considerable power as they transition to virtual-states (see Table 1).

Like market-states, virtual-states (al-Qaeda, Nigeria's MEND, and others) are the realized adaptive response of older organizational structures to the

8. Bobbit, P. (2003), p. 815.
9. Bobbitt, P. (2002) 'Get Ready for the Next Long War', *Time*, September 1.

emergence of a new global platform. This new platform allows goods, services, people, resources, and ideas to flow more freely and faster than ever before. While these newly accelerated flows have diminished the power of the nation-state by the destruction of sovereignty and independence, it has strengthened the hand of non-states since these structures now have the ability to:

- Avoid detection and elimination by living in the growing interstitial spaces between states (i.e. 5th dimensional battlespace)
- Develop economies that thrive on illegal flows of goods, services, people, resources, and ideas (intellectual property) made possible by the loss of state control
- Gain military power through utilization of new forms of Internet-enabled cooperation, development of new networked organizational types, access to rapid advances in commonly available technologies, and leveraging global transportation systems

Like the emerging market-states, virtual-states will ride the growth of the emerging global superinfrastructure. However, given their size, they may prove much better at adapting to the new environment than market-states. This has broad implications for the developing market-state framework posed by Bobbitt. It means that the emerging threats, and their ability to create system shocks, are substantially more dangerous than proposed in his scenarios.

The rise of the virtual-state as a competitive organizational form began in earnest in the 1990's with the growth of globalization. As globalization's flows began the process of unlocking the world from the stultification of isolated nation-states, fissures developed. Areas of ungoverned space, interstitial areas between and within states, emerged. Further, new pressures driven by the rapid expansion of the global superinfrastructure has created a self-awareness of the gaps in coverage within states by impacted groups. In addition new burdens on previously isolated identities (ethnic, religious, tribal, etc.) have emerged. For these groups, it was clear that their opportunity (however they defined it) was not being served by the prevailing state structures.

As a result, previously weak organizational forms are emerging to fill the "opportunity" void faster than transitioning nation-states and the community of states can adapt. Unlike most nation-states, these new organizational structures are based on a clean set of primary loyalties: to the tribe, clan, religion, gang, sect, or ethnicity. If looked at from an historical vantage point, this may represent a major reversal of legitimacy. Whereas nation-states consider virtual-states illegitimate, based on rules they established themselves, the success of these virtual-states may prove the opposite is true, that is, that nation-states, due to their inability to provide political goods and security, are illegitimate. As these virtual-states continue to generate success, in economics and warfare, nation-states will be forced to recognize them as equals.

The Virtual-state Economy

One major reason these groups have become autonomous is the growth of a global criminal economy. To really understand how this "black globalization" operates, the work of Moises Naim, the editor of *Foreign Policy* journal, is a good place to start. In his book *Illicit*, he identified the five flows of global smuggling:[10]

1. Weapons
2. Drugs
3. People
4. Knock-off products
5. Finance

In the past, illicit flows in these areas were relatively small in comparison to the vast bulk of the aggregate global economy, most of which occurred within rather than between states. Globalization changed that equation. The growth of global trade required the loosening of border controls and oversight. Further, the speed and volume of its growth outstripped the limited controls that were in place. As a result, the volume of smuggling in illicit goods blossomed. It is now, according to Moises, a $2.5 trillion economy growing at 7 times the growth in legal international trade.

The rapidity of this economy's growth also forced a change in how it was serviced. It quickly outgrew the capacity of the previous supply structure, a combination of organized criminal syndicates and independent freelancers that specialized in specific products. In its place, a new more complicated structure emerged. This new structure is characterized by a complex network of specialists in each aspect of global supply chain management, from warehousing to air transportation to cross border operations to payments to communications. Furthermore, this new supply chain is undifferentiated, in that it can handle any type of major flows listed above.

The new loose structure of this global black economy opened up the floodgates for new entrants. Without criminal syndicates as gatekeepers, a diverse set of groups could now enter this new economy as long as they could provide valuable services. Virtual-states have been happy to oblige.

The Virtual-state War Machine

The second major advance in the autonomy of virtual-states has been in their ability to fight and win wars. The most recent example of this new ability was seen during the summer of 2006, when the Israeli Defense Force (IDF) ran into Hezbollah in southern Lebanon. Hezbollah, an outgrowth of the earlier Israeli

10. Naim, M. (2005), *Illicit: How Smugglers, Traffickers and Copycats are Hijacking the Global Economy*, Doubleday, New York.

occupation of southern Lebanon, had undergone a substantial improvement in capability over the last decade.

First, it had taken the decade to improve its economic position by both participating in global criminal markets as well as making an alliance with a nation-state (Iran). Second, it built a force, armed with the correct weaponry, and a defensive strategy capable of defeating the IDF in battle. Third, it had improved its domestic position by providing political goods to the neglected Shiite subset of the Lebanese population. The result was that within the context of southern Lebanon, it was nearly unassailable.

The clash in the Summer of 2006 proved the point. To win its victory, Hezbollah focused on two weaknesses of the modern state to win the battle. The first was the increasing inability of Western militaries to accept casualties in battle. By deploying its small autonomous teams in a dispersed pattern, building defensive fortifications, training them in anti-tank operations, and listening in on Israeli battlefield communications, the Hezbollah strategy was simple: to trade territory for the blood of Israeli soldiers. The result was predictable, as IDF casualties exceeded 100 (with a substantial loss of armor) for little in gains of either territory or enemy casualties, the offensive bogged down politically. The loss of soldiers exceeded the tertiary goals upon which the war was launched.

The second Hezbollah method focused on the insensitivity of the modern Israeli state to prolonged economic damage. To accomplish this, Hezbollah assembled a substantial arsenal of unguided rockets with which it could strike at northern Israel. During the entire engagement, Hezbollah's rockets rained down on towns and cities in northern Israel at a great economic cost - early government estimates put the damage at 1.5% of Israel's GDP or $5.3 billion.[11] The combination of these methods resulted in a vice grip on Israeli strategy, in that the longer the war went on, the greater the economic damage via rocket attacks, and the faster the ground forces pushed to clear the area of rockets, the higher the IDF casualty counts. The end result was predictable. The Israelis stopped the offensive before attaining any meaningful gains.

Another example of virtual-state improvement can be seen in the US experience in Iraq, although with substantial differences from the Hezbollah example. While Hezbollah took a cohesive organizational approach, albeit decentralized, the Iraqi approach has been to completely dispense with organizational hierarchy. This new approach, one that is fully explored in the upcoming book, *Brave New War*[12] is best termed open source warfare. In this organizational approach, micro virtual-states composed of gangs, tribes, religious sects, etc. (nearly any source of loyalty that is stronger than a loyalty to the state), were used in a extremely loose configuration to defeat US forces in Iraq.

11. Chu, H. & Bekker, V. (2006), 'Israel Adds Up War's Damage to Its Economy', *Los Angeles Times*, August 18, http://www.latimes.com/news/nationworld/world/la-fg-economy18aug18,1,3441529.story

12. Robb, J. (2007), *Brave New War*, Wiley, New York, in press.

Like open source development in the software industry, a movement of this type is organized around what is called a *plausible promise*. In software, a plausible promise is a prototype of a software product that points to what is possible. Developers from across the spectrum – for reasons entirely their own – come together to improve the product and advance it from idea to reality. The process is fast, innovative, and effective. In warfare, groups that reflect a wide spectrum of primary loyalties come together to advance a central concept. In the case of Iraq, that was at first the expulsion of the US military. Since then, it has mutated to include the destruction of the central Iraqi government. Innovations that have been produced by this organizational structure include improvised explosive devices or IEDs (to include a rapid process of improvement in technology and employment), system disruption (the destruction of critical systems upon which both reconstruction and the Iraqi government rely), and social chaos (a process that fractures societal cohesiveness and in turn feeds the open source war through the development of new groups).

The results of the attempted reconstruction of Iraq speak for themselves. Not only is the US military and political apparatus on the verge of withdrawal, Iraq is in chaos. Iraq's social systems are in full collapse, its economy is in shambles due to system failures, and the new Iraqi army is more a collection of militias than a cohesive instrument of state policy. Unfortunately, this new method of warfare is now on the march globally, recently emerging in Nigeria (where 25% of the country's oil output has been disrupted due to a open source insurgency) and Balochistan (which has disrupted natural gas output and forced the Pakistani government to declare a truce with the Taliban affiliated rebels in Waziristan).

We can expect to see more of this in the future as globalization extends the economic capabilities of non-state groups, while at the same time providing them access to modern technologies (including weapons).

The Conflict

The rise of the virtual-state will complicate the transition of nation-states to market-states. Already, we see a general abdication of responsibility for policing/controlling the growth of global smuggling networks. Market-states, without the benefits of nation-state powers of internal control, are at a loss as to methods by which to successfully achieve such control. Methods such as legalization, decentralized innovation, transparency, and market incentives are thin on the ground as western states still cling to increasingly out-dated notions of sovereignty. The global system of nation-states, as it is currently designed and operated, is insufficient to the challenges presented by this new threat.

The ultimate result of this is clear. This parallel global economy will continue to quickly advance and will increasingly corrupt formerly legal trade as its profits are reinvested. It will become ever more difficult to see where the edges of the illegal economy ends and the legal one begins. Further, the label "illegal" may even become something meaningless as the percentage of the global economy so labeled reaches critical mass. We are already seeing this in many developing nations where large sections of the government are openly allied with this parallel economy. The wealth of this uncontrolled economy will, in turn, attract a bewildering variety of sub-groups into its web of transactions since it is not judgmental in regards to the political status of its participants. The tacit acceptance of this new state of affairs will eventually morph into open acceptance of these economic flows in order to slow the encroachment of virtual-states. It poses the question: would the states of Bolivia and Colombia be stronger and more legitimate if cocaine was legalized?

Armed with this huge and growing economic strength, these newly empowered groups will often find themselves in conflict with states in transition. The early tests of this conflict are not encouraging. The entrepreneurial model of *pax Americana* has fallen flat in the killing fields of Iraq, Afghanistan, and Lebanon. As a result, Asian states (China and Russia in particular) have forcefully opted out of the conflict and instead have adopted an ecumenical approach to global trade that avoids judgment. This approach is in line with the mercantile approach of those countries. Europe's managed approach is also falling flat in any region outside of Europe, since the global pace of disintegration towards culturally cohesive statelets is beyond the capacity of the international system to comprehend.

What we are left with is a chaotic global system with none of the three of Bobbitt's proposed systems of market-state cooperation and development dominant in anything but a subset. This mixed system will likely produce a hybrid that reflects the growth of the global economy dominated by virtual-states (this is my own contribution to Bobbitt's taxonomy of scenarios): *The Wilderness* scenario.

The Wilderness Scenario

The early years of this scenario were dominated by a series of conflicts set in motion by 9/11. In these conflicts, the US took the lead as the primary enforcer of global security. However, the emergence of virtual state systems that could defend themselves outstripped the limited resources the US could apply to the conflicts. Unprepared for the fact it was unable to defeat these forces through standard counter-insurgency, the US falsely analyzed the failures as counter-pressure from what it termed rogue-states. As a result, the US, with a rapidly decreasing amount of support from the international community of states, launched an attack on what it saw as the primary sponsor of its defeats—Iran.

The chaos birthed by this attack, created an arc of instability from the deserts of the Sudan to the mountains of the Hindu Kush. States within this area were operating at the edge of failure and, within each, strong virtual-states emerged to challenge their dominance. In each case, efforts at counter-insurgency and disaster relief sponsored by the US failed when placed into conflict with the virtual-states employing new means of defense. Out gunned and beset by exhaustion, the US withdrew from the area of conflict to focus on the more troubling problem of the failure of Mexico.

Mexico's failure was a combination of the depletion of easy money from oil (inevitable due to the failure of the super-giant Cantarell oil field) and the influx of pressures from globalization. These events forced the government into collapse during the 2006 Summer elections. The state limped along, from crises to crises, until 2009 when it fell into full failure. Virtual-states emerged throughout the country in overlapping zones of control. Some cooperated but in general they fell into competition for the residual wealth of the country and access to crucial cross border smuggling routes into the US.

The US, beset by the heavily armed gangs crossing into southern regions of the country that accompanied the mass influx of new illegal immigrants (some estimates claimed that the new waves involved 10 million new arrivals a year) from the south, began a crash program of deportation, border barriers, and internal controls. The result was several ugly incidents along the border that resulted in the mass slaughter of illegal immigrants. Since protests against these actions were banned, and tight legal restrictions on immigration turned illegal immigrants and their supporters into felons, a large number within the Hispanic community became radicalized. This radicalization resulted in the emergence of virtual-states within the borders of the US that derived its logistical basis from a robust parasitic existence within the domestic economy of the US and uncontrolled cross-border smuggling. Further, these groups were quickly able to purchase and employ weapons and methods of warfare that made them very effective against the National Guard and police units sent to confront them.

The US wasn't alone with internal problems. China, Russia, and Europe were all feeling similar effects as large sections of their geographies and ubiquitous sub-groups fell into an uncontrolled status and held primary loyalties to groups other than the state. Those states most able to defend themselves were tightly controlled microstates like Singapore. These states, through robust applications of technology applied to manageable geographies and populations, succeeded where the large states could not. By 2027, these original microstates and those that arose to emulate their success became islands of stability in a sea of robust disintegration.

Economically, the oil crisis precipitated by the war with Iran was an accelerator of the collapse of formal globalization. Even as states began to turn to protectionist measures to save sections of their struggling economies, they found that these measures were nearly impossible to implement. The more restrictive the measures, the greater the wealth transfer to the smuggling economy owned by virtual-states and their state allies. Globalization continued its robust growth but it was increasingly outside the control of the states that initiated it.

During this time, the Internet was left relatively unmolested by the growth in global chaos. Every attempt at control was quickly countered by numerous technologies and methodologies that eliminated their effectiveness. The Internet served as a means of continuing the advance of technology as virtual corporations and open source movements used it to coordinate advances. To protect themselves against both physical threats and the encroachment of these virtual competitors, state franchised corporate structures adopted aggressive security measures. Many of the largest companies bought private military companies that had grown quickly during the US military outsourcing of the wars in the Middle East. The companies quickly became prime suppliers of internal and external security across the globe, in both large state and small states. Further, they increasingly became useful as a means for self-protection, market-share growth, and intellectual property enforcement in global markets.

During this time, we saw rapid advancements across a wide variety of technologies. The growth in computing power and the reduction of most science to information manipulation moved technology forward quickly. However, with each advance in technology, the power continued to shift towards virtual-states due to the accessibility of most of these advances.

Finally, despite the structural complexity, businesses adapted, and economic progress was quick due to the lack of barriers to interconnectivity. However, the distribution patterns of security and economic progress were substantially different than in the past. Islands of prosperity and tranquility emerged in the most unexpected locations while pockets of extreme chaos developed in formerly stable nation-states.

Epilogue

It's clear from this extrapolation that the situation that the world will find itself in twenty to thirty years from now will be incredibly different than today. History did not end with the victory of capitalist democracy over socialism. Instead, quite the opposite occurred. It set the stage for a rapid transition to new forms of more responsive governance.

The big challenge, for nation-states across the board, is how quickly they can develop into market-states to provide competition to virtual-states. The problem will be particularly acute for large "melting-pot" countries since virtual-states can quickly cleave them into competitive subgroups at the first sign of weakness (think China). Size, in this competition, isn't an asset. It is a liability.

Defining Criminal-states

Robert J. Bunker & Pamela L. Bunker

Robert J. Bunker, Ph.D., is CEO of the Counter-OPFOR Corporation. He has been a member of the Los Angeles County Terrorism Early Warning Group since 1996 and has counter-terrorism operational planning experience. He is a past Counter-OPFOR consultant, National Law Enforcement and Corrections Technology Center-West (NLECTC-West), a program of the National Institute of Justice (NIJ). He is also a former Adjunct Professor, National Security Studies Program, California State University San Bernardino; past Fellow, Institute of Land Warfare, Association of the United States Army; and former Professor, Unconventional Warfare, American Military University, Manassas Park, Virginia. Professional LE related training includes Intelligence Support to Force Protection, Anti-Terrorism Course & Force Protection Operations Course, and Mirror Image (Jihadi) Course. Dr. Bunker has provided 150 briefings and presentations on terrorism, future warfare & conflict, suicide bombers, less lethal weapons and directed energy weapons. He has written over 100 essays in publications such as *The Police Chief, The Tactical Edge, California Journal of Law Enforcement, Parameters, Military Review, Marine Corps Gazette, Special Warfare, Airpower Journal, Naval Institute Proceedings*, and numerous military encyclopedias. He is the editor of a series of law enforcement booklets, *Non-State Threats and Future Wars* (Frank Cass: 2003), and *Networks, Terrorism and Global Insurgency* (Routledge: 2005).
Pamela L. Bunker is a senior officer of the Counter-OPFOR Corporation. Research interests include less lethal weapons (LLW) and CONUS OPFORs (radical environmental and fringe groups and religious cults). Her work has been presented in policing and academic conferences in Alaska, Australia, and Germany. She was a contributor to the *Encyclopedia of World War I* (ABC-CLIO, 2005), has written on less lethal weapons for a NLECTC-West project, and has fired LLW on the South Australia Police (SAPOL) Range. She graduated from California State Polytechnic University Pomona with a B.S. in anthropology/geography and a B.S. in social science and from The Claremont Graduate University with a M.A. in public policy with additional post-graduate work completed in comparative politics and government. Past professional experience includes research and program coordination in University, Non-Government Organization (NGO), and City Government settings.

Since the 9/11 attacks, the US has been in a constant state of war; one that Fourth Epoch War theorists have repeatedly stated represents 'a war over [humanity's] future social and political organization.' As a result, new definitions are required to better understand and respond to this conflict, the new threats that have emerged, and their interrelationship with evolving forms of global criminality. We appear to still be in the early stages of an Epochal transformation from the Modern to the Post-Modern era. During periods of such transformation, old state structures and institutions break apart and the dominant state form finds itself in conflict with emerging non-state (criminal) entities. These periods of de-institutionalization also witness the increasing privatization of state functions and the rise of mercenary and private-security corporations to contend with the new threats that have developed.

Within this background of Epochal change, our ability to fully define the new threat of 'Criminal-states' that we now face will be impeded until the new security environment is openly recognized as merging with global criminality and when it is accepted that this security environment is being increasingly populated with highly adaptive 'small, fast, and ruthless' challengers to the nation-state form.[1] Nonetheless, it is imperative, given the nature and potential scope of this threat, that we make some first attempts at such a definition and, to that end, this essay outlines four distinct criminal-state forms. Further, it seeks to impart a recognition that the moral values inherent in such definitions, and the perceptions behind them, ultimately will shape US foreign, and increasingly domestic, security policies.

Belligerent and Near-belligerent States

The governments and leaders of states have engaged in pejorative labeling, categorization, and name calling of other states since the rise of the earliest political forms. This has been done for both legitimate political needs and expediency. The reasons for so doing include disgracing an opposing state and/or its activities, discrediting its leadership, and bolstering the domestic and foreign policies of one's own state and allies in times of war. Defining another state, or group of states, in the pejorative is thus a useful tool and has been employed by American and Western governments in their foreign policies.

The granting of these negative titles have been reserved almost exclusively for belligerent states and near-belligerent states. Belligerent states fall into two categories – those formally declared and those not formally declared. For America, the Central Powers in World War I and North Vietnam in the

1. The al Qaeda OPFOR (Opposing Force) represents but one of the new threats that we face. For a recently released declassified perspective on this threat see *Trends in Global Terrorism: Implications for the United States (U)* (2006) National Intelligence Estimate (NIE 20006-02D), United States of America, National Intelligence Council, Washington, DC, April 2006, [online]. Available at: www.dni.gov/press_releases/cover.pdf

Vietnam War represent each example, respectively. Both categories of belligerents can be placed cleanly into the category of the enemy. Near-belligerent states are far more problematic because of their ambiguous status. They may be viewed as dangerous to only their own people, to other states, or to both their own people and to other states Because hostilities are not in effect (or may never be), are being carried out by proxies, or are taking place below the threshold of conventional warfare – at terrorist (pre-9/11) and insurgent levels – these states have not been formally designated as the enemy. Belligerent (enemy) states are normally labeled more harshly than near-belligerent (possible enemy) states but this is not always the case. In 1982, during the height of the Cold War, the Soviet Union was termed "The Evil Empire" by the Reagan administration but no formal belligerent status ever existed because of the dangers inherent in the strategic nuclear capabilities of both superpowers.

Dangerous States

US views on belligerent and near-belligerent states, that is to say dangerous states, have changed over the decades. During the Cold War, its focus was on the proxy and client states of the Soviet Union. These included Afghanistan, Angola, Cuba, Grenada, Nicaragua, Vietnam, and Warsaw Pact Members. Various terms existed

Table 1 US Terms for dangerous states[2]

Name	Reason and Examples
Soviet Proxy and Client States (Cold War) Evil Empire (1982)	*Allegiance to the Soviet Union* *Communism-Socialism* *Terrorist and Guerilla Support* Afghanistan, Angola, Cuba, Grenada, Nicaragua, Vietnam and Warsaw Pact Members
Pariah & Outlaw States (Pre-1980)	*Objectionable Internal Behavior* Cambodia, South Africa and Uganda
State Sponsors of Terrorism (1979)	*WMD Pursuit/Acquisition* *Objectionable External Behavior* Cuba, Iran, Iraq, Libya, North Korea, South Yemen, Sudan and Syria
Renegade States (1992) Backlash States (1994) Rogue States (1994, 2002) States of Concern (2000)	*WMD Pursuit/Acquisition* *Terrorism as an Instrument of State Policy* *Regional Threats to US Interests* Cuba, Iran, Iraq, Libya, & North Korea
Axis of Evil (2002)	*Arming to Threaten the Peace of the World* Iraq, Iran and North Korea
Undeclared Rogue States (Pre-9/11)	*Objectionable Internal Behavior* Afghanistan and Serbia

2. Henriksen, T. H. (2001) 'The Rise and Decline of Rogue States', *Journal of International Affairs*, vol. 54, no. 2, pp. 349–373; Litwak, R. S. (2001) 'What's in a Name? The Changing Foreign Policy Lexicon', *Journal of International Affairs*, vol. 54, no. 2, pp. 375–392; and Minnero, P. (2002), pp. 1–8.

for these and other dangerous states (see Table 1). The reason for this labeling was initially derived from their allegiance to the Soviet Union. Later, objectionable internal or external behaviors including human rights violations, the support of terrorism, and the pursuit and acquisition of weapons of mass destruction were the cause. Over time, different terms tended to be favored by successive administrations when labeling dangerous states. Reagan's officials used "outlaw states", the first Bush's officials used "renegade states", and Clinton's officials used the terms "rogue states" and "states of concern" to describe many of these states. The second Bush's officials used "rogue states" to describe them and he himself called them the "axis of evil".[3,4]

In 1994, Anthony Lake, Clinton's Special Assistant for National Security Affairs, developed the concept of 'backlash states' – a listing of problematic states opposed to US policies as well as a few unrepentant and unreformed Soviet Allies dating back to the Cold War; Cuba, Iran, Iraq, Libya and North Korea. These types of states were described by Lake as:

- Often defiant and aggressive behavior.
- Ruled by cliques that control power through coercion.
- Suppress basic human rights and promote radical ideas.
- Leaders share common antipathy toward popular participation.
- Chronic inability to engage constructively with the outside world.
- Do not function effectively in alliances.
- Often defensive, increasingly criticized and targeted with sanctions in international forums.
- They share a siege mentality.
- Embarked on ambitious and costly military programs – especially in weapons of mass destruction (WMD) and missile delivery systems.[5]

While a considerable amount of thinking by presidential administration officials went into 'rogue state' and affiliated term development, these pejorative labels and definitions, created as they were for belligerent and near-belligerent states during the Cold War and post-Cold War eras, are no longer adequate for the new reality of the post-9/11 world. However, the early perception concerning

3. Litwak, R. S. (2000) 'A Look at Rogue States: A Handy Label but a Lousy Policy', *The Washington Post*, February 20, p. B3.
4. Minnero, P. (2002) 'Rogue States – State Sponsors of Terrorism?' *German Law Journal*, September, p. 2, [online]. Available at: www.germanlawjournal.com.
5. Lake, A. (1994) 'Confronting Backlash States', *Foreign Affairs*, vol. 73, no. 2, pp. 45–55. Criticism has been directed by the left against the US as being a rogue state as well. See Klare, M. (1995) *Rogue States and Nuclear Outlaws: America's Search for A New Foreign Policy*, Hill and Wang, New York; Blum, W. (2000) *Rogue State: A Guide to the World's Only Superpower*, Common Courage Press, Monroe; and Chomsky, N. (2000) *Rogue States: The Rule of Force in World Affairs*, South End Press, Cambridge. The term itself has also come into question; see Thompson, J. (2002) 'Is There Such a Thing as a Rogue State?' *The Centre for Applied Philosophy and Public Ethics Working Paper*, no. 8, University of Melbourne, Melbourne, [online]. Available at: www.cappe.edu.au.

the underlying 'non-state' aspect of those entities as expressed by one academic scholar has become even more valid:

> Rogue states are those 'which are alleged to have removed themselves somehow from the international legal system and who supposedly act as if they were, in fact, not states, but non-state entities that are unrestrained by an expectation to profit from the benefits of membership in the international system and similarly unconcerned about countermeasures that may result from exceeding the rules of the system'.[6]

A New Form of Dangerous State – the 'Criminal-state'

Post 9/11 national security threats to the United States are no longer solely derived from individual nation-states or their coalitions. This threat goes beyond President Bush's 2002 State of the Union Address which only modified earlier rogue state thinking with the addition of non-state groups placed in a supporting role – "States like these [North Korea, Iran, and Iraq], and their terrorist allies, constitute an axis of evil, arming to threaten the peace of the world."[7] Rather, belligerent non-state entities and their networks, which are at war with the nation-state form, must now be dominantly factored in and a new term – 'Criminal-states' – that better addresses those threats articulated.[8] This focus on the non-state over the state elements of the threat is still difficult for the United States government to comprehend but, in retrospect, it was not a North Korea, Iran or Iraq that ultimately dropped the World Trade Towers but al Qaeda: *a new warmaking-entity*.

Recent movement has been made in US governmental understanding of this new threat.[9] President Bush's *Address to the Nation* on the fifth anniversary of

6. Weller, M. (1988) 'The Changing Environment for Forcible Responses to Nontraditional Threats', *American Society of Law Annual Proceedings*, vol. 92, April 1-4, pp. 177–178. Cited in Mertus, J. (2001) 'Serbia: Reimagining Europe's Outlaw Nation', *Journal of International Affairs*, vol. 54, no. 2, p. 489.

7. Office of the Press Secretary, The White House (2002) 'President Delivers State of the Union Address', January 29, [online]. Available at: www.whitehouse.gov.

8. A cursory survey suggests that the term 'criminal-states' was used as early as December 1917 in a speech given by the Prime Minister of Great Britain when describing Imperial Germany. Section of speech quoted in *Georges Clemenceau's Letter of Reply to the Objections of the German Peace Delegation, May 1919*. Posted June 12 2004, [online]. Available at: www.firstworldwar.com. The term has also been contemplated in regards to international law – 'It can certainly be sustained that states can be held 'criminal' in a sense which is close to the penal meaning of the term: Nazi Germany and Saddam Hussein's Iraq can be called 'criminal states' and have been treated as such by the international community', Pellet, A. (1999) 'Can a State Commit a Crime? Definitely, Yes!' *European Journal of International Law*, vol. 10, no. 2, p. 433 [online]. Available at: www.ejil.org. The use of the term or a similar one to now describe non-state entities criminalizing states/criminal-state forms may already be starting to develop, albeit haphazardly, by US governmental officials. See Haiti 'could be criminal state' (US Senate) (2004) *News24*, September 26 [online]. Available at: www.haiti-info.com; and the Associated Press, 'U.S. Calls North Korea 'Criminal Regime'', December 7, 2005, 1 p [online]. Available at: www.nytimes.com.

9. This section concerning the need for the term 'Criminal-states' was written over six-months prior to President Bush's September 11, 2006 commemorative address. It has been updated to reflect new executive office threat perceptions.

9/11 shows a maturing of threat perceptions concerning the dire threat posed by networked non-state opponents:

> Since the horror of 9/11, we've learned a great deal about the enemy. We have learned that they are evil and kill without mercy - but not without purpose. We have learned that they form a global network of extremists who are driven by a perverted vision of Islam - a totalitarian ideology that hates freedom, rejects tolerance, and despises all dissent. And we have learned that their goal is to build a radical Islamic empire where women are prisoners in their homes, men are beaten for missing prayer meetings, and terrorists have a safe haven to plan and launch attacks on America and other civilized nations. The war against this enemy is more than a military conflict. It is the decisive ideological struggle of the 21st century, and the calling of our generation.[10]

In addition, the term "terrorist states" [not "state sponsor of terrorism"] was mentioned in this address as another aspect of the threat along with "terrorist networks."[11] No further elaboration of the term "terrorist states" was made so whether these states were derived from terrorist (insurgent) take over of pre-existing states and their territories (e.g. Afghanistan and Southern Lebanon, respectively) or if they were solely states that engage in direct terrorist activity (e.g. Iran) is unknown.

Still, these new US executive office perceptions fit well within the usage of the term 'Criminal-states.' Four criminal-state forms derived from jihadi insurgency, state failure - lawless zones, criminal takeover, and oligarchic regimes have been identified and can be used to further illustrate the need for this new term and its general parameters.[12] All of these criminal-state forms share a common dependence on criminal economic activity or, in a few instances, the criminal takeover of legitimate activities (such as the oil and gas industry) for logistical support.[13] At that point, the similarities diverge greatly (see Table 2).

Jihadi Insurgency

Taliban and al Qaeda-controlled Afghanistan, one of the main targets in the United States Global War on Terrorism (GWOT), represents one of the archetypes

10. Office of the Press Secretary, The White House (2006) 'President's Address to the Nation', September 11. Available at: www.whitehouse.gov.

11. Ibid.

12. Some overlap between the criminal-state forms is expected with global groups such al Qaeda. Concerning the blurring of crime and terrorism see Shelley, L. (2005) 'The Unholy Trinity: Transnational Crime, Corruption, and Terrorism', *Brown Journal of World Affairs*, vol. 11, no. 2, pp. 101-111.

13. Oil and natural gas reserves represent legitimate economic activities that have been criminalized. These legitimate activities may greatly supplement criminal economic endeavors or even provide the foundation of the criminal-state's economy. Saddam Hussein's regime was fortunate to have immense Iraqi oil resources, however, once international trade sanctions were emplaced he was forced to engage in black market oil smuggling for revenue purposes. For more on the illicit activities of criminal-states see Naim, M. (2005) *Illicit: How Smugglers, Traffickers and Copycats are Hijacking the Global Economy*, Doubleday, New York; and Mike Arena's contribution on 'Hizballah's Global Criminal Operations' in this work on 'Criminal-states and Criminal-soldiers'.

Table 2 Criminal-state forms

Form	Derived From	Description	Examples
Jihadi Insurgency (Extremist Religious-political Fusion)	Conquest of state territory by Islamic terrorist and/or insurgent group. Centralized and/or decentralized criminal activity	Jihadi groups seek to create Caliphate lands and spur the arrival of the Mahdi Groups dependent on illegal economic activities Radical Islamic law. Beheadings and suicide bombings/assaults (blood sacrifices)	Parts of Iran (Ayatollahs Ruling Under Mahdi Mandate)[1] Afghanistan (Taliban and al Qaeda) Southern Lebanon (Hizballah)[2] Parts of Iraq (al Qaeda and Iranian backed groups) Palestine (Hamas led government) Parts of Somalia (Islamic Courts)
State Failure-lawless Zones (Anarchy)	State, regional or local failure to maintain law and governmental order Governmental collapse Decentralized criminal activity	Regional warlords, armed gangs, drug cartels, outlaw mercenaries, pirates, and human trafficking groups emerge in power vacuum Groups dependent on illegal economic activities No or weak legal system Torture, rape, and random violence	Haiti Tri-Border Region (Ciudad del Este) Parts of Mexico (Sinaloa & Quintana Roo) Mexican-American Border (Segments) Palestinian Authority (Secular & Corrupt) Parts of Somalia/Coast (Warlords & Piracy)

(*continued*)

Table 2 - *Continued*

Form	Derived From	Description	Examples
Criminal Takeover (Illegal Business)	Governmental takeover by criminal groups External Capture Centralized criminal activity	Transnational criminal groups run the government Mafia in uniform Economy dependent on illegal activities Corrupt legal system	Bolivia (Meza) Chechnya (Dudaev) Transdniestria (Smirnov)
Oligarchic Regimes (Dynastic)	Corruption of state institutions (political, military and economic) Internal Capture Centralized criminal activity	Centralized state run by ruling families/kinship groups for private benefit Economy dependent on illegal activities National police and special forces merge with organized crime No due process/widespread use of torture for suppression	Iraq (Hussein)[1] North Korea (Jong Il) Numerous States in Africa (Cameroon, Central African Republic, Chad, etc) Panama (Noreiga) Parts of Russia (Yeltsin & Putin)[1] Serbia (Milosevic) Syria (Assad)

1) With the addition of oil and natural gas revenues; 2) With the addition of diamond trade revenues

of this new type of threat.[14] Afghanistan represented a state conquered by Jihadi groups. Rather than being viewed as a "state sponsor of terrorism" – the more traditional viewed held by the US State Department – it should be thought of as a belligerent "jihadi-" or "terrorist-state." Such a state is anathema to the modern state-form and criminal in its orientation because, ultimately, it was to merge with other conquered territories to form the new Caliphate envisioned by al Qaeda. The term used by Secretary General Lord Robertson of NATO for such threats are "...criminal terrorists and criminal states...."[15] Prior to Taliban and al Qaeda successes, the terrorist group Hizballah had emerged as the dominant force in Southern Lebanon and set up a quasi-state.[16] That "terrorist state" is directly supported by Iran, intent on the destruction of Israel, and seeks to create a Khomeini-style Islamic state throughout all of Lebanon. In Iraq, we are now seeing both al Qaeda terrorists and Iranian backed terrorists attempting to take control of some of the provinces within that state, however, they represent competing Sunni and Shiite visions of theocracy. Criminal activity for this state form has fluctuated between centralized and decentralized approaches. This is even evident within al Qaeda during different time periods. Early al Qaeda engaged in more centralized operations, both militarily and logistically. After the loss of its base in Afghanistan, it has been forced to decentralize both its attack planning and implementation and criminal economic activities.

State Failure - Lawless Zones

The process involves the territorial shell of a dead nation-state, one with no central authority and devoid of state institutions, being overrun by non-state groups – such as warlords, armed gangs, and drug cartels – that fill the power vacuum that develops.[17] Another aspect of this criminal-state form is based on lawless zones. These zones can exist within a state, such as a failed-region, or even on a smaller scale within a failed-section of a city such as a sprawling slum.[18]

14. Just coming up with a term for this 'bad guy' subset has been problematic for the Bush White House. Possible terms of use have included "Islamism," Jihadism," "Militant Jihadism," "Evil Islamic Radicalism," and now the more popular "Islamofascism" or "Islamic Fascists." See Wolffe, R. and Bailey, H. (2006) 'The 'Islamofascists'', *Newsweek*, pp. 24-25.

15. 'Opening Statement by Secretary General Lord Robertson at the Informal Meeting of the North Atlantic Council at the Level of Defence Ministers' (2002) *NATO Speeches*, p. 1 [online]. Available at: www.NATO.int.

16. Aboul-Enein, Y. H. (2003) 'The Hezbollah Model: Using Terror and Creating a Quasi-State in Lebanon', *Marine Corps Gazette*, June 2003, pp. 34-35.

17. Many of these non-state groups have been have been characterized as "para-states" – entities that challenge the legitimate monopoly on violence held by states through various forms of direct action – by the Federation of American Scientists. Unfortunately this usage of the term 'direct action' results in its ranging from application of illegal forms of protest through terrorist bombings. The para-state listing includes 'nasty and nice' entities so that it does not become politicized. See 'Para-states - Scope Note', [online]. Available at: www.fas.org.

18. Such lawless zones can temporarily emerge in stable environments due to natural and man-made disasters such as the recent Los Angeles Riots in 1992 and Hurricane Katrina in New Orleans in 2005. A tactical nuclear attack by a terrorist group (hypothetical) could conceivably result in a lawless zone that would exist for much longer periods. Insight derived from discussions with John P. Sullivan.

Examples of such fragmented criminal-states and -regions can be readily found in Haiti, parts of Mexico, the tri-border region of South America, and Somalia. Criminal activity is decentralized, the legal system is weak if not altogether non-existent, and illegal economic activities dominate. The US Senate in a unanimously approved resolution in September 2004 said "The failure to establish a secure and stable environment and to conduct credible and inclusive elections will likely result in Haiti's complete transition from a failed to a criminal state."[19] Years earlier, the potential for a third phase cartel (criminal state successor) to emerge in parts of Mexico (Sinaloa and Quintana Roo), Haiti, and the tri-border region (Ciudad del Este) had been identified by global crime researchers Bunker and Sullivan.[20] A failed-Somalia overrun with Warlords and their kat (narcotic drug) chewing gangsters is the image similarly presented in Mark Bowden's celebrated work *Blackhawk Down.*[21]

Lawless zones can also be extended into cyberspace because most of it defies traditional notions of sovereignty and remains unregulated. Cyberspace itself represents a fifth-dimensional (beyond normal space-time) informational frontier. Virtual-cities, -tribes, and -communities have emerged, been discussed in numerous writings, and even promoted as a form of denationalization.[22] In retrospect, the historical expansion of the Crips and Bloods throughout the United States in the 1980s and early-1990s and the current rise of the MS-13 (*Mara Salvatrucha*) and MS-18 gangs in the Western Hemisphere can be viewed in some ways as the evolution of early cyber-tribes.[23] Of greatest concern is the development of belligerent virtual-states that are geographically patched together from clusters of failed-states and lawless zones. Such virtual-states, reminiscent of pre-Westphalia states such as that patchwork of estates forming early Brandenburg-Prussia, now have the potential to arise with the advent of

19. Haiti 'could be criminal state' (US Senate). *Op. Cit.*, See In THE SENATE OF THE UNITED STATES – 108th Cong., 2nd Session. September 24 2004. Making Appropriations for foreign operations, export financing, and related programs for the fiscal year ending September 30, 2005, and for other purposes. INTENDED to be proposed by Mr. Leahy (for himself and Mr. DeWine, Mr. Dodd, Mr. Coleman, Mr. Nelson, Mr. Harkin, and Mr. Feingold) At the appropriate place in the bill, insert the following: IMPROVING SECURITY IN HAITI SEC. (b) Congress - 6) notes that the failure to establish a secure and stable environment and to conduct credible and inclusive elections will likely result in Haiti's complete transition from a failed state to a criminal state; [online]. Available at: www.haitipolicy.org.

20. See Bunker, R. J. & Sullivan, J. P. (1998) 'Cartel Evolution: Potentials and Consequences', *Transnational Organized Crime*, vol. 4, no. 2, pp. 55–74.

21. Bowden, M. (1999) *Blackhawk Down: A Story of Modern War*, Atlantic Monthly Press, New York.

22. For an introduction, see Sassen, S. (2002) 'The Global City: The De-Nationalizing of Time and Space', Bridging The Gap [online]. Available at: www.btgjapan.org; and 'The global city: strategic site/new frontier', July 2001, Globalization seminar [online]. Available at: www.india-seminar.com; Works challenging the 'obsolescing structure' of nation-states have also appeared. See Greenfield, A. (2003) *The minimal compact: A manifesto for virtual states*, February 25 [online]. Available at: www.v-2.org.

23. The initial expansion of the Crips and Bloods was facilitated by failed gang member relocations by families that helped to spread the social cancer that the gangster lifestyle represented across the United States. A map of gang nodes that have emerged in the US between 1960 and 1992 can be found in Klein, M. W. (1995) *The American Street Gang*, Oxford University Press, New York, pp. 92–95. MS-13 expansion in the Western Hemisphere was facilitated by gang member deportations to Central America and the emergence of the cell phone and internet that allowed for social networks to be maintained.

maturing forms of cyberspace. Phillip Bobbitt appears to be in agreement and has said al Qaeda "...represents a new and profoundly dangerous kind of organization – one that might be called a 'virtual state'".[24]

Criminal Takeover

The next form is derived from Phil William's concept of the "captured state" used "... to describe situations in which criminal influence has become so pervasive that the state effectively becomes a partner with organized crime."[25] The process involves the government of a weakened-state being taken over by criminal groups. William also uses the term "criminal-states" to describe these captured states. Such criminal state-forms see more centralized criminal activity as opposed to the decentralized criminal activity found in failed-states and lawless zones. The *International Crime Threat Assessment* warns:

> The world in 2010 may see the emergence of "criminal states" that are not merely safehavens for international criminal activities, but support them as a matter of course. The involvement of "criminal states" in the community of nations could undermine international finance and commerce and preclude effective international cooperation against organized crime. "Criminal states" may also adopt the political agendas of states of concern and terrorist groups, thereby weakening US political, economic, and security interests around the world.[26]

Examples of this criminal takeover are Bolivia under General Luis Garcia Meza (1980–1981) whose coup was funded largely by drug traffickers and Chechnya under Djokhar Dudaev (1991–1996) who helped defraud the Russian State Bank of $700 million and allowed bandit and drug gangs to run freely.[27]

24. Bobbitt, P. (2002) 'Get Ready for the Next Long War: Virtual states are new, elusive threat', *Time*, Sunday, September 1 [online]. Available at: www.time.com; For more on the threat posed by virtual-states see John Robb's 'Nation-states, Market-states, and Virtual-states' in this work on 'Criminal-states and Criminal-soldiers'.

25. Lahneman, W. J. (2000) 'Summary of Proceedings', *Conference on the Evolution of the Nation-State Through 2015*, University of Maryland, April 18, College Park [online]. Available at: www.cissm.umd.edu.

26. US Government interagency working group, *International Crime Threat Assessment*, Chapter V: The Future of International Crime. Washington, DC: US Government Printing Office, December 2000. Final paragraph quoted. Clinton administration released the "first ever unclassified threat assessment of international crime to the United States." See THE WHITE HOUSE, Office of the Press Secretary, December 15, 2000. PRESS BRIEFING BY NATIONAL COORDINATOR FOR SECURITY INFRASTRUCTURE PROTECTION AND COUNTERTERRORISM FOR NSC RICHARD CLARKE, ASSISTANT SECRETARY OF STATE FOR INTERNATIONAL NARCOTICS AND LAW ENFORCEMENT RAND BEERS, DEPUTY ASSISTANT SECRETARY OF TREASURY FOR ENFORCEMENT JOSEPH MYERS, AND NSC DIRECTOR OF INTERNATIONAL CRIME GROUP FRED ROSA. The James S. Brady Press Briefing Room, 11:12 A.M. EST, [online]. Available at: www.usembassy.it.

27. Galeotti, M. (2002) 'Underworld and Upperworld: Transnational Organized Crime and Global Society', in *Non-State Actors in World Politics*, eds. W. Wallace & D. Josselin, Palgrave Macmillan, New York, p. 211.

Oligarchic Regimes

These secular regimes witness a corruption of state institutions from the top down and exist for the private benefit of ruling families and kinship groups. In the past, quite a few of these regimes have been at odds with the United States and, as a result, have been labeled as rogue states. Where state police forces end and the mob begins is fully blurred within these regimes. Terms for this criminal-state form include kleptocracy, thugocracy, and Soprano state. While never mentioned as a reason for invasion by the US, the sexual deprivations, infliction of torture, and mass murders carried out by Hussein's sons Uday and Qusay suggest that, once the princes of that criminal-realm came to power in Iraq, the sins of the sons might have made those of the father look pale in comparison. A state that is even more criminal in nature is that of North Korea under Kim Jong Il – another son born into the 'family business' and about as cruel, ruthless, and self-indulgent as they come. The criminal sector may account for 40% of the state's exports and includes production and overseas distribution of narcotics, production and international distribution of counterfeit currency (e.g. Supernotes), the smuggling of internationally sanctioned items (e.g. conflict diamonds and endangered species and species items), money laundering, weapons smuggling, and WMD transfers.[28] Syria under Bashar Assad, still another son that has learned the family business,[29] and a host of African states have also been identified as oligarchic regimes directly engaging in criminal activity.[30] In addition, large sectors of Russia under Boris Yeltsin and Vladimir Putin became criminalized during the process of reforming the outdated Soviet bureaucracy (including police and military forces) and privatizing former Soviet industries and natural resource holdings.[31]

Moral Considerations

> Our country! In her intercourse with foreign nations, may she always be in the right; but our country, right or wrong.
>
> Stephen Decatur[32]

28. Asher, D. L. (2005) 'The North Korean Criminal State, its Ties to Organized Crime, and the Possibility of WMD Proliferation', *Policy Forum Online*, 05-92A, November 15 [online]. Available at: www.nautilus.org; and ''Soprano state': N. Korean economy called dependent on organized crime' (2005) *East-Asia-Intel*, November 30.
29. See Whitelaw, K. & Omestad, T. (2005) 'Twilight for Assad?' *U.S. News & World Report*, October 17, pp. 26, 28; and Ajami, F. (2005) 'Syria's Sopranos', Commentary, *U.S. News & World Report*, November 7, p. 57.
30. Bayart, J.-F., Ellis, S. & Hibou, B. (1999) *The Criminalization of the State in Africa*, in African Issues Series, eds. A. de Waal and S. Ellis, Indiana University Press, Bloomington.
31. Satter, D. (2003) *Darkness at Dawn: The Rise of the Russian Criminal State*, Yale University Press, New Haven.
32. Quote background; "Naval commander Stephen Decatur originated the phrase in a toast given at an April 1816 banquet in Norfolk, Virginia, to celebrate his victory over the Barbary pirates. (The action in Algeria also gave the U.S. Marine Corps anthem its 'to the shores of Tripoli' phrase, saluting their first renowned military action.)" See Quint, B. (2002) 'My Country, Right or Wrong', *Searcher*, vol. 10, no. 6, June [online]. Available at: http://www.onlineinc.com/searcher/jun02/voice.htm.

> Our country right or wrong. When right, to be kept right; when wrong, to be put right.
>
> Carl Schurz[33]

The original quote dates to April 1816 and was used at a banquet in Norfolk, Virginia celebrating the US victory over the Barbary pirates in Tripoli. The second quote is a mid-19th century moral clarification of the original. It means that while we will always support our country, even if our foreign policies are initially wrong, we (the people – including military personnel) have an ethical obligation to make sure that those policies are put right.[34]

This moral clarification is important and has helped to allow us to recognize that our foreign policies should ultimately strive towards some sort of higher ethical standard. This has not always been the case. Historically, states, including the United States, have at times defined and labeled other states in the pejorative for less than noble reasons such as for the annexation of their peoples, resources, and territories. In developing these definitions, therefore, some consideration needs to take place concerning the effects that these new terms and perceptions might have on our government policies. In no way should we seek to become intolerant and engage in atrocities, such as beheadings or mass executions, like our enemies, or, for that matter, turn on ourselves and go down the path of becoming a police state.

Such concerns are justified. At the criminal-soldier level, Jose Padilla, former gang member and al Qaeda member tied into a 'dirty bomb' plot, has been held in military detention for four years now without being charged. His detention has been intentionally harsh and issues of mistreatment have been alleged.[35] If we are willing to treat individual criminal-soldiers, such as Padilla, as well as groups of other unlawful enemy combatants at Gitmo (US Naval Air Station Guantanamo Bay) in a morally questionable manner, then would we be any more likely to treat identified 'Criminal-states' any less so?

Conclusion

We face a far greater threat than most of our citizens realize and must be prepared to adequately defend ourselves against the highly adaptive criminal entities that have come into being and which continue to emerge, evolve, and threaten our people and its government. This essay has been a first attempt at defining criminal-states and discussing the issues inherent in so doing.

33. Quote background; "Fifty-five years later, Carl Schurz, German-born U.S. general and U.S. senator, clarified the concept..." Ibid.

34. For a useful discussion on ethics and the war on terrorism see 'Moral Clarity', *Wikipedia*, n.d., [online]. Available at: http://en.wikipedia.org/wiki/Moral_clarity.

35. Refer to Brian Levin's essay on 'Military Tribunals or Civilian Prosecution: The Dilemma of Unlawful Enemy Combatants' in this work on 'Criminal-states and Criminal-soldiers' for further information on the Jose Padilla case and the evolving legal status of Criminal-soldiers.

The US has already engaged three out of the four criminal-state forms identified above. We first crossed paths with the Shi'ite jihadi insurgency form in Beirut in April and October 1983 with the suicide bombings directed against the US Embassy and the Marine Barracks. Since that time, global operations have taken place by and against al Qaeda (the Sunni form) since its first attack on the World Trade Towers in February 1993. In post-Hussein Iraq, both Shi'ite and Sunni insurgents have been engaged by US forces. US stability and support operations (SASO) have repeatedly taken place in the state failure – lawless zones criminal-state form. These operations include those taking place in the states of Haiti (1994–1995) and Somalia (1992–1994), and are ongoing along segments of the US-Mexico border. The Oligarchic regime criminal- state form has been engaged in Panama (1989–1990), Serbia (1999), and Iraq (1990–1991, 2003). Of all the criminal-state forms, this has been the easiest to defeat because it most resembles a traditional nation-state and, as a result when devoid of nuclear weaponry, is usually no match against overwhelming US conventional force. The criminal takeover state form has not as of yet been directly engaged by the US.

Much work needs to be done in understanding the new 'half-criminal, half-political' entities (and their 'half-criminal, half-religious,' 'half-criminal, half-social [tribal]' and 'hybrid' brethren) that are evolving. Even more work is required in understanding how our definitions of such entities will – if at all – affect the moral components of our foreign policies. Are such criminal-soldiers and criminal-states considered anathema and, once labeled as 'enemies of the state,' subject to harsher treatment than traditional soldiers/states? Our choice of definition may ultimately determine the individual and organizational rights allowed to those so designated and should not be taken lightly. The word on the 'cyber-street' is "You don't defeat the enemy by becoming him."[36]

Acknowledgements

Special thanks to Mark Galeotti, William C. Green, and John P. Sullivan for comment and review of the typology of criminal-state forms.

36. Green, S. (2004) 'Game Plan', *The Command Post-Op Ed Page*, August 10 [online]. Available at: http://www.command-post.org/oped/2_archives/cat_military_strategy.html.

Military Tribunals or Civilian Prosecution: The Dilemma of Unlawful Enemy Combatants

Brian Levin

Over the centuries Europeans, and later the Americans, instituted rules, laws and mechanisms to address certain forms of violence by soldiers, guerillas, terrorists and those under military occupation. In the United States, a fairly well developed body of law evolved to govern the activities of its soldiers and civilian support

Brian Levin is a criminologist, civil rights attorney, and an associate professor of criminal justice and Director of the Center for the Study of Hate & Extremism at California State University, San Bernardino where he specializes in analysis of terrorism and legal issues. Previously, Professor Levin was Associate Director-Legal Affairs of the Southern Poverty Law Center's Klanwatch/Militia Task Force in Montgomery, Alabama and before that was a corporate litigator. The son of a WWII prisoner of war, he was also a New York City Police Officer. Mr. Levin is a graduate of Stanford Law School, where he was awarded the Block Civil Liberties Award. He is the author or co-author of books, scholarly articles, Supreme Court briefs and studies on extremism and hate crime. His book, The Limits of Dissent (co-authored with Thomas Halpern) is about the Constitution and domestic terrorism. Mr. Levin is a court certified expert on extremism in the United States and England. He has appeared on every network morning and evening news broadcast and various network magazine shows on the subjects of civil rights, criminal law, and extremism. He has also appeared in every major American newspaper, newsmagazine, and wire service.

personnel in both wartime and peacetime. In addition, treaties addressed the treatment of those held by the military pursuant to armed conflict. As twenty first century America grapples with an increasingly amorphous yet sophisticated terrorist threat, it is illuminating to examine the evolving role of military and civilian courts and laws in our history and their relationship to due process and civil liberties during times of conflict. The Supreme Court noted in a recent case involving a Guantanamo detainee that military tribunals, other than standard courts-martial, have emerged during three situations. First, military tribunals have been conducted in lieu of civilian courts during times of martial law. Next, military tribunals operated during instances of armed occupation over captured or recovered territory when civilian courts were not operational. Lastly, the Court noted that tribunals operated as an incident to the conduct of war when there is a need to seize and punish those who were engaged in impeding the war effort or engaging in violations of accepted rules of the law of war. Today most of those designated as unlawful enemy combatants are the latest to fall within this third category.[1]

The Evolving Role of Military and Civilian Courts and Laws

Military law started with the goal of regulating only those associated with the Armed Forces. Rules and punishments relating to discipline and conduct by those in a state of war and other armed conflict date back centuries. Britain's King Richard II compiled 26 directives for members of his armed services in 1385 while Sweden's King Gustavus Adolphus went even further by disseminating a 167 point Articles of War in 1621. Of particular relevance for this essay are those foundational provisions concerning the protection of civilians during the course of hostilities.[2]

Sweden's Articles 96 and 97 ordered that "No man shall presume to pillage any Chuch or Hospitall," nor "set fire upon any Hospitall, Churche, Schoole, or Mill, or spoyle them any way, except he be commanded." Article 113 concerned the protection of civilians: "Our Commanders shall defend the countrey-people and Ploughman that follow their husbandry, and shall suffer none to hinder them in it." In order to ensure compliance, the articles further mandated punishments and regular readings to troops. The Swedish Articles were the basis for future provisions subsequently established for British and American forces.[3]

In the early 1700s, the British Articles of War were revised with regard to the limited circumstances under which civilians could be tried by military courts. Servants of officers and certain merchants at military posts were among those civilians who could be hauled before military tribunals. As tensions escalated

1. Hamdan v. Rumsfeld, 548 U.S. _; 126 S. Ct. 2749; 165 L. Ed. 2d 723; 2006 U.S. LEXIS 5185 (2006).
2. Fisher, M. (2005) *Military Tribunals & Presidential Power*, University of Kansas Press, Lawrence.
3. Ibid; Glazier, D. (2005) 'Precedents Lost: The Neglected History of the Military Commission', *Virginia Journal of International Law*, vol. 46, no. 1.

between the American colonies and the British, the methods of the crown in prosecuting colonists accused of crimes became a divisive issue. In October 1774, the First Continental Congress complained about the practice of colonists being transferred to Britain where they were "tried upon accusations for treasons and misprisions, or concealments of treasons committed in the colonies" without the benefit of a jury.[4]

After some of the colonies individually proceeded, the Continental Congress set forth their own statutory system of regulation for the armed services that was heavily based on those used by their English adversaries. In 1775, the Continental Congress set forth rules in the Articles of War relating to which offenses were covered by military court-martial and set limitations on punishment. George Washington mandated that troops be informed of the rules and in, 1777, published proscriptions preventing troops from "plundering any person whatsoever, whether Tories or others." He further directed that "humanity and tenderness to women and children will distinguish brave Americans." Noting the poor conduct of some British toward colonial war prisoners, Washington noted that "their wanton Cruelty injures rather than benefits their cause" and discouraged in kind retaliation by his subordinates. Among the "abuses and usurpations" protested in the Declaration of Independence were the English practices of holding military authority independent and superior to civilian authority as well as unfair overseas trials without juries.[5]

Throughout the Revolutionary period, spies and saboteurs were not afforded the benefits that captured soldiers enjoyed. Continental Army Captain Nathan Hale was executed after his September 1776 capture in Long Island, New York by British authorities. Hale was carrying documents relating to English installations while dressed in civilian attire. The Americans had their own rules for similar situations. In August 1776, the Continental Congress resolved that those enemies "found lurking as spies in or about the fortifications or encampments of the armies of the United States" shall be subject to court-martial and possible execution. The Americans made good on their promise in 1780 when they caught and executed English Major John André for being a spy, despite his protestation that he should be held as a prisoner of war. At the time of his capture, André was in communication with American traitor Benedict Arnold, who escaped, about a plot to hand over strategic West Point to the British.[6]

As scholar Louis Fisher observed: "America inherited military tribunals from British precedents and its own experience during the Revolutionary War, but it

4. Fisher, 2005; Glazier, 2005; Winthrop, W. (1920) *Military Law and Precedents*, rev. 2d ed., War Department, Washington, DC.
5. Baldrate, B. C. (2005) 'The Supreme Court's Role in Defining the Jurisdiction of Military Tribunals: A Study, Critique, & Proposal for *Hamdan v. Rumsfeld*', vol. 186, Winter, 2005, pp. 1–116, [online]. Available at: http://www.loc.gov/rr/frd/Military_Law/Military_Law_Review/2005.htm; Glazier, 2005; Fisher, 2005.
6. Baldrate, 2005; Glazier, 2005; Fisher, 2005.

also adopted the fundamental principle that military tribunals and the war powers flowed from legislative judgments reached by the people's representatives."[7]

The Constitution established the roles of the coequal branches, as well as the protections that citizens and states would have from the authority of a centralized federal government. Its preamble highlighted important goals for the document to inter alia "establish justice, insure domestic tranquility, provide for the common defense, [and] promote the general welfare." The first three articles set forth the duties and authority of the coequal branches of government, the Congress (Article I), the President (Article II), and the Judiciary (Article III) (Table 1).[8]

Article II addresses the authority of the president, which includes the position of Commander-in-Chief of the military (then "Army and Navy") and of the national guard ("militia") when called into federal service. Article III sets forth the authority of the Supreme Court and also defines the crime of treason- rendering aid and comfort to an enemy: "The judicial power shall extend to all cases, in law and equity, arising under this Constitution, the laws of the United States, and treaties....to all cases of admiralty and maritime jurisdiction; to controversies to which the United States shall be a party... [and to cases involving] foreign states, citizens or subjects."

Congress' Article I authority to "make rules for the Government and Regulation of the land and naval Forces" led to new statutory provisions in 1789. These laws placed present and future military governance under congressionally authorized provisions including the "rules and articles of war." Nineteenth century Supreme Court Associate Justice Joseph Story observed that such action was consistent with the Constitution's vesting of other powers over the military in the legislature. Moreover, Story believed that Congressional authority over tribunal rules was a check against "summary and severe punishments" inflicted at the "mere will of the executive." In April 1806, Congress passed legislation regarding courts-martial in 101 Articles of War. In the next decade, and again in 1830, legislation was passed to limit abuse, clarify which officials have authority over tribunals, and address possible conflicts of interest.[9]

The First Ten amendments, otherwise known as the Bill of Rights, were ratified on Dec. 15, 1791 as a response, in part, to the kind of substantive and procedural deprivations that the Crown meted out to colonists accused of crimes. For the most part, these provisions protect individual rights, particularly in the area of criminal procedure, except for slaves until the 1860s, when slavery was outlawed (Table 2).

In the pre Civil War period, military tribunals were the subject of controversy. During his service as a general in 1815, future President Andrew Jackson instituted martial law in New Orleans and continued its use even after the British had

7. Ibid.
8. *United States Constitution.*
9. Ibid; Fisher, 2005.

Table 1 Article 1: Provisions on congress' role in national security/civil liberties

To constitute tribunals inferior to the Supreme Court;
To define and punish piracies and felonies committed on the high seas, and offenses against the law of nations;
To declare war, grant letters of marque and reprisal, and make rules concerning captures on land and water;
To raise and support armies, but no appropriation of money to that use shall be for a longer term than two years; to provide and maintain a navy;
To make rules for the government and regulation of the land and naval forces;
To provide for calling forth the militia to execute the laws of the union, suppress insurrections and repel invasions;
To provide for organizing, arming, and disciplining, the militia, and for governing such part of them as may be employed in the service of the United States, reserving to the states respectively, the appointment of the officers, and the authority of training the militia according to the discipline prescribed by Congress;
The privilege of the writ of habeas corpus shall not be suspended [by Congress], unless when in cases of rebellion or invasion the public safety may require it.

withdrawn. Jackson charged a state legislator Louis Loullier with inciting mutiny and spying after he authored a newspaper entry critical of the general. When federal district judge Dominick Augustin Hall ordered Loullier's release pursuant to a writ of habeous corpus, the undeterred Jackson had the judge arrested as well for "aiding, abetting and exiting mutiny." The military tribunal set aside the charges against Lollier on the grounds that the court could not establish jurisdiction over a civilian and that a spy would not generally advertise his views in a newspaper. Jackson nonetheless retained custody briefly over Lollier and, on March 12, unceremoniously expelled the judge from the city until martial law was withdrawn after news of a peace treaty was confirmed. The next day, Lollier was released after martial law was lifted.[10]

In the weeks that followed, Jackson was defending himself before a civilian court. He appeared in federal court and was eventually held in contempt by Hall for his treatment of the Judge and fined $1000—not an insignificant amount in 1815. Three decades later, Congress reimbursed Jackson the amount of the fine.

In 1818, Jackson faced controversy, yet again, over his handling of military tribunals during the Seminole War in Florida. Two British citizens were tried on a variety of charges relating to their assistance of Native Americans in warfare against the United States. One defendant, Alexander Arbuthnot, was also charged with incitement to murder and spying. Arbuthnot was found guilty of all charges except spying and was sentenced to death and executed. The other defendant, Robert Ambrister, did not fare much better. After he was found guilty on all charges, except one, he was initially ordered executed. Ambrister's death sentence, however, was rescinded after a rehearing and his punishment

10. Baldrate, 2005; Glazier, 2005; Fisher, 2005.

Table 2 Amendments 1 - 10: The bill of rights- selected portions on protections of civil and criminal rights

First Amendment guarantees freedom of speech and religion and right of assembly for peaceful political purposes.
Fourth Amendment protects people against unreasonable searches and seizures and sets forth the requirement of probable cause for searches, seizures and arrests.
Fifth Amendment requires indictments in many circumstances, prohibits double jeopardy, compelled self incrimination and deprivations of life or limb without due process.
Sixth Amendment provides for speedy public trials by impartial juries for criminal cases with various procedural safeguards including notice of the charges and the right to counsel.
The Eighth Amendment prohibits the imposition of excessive fines as well as cruel and unusual punishment. Today, the death penalty is available in cases involving killings, narcotics trafficking, espionage and for treason.

downgraded to one year imprisonment at hard labor and whippings. Jackson intervened to reverse the tribunal's decision and Ambrister was executed.[11]

After President James Monroe mentioned the trial in his 1818 State of the Union address, Congress investigated the matter. A House committee criticized the proceedings for its adjudication of offenses not specifically enumerated by statute and its inapplicable use of the general label of outlaw and pirate. The legislators concluded that the only possible available charge was spying-which had resulted in an acquittal. The Committee also found the punishments overly severe:

> [W]here the war is with a savage nation, which observes no rules, and never gives quarter, we may punish them in the persons of any of their people whom we may take, (these belonging to the number of the guilty,) and endeavor, by this rigorous proceeding, to force them to respect the laws of humanity; but wherever severity is not absolutely necessary, clemency becomes a duty.[12]

Nevertheless, Congressional censure votes against Jackson for his actions against Arbuthnot and Ambrister failed by wide margins.

Most historians contend that the modern roots of contemporary military tribunals began in the 1840s during the Mexican-American War. For the first time, the American military exerted substantial control over foreign territory. The Mexican War commander of American forces, General Winfield Scott, a lawyer in civilian life, faced a difficult situation. He needed the support of Mexican citizens for supplies and also to limit attacks by civilians upon his troops. In order to maintain order within conquered territory, Scott needed the ability to punish offenses by both his soldiers as well as Mexican citizens.[13]

Unfortunately, the Articles of War did not cover crimes by soldiers against Mexican citizens or crimes by Mexicans within their own country. When both the administration and Congress failed to authorize new tribunals, Scott declared

11. Baldrate, 2005; Glazier, 2005; Fisher, 2005.
12. Ibid.
13. Baldrate, 2005; Glazier, 2005; Fisher, 2005.

martial law in the Mexican territories. Pursuant to the martial law order, he established military commissions on his own on a temporary basis until Congressionally approved courts could be created. That never happened. These commissions, distinct from courts-martial, presided over cases involving American soldiers and Mexican citizens accused of common law offenses. Scott also created another entity called "Council of War", to prosecute what is now known as war crimes committed by American soldiers and Mexican citizens. After 1848, this tribunal was collapsed into existing military courts (Table 3).[14]

The Supreme Court was never required to directly rule on the legitimacy of Scott's criminal military tribunals- although it did make reference to it. Before the Civil War, the High Court had a relatively small number of cases involving courts-martial or other military tribunals. While the Supreme Court often deferred to military courts, it sometimes limited their authority to try certain civilians and government officials. In one instance, the Court denied that tribunals had authority to prosecute a justice of the peace for avoiding military service because Congress expressly exempted government officials.[15]

In another case, Jecker v. Montgomery, the Court held that neither the President nor the military could create courts in foreign territories to adjudicate claims related to seized property, the rights of the United States, or to administer the laws of nations. In Jecker, the Court distinguished American "prize courts" in Mexico which impermissibly adjudicated claims about confiscated property from those established by Scott during the war:

> The courts, established or sanctioned in Mexico during the war by the commanders of the American forces, were nothing more than the agents of the military power, to assist it in preserving order in conquered territory, and to protect the inhabitants in their persons and property while it was occupied by the American arms...They were not courts of the United States and had no right to adjudicate upon a question of prize.[16]

The Civil War and Reconstruction period that followed was a time when the military exercised widespread authority to detain and prosecute individuals outside of civilian courts. In 1861, shortly after the start of the Civil War, fear of violence and sabotage by confederate sympathizers in border and northern states induced President Abraham Lincoln to take unilateral action while Congress was out of session. He suspended the writ of habeas corpus - the constitutional guarantee giving prisoners the right to challenge their detention through independent judicial review. He also ordered military authorities to arrest and detain those of questionable loyalties and seize railroad and telegraph lines. Lincoln's "Suspension of the Writ of Habeas Corpus Relating to the Events in Baltimore" was signed in Washington on April 27, 1861. Following is the text of the

14. Baldrate, 2005; Glazier, 2005; Fisher, 2005.
15. Baldrate, 2005; Glazier, 2005; Fisher, 2005.
16. Jecker v. Montgomery, 54 U.S. 498, 515 (1851), [online] Available at: http://supreme.justia.com/us/54/498/case.html.

Table 3 Persons tried by the military in late 1840s in Mexican territories/California

	Total	Americans	Mexicans	Other/Unspecified
Military Commissions	409	303	88	18
Council of War	21	1	18	2

suspension sent to the Commanding General of the Army of the United States: "You are engaged in repressing an insurrection against the laws of the United States. If at any point on or in the vicinity of the military line which is now used between the city of Philadelphia via Perryville, Annapolis City and Annapolis Junction you find resistance which renders it necessary to suspend the writ of habeas corpus for the public safety, you personally or through the officer in command at the point where resistance occurs are authorized to suspend that writ."[17]

Thereafter, Confederate spies, those aiding the rebel cause, resisting the draft, or those who "were guilty of any disloyal practice" were denied the writ of habeas corpus and detained until the war's conclusion. Lincoln ordered that persons thus arrested could be tried and punished by military courts. In defending his action, Lincoln declared that regular civilian courts were inadequate during a rebellion and those opposing the Union endangered "the public safety." As the war raged on, President Lincoln defended his unilateral actions and urged Congressional approval before a special session of Congress on July 4, 1861: "Are all laws but one to go unexecuted and the government itself go to pieces less that one law be violated?"[18]

John Merryman, a farmer, militia member, and Confederate sympathizer who lived outside Baltimore, was one agitator caught up in Lincoln's exercise of executive authority. Merryman was suspected in a conspiracy to sabotage a railroad but never charged. Almost immediately after his arrest, Merryman petitioned the federal courts for relief. United States Supreme Court Justice Roger Taney, a Maryland native sitting temporarily on a lower federal appeals court, ruled that Merryman should be released. Merryman's detention was illegal because, in Taney's view, only Congress had the authority to suspend the writ of habeas corpus. But Taney was powerless to enforce his order. While the justice may have had the law on his side, Lincoln commanded the troops. As the Latin expression holds, *silent leges inter arma*- "laws fall silent when weapons speak."– military commanders simply ignored Taney's command that Merryman be released.[19]

17. Lincoln, A. (1861) *Suspension of the Writ of Habeas Corpus Relating to the Events in Baltimore, 1861*. With Winfield Scott. Headquarters of the Army, Washington, April 27, [online]. Available at: http://www.civilwarhome.com/Writ.htm.
18. Miller, M. M. (ed) (1907) *Life and Works of Abraham Lincoln (centenary edition)* [online]. Available at: http://ehistory.osu.edu/uscw/library/books/lincoln/index.cfm.
19. Ex parte Merryman, 17 Fed. Case. No. 9, 487, p. 144 (1861).

Eventually, Congress ratified Lincoln's suspension of habeas corpus and his seizure of rail and telegraph lines, but not before military commanders had detained many people like Merryman in the name of national security. While courts-martial had a Congressional mandate before hostilities erupted, it was not until 1862 that Congress enacted a limited authorization for military tribunals to address offenses by those who were under the jurisdiction of the Articles of War. The following year, Congress expanded the scope of Articles of War to include various common law offense like rape, murder, battery, and arson that occurred in "times of war or rebellion" by those in the military—not civilians. Congress' action approved of tribunals similar to those unilaterally created by the military during the Mexican-American War. The 1863 statute also outlawed draft resistance and provided for military trials for those accused of espionage. Congress also enacted legislation mandating notification by the President to the federal judiciary of the identities of all military prisoners and permitted judicial intervention in certain instances. By 1864, federal law was expanded further to permit the use of "military commissions upon guerillas for violation of the laws and customs of war."[20]

President Lincoln specifically authorized military commissions by proclamation on September 24, 1862:

> [D]uring the existing insurrection, and as a necessary measure for suppressing the same, all Rebels and insurgents, their aiders and abettors within the United States, and all persons discouraging volunteer enlistments, resisting militia drafts, or guilty of any disloyal practice, affording aid and comfort to Rebels against the authority of the United States, shall be subject to martial law and liable to trial and punishment by Courts Martial or Military Commissions.[21]

Confederate operatives and sympathizers were not the only ones to face American military tribunals during the Civil War period. In 1862, five weeks of hostilities broke out between Native American Dakota Indians and white settlers and soldiers in Minnesota. By the time the violence subsided, over 450 whites and over two dozen Dakotas were killed. The subsequent military tribunals took place in an atmosphere of revenge, prejudice, and desire for the spoils of victory. Of the over 300 initially sentenced to death, President Lincoln approved of little more than three dozen executions. It was important to the President to distinguish those who killed in battle as opposed to those who raped or killed in massacres. It was the later whose harsh punishment he allowed.[22]

While President Lincoln sometimes did not depend on Congressional or judicial authorization for his actions, it would be incorrect to conclude that he allowed the military to act without oversight. Lincoln reigned in generals who sought to confiscate property or summarily execute people during the imposition of martial law. The President, through the adjunct general, also regularly conducted

20. Baldrate, 2005; Glazier, 2005; Fisher, 2005.
21. Miller, 1907.
22. Fisher, 2005.

oversight of military tribunals and on numerous occasions reversed its death sentences. Tribunals were further limited by the fact that they could only be convened by generals and were used to prosecute serious transgressions of the customs of "laws of war." Thus, these hearings were usually reserved for violent guerilla warfare types of activities committed in jurisdictions under occupation or martial law.[23]

One case where the hearings appeared to involve political rather than security goals was the trial of Ohio politician Clement Vallandigham. Following an order handed down by the military commander in Ohio outlawing declarations of sympathy for the enemy, Vallandigham was arrested and prosecuted by a military tribunal. The Supreme Court held that it had no jurisdiction over the case or to review the tribunal's decisions because these commissions were not courts of the kind addressed in Article III of the Constitution or by the Judiciary Act of 1789. Congress simply never assigned any authority to the federal bench to take such appeals, the justices maintained.[24]

However, when the military sought to expand its authority to include civilians in areas not under martial law or occupation, it faced a stern, albeit late, rebuke from the United States Supreme Court. In 1864, a Democratic partisan, Lambdin Milligan, was arrested by United States Army officers and charged with conspiring to steal explosives from Union arsenals and planning a raid on prison camps in Indiana. Notwithstanding the facts that federal civilian courts were operational and Indiana was outside of the field of military operations, Milligan was tried before a military tribunal and sentenced to death.[25]

The Supreme Court released its decision, sparing Milligan's life in December 1866, perhaps not accidentally, after the war had ended. The Court unanimously held that the president does not have the authority to create military tribunals to try citizens in jurisdictions where civilian courts are in operation. Justice David Davis explained that the Constitution could not be suspended due to exigency and that it existed as:

> [A] law for rulers and people, equally in time of war and peace and covers with the shield of its protection all classes of men, at all times, and under all circumstances. No doctrine, involving more pernicious consequences, was ever invented by the wit of man than any of its provisions can be suspended during any great exigencies of government. Such a doctrine leads directly to anarchy or despotism.[26]

Davis contended that Milligan's trial by military authorities violated his right to a grand jury indictment and a public trial. Four justices contended that the military tribunal at issue was only unconstitutional because Congress failed to ratify their

23. Ibid.
24. Ex parte Vallandigham, 1Wall. 243, 251 (1864); Baldrate, 2005; Glazier, 2005; Fisher, 2005.
25. Ex parte Milligan, 71 U.S. 2 (1866).
26. Ex parte Milligan, 71 U.S. 2, 120–1 (1866).

existence, while the remaining five held that the government lacked the authority even in instances of Congressional assent.[27]

Military tribunals were created in the immediate postwar period to address mistreatment of prisoners of war and the assassination of President Lincoln. Half of the eight people tried by the military commissions for their role in the assassination were sentenced to death while the rest received sentences of life imprisonment. Despite the fact that civilian courts were in operation, President Johnson opted for military tribunals because the capitol was under martial law at the time of the assassination. Mary Surratt's habeas corpus filing was initially accepted by a federal judge. After President Johnson personally persuaded the judge that habeas corpus was inapplicable to the assassination case, he stepped aside and Surratt gained the dubious distinction of being the only female executed in connection with Lincoln's murder. Shortly after Surrat's execution and despite conflicting evidence a military commission sentenced Henry Wirz to hang for his role in the deaths of Union prisoners of war held at an Andersonville, Georgia prison camp. He was one of eight called before the tribunal for their role in maintaining the prison camp.[28]

During Reconstruction, military occupiers ruled over the defeated Confederate states. While the military authorities operated tribunals, Congress also acted by passing civilian federal criminal laws aimed at those who sought to deprive individuals of their civil rights through force or threats. In particular, Congress targeted conspiracies such as those committed by Ku Klux Klan members and misconduct by government officials.[29]

Perhaps the most crucial development of the Civil War period relating to the status of modern day terrorists was the work of German immigrant scholar Francis Lieber. Lieber was injured during battle and later imprisoned for his political views in Europe before coming to the United States. By the Civil War, Lieber was one of the Union's most prominent advisors. Lieber issued a lengthy protocol for the military, General Orders 100: "Instructions for the Government of Armies of the United States in the Field" in April 1863. The directives were divided into 157 articles spread throughout ten main sections. The goal of the work was to provide humane standards of conduct on the one hand, while providing military officials flexibility in combating the nation's enemies. With regard to hearings, Lieber noted that authority for the military to prosecute cases came from statutes, which were primarily used with regard to courts-martial, while other "common law" violations were addressed by military commissions.[30]

In the decades that followed, there were minor changes to the Articles of War and the United States became a signatory to the Hague Treaty of July 1899. Borrowing from Lieber's earlier work, the treaty established humane rules for prisoners of war (POWs), as well as general limitations on their being tried.

27. Ex parte Milligan (1866).
28. Baldrate, 2005, Glazier, 2005; Fisher, 2005.
29. 18 USC §241, 242.
30. Fisher, 2005.

Civilians who officially accompanied armies, such as contractors or journalists, were also afforded POW status. However, those operating as spies could be tried and were not subject to the protections of POW designation. In the last decades of the 19th century, the location of tribunals mirrored America's expansion, from newly conquered Indian territory to Cuba, Puerto Rico and the Philippines. Tribunals in the Philippines around the turn of the century were particularly noteworthy. These tribunals not only addressed traditional crimes, but were also applied to violent insurgent guerillas who slaughtered natives friendly to Americans.[31]

In 1916, legislation was enacted that expanded the military's authority to crimes committed by soldiers during peacetime, but also allowed for civilian prosecutions. The legislation allowed courts-martial against "any other person who [is designated] by statute or the laws of war" In order to allow for both courts-martial and other military tribunals, Article 15 of the 1916 Articles of War stated:

> Not Exclusive—the provisions of these articles conferring jurisdiction upon courts-martial shall not be construed as depriving military commissions, provost courts, or other military tribunals of concurrent jurisdiction in respect of offenders or offenses that by the law of war may be lawfully triable by such commissions, provost courts, or other military tribunals.[32]

Also, in 1916, a German saboteur named Lothar Witzke was tried in secret in Texas and sentenced to death after he entered America illegally via Mexico. President Woodrow Wilson, however, lessened the sentence to life imprisonment after Attorney General Thomas Watt Gregory challenged the constitutionality of the hearings in a secret memoranda. Gregory maintained that the military had no authority to try someone charged with activities outside of areas of military operation or martial law except for soldiers and their assistants. Witzke was eventually returned to Germany after performing heroic acts during a fire at Leavenworth penitentiary.[33]

The United States was not so generous when it dealt with other German saboteurs three decades later. In ex parte Quirin, the Supreme Court unanimously upheld the right of the President to try enemy belligerents who violate the rules of war before military tribunals. The Court based its decision on the President's authority as Commander-in-Chief and Congress' approval of such tribunals. The case related to the capture of eight German saboteurs who made secret nocturnal beach arrivals at Amagansett Beach, Long Island, and Ponte Vedra, Florida as part of a plan to commit violence and acts of sabotage. The Germans landed in two groups of four after disembarking from German submarines in June 1942. Upon their arrival, they changed into civilian attire and buried their military uniforms and cache of explosives. The beaches and surrounding waters had been previously designated as areas under military authority. After being arrested in New York and

31. Glazier, 2005.
32. *Articles of War, 1916.* Act of Aug. 29. 1916, ch. 418.
33. Fisher, 2005.

Chicago, all eight were charged with violation of the laws of war, Articles of War violations of aiding the enemy and spying, and conspiracy.[34]

The Court noted the relevance of common law rules of law which outlawed the actions of an enemy combatant who "without uniform comes secretly through the lines for the purpose of waging war by destruction of life and property...." The Court also held that even a citizen could be tried as a belligerent. One of those captured, Herbert Haupt, maintained he was an American citizen, despite his service to the enemy. The Court additionally held that the mere secret presence of the enemy combatants and their hostile intent was enough to charge and convict them. The Court ignored various procedural and review alterations implemented unilaterally by the President that some maintained exceeded his authority. Without deciding the culpability of the Germans, the Supreme Court found that the Constitution gave the President, with Congress' assent, the authority to convene military tribunals against the saboteurs. The President's reliance on common law laws of war gave him flexibility on crucial issues that Congress did not explicitly establish, the Court maintained. The Court further found that the Sixth Amendment guarantee of a trial by jury did not extend to military tribunals.[35]

Soon after the Supreme Court ruled, six of the eight saboteurs were executed, including Haupt. The Court's decision in Quirin became the legal basis used in President George W. Bush's designation of al Qaeda captive's designation as enemy combatants after 9/11. While the Supreme Court held in favor of President Roosevelt in the case at hand, it also set the precedent that federal courts have the authority to review the jurisdiction and authority of such tribunals.

Constitutional guarantees for thousands of citizens and residents also yielded to wartime fears. Following the devastating attack on Pearl Harbor that killed in excess of 2400 Americans, Hawaii was placed under martial law. In addition, President Franklin D. Roosevelt signed an executive order that permitted military leaders to designate areas "from which any or all persons may be excluded." Citizens or not, and without trial or proof of individualized suspicion, over 110,000 persons of Japanese ancestry on the continental Pacific coast were involuntarily removed from their residences and imprisoned in inland internment camps. A far smaller number of German and Italians were also held. Citing wartime exigencies, the Supreme Court upheld the removals by a 6-3 vote - a decision that dissenting Justice Murphy termed "one of the most sweeping and complete deprivations of constitutional rights in the history of this nation." While acknowledging for the first time that governmental classifications based on race were indeed "suspect," the Court nonetheless upheld the discriminatory forced removal of those of Japanese ancestry from military designated zones. As a technical matter, the Court did not rule on the internment camps themselves,

34. Ex Parte Quirin, 317 U.S. 1 (1942).
35. Ibid.

but rather on the reporting and removal requirements that led to the imprisonments.[36]

Justice Murphy's majority concurrence in Ex parte Mitsuye Endo echoed his earlier dissent in Koramatsu: "I am of the view that detention in Relocation Centers of persons of Japanese ancestry regardless of loyalty is not only unauthorized by Congress or the Executive, but is another example of the unconstitutional resort to racism inherent in the entire evacuation program...-racial discrimination of this nature bears no reasonable relation to military necessity and is utterly foreign to the ideals and traditions of the American people.." In Endo, a unanimous United States Supreme Court ordered the release from an internment camp of a Japanese American woman because the government failed to allege any evidence of disloyalty. Justice Douglas' majority opinion explained: "A citizen who is concededly loyal presents no problem of espionage or sabotage. Loyalty is a matter of the heart and mind, not of race, creed, or color."[37]

Future Supreme Court Justice Tom Clark, who represented the government in the wartime relocations cases, echoed these thoughts in a later writing: "The truth is - as this deplorable experience proves - that constitutions and laws are not sufficient of themselves...Despite the unequivocal language of the Constitution of the United States that the writ of habeas corpus shall not be suspended, and despite the Fifth Amendment's command that no person shall be deprived of life, liberty, or property without due process of law, both of these constitutional safeguards were denied by military action..." Decades later Japanese who had been detained were awarded $20,000 in compensation.[38]

After World War II, the Allies convened international tribunals to prosecute Axis officials for violence and misconduct that violated traditional laws of war. This was the first time an international tribunal convened to try prominent officials of violations relating to the nature of their warfare. In Nuremberg, Germany on November 20, 1945, the trials of two dozen German nationals commenced pursuant to an International Military Tribunal consisting of representatives from the United States, France, the United Kingdom, and the Soviet Union.[39]

Among the most notable features of the proceedings was the fact that it was a public trial and one where influential lawyers and judges held prominent positions. The lead prosecutor for the United States was Supreme Court Chief Justice Robert Jackson. The main evidence presented included captured documents, witnesses, and photographs. A few Nazi leaders, including Adolph

36. *Executive Order 9066: The Internment of 110,000 Japanese Americans*, (1942), [online] Available at: http://www.sscnet.ucla.edu/aasc/ex9066/; Korematsu v. United States, 323 U.S. 214 (1944).
37. Ex Parte Mitsuye Endo, 323 U.S. 283 (1944); Korematsu v. United States, 323 U.S. 214 (1944).
38. *Executive Order 9066:The Internment of 110,000 Japanese Americans* (1942).
39. Fisher, 2005; *Trial of the Major War Criminals Before the International Military Tribunal*, (IMT) Nuremberg, 14 November 1945-1 October 1946, [online] Available at: http://www.archives.gov/iwg/research-papers/trial-of-war-criminals-before-imt.html.

Hitler, Heinrich Himmler, and Joseph Goebbels, chose suicide over execution. There were four basic charges levied against the defendants: conspiracy, crimes against peace and the waging of wars of aggression, war crimes, and a Holocaust related "crimes against humanity". Of the twenty-two defendants in custody at the trial's close, twelve were sentenced to hang and seven more to prison. Thousands of other lower level individuals were tried for war-era crimes across Europe and similar tribunals were held for 25 Axis leaders and thousands of their subordinates in the Pacific theater. The conviction of Japanese General Yamashita before a military tribunal was affirmed by a 6-2 vote of the United States Supreme Court in 1946. Yamashita was held responsible by a tribunal for the brutality of his troops against Filipinos and Americans, despite an assertion that he was unaware of the conduct of his subordinates and irregularities in the process against him.[40]

The Geneva Conventions are a series of treaties that establish rules for the civilized treatment of civilians and combatants during armed conflicts. The first treaty, introduced in 1864, governed the treatment of the sick and wounded. Similar rules addressing acceptable methods of warfare were established in 1899 and 1907 as the Hague Conventions, and other refinements to the Geneva rules were made in 1906 and 1929. In 1949, various previous Geneva and Hague convention rules were revised and additions made under the title of the Geneva Conventions of 1949. These post World War II Geneva Conventions define various categories of protected classes of people and details how they are to be treated by signatories during periods of hostilities, irrespective of whether war is officially declared. Three additional protocols were introduced in subsequent decades. While the sick and wounded on land and at sea, prisoners of war, and civilians are specifically addressed, the Conventions provide a minimal level of care for all people who come under the jurisdiction of a party in a conflict. Under Article 3, those who are no longer participants in a conflict must be cared for humanely. Criminal cases must be tried fairly before a "regularly constituted court."[41]

Article 3 also mandates humane treatment as well as specific rights and protections to those designated as POW. POWs are entitled to adequate housing, clothing, a reasonable diet, medical care, and the exercise of their religious faith. While in captivity, POWs need only provide pedigree information such as name, rank, and identifying serial number and are protected from coercive questioning techniques. The POW's government are to be notified of their status and the POWs may send and receive correspondence. A humanitarian organization, such as the Red Cross, may have access to facilities. Discipline that is inhuman, brutal, or dangerous is prohibited. Torture and cruelty is also proscribed.[42]

While POWs may be tried, Article 3 details significant requirements on the type of charges, investigative techniques, and procedural methods for trials.

40. Fisher, 2005; Baldrate, 2005; In re Yamashita, 327 U.S. 1, 11 (1946).
41. *Geneva Convention (III) Relative to the Treatment of Prisoners of War* (1949) Aug. 12 [1955] 6 U. S. T. 3316, T. I. A. S. No. 3364 (Third Geneva Convention).
42. Ibid.

Generally, Article 3 requires that POWs be afforded similar treatment of the kind that is extended to military and civilian defendants who are residents of the detaining power. A baseline requirement of notice, representation by counsel, translation, access to witnesses, and appeal is mandated. In addition, charges must relate to offenses found in civilian or military statutes or violations of the laws of war.[43]

On May 31, 1951, a new body of military law became effective for the American military. The Uniform Code of Military Justice (UCMJ) created a uniform set of laws for all the branches of the American armed forces and a system of official appeals, including a civilian appellate court. Most of the UCMJ provisions were not actually new but adapted or revised from the Articles of War and other sources. Like previous incarnations of military law, the UCMJ allows for both military tribunals and courts-martial.[44]

September 11 and Beyond

The terrorist attacks of September 11, 2001, and the national anthrax scare that followed, once again exacerbated the tension between civil liberties and police power in America. On September 18, 2001 a joint resolution of Congress was passed giving the President authority to use force against those responsible for the September 11 attacks:

> That the President is authorized to use all necessary and appropriate force against those nations, organizations, or persons he determines planned, authorized, committed, or aided the terrorist attacks that occurred on September 11, 2001, or harbored such organizations or persons, in order to prevent any future acts of international terrorism against the United States by such nations, organizations or persons.[45]

For those advocating broad presidential powers in the War on Terror, the Authorization for Use of Military Force (AUMF) was seen not only as approval for a military response against the Taliban and al Qaeda, but of Congressional deference to the administration on a range of other matters, from aggressive intelligence gathering to foreign detainee treatment.[46]

Domestically, in the six weeks that followed the terrorist attacks, civilian authorities arrested or detained more than 1,000 people within the United States. The aggressive enforcement of existing law and traditional detention methods such as immigration violations, various criminal charges, and material witness designation spread fear throughout immigrant communities and condemnation from advocacy organizations like the American Civil Liberties Union (ACLU). Some commentators drew comparisons to previous eras where individual liberties were

43. Ibid.
44. *Uniform Code of Military Justice (UCMJ)* (1951) 10 U.S.C. § 801 et seq.
45. *Authorization for Use of Military Force (AUMF)*, 115 Stat. 224 (2001).
46. Ibid.

curtailed such as the Alien & Sedition Acts period, the post World War I "Red Scare", and the internments of Japanese Americans, while others claimed such analogies were exaggerated. In June 2002, the Department of Justice reported that more than 1,200 people had been arrested or detained since the attacks-752 of whom were held on immigration charges and the remainder for various other charges. At least 74 people were still detained into June 2002, including 38 who were being held on charges involving immigration violations.[47]

FBI Director Robert Mueller responded to critics who suggested that federal authorities engaged in racial profiling, "I do not agree with the predicate that we are racial profiling." He acknowledged, however, that many individuals of interest in connection to post September 11 investigations involving international terrorism "share a common ethnic and religious background."[48] The Constitution's Fourteenth Amendment prohibits using race as a general criteria for criminal suspicion. However, race can be used to the extent that it is part of an individualized description of a particular suspect.[49]

Civil libertarians have also criticized a wide ranging anti-terrorism legislative package enacted in October 2001 - the Patriot Act.[50] While many key parts of the Act-were subject to a "sunset" provision that required reauthorization by the end of 2005, nearly all were reinstituted by Congress in early 2006. The act streamlines and relaxes warrant, investigative, and immigration detention requirements and gives federal agents expanded authority to track the flow of Internet and telephone communication. It also allows for secret information retrieved under the Foreign Intelligence Surveillance Act (FISA) to be shared across various law enforcement and intelligence agencies; the limited transfer of information from traditionally secret grand jury proceedings; the use of "sneak and peek" warrants, the use of various mechanisms for more speedy deportation hearings; increased time for the Immigration and Naturalization Service to detain non-citizens; enhanced authority for phone record searches; the retrieval of electronic evidence; and the use of roving wiretaps. These wiretaps follow a particular targeted person thus allowing phone intercepts of multiple phones across numerous jurisdictions. The Patriot Act allows one federal court to have nationwide authority to approve roving wiretaps, phone record searches, and retrieval of electronic evidence. While the Patriot Act had no effect on military tribunals or the basic requirements for civilian trials of citizens it did affect non citizen immigrants. It provides for expedited deportation proceedings and allows for one week detentions of foreigners alleged to be terrorists. The Attorney General is required to certify foreigners as security risks every six months if they remain in custody after that one week limit.[51]

47. Siemaszko, C. (2002) 'Most 9/11 Detainees Were Freed', *New York Daily News*, July 12, p. B18.
48. Mueller, R. (2002) 'Remarks at the Stanford Law School', Stanford, CA., October 18.
49. *United States Constitution.*
50. *Providing Appropriate Tools Required to Intercept and Obstruct Terrorism (PATRIOT) Act of 2001* (2001) Pub. L. 107-56, 115 Stat. 272 (October 26).
51. U.S.C. §1862; 18 U.S.C. §§3121-3127; 50 U.S.C. §1852; Patriot Act §218; §219, §220 and §206.

"These new and unchecked powers," said Gregory Nojeim, the associate director of the ACLU's Washington office, "could be used against American citizens who are not under criminal investigation, immigrants who are here within our border legally and also against those whose First Amendment activities are deemed to be threats to national security by the attorney general."[52] These debates continued for some time, both in the public and in Congress.

Even with the passage of the Patriot Act, the Bush administration was left with the issue of how to handle suspected stateless or American terrorists who may belong to clandestine overseas entities. That situation deviated from traditional military conflicts and declared wars which had defined end points, uniformed soldiers, and direct state affiliation. The situation also differed from standard criminal cases in that many were captured abroad by the military, intelligence operatives, or foreign governments. Furthermore, the administration was as interested in obtaining intelligence from captives as it was in their incapacitation. In the period after 9/11, an internal debate on the status of captured detainees occurred within the Bush administration with officials from the State Department and career military on one side and the Vice President and some civilian lawyers on the other.

On November 13, 2001, President George W. Bush, relying in part on the Quirin case and Roosevelt's 1942 order, issued an Executive Order authorizing military tribunals to prosecute certain types of international terrorists under his authority as Commander-in-Chief. In January 2002, foreign captives arrived at a prison holding facility at a United States military base at Guantanamo Bay, Cuba. In February 2002, President Bush labeled the detainees as "unlawful combatants" rather than POWs. By June, government officials maintained that the President had the power to hold these captives indefinitely without judicial review or counsel (Figure 1).[53]

A key figure in sculpting the administration's position was a young Justice Department lawyer and scholar named John Yoo. Yoo's overall position was that the President had wide authority to prosecute the War on Terror by virtue of his constitutional powers as evidenced by precedent, wartime exigencies, and the AUMF. Yoo, along with Vice Presidential advisor David Addington, prevailed in convincing the administration that it had broad authority over the interrogation, treatment, and trial of detainees without regard to the Geneva Conventions or additional approvals from the other coequal branches of government. Among the more controversial proposals presented to the administration were the implementation of limited trial rights and approval of interrogation methods as long as they did not cause lasting "psychological harm" or pain "akin to that which accompanies serious physical injury such as death or organ failure." These legal positions emboldened the administration to pursue an aggressive strategy

52. Eggen, D. (2001) 'Tough Anti-Terror Campaign Pledged', *Washington Post*, October 26, p. A1.
53. 'Detention, Treatment, and Trial of Certain Non-Citizens in the War Against Terrorism', *Federal Register*, vol. 56, 57833, November 13, 2001.

Figure 1 Two US Army (USA) Military Police (MP) escort a detainee, dressed in his new orange jumpsuit to a cell at Camp X-Ray, Guantanamo Bay Navy Base, Cuba. Camp X-Ray is the holding facility for detainees held at the US Navy (USN) Base during Operation ENDURING FREEDOM. (Released to Public) DoD photo by: PH1 SHANE T. MCCOY, USN Date Shot: 11 Jan 2002.

regarding captured combatants that was eventually challenged by allies, civilian lawyers, the Supreme Court, and Congress.[54]

After significant input from Congress, the American Bar Association, and our allies, the Department of Defense issued an order on March 21, 2002 detailing the composition and standards for tribunals. These tribunals include juries composed of three to seven military officers. For death penalty tribunals they must number seven and vote unanimously to render a death penalty verdict. An automatic post trial appeal of death sentences before military reviewers was required. Non-capital verdicts would require that two thirds of the jurors to agree on guilt by a standard of beyond a reasonable doubt. Defendants would also be entitled to a presumption of innocence, discovery, protection against self-incrimination, access to paid military legal counsel, and protections against double jeopardy. Trials would be open to the public, with certain exceptions, but could be held outside the territory of the United States. Rules of evidence would be relaxed and appeals to civilian courts were disallowed.[55]

Almost one year later, in February 2003, a draft guide "Crimes and Elements for Trials by Military Commission" was published that proposed two dozen such

54. Golden, T. (2005) 'The Advocate: A Junior Aide Had a Big Role in Terror Policy', *New York Times*, December 23, p. A1.
55. US Department of Defense (2002) Military Commission Order No. 1, March 21.

offenses including attacking civilians, hostage taking, hijacking, and use of poisons, along with the inclusion of other offenses found traditionally in the Articles of War. The UCMJ was not referenced presumably because of its Article 36 directive for military tribunals to, as much as is practicable, resemble proceedings in federal court. In July 2003, the President authorized six Guantanamo captives to face military tribunals including Salim Ahmed Hamdan, a chauffer and alleged bodyguard for Usama bin Laden. Hamdan's case would eventually end up before the United States Supreme Court in 2006. In late 2003, as other detainee cases proceeded through the civilian federal court system, the Bush administration reversed its prohibition on detainees having access to counsel.[56]

The detention of enemy combatants resulted in the United States Supreme Court accepting three appeals between November 2003 and February 2004. In all the cases, the President's Authority under Article II of the Constitution as Commander-in-Chief was pitted against the right of detained persons to have the government account for such detention.

One of the detainee appeals involved an American citizen named Yaser Hamdi, who was captured on a battlefield in Afghanistan by Northern Alliance forces and subsequently detained by the United States military at Guantanamo Bay. Hamdi was born in Louisiana while his father was studying in the United States, but he and his parents soon returned to Saudi Arabia. The Constitution's Fourteenth Amendment, ratified in February 1868, confers American citizenship to all persons born or naturalized within the United States, even if their parents are non-citizens. A 2003 decision by the United States Court of Appeals for the Fourth Circuit in Virginia held that Hamdi's indefinite detention was constitutional as a proper exercise of the President's authority as Commander-in-Chief. The Court held that a defense department official's summary declaration of the propriety of Hamdi's designation was sufficient to maintain his continued open-ended detention without granting him access to courts.[57]

In its ruling in Hamdi v. Rumsfeld, issued on June 28, 2004, the Supreme Court did not upset the holding of World War II era caselaw that maintained American citizens who act against their country can, in fact, be held as enemy combatants. However, the Court held by an 8-1 vote that such an individual is entitled to notice of the factual basis of the enemy combatant classification and an opportunity to rebut the classification before a neutral decision-maker. To fail to do so, particularly within a reasonable period of time, deprived Mr. Hamdi of his constitutional right to due process pursuant to the Fifth Amendment. The exact standards or configuration of such hearings was left open-ended, but the Court's controlling opinion indicated that military hearings with lower governmental burdens may suffice. The justices were also in disagreement as to whether

56. Fisher, 2005; Greenhouse, L. (2006) 'Justices, 5-3 Broadly Reject Bush Plan to Try Detainees/Accompanying Charts', *New York Times*, June 30, p. 1.
57. Hamdi v. Rumsfeld, (2004).

Congressional approval of the AUMF was sufficient to overcome the requirements of a 1971 law prohibiting detention of American citizens absent the enactment of specific legislation. A narrow plurality of five Justices maintained that the AUMF resolution extended the government's authority to detain Hamdi. Hamdi was released to Saudi Arabia in late 2004 after renouncing his citizenship and promising never to come back to the United States.[58]

In two companion cases, Rasul v. Bush and Odah v. United States, also decided on June 28, 2004, the Supreme Court held 6-3 that non-citizen enemy combatants are entitled to federal judicial review of habeas petitions. The majority opinions by Justice Stevens held that neither the foreign citizenship of a detainee or the detention camp's geographic presence in Cuba barred a detainee from challenging his detention. The cases involved 16 citizens of Britain, Australia, and Kuwait.[59]

One month after the Supreme Court ruled that detainees had the right to contest their detention, the Defense Department allowed for hearings before a panel of military officers. Salim Hamdan became the first captive to go before such a tribunal in August 2004. From August 2004 through March 2005, the military judged the cases of 558 detainees and reclassified only 38 of them to non-enemy combatant status. The government also released many prisoners due to diplomatic pressure. In the months after four Britons were released in January 2005 at the request of United Kingdom Prime Minister Tony Blair, every European captive was released for a total of nearly 100. Hamdan was not quite as fortunate. In November 2004, a federal court stopped Hamdan's proceedings on the grounds that it contravened requirements of both domestic military law and the Geneva Conventions. In July 2005, a panel of the United States Court of Appeals for the District of Columbia Circuit unanimously overturned the district court. The panel, which included future Supreme Court Chief Justice John Roberts, contended that the military tribunal was authorized by Congress and that the Geneva Conventions allowed nations, not individuals, to enforce its provisions, precluding Hamdan from doing so individually. In November 2005, the United States Supreme Court accepted Hamdan's appeal and heard oral arguments four months later.[60]

On December 30, 2005, the Detainee Treatment Act (DTA) was enacted. The DTA established new guidelines for the questioning and treatment of detainees and established procedural safeguards for Americans accused of improper conduct during interrogations. The DTA further established various procedures for tribunals and a requirement of Congressional notification by the Pentagon regarding procedural practices. The DTA's language, aimed at denying detainees

58. Ibid.

59. Rasul v. Bush, 542 U.S. 466 (2004); *Odah v. United States*, 542 U.S. 466 (2004).

60. Hamdan v. Rumsfeld, (2006); Combatant Status Review Tribunal Summary, March 2005, [online]. Available at: http://www.defenselink.mil/news/Mar2005/d20050329csrt.pdf; Linzer, D. & Kessler, G. (2006) 'Decision to Move Detainees Resolved Two-Year Debate Among Bush Advisers', *Washington Post*, Friday, September 8, p. A1.

access to the federal court appeals, did not prevent the Supreme Court from deciding Hamdan's case.[61]

On June 29, 2006, in a sharp rebuke to the Bush administration, the United States Supreme Court ruled in favor of Hamdan. First, the Court held that a detainee's rights were protected by the Geneva Conventions and were enforceable through the federal courts pursuant to habeas corpus procedures. Second, the Court maintained that the President lacked the necessary Constitutional authority or specific Congressional approval for the tribunals he created. Without specific Congressional approval, the President was bound by existing law, including the UCMJ and the laws of war, which include the Geneva Conventions. Restrictive evidentiary rules for the defense and Hamdan's compelled absence on national security grounds from portions of his trial contravened provisions of both these controlling authorities, thus making his trial unlawful.[62]

In the months after the Hamdan ruling, sweeping changes took place regarding the treatment of detainees suspected of terrorist connections. In July 2006, the Bush administration announced that all suspected terrorists held by the military or CIA would be treated in conformance to the standards of the Geneva Conventions. In September 2006, the Army introduced a revised Army Field Manual that was governed by such standards and prohibited such practices as lengthy solitary confinement, aggressive use of dogs, and simulated drowning. On Labor Day weekend the government transferred the 14 remaining detainees in CIA custody from secret overseas locations to the United States military camp at Guantanamo Bay. Among those turned over to the Defense Department for future trials was Khalid Shaikh Mohammed- the alleged mastermind of the 9/11 terror attacks.[63]

Because the Supreme Court allowed for Congress to legislate changes to the tribunal process for Guantanamo detainees, intensive negotiations between Congress and the administration continued into the Fall of 2006. On October 17, 2006, President Bush signed a compromise bill, the Military Commissions Act (MCA), into law. The MCA set rules and standards for military tribunals and placed restrictions on certain types of aggressive interrogation. The MCA allows the government to introduce hearsay evidence and coerced statements at trials of suspected al Qaeda detainees. It also allows the military to bar detainee defendants from trials when classified material is used. While the MCA disallows habeas appeals to federal district courts, it provides for a review of enemy combatant status by a three person panel of military officials. The MCA further provides that those designated as unlawful enemy combatants may be subject to open ended periods of detention. The MCA states that those who merely provide material support to a hostile enemy can be classified as an unlawful enemy combatant without any requirement of active participation in armed conflict.

61. *Detention Treatment Act* (2005) 119 Stat. 2739–2740.
62. Ibid.
63. Greenhouse, 2006; Linzer & Kessler, 2006; White, J. (2006) 'New Rules of Interrogation Forbid Use of Harsh Tactics', *Washington Post*, Thursday, September 7, p. A1.

While accepting the general restrictions on torture and inhumane treatment found in Geneva's Article 3, the MCA limits the provision's application to only certain types of treatment. The act establishes a defense for government employees accused of aggressive questioning techniques from 2001 to 2005, when another law banned such practices. Lastly, the MCA prohibits United States citizens from being detained as unlawful enemy combatants. Even before the legislation was signed, advocacy groups pledged to challenge the MCA in federal court.[64]

Perhaps the most confusing case relating to the military's authority to detain is the circuitous saga of Jose Padilla. Lawyers filed a habeas corpus case in United States District Court in New York in September 2002 on behalf of Jose Padilla, an American citizen, detained at a South Carolina military base. Mr. Padilla, an alleged al Qaeda associate, was arrested by federal agents on a material witness charge at Chicago's O'Hare airport in May 2002 upon his arrival from overseas. Mr. Padilla, a former gang member and Muslim convert, was turned over to military authorities who maintained they could incarcerate him indefinitely without charges or access to counsel on national security grounds. During his military confinement Padilla's lawyers allege he was shackled, had his sleep disrupted, and subjected to threats and intense questioning without access to an attorney.

Mr. Padilla is allegedly connected to a plot by foreign terrorists to detonate a radiological "dirty bomb" in the United States, but the actual extent of the plot is subject to debate. Public reports based on material recovered in Afghanistan indicate that al-Qaeda is interested in obtaining weapons of mass destruction for use against civilians. In June 2004, the Supreme Court by a 5-4 vote, made no substantive ruling in Padilla's case because it held the case was wrongfully filed at a federal district court in New York, rather than in South Carolina, where Padilla was incarcerated. In March 2005, a federal district court judge in South Carolina ruled that the government must either charge Padilla with a crime or release him shortly.[65] As Padilla's challenge to military detention wound its way back up through the federal appellate courts, the Bush administration pursued a criminal indictment in civilian courts, which was issued in November 2005. Critics alleged that the late change in custody status was a last minute tactic by the Bush administration designed to avoid a Supreme Court hearing on the merits that could result in yet another legal loss.[66]

The United States Supreme Court allowed his physical transfer to civilian courts and Padilla was brought before a federal district court judge in January 2006. He was charged with offenses of providing material support to terrorists and conspiring to murder Americans. The charges, however, are not directly related to the dirty bomb plot for which he was initially detained. In April 2006, the United

64. Military Commissions Act of 2006, Pub. L. No. 109-366, 120 Stat. 2600 (Oct. 17, 2006); Richey, W. (2006) 'New lawsuits challenge Congress detainee act', *Christian Science Monitor*, October 6, [online]. Available at: http://www.csmonitor.com/2006/1006/p01s03-uspo.html

65. Rumsfeld v. Padilla, 542 U.S. 426 (2004).

66. Greenhouse, 2006.

States Supreme Court, by a single vote, refused to hear Padilla's appeal, apparently on the grounds that he was no longer in military custody. In an unusual explanation accompanying their denial of his appeal, three justices warned the government that its victory was not a blank check. Chief Justice Roberts, joined by Justices Kennedy and Stevens,indicated that Padilla was entitled to the full rights of a criminal defendant including a speedy trial. They also pointed out that the Supreme Court would not ignore further government attempts "to change the status or conditions of Padilla's custody." Padilla's civilian criminal trial date, set for 2007 in federal district court in Miami, means that he faced almost 5 years imprisonment before the government took him before a jury.[67]

Studies and a series of high profile cases in civilian federal courts have shown that traditional criminal laws are being used against suspected terrorists and extremists with mixed results. Part of the reason for these mixed results is that the FBI and federal prosecutors have changed their strategy from post event response to interdiction of terrorist acts before they occur. A report by the Washington Post in 2005 revealed that the most common type of charges in post 9/11 terrorism related cases upon which defendants pled guilty or were convicted involved lying to investigators, followed by terrorism and national security offenses, using illegal travel documents, and conspiracy.[68]

A 2006 study of Justice Department records by a Syracuse University affiliated research center found that of the 1,391 cases of international terrorism referred by federal law enforcement to prosecutors after 9/11, 817 were declined for prosecution for reasons including a subsequent request by investigators (117), evidence issues (205), no chargeable federal offense (86), and other reasons (273). Another 239 cases were pending referrals, while 335 more resulted in prosecutions. Of the 335 cases sent to federal district court for criminal trials, 66 resulted in dismissal or not guilty verdicts, 56 were still pending, and 213 resulted in convictions. The study found the overwhelming majority of sentences were quite short with 90 resulting in no prison time and 91 more resulting in less than one years incarceration. Only 14 resulted in sentences of five years or more. The study also revealed that, in most recent years, terrorism related prosecutions dropped sharply, along with the length of sentences. For cases commenced in the two years following 9/11, the median sentence was only 28 days, compared to a median sentence of 41 months for those cases commenced in the two years prior to 9/11.[69]

The government prevailed in high profile cases like that of the "Lackawanna Six" (participation in al Qaeda terror training), attempted airline "shoebomber" Richard Reid, al Qaeda member Zacarias Moussaoui, attempted terror camp organizer James

67. Padilla v. Hanft, No. 05-533 (2005); 'Jose Padilla', Updates, *Jurist*, 2006, [online] Available at: http://jurist.law.pitt.edu/currentawareness/padilla.php.

68. Eggen, D. & Tate, J. (2005) 'U.S. campaign Produces Few Convictions on Terrorism Charges/Accompanying Charts', *Washington Post*, June 12, p. A1.

69. Trac Reports (2006) *Criminal Terrorism Enforcement in the United States During the Five years Since the 9/11/01 Attacks*, Transactional Records Access Clearinghouse, Syracuse; Lichtblau, E. (2006) 'Study Finds Sharp Drop in the Number of Terrorism Cases Prosecuted', *New York Times*, September 4, p. A9.

Table 4 High profile post 9/11 cases alleging ideological connections to Middle East extremism

John Walker Lindh, US	Aiding Taliban, weapons, VA	Plea, 20 years, 2002
James Ujamma, US	Aiding al Qaeda, training, WA	Plea, 2 years, 2003
Iyman Faris, US	Aiding al Qaeda, bridge plot, VA	20 years, 2003, On appeal
"Lackawana Six" US	Aiding al Qaeda, training, NY	7-10 years, 2003
Richard Reid, UK	Attempted aircraft "shoe bomber," MA	Life, 2003
Zacarias Moussaoui, Alg.	Terrorist Conspiracy relating to 9/11, VA	Life, 2006
Hamid Hayat, US	Aiding al Qaeda, lying to agent, CA	On appeal of up to 39 year sentence, 2006
Jam'yyat Al-Islam Al-Saheeh (JIS) US/Pak.	Robberies to fund domestic terror by homegrown, CA	Trial Pending, 2006
Sami Al Arian US/Kuw.	Conspiracy to aid Palestinian Islamic Jihad, FL	Plea, 57 months, 2006
Lynne Stewart, US	Communicating with Egyptian extremists, NY	28 months, 2006

Ujaama, New York City bridge bomb plotter Iyman Faris, Jewish Defense League leader Irv Rubin, and white supremacist Matt Hale. The government's efforts have not always been successful or without controversy. Terror related actions against Internet webmaster Sami Omar al-Hussayen, attorney Brandon Mayfield, Army Chaplain James Yee, and two Detroit "sleeper cell" defendants failed and resulted in criticism. In the al-Hussayen case, the government faces litigation from an American Islamic convert who was seized as a "material witness" for over two weeks, but never presented to render testimony. The ACLU maintains that scores of improper material witness seizures took place as a means to improperly detain civilians without substantive cause. In the Detroit "sleeper case" charges were filed against the former federal prosecutor for misconduct relating to the trial. In some other cases, the government faced criticism from civil libertarians despite convictions or guilty pleas. In the case of Hamid and Umer Hayat of Lodi, California authorities faced criticism for initially suggesting an ominous direct al Qaeda nexus to the case. In the case of "American Taliban" John Walker Lindh, prosecutors dropped most charges amid allegations relating to rough treatment and denial of counsel while he was in custody abroad (Table 4).[70]

One of the most unusual charges involves Adam Gadahn, also known as Azzam the American. The young California native was indicted in October 2006 on

70. Findlaw (2006) 'Special Coverage: War on Terrorism' [online]. Available at: http://news.findlaw.com/legalnews/us/terrorism/cases/index.html; Eggen, D. (2006) Ashcroft Is Denied Immunity in Case', *Washington Post*, Friday, September 29, p. A12; Richey, W. (2006) 'Torture of detainees? No. 'Coercion'? It depends', The Christian Science Monitor, October 19 [online]. Available at: http://www.csmonitor.com/2006/1019/p02s01-usju.html; 'The Enemy Within', *PBS Frontline*, aired Oct 10, 2006 [online]. Available at: http://www.pbs.org/wgbh/pages/frontline/enemywithin/; Lichtblau, E. (2006) 'Ex-Prosecutor in Terror Inquiry Is Indicted', *New York Times*, March 30, p. A8, [online]. Available at: http://travel2.nytimes.com/2006/03/30/washington/30prosecutor.html.

Table 5 United States federal terrorism related trials by type of offense charged[71]

Crime	No. Convictions
Lying to Investigators	75
Terrorism/National Security	46
Travel Documents	30
Conspiracy	29
Racketeering	27
Immigration	22
Firearms	21
Food & Drugs	8
Bank fraud	6
Public Health	6
Mail Fraud	5
Other	5
Foreign Relations	4
Identity Fraud	4
Explosives	3
Trafficking in Contraband	3
Treason/Sedition	3
Financial Crimes	2
Stolen Property	2
Tax Code	2
Customs	1
Forgery	1
Total cases	**330**

Note: Some individuals were convicted of more than one type of crime.

charges including treason. Gadahan, a Muslim convert, left the United States in the late 1990s and in 2004 emerged as an al Qaeda spokesperson who delivered a series of fiery videotaped threats over the Internet. If Gadahan is captured by the United States and convicted, he could face execution. Treason, providing aid and comfort to an enemy, is the only modern offense whose requirements are set forth in the Constitution. Gadahan is the first person charged with treason since the World War II era (see Table 5).[72]

Conclusion

In the immediate period following 9/11, the President invoked broad authority under both civilian criminal law and his role as Commander-in-Chief to investigate and detain those suspected of terrorism. Five years after those attacks, Congress, the Supreme Court, the American public, and America's allies reigned in the Bush

71. Eggen D. & Tate, J. (2005) 'In Terror Cases, Few Convictions; U.S. Often Depends on Lesser Charges', *Washington Post*, June 12, p. A1.
72. Krikorian, G. (2006) 'So Cal Man Indicted on Federal Charges of Aiding Al Qaeda', *Los Angeles Times*, October 11, [online]. Available at: http://www.latimes.com/news/local/la-101106treason,0,29774.story?coll = la-home-headlines

administration from implementing its expansive doctrine of executive authority over detainees. As history has shown, in the wake of armed conflict, executive authority is often enhanced and tolerated in the name of national security. However, when these broadened powers cease to be regarded as an immediate necessity, the levers of politics, the Courts, and diplomacy invariably act to define both the limits of governmental authority as well as the extent of individual protections. In the case of detainees, it means that if the military is going to hold them indefinitely, it must provide them with a basic standard of care and some kind of hearing to challenge their status. Government critics maintain that the most recent reforms are hollow protections that are more consistent with totalitarian regimes, while government officials contend that it is an appropriate response based on precedent to an evolving threat. This process of broadened powers, moderated by eventual limits on governmental authority, is not a static one and will certainly begin anew when the American homeland is once again attacked on a significant scale by al Qaeda or another terrorist group utilizing unlawful enemy combatants.

Appendix I. Selected Civilian Offenses[73]

Federal Crimes of Terrorism: Section 2339A criminalizes providing material support or resources with the intent that they be used for the commission of specific designated violent crimes (predicate offenses). Section 6603 lengthened the list of predicate offenses to include those federal crimes of terrorism cited in 18 U.S.C. 2332b(g)(5)(B).

Section

2339A already covered assistance rendered for the commission of the following:
18 U.S.C. 32 (destruction of aircraft)
18 U.S.C. 37 (violence at international airports)
18 U.S.C. 81 (arson within a federal enclave)
18 U.S.C. 175 (biological weapons offenses)
18 U.S.C. 229 (chemical weapons offenses)
18 U.S.C. 351 (murder, kidnapping, or assault upon Members of Congress)
18 U.S.C. 831 (nuclear material offenses)
18 U.S.C. 842(m) or (n) (plastic explosives offenses)
18 U.S.C. 844(f) or (i) (bombing federal property or property in or affecting commerce)

73. Doyle, C. (2006) *Material Support of Terrorists and Foreign Terrorist Organizations: Sunset Amendments in Brief*, CRS Report for Congress, Order Code RS22222, Updated March 17 [online]. Available at: http://www.fas.org/sgp/crs/terror/RS22222.pdf

18 U.S.C. 930(c) (homicide with dangerous weapon in a federal facility)
18 U.S.C. 956 (conspiracy to commit certain violent crimes overseas)
18 U.S.C. 1114 (murder of a federal officer or employees)
18 U.S.C. 1116 (murder of a foreign dignitary)
18 U.S.C. 1203 (hostage taking)
18 U.S.C. 1361 (destruction of federal property)
18 U.S.C. 1362 (destruction of communications property)
18 U.S.C. 1363 (destruction of property within a federal enclave)
18 U.S.C. 1366 (destruction of an energy facility),
18 U.S.C. 1751 (murder, kidnapping or assault of the President, etc.)
18 U.S.C. 1992 (train wrecking)
18 U.S.C. 1993 (violent attacks on mass transit)
18 U.S.C. 2155 (destruction of national defense material)
18 U.S.C. 2156 (production of defective national defense material)
18 U.S.C. 2280 (violence against maritime navigation)
18 U.S.C. 2281 (violence against maritime fixed platforms)
18 U.S.C. 2332 (violence against Americans overseas)
18 U.S.C. 2332a (weapons of mass destruction offenses)
18 U.S.C. 2332b (multinational terrorism)
18 U.S.C. 2332f (bombing public places or facilities)
18 U.S.C. 2340A (torture)
42 U.S.C. 2284 (atomic weapons offenses)
49 U.S.C. 46502 (air piracy)
49 U.S.C. 60123(b) (destruction of gas pipeline facilities)
With the addition of the federal crimes of terrorism not already among the enumerated, section 2339A now also condemns assistance relating to:
18 U.S.C. 175b (unlawful possession biological materials)
18 U.S.C. 175c (smallpox virus offenses)
18 U.S.C. 1030(a)(1), (5)(A)(i)(certain computer fraud and abuse offenses)
18 U.S.C. 2332 g (anti-aircraft offenses)
18 U.S.C. 2332 h (radiological dispersal device offenses)
18 U.S.C. 2339 (harboring terrorists)
18 U.S.C. 2339C (financing of terrorism)
42 U.S.C. 2122 (atomic weapons offenses)
49 U.S.C. 46504 (2d sentence) (assault on a flight crew with a dangerous weapon)
49 U.S.C. 46505(b)(3) or (c) (explosive or incendiary devices, or endangerment of human life by means of weapons, on an aircraft within U.S. jurisdiction)
49 U.S.C. 46506 (homicide or attempted homicide aboard an aircraft within U.S. jurisdiction).

Section 6603 also introduced two crimes 18 U.S.C. 1361 (destruction of federal property) and 18 U.S.C. 2156 (production of defective national defense material) into the family of federal crimes of terrorism. Both crimes were already predicate offenses in section 2339A.

Does Clausewitz Apply to Criminal-States and Gangs?

Mark T. Clark

Bunker and Bunker have worked to develop a taxonomy of agencies and entities that they label as Criminal-States. Although they point to the fact that states and state leaders use pejorative terms to label belligerent and near-belligerent states and groups, there may be something deeper in the meaning of the terms than mere antipathy. It may be a way for policy-makers to grapple with behavior that states must engage. Labeling an entity gives leaders a way to talk about complex issues with simple language; language that can help galvanize the state to political action or ignore it to the state's peril.

The question posed for this essay is whether the theory and ideas of a Prussian General, Karl von Clausewitz, apply to a non-state entity that Bunker and Bunker

Mark T. Clark, Ph.D., is professor of political science and director of the National Security Studies program at California State University, San Bernardino. He serves on the Nuclear Strategy Forum (Washington, D.C.) and is an adjunct fellow with the Claremont Institute for the Study of Statesmanship and Political Philosophy. He authored and received a multimillion dollar grant from the National Geospatial Agency (NGA) as part of the Office of the Director of National Intelligence's efforts for long-term intelligence reform. He now directs a seven-campus Consortium of the California State University as an Intelligence Community Center of Academic Excellence. Clark has been published on traditional issues of national security such as strategic intelligence, arms control, strategic nuclear forces, the just war tradition, American foreign and military policy, and collective security. He has also written on the contributions of Carl von Clausewitz in other venues. This is his first sally into nontraditional warfare. Clark served in the U.S. Marine Corps, 1973–1977 in the infantry and in intelligence.

have identified as the Criminal-State. Though this may seem moot, there may be more at stake than simple disputation between members of the academy. What may be at stake is whether – and how – we may be compelled to fight such entities. Under a certain set of conditions, it will be argued here that some of the theories and ideas of Clausewitz do apply to Criminal-States, and, when they do, they will have large implications for how states – and state leaders – may be called upon to act. When the ideas of Clausewitz are inapplicable, different implications will follow for how we may need to treat such entities.

The argument will develop along the following lines. First, I will examine the key components of Clausewitz's argument in his famous work, *Vom Kriege* (On War). Such ideas will include how Clausewitz understood his theory of war and his relation between war and politics. Second, I will evaluate what may be understood as the political and how it would apply to war making entities. Last, I will examine what conditions would be required of Criminal-States (or even criminal-non-state actors) for his theory to work, with a brief analysis of the implications of this when it does.

On War

Karl von Clausewitz wrote *On War* – the finest work ever produced on the subject of war and politics – in the early nineteenth century. One of the ablest translators of Clausewitz's work wrote that "Abraham Lincoln or Georges Clemenceau did not need to read [him] to discover the relationship between the military objectives and political purpose of wars they were fighting."[1] While that may be true, we tend to forget it. We seem to have largely forgotten the political purposes for which wars are fought. Military strategists for centuries have studied the subject of war apart from its broader political purposes, as if it were a problem reducible to a set of theorems. That continues today with the study of tactics and strategy as "military science" in Reserve Officers Training Corps (ROTC) programs at civilian universities and in the military service academies. At the same time, most western political leaders today have never participated in military service, and few if any have ever studied the subject of war as a means to political ends. It is as if without war, we tend to ignore or forget the linkage between the political goals and military means in war.

In part, this is the defining problem of modernity. Since the Enlightenment, modernity is understood to hold to the fact/value distinction. Facts are objective and worthy of research; values are subjective and are left to personal opinion. Most of our contemporary science as well as academic research are modern. Our theories in international relations on the workings of international politics hew to this line as well. Modern states wage war as if it was a technical problem of how

1. See Peter Paret's comment in von Clausewitz, C. (1976) *On War*, Princeton University Press, Princeton, [Michael Howard & Peter Paret (ed) and trans], published by Alfred A. Knopf (1993) (hereafter, cited as *On War*), p. 211.

many men and the type of equipment will be enough to defeat an enemy army. However, throughout history, and in most of the world still, the pre-modern view held or holds sway: that values are also facts. That is, the moral justification for doing things is as important as the technical means to do them. We shall have occasion to return to this shortly.

On War is one of the most widely quoted though least read books on war. Clausewitz, a Prussian military officer, wrote his classic after Napoleon Bonaparte waged aggressive wars in Europe and radically changed how – and to what extent – wars were fought. Clausewitz never actually completed his work despite spending some twelve years on it. At the end of his life, he considered only Chapter One of Book I completely finished.[2] He died at a fairly young age and it was left to his wife, Marie von Clausewitz, to publish his work posthumously.

On War consists of eight books with a total of 128 chapters and sections. The prose is stilted and difficult to read at times, in part because it was never finished. The material is nonetheless logically organized. Book I defines the general nature of war and Book II develops his methods of theorizing, a method that led Frederich Engels to comment that it was a "peculiar way to philosophize but in essence very good".[3] Book III discusses strategy in general and the psychological dimensions while Book IV treats the essential of military activity, fighting. Books V through VII treat the more conventional aspects of war and Book VIII takes up the theme of the relationship of war to politics, first explored early in Book I.

Only recently has controversy developed over whether *On War* remains relevant to modern war or whether it has become dated, fatally so. In a way, there is nothing really new in this problem; his work has been selectively cited, quoted, and used or misused by generations of military officers and military historians – as well as occasionally being understood properly. Before World War I, the military establishments of Germany, France and Italy fatally misinterpreted *On War* to suit their doctrinal preferences at the time, usually for offensive military action.[4] After the war, two of the more famous British military historians (and officers), Major General J.F.C. Fuller and Captain B.H. Liddell Hart, blamed Clausewitz for the slaughter that occurred during the Great War and for failing to look beyond war to the peace that would ensue.[5] Since the end of the Cold War, a number of scholars and critics have assiduously worked to denigrate the continuing value of *On War*.[6] Of these, the two most widely quoted and read are military historians Martin van Creveld, an Israeli, and John Keegan, a Briton. Van

2. See Clausewitz' comment in Unfinished Note, 1830, in *On War*, p. 79.
3. Quoted in comments by A.S. Bubnov on V.I. Lenin's critique of *On War*, Davis, D. E. & Kohn, W. S. G. (1977) 'Lenin's "Notebook on Clausewitz"', in *Soviet Armed Forces Review Annual*, ed. David R. Jones, Academic International Press, Gulf Breeze, p. 192.
4. See the chapters in Section III: Clausewitz Misperceived, Handel, M. I. (1986) *Clausewitz and Modern Strategy*, Frank Cass, London, pp. 197–324.
5. See the perceptive analysis in Luvaas, J. (1999) 'Clausewitz, Fuller and Liddell Hart', Handel, *Clausewitz*, pp. 197–212.
6. For an analysis of the emerging criticisms, see Clark, M. T. (1998) 'The Continuing Relevance of Clausewitz', *Strategic Review*, vol. 26, no. 1, pp. 54–61.

Creveld's *The Transformation of War*[7] was published in 1991, soon after the demise of the Warsaw Pact, before the 1991 Gulf War, and shortly after the beginning of the Intifada (uprising) in Palestine. Keegan's *A History of Warfare*[8] was published a little later, in 1994. Both authors in part seek to demonstrate the irrelevance of Clausewitz's work to contemporary war. Van Creveld argues that modern, non-state warfare (i.e., terrorism, guerrilla warfare, and other types of warfare labeled by the Pentagon as "Low-Intensity Conflict") is similar to pre-modern forms and that Clausewitz wrote solely for the type of warfare waged by a state against another state. Keegan, on the other hand, argues that culture – not politics – drives warfare and that the modern, western way of war as defined by Clausewitz has outlived its usefulness.

Clausewitz opens his work with the only fully complete chapter in Book I with the title in the form of a question, "What is War?" He tells the reader that he will proceed from the simple to the complex and will look at the nature of the whole. In its simplest form, he starts by using the analogy of a duel between opposing forces and depicts war as a duel on a larger scale with many duels making a war. Because each actor tries to make his opponent incapable of further resistance, he argues "War is thus an act of force to compel our enemy to do our will".[9] In compelling an opponent, the aim will be to disarm him forcefully. He then goes on to argue a point that has since repeatedly gotten him into trouble with softer souls. Under the section titled "Maximum Use of Force," Clausewitz says that "Kind-hearted people might of course think there was some ingenious way to disarm or defeat an enemy without too much bloodshed, and might imagine this is the true goal of the art of war. Pleasant as it sounds, it is a fallacy that must be exposed".[10] "The thesis, then, must be repeated: war is an act of force, and there is no logical limit to the application of that force." Because of statements like this, Liddell Hart says his theory was "a Prussian Marseillaise – which inflamed the blood and intoxicated the mind".[11] Van Creveld believes "Clausewitz himself seems to have looked at war's barbarities with quiet resignation".[12] The historian, Keegan, adds:

> And although this catastrophic outcome [WW I] must not be laid at the door of Clausewitz's study, we are nevertheless right to see Clausewitz as the ideological father of the First World War, just as we are right to perceive Marx as the ideological father of the Russian Revolution. The ideology of 'true war' [*absolute war*] was the ideology of the First World War's armies; and the appalling fate that those armies brought upon themselves by their dedication to it may be Clausewitz's enduring legacy.[13]

Clausewitz, however, is not finished.

7. van Creveld, M. (1991) *The Transformation of War*, The Free Press, New York.
8. Keegan, J. (1994) *A History of Warfare*, Alfred A. Knopf, New York.
9. Clausewitz, *On War*, p. 83.
10. Clausewitz, *On War*, pp. 83-84.
11. Liddell Hart, B. H. (1967) *Strategy*, 2nd edition, Frederick A. Praeger, New York, p. 355.
12. van Creveld, *Transformation*, p. 65.
13. Keegan, *History*, p. 22.

Clausewitz makes clear that he will establish what war is, in its essence or by its nature. He calls it theory, but it is a form of theory that appears strange to the modern eye. It is a form of theory that few of his critics like. Keegan apparently believes that war will not admit of any theory at all. He believes that war cannot "be understood in terms of abstractions about the 'nature of war' itself, since there is no such thing." He also argues that "'Without a theory the facts are silent,' the economist F.A. Hayek has written. That may be true of the cold facts of economics, but the facts of war are not cold. They burn with the heat of the fires of hell".[14] Van Creveld goes further and implies a conclusion or prescription that Clausewitz did not make, that war ought to be fought a certain way. Van Creveld blames Clausewitz for developing normative war-fighting theory:

> *Vom Kriege* is mainly deductive in character: starting from first principles, the nature of war and the goal that it serves, the book seeks to progress step by step towards the most important question of all – namely, how armed conflict ought to be conducted. Given this axiomatic method, the role played by military history was limited. It was used as a source of examples (many of which have long become dated), and also as a kind of control designed to prevent theory from straying too far away from reality. However, no very great value was put on the past as such.[15]

It is no small irony that van Creveld, in an essay he wrote only five years before titled "The Eternal Clausewitz," argued that because Clausewitz avoided prescribing how wars ought to be fought he remained relevant for future generations.[16]

Clausewitz developed a form of theory that draws on philosophy, though he was not steeped in philosophy himself.[17] He starts with the simple and moves to the complex. He establishes the simple as *absolute war*, or war without bounds or limits, as logic alone would imply. He soon contrasts *absolute war* with *real war*, or war in reality. It is the difference between how war may be planned and how it is actually fought. *Absolute war* is an intellectual exercise in understanding the nature of war without regard for the variety of forms war actually takes in practice. Like any noun except personal names, the noun "war" is an abstraction. As an abstraction, it communicates a generality. It is the essence or universality of "war-ness" that Clausewitz identifies. Like the noun chair, which is universal but which differs in particular chairs, war has a nature or essence in the abstract that allows us to identify all wars. Clausewitz gives us a universal abstract definition of war in order that we might be able to identify any war in particular. With this abstract noun, we add adjectives to modify the kind of war we talk about: inter-state war, revolutionary war, guerrilla war, unconventional war, and the like.

14. Keegan, *History*, p. 6.
15. van Creveld, *Transformation*, p. 35.
16. van Creveld, 'The Eternal Clausewitz', *Clausewitz and Modern Strategy*, pp. 35–50.
17. For a discussion of Clausewitz's use and understanding of German philosophy, see Paret, P. (1976) *Clausewitz and the State*, Oxford University Press, Oxford, pp. 147–208.

In the abstract sense of war, Clausewitz identifies its character. Because opponents in *absolute war* will seek to disarm each other, there will be no logical limit to the exertion of force by the combatants. In a kind of dialectic. he then introduces his "reciprocals," actions that have equal and opposite force. As one opponent tries to disarm the other, the second will try equally to avoid being disarmed and simultaneously work to disarm his opponent. If the aim of war is to disarm the enemy, another reciprocal will occur. Clausewitz states: "So long as I have not overthrown my opponent I am bound to fear he may overthrow me." This reciprocal pushes the interaction to a further extreme. Finally, a third extreme is introduced. To overcome an enemy "you must match your effort against his power of resistance, which can be expressed as the product of two inseparable factors, viz. the total means at his disposal and the strength of his will".[18] Again, these are simply *logical* relations among the elements of war in general, not actual relations in practice. It is the character of the relations among its logical, though abstract, components that leads war into its most extreme form.

After setting up *absolute war*, but before comparing it to *real* war, he introduces things that modify the extreme or the abstract in practice. Clausewitz argues:

> From a pure concept of war you might try to deduce absolute terms for the objective you should aim at and for the means of achieving it; but if you did so the continuous interaction would land you in extremes that represented nothing but a play of the imagination issuing from an almost invisible sequence of logical subtleties....
>
> But move from the abstract to the real world, and the whole thing looks quite different.[19]

Clausewitz notes that for war to reach the extremes found in *absolute war* it would have to meet three conditions that he rules out. One, war would have to be a completely isolated act, occurring suddenly and without reference to the politics preceding it; two, war would have to consist of a single short blow, a single decisive act; and three, the outcome would have to be final. Because these three have never been found in the world of *real war*, though sometimes they can be approximated, he then shows how wars are far more a function of probabilities than the extremes found in *absolute war*.

Clausewitz introduces many variables that modify *absolute war*. Friction, uncertainty and chance play a great role in warfare and he shows how they can make the simple become complex. These things make real war different from the plans one makes for war. But more than any other variable, Clausewitz argues that politics modifies or shapes how any particular *real war* is conducted and modifies the degree to which it is fought. Earlier, Clausewitz had shown that the aim or object of war is to "impose our will on the enemy." But in considering *real war*,

18. Clausewitz, On War, p. 86.
19. Clausewitz, *On War*, pp. 86-87.

the political object or goal must be given primacy because politics, we shall see, drives war:

> If it is all a calculation of probabilities based on given individuals and conditions, the *political object*, which was the *original motive*, must become an essential factor in the equation. The smaller the penalty you demand from your opponent, the less you can expect him to try and deny it to you; the smaller the effort he makes, the less you need make yourself. Moreover, the more modest your own political aim, the less importance you attach to it and the less reluctantly you will abandon it if you must....
>
> The political object – the original motive for the war – will thus determine both the military objective to be reached and the amount of effort it requires....The same political object can elicit *differing* reactions from different peoples, and even from the same people at different times....
>
> Thus it follows that without any inconsistency wars can have all degrees of importance and intensity, ranging from a war of extermination down to simple armed observation.[20]

Clausewitz argues that the intensity of any particular war is largely a function of the politics that produce it, both by nature of the aggressor's goals and the defender's will to resist. The universal definition of war can help us understand particular types of wars of every kind along the continuum from so-called "total war" to contemporary peacekeeping operations, from inter-state to civil wars, each of which varies in degree of intensity and strength of will to accomplish the desired political object.

In one of his more famous quotations, Clausewitz stakes his claim to fame. He says: "We see, therefore, that war is not merely an act of policy but a true political instrument, a continuation of political intercourse, carried on with other means".[21] He argues "When whole communities go to war – whole peoples, and especially *civilized* peoples – the reason always lies in some political situation, and the occasion is always due to some political object. War, therefore, is an act of policy." In a note of July 10, 1827 Clausewitz emphasized the importance he attached to the political element. "If this is firmly kept in mind throughout [the statement that war is a continuation of politics by other means] it will greatly facilitate the study of the subject and the whole will be easier to analyze".[22]

Clausewitz created another useful analytic tool for understanding the relationship of politics to war: the trinity or the trifold analysis of politics in relation to war. If war is an act of policy, a political instrument, politics and the influence it holds over war is also conditioned or affected by a remarkable, or wonderful, or paradoxical trinity. In his own words:

20. Clausewitz, *On War*, pp. 90–91.
21. Clausewitz, *On War*, p. 99.
22. See Note of 10 July 1827, in Clausewitz, *On War*, p. 77.

> As a total phenomenon its dominant tendencies always make war a paradoxical trinity – composed of primordial violence, hatred, and enmity, which are to be regarded as a blind natural force; of the play of chance and probability within which the creative spirit is free to roam; and of its element of subordination, as an instrument of policy, which makes it subject to reason alone.
>
> The first of these three aspects mainly concerns the people; the second the commander and his army; the third the government. The passions that are to be kindled in war must already be inherent in the people; the scope which the play of courage and talent will enjoy in the realm of probability and chance depends on the particular character of the commander and the army; but the political aims are the business of government alone.
>
> These three tendencies are like three different codes of law, deeply rooted in their subject and yet variable in their relationship to one another.[23]

These tendencies of the "trinity," a term from which modern critics belittle Clausewitzian warfare as "trinitarian," are not iron laws but more like magnets, constantly pushing and pulling at one another with varying degrees of intensity. One scholar argues:

> the image is *not* that of any kind of Euclidean triangle or triad, despite its understanding as such by many readers....Clausewitz's message is not that there are three passive points, but three interactive points of attraction that are simultaneously pulling the object in different directions....The nature of war should not be conceived as a stationary point among the members of the trinity, but as a complex trajectory traced among them.[24]

That trajectory is made difficult to predict by virtue of the three components of the trinity of the people (passion, anger), the state (intentionality, politics) and the commander (the genius). These three things characterize war in all its forms. But, "If war is one part passion, one part chance, and one part reason, then two of the three elements in its nature are by definition wanton, even uncontrollable....the first thing one notices about Clausewitz' trifold analysis of the nature of war is how the deck is stacked against war's being a rational endeavor".[25] War is preeminently an uncertain project, made more so by its unpredictable nature. Van Creveld noted this in his earlier essay: "Clausewitz more than anybody else emphasizes that war is the domain of anger and fear, boldness and passion, in short, of the most violent emotions known to man, and that any analysis of it which does not take these emotions into account will be completely without value".[26] No war, then, in its almost infinite variety, can be understood apart from the politics that drives it and the influences these three things bring to bear on it.

23. Clausewitz, *On War*, p. 101.
24. Beyerchan, A. (1992) 'Clausewitz, Nonlinearity, and the Unpredictability of War', *International Security*, vol. 17, no. 3, pp. 70–71.
25. Herbig, K. L. (1999) 'Chance and Uncertainty in *On War*', *Clausewitz and Modern Strategy*, p. 98.
26. van Creveld, 'The Eternal Clausewitz', p. 38.

The Political

Both John Keegan and Martin van Creveld take issue with Clausewitz over the political. In fact, both believe that Clausewitz erroneously conflates the modern state with politics. Keegan argues that "War is not the continuation of policy by other means..., Clausewitz's thought is incomplete. It implies the existence of states, of state interests and of rational calculation about how they may be achieved. Yet war antedates the state, diplomacy and strategy by many millennia".[27] Van Creveld, on the other hand, argues that:

> Clausewitz's ideas on war were wholly rooted in the fact that, ever since 1648, war had been waged overwhelmingly by states. A brief period of revolutionary fervor and guerrilla uprisings apart, these ideas turned out to be even more applicable during the nineteenth century. It was a period when the legal separation between governments, armies, and peoples became, for various reasons, even stricter than before: 1848-9 marked the end of armed uprisings. Intrastate political violence was largely restricted to the anarchists, a term that speaks for itself.[28]

Keegan believes culture, not politics, makes war. He boldly opens his book with the first sentence: "War is not the continuation of policy by other means." He argues "The original German expresses a more subtle and complex idea than the English words in which it is so frequently quoted," but then fails to tell the reader what he thinks it means. He quotes Aristotle's famous expression that man is a political animal and argues that neither he, nor Clausewitz after him, "dared confront the thought that man is a thinking animal in whom the intellect directs the urge to hunt and the ability to kill." However, here Keegan flatly contradicts Aristotle, who complained that "without virtue, he [man] is the most savage [of the animals], and he is the worst with regard to sex and food [a reference to incest and cannibalism]" and that "just as man is the best of animals when completed, when separated from law and adjudication he is the worst of all".[29] It becomes ironic if the story is true that his most famous student was Alexander the Great, a notorious warrior himself. Van Creveld also believes Clausewitz fatally misunderstood politics and the formulation that war is a continuation of policy. He suggests that:

> Whatever the exact meaning of the term 'politics,' it is not the same as 'any kind of relationship involving any kind of government in any kind of society.' A more correct interpretation would be that politics are intimately connected with the state; they are, indeed, the characteristic form that power-relationships assume within the kind of organization known as the state. Where there is no state, as was the case during most of human history, politics will be so mixed in with other factors as to leave room neither for the term nor for the reality behind it.

27. Keegan, *History*, p. 3.
28. van Creveld, *Transformation*, pp. 41-42.
29. Aristotle (1984) *The Politics*, University of Chicago Press, Chicago [trans, Carnes Lord], hereafter cited as *Politics*, 1253^{a1} 35-37, 31-33.

> Even where the state does exist, only some of its actions are political by nature, whereas the rest are administrative or juridical. Thus, strictly speaking, the dictum that war is the continuation of politics means nothing more or less than that it represents an instrument in the hands of the state, *insofar as the state employs violence for political ends* [emphasis original]. It does not mean that war serves any kind of interest in any kind of community; or, if it does mean that, then it is little more than a meaningless cliché.[30]

Though Clausewitz was no political philosopher, he nonetheless leaves the reader with the impression he grasps its significance. Clausewitz said that "Policy, of course, is nothing in itself; it is simply the trustee for all these interests [all aspects of internal administration and spiritual values] against other states. That it can err, subserve the ambitions, private interests, and vanity of those in power, is neither here nor there. In no sense can the art of war ever be regarded as the preceptor of policy, and here we can only treat policy as representative of all interests of the community".[31] While it is true that Clausewitz does not spend much time on politics, that is to say, what politics is and how its exercise in a political community can lead to wars against another political community, he does leave us with a general enough description of policy to grasp its connection to and direction over wars. As Peter Paret, one of the leading scholars on the works of Clausewitz, points out, Clausewitz theorizes about war and not politics. Even the "Morality of going to war, Clausewitz thought, was a question of political ethics, not one that concerned the theory of war. War is a social act, and the decision to resort to it lies beyond war itself".[32]

To claim that the policy or politics of Clausewitz apply only to the state, and primarily to states of his time, misconstrues the notion of policy and politics. The root words for politics or policy come from the Greek words politeia, politike, politikos, politeuma and polis, words that were developed long before the thing we call a state existed. Clausewitz understood that policy and politics involved the public sphere of activities of a political community that included internal administration, material interests, even spiritual or religious values. Aristotle wrote that the notion of a political community (polis) must already exist before the formalization of it can occur. In other words, there has to be some kind of association beyond mere family, and in his time the tribe, for a political association of any form to develop. It is the ends (telos) of men to live politically; for their lives to be lived as fully human they find their greatest expression or fulfillment in political communities, even more in stable ones. When Aristotle lived, the form or concrete expression of the polis was the city, though he was familiar with empires. But political communities have evolved over time and varied across cultures and will continue to evolve so long as these belong

30. van Creveld, *Transformation*, p. 125.
31. Clausewitz, *On War*, p. 733.
32. Paret, P. (1986) 'Clausewitz', in *Makers of Modern Strategy: From Machiavelli to the Nuclear Age*, ed. P. Paret, Princeton University Press, Princeton, p. 209.

"among the things that exist by nature, and that man is by nature a political animal".[33]

The heart of the problem is that many shoehorn politics and war into the narrow confines of the nation-state. However, Clausewitz envisions a broader conception of the political. We might even say that Clausewitz included non-state actors in his analysis. He assumed both that such non-state actors had their own version of politics and that they varied in their method of warfare. He acknowledges that "The semibarbarous Tartars, the republics of antiquity, the feudal lords and trading cities of the Middle Ages, eighteenth-century kings and the rulers and peoples of the nineteenth century – all conducted war in their own particular way, using different methods and pursuing *different aims* [emphasis mine]".[34] He noted too how different from the nation-state were many of the previous political entities, especially during the Middle Ages:

> Europe, essentially, had broken down into a mass of minor states. Some were turbulent republics, others precarious small monarchies with very limited central power. A state of that type could not be said to be genuinely united; it was rather an agglomeration of loosely associated forces. Therefore we should not think of such a state as a personified intelligence acting according to simple and logical rules.
>
> This is the point of view from which *the policies* [emphasis mine] and wars of the Middle Ages should be considered.[35]

Clausewitz, despite his critics' charge that his trifold analysis of politics was irrelevant to most events throughout history, even noted that one part of the trinity, the people, was almost completely irrelevant to the policies of the states in the eighteenth century. "War thus became solely the concern of the government to the extent that governments parted company with their peoples and behaved as if they were themselves the state".[36]

Though Clausewitz leaves the reader with a broad understanding of politics, he avoids exploring politics proper. But to understand the essence of the political, the glue that holds the polis together as a political community, we must turn to Aristotle himself. As a pre-modern, though, Aristotle will examine values as if they are as important as facts. As we shall soon see, many of the non-state actors we may be called upon to fight will also hold to similar ideas, and so we should be prepared to understand them.

In his fifth book of *The Politics*, Aristotle examines the subject of revolutions, that is, what causes the disuniting and overturning of political entities. However, given our modern understanding of the term from the English, American, French and Russian revolutions, we should note for "Aristotle revolution means primarily

33. *Politics*, 1253[a1] 37.
34. *On War*, pp. 708–709.
35. *On War*, pp. 710–711.
36. *On War*, pp. 712–713.

the process whereby one regime is replaced by another, as one or another group gains power within the same regime, or as the regime is altered so as no longer to be the same".[37] Regime change is probably a better term to use here, though certainly revolution in the modern sense would also apply.

By Book V of *The Politics*, Aristotle has evaluated the various kinds of regimes that can come into existence. For him, there were three good and three aberrant regimes, regimes that deviate from the good. The good regimes allow for some element of the ruled to participate in some way of ruling. The best regime, the regime in which the ruled participate rightly, is polity. "Book III addresses the reason, the main reason, for the variety of regimes: that they are based on different principles by which men justify their claims to supremacy".[38] Each regime differs greatly from others by the different conception of justice men have in the regime. The key distinction between correctly and incorrectly constituted regimes lies in the fact that in deviant regimes, the rulers do not act for the common interest but for themselves, much like modern mafias and criminal gangs.

Aristotle demonstrates how regimes can change. The core issue for regime change or revolution is the same thing that makes for differences among the various types of regimes: different conceptions of justice. The key difference in conceptions of justice is based upon the understanding of equality and inequality. Aristotle argues "Now while there is agreement that justice in an unqualified sense is according to merit, there are differences, as was said before: some consider themselves to be equal generally if they are equal in some respect, while others claim to merit all things unequally if they are unequal in some respect".[39] That is to say, those who believe themselves unequal in say birthright thereby believe they are unequal in other areas as well, in their minds thereby establishing their right to rule over lesser mortals. The aberrant variations are usually based on this misconception of inequality, and similar misconceptions of its polar opposite: equality. Aristotle notes that apart from the good regimes and the best in particular, "All have a certain sort of justice, but all tend to err in some respects. When certain groups do not share in the regime on the basis of the conceptions they have, they engage in factional conflict".[40]

Aristotle shows that there are many reasons to engage in factional conflict leading to regime change. "Some engage in factional conflict because they aim at equality, if they consider that they have less in spite of being equal to those who are aggrandizing themselves; others, because they aim at inequality and preeminence, if they conceive themselves to be unequal but not to have a greater share, but an equal or lesser one".[41] Others may fight because they are reacting to the arrogance and self-aggrandizement of the rulers; others when certain factions

37. Jaffa, H. V. (2000) 'What is Politics? An Interpretation of Aristotle's *Politics*', in *The Conditions of Freedom: Essays in Political Philosophy*, ed. H. V. Jaffa, the Claremont Institute, Claremont, p. 65.
38. Jaffa, 'What is Politics?', p. 61.
39. *Politics*, 1301bl 35–38.
40. *Politics*, 1301al 26–29.
41. *Politics*, 1302al 25–29.

or people are dishonored or see others honored unjustifiably; others through fear, either because they acted unjustly and are about to be punished or are about to suffer an injustice themselves; still others when leading factions in the regime hold others in contempt; and sometimes through disproportionate growth of a part of the body politic. "Factional conflicts arise, then, not over small things but from small things – it is over great things that [men] engage in factional conflict".[42]

A commonly held conception of justice preserves the regime, just as differently held conceptions can undo it. More importantly, "Aristotle makes clear...that justice in the fullest sense exists only in a community of relatively free and equal men whose relations are regulated by law." He also "registers his disagreement with the sophistic view that, because all just things are subject to variation or change, justice exits only by convention; in his view, while it is true that the just things like all human things are subject to change, there are things nevertheless just by nature".[43] In other words, every political regime has some kind of conception of justice, but that only some of these conceptions are by their very nature just. In the homage vice pays to virtue, even tyrannies must find some way to justify their regime, such as the Marxist ideological claim to leadership over the proletariat or the medieval claim to rule by divine right or the modern claim by Usama Bin Laden (UBL) to rule over a renewed Islamic regime.

Justice lies at the heart of politics and different conceptions of justice lie at the heart of factional conflict. But if it lies at the heart of politics and factional conflict, then according to Clausewitz it must also lie at the heart of international conflict and war where two or more political systems interact. And in fact, Aristotle believed that justice was at the heart of the war between Sparta and Athens. In an aside, he comments in *The Politics* that "All regimes are overturned sometimes from within themselves and sometimes from outside, when an opposite sort of regime is either nearby or far away but powerful. This is what happened in the case of the Athenians and the Lacedaemonians: the Athenians overthrew oligarchies everywhere, and the Spartans democracies".[44] In Aristotle's interpretation of the conflict between the major competing powers in the Peloponnesian War, Sparta and Athens each had their own interpretation of the just regime and sought to impose them on those nearby or, at the very least, to get rid of those regimes that were hostile to their own conception of justice. For the Spartans, it was their concept of oligarchy and for the Athenians, their concept of democracy. The core concept of any political regime, or community, is its concept of the just.

And the core issue in wars is over the question of justice, or what is just. Earlier in *On War*, Clausewitz argued that the degree of intensity in war corresponds to the degree of intensity found in the political object. Because politics drives wars,

42. *Politics*, 1303^{bl} 16–17.
43. Lord, C. (1987) 'Aristotle', in *History of Political Philosophy*, eds. L. Strauss & J. Cropsey, 3rd edn, The University of Chicago Press, Chicago, p. 128.
44. *Politics*, 1307^{bl} 20–23.

the intensity or earnestness of the political goal dictates the intensity of the means to accomplish it; thus particular wars may be as variously intense as one in which at least one side seeks to exterminate the other, while in another war may simply consist of armed observation. One reason for the intensity of political objects may be because of the outrage to the justice of the political community as well. This helps explain why the United States could demand no less than unconditional surrender from Hitler's Germany at the end of World War II but required only an armistice from Kaiser's Germany at the end of an earlier one. There could be no reconciliation with the racist Nazi regime short of its total annihilation as a functioning political entity; and, despite the destructiveness of the Great War, the US could live with a successor regime and leave Germany's army intact after the armistice.[45] An extreme outrage to a nation's sense of justice demands intolerance.

War, Politics and Some Non-state Actors

The understanding of the political goes beyond merely Clausewitz's theory and time. Beyond the work of Thucydides, the ancient Chinese philosopher of war Sun Tzu also understood that war and politics went hand in glove. Sun Tzu's classic, *The Art of War*, opens with the statement: "War is a matter of vital importance to the State; the province of life or death; the road to survival or ruin".[46] Sun Tzu anticipated Clausewitz's statement that war is a continuation of policy by at least two millennia, though the modern state did not yet exist; in fact, he wrote for an Emperor. He argues further that because war is serious, it must be carefully planned and appraised by several things. The first and most important thing he enjoins the reader to understand is moral influence or, to put it in terms we have been using, the justice of the regime. Sun Tzu says "By moral influence I mean that which causes the people to be in harmony with their leaders, so that they will accompany them in life and unto death without fear of mortal peril." According to the translator, Samuel Griffith, the term Tao is translated "moral influence," but is usually translated as "The Way" or "The Right Way." Griffith says that "Here it refers to the morality of government; specifically to that of the sovereign. If the sovereign rules justly, benevolently, and righteously, he follows the Right Path or the Right Way, and thus exerts a superior degree of moral influence".[47] In other words, for the ruler to have any effective influence on the course of the campaign, the people he commands, and the subjects he rules, his subjects and soldiers must see him and his regime as just. Sun Tzu even urges just treatment of captives, a form of justice in war.

Sun Tzu's greatest disciple more than 2,000 years later, Mao Tse-tung, also understood war and politics in the same way, though with a communist political

45. Brodie, B. (1973) *War and Politics*, The Macmillan Co., Chicago, pp. 38–39.
46. Tzu, S. (1963) *The Art of War*, Oxford University Press, London, p. 63 [trans S. B. Griffith].
47. *The Art of War*, p. 63, fn. 4.

twist. Mao picks up the proletarian – that is city and worker – base of V. I. Lenin's revolutionary communism and transforms it to a peasant-based revolution. And though Lenin was not the first Marxist to read and understand Clausewitz's dictum of the relationship of war to politics (both Marx and Engels had read him), he was perhaps its greatest exponent. Lenin's use of Clausewitz is famous. His notes and commentary on *On War* demonstrate a keen understanding of the Prussian's work. Lenin's understanding of Clausewitz also becomes the basis for Soviet military doctrine.[48] As a student of the Bolshevik revolution, Mao clearly read Lenin's understanding of Clausewitz, as well as Clausewitz's dictum into his modified form of revolutionary war.

Mao's work on guerrilla warfare proves that war and politics are not just a function of a nation-state in the modern sense or of ancient political entities like the city-states of Greece or imperial powers of China. Unconventional war in the form of guerrilla war is another form of war that expresses the linkage between politics and war. Guerrilla warfare is really a set of tactics such as hit and run, sabotage and deception that pits a small, revolutionary group against the strengths of a conventionally armed "legitimate" political entity. It is a form of "asymmetrical warfare," a type of warfare in which at least one opponent refuses to fight against an enemy on equal terms because he would lose in a conventional conflict. It turns his weaknesses – his lack of manpower and resources – into strength – mobility and stealth; and turns the strength of conventional power – technical prowess – into a weakness – fighting defensively from fixed positions.

Mao approached the subject from a Clausewitzian perspective. He understood the relation of war to politics very well and indeed quotes Clausewitz's famous maxim frequently. And, like a good communist, he supercharges the political element. As Griffith, who was a Captain in the US Marine Corps when he translated Mao's *On Guerrilla Warfare* in 1940, said:

> In the United States, we go to considerable trouble to keep soldiers out of politics, and even more to keep politics out of soldiers. Guerrillas do exactly the opposite. They go to great lengths to make sure that their men are politically educated and thoroughly aware of the issues at stake.
>
> Guerrilla leaders spend a great deal more time in organization, instruction, agitation, and propaganda work than they do fighting, for their most important job is to win over the people.[49]

Revolutionary armies understand the importance of the political in a way that modern states forget.

The political object is central to effective guerrilla warfare. To Mao, war was "politics with blood." Mao writes "'War is the continuation of politics.' In this

48. See Davis & Kohn, 'Lenin's "Notebook on Clausewitz"', *Soviet Armed Forces Review Annual*, pp. 189–229.
49. Tse-tung, M. (1961) *On Guerrilla Warfare*, Frederick A. Praeger, New York, p. 8, cf. Translator's Note, pp. 37–38 [trans. S. B. Griffith].

sense war is politics and war itself is a political action; since ancient times there has never been a war that did not have a political character....In a word, war cannot for a single moment be separated from politics. Any tendency among the anti-Japanese armed forces [the communists and the nationalists] to belittle politics by isolating war from it is wrong and should be corrected".[50] Mao also complained that "There are some militarists who say: 'We are not interested in politics but only in the profession of arms.' It is vital that these simple-minded militarists be made to realize the relationship that exists between politics and military affairs. Military action is a method used to attain a political goal. While military affairs and political affairs are not identical, it is impossible to isolate one from the other".[51] Indeed, without political direction, the rational element of the Clausewitzian trinity, guerrilla warfare cannot contribute to victory.[52]

As did Sun Tzu, Mao also argues for just war, though it is a Marxist interpretation of justice. The goal or object of the war must be for a just regime, one of course based on Mao's interpretation of the communist political regime. He writes that "History knows only two kinds of war, just and unjust. We support just wars and oppose unjust war. All counter-revolutionary wars are unjust, all revolutionary wars are just".[53] Like Marxists generally, Mao's political communism was a stated goal of universal equality, something that would appeal to a peasant population brutally treated for centuries under warlords, bandits, and petty local bosses. He could thus write with some degree of credulity among the peasants that "China's war is progressive, hence its just character. Because it is a just war, it is capable of arousing the nation to unity, of evoking the sympathy of the people in Japan and of winning the support of most countries in the world".[54] Note here too, as in Aristotle, that the idea of justice has to do with equality, however aberrant that equality is in fact. As well, Mao enjoins the guerrillas to treat prisoners justly. But that just treatment is also prudent, for by treating such people justly the guerrillas hope to win them over to their side. He thus instructs that guerrilla bands in the northern, colder and wetter, part of China must have their own overcoats because they "cannot depend on captures made from the enemy, for it is forbidden for captors to take clothing from their prisoners".[55] A student of Mao's writings, North Vietnamese General Vo Nguyen Giap, argued for a similar understanding of war and politics in his *People's War, People's Army*[56] as did the hapless Che Guevarra.[57]

50. Tse-tung, M. (1972) 'On Protracted War (1938)', in *Six Essays on Military Affairs*, ed. M. Tse-tung, Foreign Language Press, Peking, p. 266.
51. Mao, *On Guerrilla Warfare*, p. 89.
52. Mao, *On Guerrilla Warfare*, p. 45.
53. Tse-tung, M. (1972) 'Problems of Strategy in China's Revolutionary War (December 1936)', in *Six Essays on Military Affairs*, ed. M. Tse-tung, Foreign Language Press, Peking, p. 7.
54. Mao, 'On Protracted War', p. 213.
55. Mao, *On Guerrilla Warfare*, p. 84.
56. General Giap, V. N. (1961) *People's War, People's Army: The Viet Cong Insurrection Manual for Underdeveloped Countries*, Foreign Languages Publishing House, Hanoi; published in the US by Frederick A. Praeger, New York, 1962.
57. Guevara, C. (1961) *Guerrilla Warfare*, Monthly Review Press, New York.

Not everyone, of course, supported the communist insurgencies in either China or Vietnam (or Bolivia). But as the scholar Roger Hilsman noted, not everyone has to. Many outright opponents were killed, both by Vietnamese and Chinese communists. Certainly every defector or traitor to the cause that was caught was killed. Even so, in a country populated by villages, only a few had to actively support the movement. Hilsman illustrates his point with the following analogy:

> Any comparison with our own world must be somewhat farfetched, but one may ask whether the citizens of Chicago 'supported' the gangs that flourished in the 1920's. The shopkeeper who was 'hit' by the 'protection' racket did not support the gangs, but he often went along with them. He thought he had a weak government, and it seemed far away, and the threats of the hoodlums were close by.[58]

But unlike the gangland wars of Chicago in the 1920s, Hilsman notes that guerrilla warfare has a political nature: "Guerrillas may be tragically misinformed and misled, but they fight with conviction, and as far as the war goes on, bringing the deaths of relatives and friends, they frequently acquire deep personal motives and sometimes a bitter desire for vengeance. Many regard it, not without some justification, as a very democratic kind of struggle – with bullets for ballots".[59]

Clausewitz's conception of the political, with modifications by Aristotle, remains useful for many, if not all, non-state warmaking entities. Do the ideas and theories of Clausewitz apply to Criminal-States? To the extent that such Criminal-States practice the political, they will. It is most easily seen in the two categories Bunker and Bunker label the *Oligarchic Regimes* and the *Jihadi Insurgency*. For *Oligarchic Regimes*, Clausewitz applies, as all but a few of them are recognizable political entities. Aristotle noted that tyrannies can remain political, and many of these regimes evince the kind of political behavior (service to the members of the regime) that is typical of tyranny. North Korea, Iraq under Saddam Hussein, and the many others wage war for political purposes, though of course their concept of the political differs from the United States. One could even argue that the Soviet Union, Communist China, and earlier, Nazi Germany, were all variants on the theme of *Oligarchic Regimes*. All had or have a political leadership, a population (with varying degrees of enthusiasm or tolerance of the regime) and an army, as well as territorial control. Clausewitz and his conceptions still apply, though unlike fighting *Jihadi Insurgencies* where the methods of warfare will be asymmetrical, the methods here have been more conventional and will probably remain so for the foreseeable future.

The prototype of the modern terrorist organization was the Palestinian Liberation Organization, which has now mutated into the Palestinian Authority. As a revolutionary political group, it did not have statehood in any modern sense of the term. However, it did have the three components of Clausewitz's trinity. The PLO trinity consisted of Palestinians (the people who supplied the passion and the

58. See comments of Roger Hilsman in Giap, *People's War, People's Army*, p. xxii.
59. Giap, *People's War, People's Army*, pp. xxiv-xxv.

resources for the war); an army (of terrorists, who waged unconventional war); and political leadership (Al Fatah as the principal, though not the only, "government"). The political leadership provided the "reason" or political direction and goals for the war, which were, ironically, statehood. The chosen methods of warfare have been unconventional, beginning with the public murder of Israeli athletes at the 1972 Olympic games in Munich to the campaign of "suicide" bombers that deliberately slaughter Israeli and non-Palestinian civilians in order to weaken Israeli rule. Of course, it usually helps bolster the apparent justness of the cause that the enemy is foreign.

There are many examples of *Jihadi Insurgency*, but Usama Bin Laden's al Qaeda is the model. Al Qaeda has all the elements of the Clausewitzian trinity (political leadership with UBL and al-Zawahiri), the people (disaffected Muslims his organization is trying to reach) and an army (terrorists), though al-Qaeda is also without a state. Usama bin Laden and his minions provide the political direction for the campaign, while radicalized Muslims provide the base of support, and the terrorists and insurgents act as the army. The tactics differ dramatically from conventional war. And bin Laden claims a lunatic interpretation of Islam to promote his conception of justice that became the spark for the war, even before the homicidal attacks of 9/11.

On November 24, 2002, the English newspaper *The Observer* published Usama bin Laden's "Letter to America".[60] His letter responded to 60 American scholars who earlier published "Why We Fight," a moral argument based on the "just war" tradition and on the basis of natural rights shared with all human beings.[61] Bin Laden articulates his concept of the just regime and just political claims against the United States. He argues that al-Qaeda has the right to fight against "disbelievers" because "believers" have been wronged and anyone who fights for anything else is fighting on behalf of Satan. Bin Laden poses two questions he proposes to answer: first, "Why are we fighting and opposing you?"; and second, "What are we calling you to, and what do we want from you?" Both are intoned for broader political support among disaffected Muslims throughout the world. He is habituating generations of young men into this cult of death[62] and his followers revel in the "freedom" such unrestrained violence grants them: freedom, that is, from traditional Islamic "just war" constraints.[63]

He also espouses a concept of just war, albeit one that is radically deficient morally. In his different communications over the years, he has at times acknowledged, and at times denied, engaging in terrorism, the deliberate

60. The letter first appeared on the internet in Arabic, and translated and circulated by Islamists in Britain. See 'bin Laden's 'letter to America'', *The Observer*, 24 November 2002. Available at: www.observer.co.uk (accessed 30 April 2003).

61. See 'What We're Fighting For: A Letter from America', 12 February 2002. Available at: www.americanvalues.org (accessed 1 November 2002).

62. For a good study of the training found in the religious schools – the madrassas – see Goldberg, J. (2000) 'Inside Jihad U.; The Education of a Holy Warrior', *New York Times Magazine*, 25 June, p. 32f.

63. See the quote of one young man from Yemen, who said 'When you have a gun, you're free. You feel as if you can do anything', Orbach, 'Usama bin Laden and Al-Qa'ida'.

attacking of noncombatants. It usually depends upon the audience and his purposes at the time.[64] As to the charge that he killed civilians in the 9/11 attacks, he argues that such citizens were equally complicit in the policies of the US government because Americans may choose their form of government and pay taxes that support it. In his 1998 declaration, he called for the killing of Americans anywhere and everywhere, but in his 1996 *fatwa* he emphasized killing American soldiers in Muslim lands. He says whatever it takes to broaden his appeal to the Islamic world at large.[65] His goal is to unite Muslims and to establish a government that follows the rule of the Caliphs, not a modern state. Apparently, bin Laden would like to rule the Caliphate himself, for his willingness to issue *fatwas* – religious rulings – despite his lack of religious training, suggests he views himself as the political and religious leader of this new, or renewed, Islamist order.

Because the bin Laden's political concept of the just regime differs so radically from the United States, this war may approach the extreme in a Clausewitzian way. That is, just as the United States had to fight Nazi Germany to the end because its concept of the just regime was so completely alien and contrary to the American concept of "All men are created equal," so too will the United States have to defeat al-Qaeda wherein only some are created equal (certain, radicalized Muslims following Bin Laden's script). The two regimes are so alien to one another that both policies will push each polis into more extreme forms of war.

Where it gets tricky is with Bunker and Bunker's concept of *State Failure-Lawless Zones* and with *Criminal Takeover*. To the extent that these regimes evince political behavior, such as seeking some kind of justification for the regime beyond simple violence and providing political reasons to gain popular support, Clausewitz's theory should apply even if the regime seeks logistical support through illegal criminal activity. The Taliban and al-Qaeda used narco-trafficking to support their regimes. Should such regimes threaten our security, it seems self-evident that Clausewitz would still apply. However, to the extent that these regimes do not evince political behavior – at least yet – they may be more

64. His most important communications include his first "fatwa" or religious ruling (of which he is not educated enough religiously to make such a rule) of 23 August 1996, titled 'Declaration of War Against the Americans Who Occupy the Land of the Two Holy Mosques'. Available at: www.Islamic-news.co.uk (accessed 11 February 2003); an interview quoted in *Nida'ul Islam* sometime in October or November 1996, available at: www.fas.org (accessed 13 November 2002); his second "fatwa" with the creation of the 'International Islamic Front for Jihad Against the Jews and Crusaders' on 22 February 1998, available at: www.pbs.org (accessed 14 January 2003); the transcript of his video tape of mid-November 2001, indicating his complicity in the 9/11 attacks, available at: www.fas.org (accessed 13 November 2002); his 'Will' published in *Al-Majallah* (London), 2 November 2002, available at: www.fas.org (accessed 13 November 2002); his response to the American scholars cited above; and his sermon for the 'Feast of the Sacrifice', 5 March 2002, *Middle East Media Research Institute*, no. 476, available at: www.memri.org (accessed 2 May 2003).

65. See Gunaratna, R. (2002) *Inside Al-Qaeda*, Columbia University Press, New York; especially Chapter 2: 'Al Qaeda's Organisation, Ideology and Strategy'; see also the excellent study by Orbach, B. (2001) 'Usama bin Laden and al-Qa'ida: Origins and Doctrines', *Middle East Review of International Affairs*, vol. 5, no. 4, available at: http://meria.idc.ac.il (accessed 30 April 2003).

susceptible to legal methods of control. However, even here, when such regimes threaten the existence of states (such as Dudayev's Chechnya), treating the regime as an enemy entity and fighting it as if it were a real war may be the only long-term solution.

Fighting such regimes, however, will not always have to be militarily. In fact, these essays all point to the problem that we tend to think about war in traditional terms, if we think about them at all. However, the center of gravity of many of these regimes is not their military, but their political rule. As Manwaring points out in an essay on street gangs, Clausewitz looks at two centers of gravity: "the personalities of the [enemy] leaders and public opinion".[66] The keys to how we will need to fight them will be found in how the leaders rule, whether justly or no, and the degree of public support for the regime. During the 1991 Gulf War, though we used overwhelming conventional superiority to re-claim Kuwait, many conscripts surrendered to our soldiers, our media, and even our unmanned aerial vehicles (UAVs) without a fight, because they did not believe in the justness of the war and the rule of Saddam Hussein.

Criminal gangs present even more complications. However, as many of the authors note, the newer, Third Generation, gangs are engaging more and more in political behavior. Such gangs mix politics and commerce in a lethal brew. More than half of the countries in the world face political challenges from such non-state actors that include these criminal gangs.[67] But whereas traditional revolutionary movements, like Mao's guerrilla war, Lenin's revolution, or even bin Laden's al-Qaeda, seek some political community, these groups seem more parasitic. Their political goals, such as they are, seem more intended to co-opt the state to gain freedom for their criminal activities.[68] However, as they take political control, their goals may mutate into more traditional political objectives. If and when this occurs, the Clausewitzian/Aristotelian view of the importance of justice as the bond of the political leaders, the community and the army will come into view. When it does, the fight will have to move from the domain of the legal to that of warfare. Our neat categories separating civil-military and military-police relations may have to change; I expect as well that should such entities threaten the core interests of strong states, like the United States, such distinctions will inevitably go by the wayside. After all, as one scholar has noted, though the state makes war, war made the state.[69]

66. Manwaring, M. (2005) *Street Gangs: The New Urban Insurgency*, U.S. Army War College, Strategic Studies Institute, Carlisle Barracks, PA, p. 40.

67. Manwaring, p. 1.

68. John P. Sullivan explores the political efforts of some gangs in Sullivan, J. P. (1997) 'Third Generation Street Gangs: Turf, Cartels, and Net Warriors', *Transnational Organized Crime*, vol. 3, no. 3, Autumn 1997, pp. 95–108. See also Manwaring, p. 7.

69. Bruce D. Porter provides a compelling case in Porter, B. D. (1994) *War and the Rise of the State: The Military Foundations of Modern Politics*, The Free Press, New York.

Conclusion

There remains much to be done in analyzing the behavior of new forms of the Criminal-State. This essay, and the companion essays in this edition, tries to get to the heart of the problem. However, the literature on these new forms is new and the theories to grapple with them are in their infancy. Even our theories of traditional international relations primarily deal with the state and its influence on international politics. When such theories treat non-state actors, they tend to emphasize the beneficial sub-state and transnational actors like the Red Cross or Doctors Across Borders and other humanitarian organizations. Some are beginning to evaluate lethal non-state actors, the dark cousins to the beneficent actors, but such evaluations remain in their infancy.[70] Nonetheless, the challenges these criminal forms pose to modern polities are enormous. Nothing less than a "Copernican revolution" in how we understand them will help us grapple with these challenges.

70. Only recently have some begun attempting to correct this. See, for example, Pollard, N. A. (2002) 'Globalization's Bastards: Illegitimate Non-State Actors in International Law', *Low Intensity Conflict & Law Enforcement*, vol. 11, no. 2/3.

Perpetual Jihad: Striving for a Caliphate

Hakim Hazim & Robert J. Bunker

Hakim Hazim is a researcher focusing on Islamic fundamentalism and eschatology, Al Qaeda, and militant cults. He is the owner of Relevant Now, a law enforcement and military consulting company. He is also a member of the management team for Walsh & Associates, Boise, Idaho. Past professional activities include that of a high school educator, correctional work, and restricted living programs for mentally ill and impaired adults with criminal backgrounds. He has a B.A. in Sociology from Washburn University, Topeka, Kansas and a M.A. in National Security Studies, California State University San Bernardino. He has given presentations and training to various military, law enforcement and private sector entities including the MG-5 East and MG-5 West Naval Intelligence Reserve Officer Courses, the Los Angeles, Inland Empire, and Orange County Terrorism Early Warning Groups, and for activities of the National Law Enforcement and Corrections Technology Center- West (NLECTC-West), a program of the National Institute of Justice (NIJ), including the briefing of law enforcement negotiators that took part in the DC sniper investigation for Chief Charles Moose. He has also lectured at California State University Long Beach. He is the author of American Realism Revisited: Lethal Minds & Latent Threats (IUniverse, 2005) and the primary researcher of Foreign OPFOR Reader: Radical Islamic and Al Qaeda Doctrine (NLECTC-West, 2002). **Robert J. Bunker**, Ph.D., is CEO of the Counter-OPFOR Corporation. He has been a member of the Los Angeles County Terrorism Early Warning Group since 1996 and has counter-terrorism operational planning experience. He is a past Counter-OPFOR consultant, National Law Enforcement and Corrections Technology Center- West (NLECTC-West), a program of the National Institute of Justice (NIJ). He is also a former Adjunct Professor, National Security Studies Program, California State University San Bernardino; past Fellow, Institute of Land Warfare, Association of the United States Army; and former Professor, Unconventional Warfare, American Military University, Manassas Park, Virginia. Professional LE related training includes Intelligence Support to Force Protection, Anti-Terrorism Course & Force Protection Operations Course, and Mirror Image (Jihadi) Course. Dr. Bunker has provided150 briefings and presentations on terrorism, future warfare & conflict, suicide bombers, less lethal weapons and directed energy weapons. He has written over 100 essays in publications such as *The Police Chief*, *The Tactical Edge*, *California Journal of Law Enforcement*, *Parameters*, *Military Review*, *Marine Corps Gazette*, *Special Warfare*, *Airpower Journal*, *Naval Institute Proceedings*, and numerous military encyclopedias. He is the editor of a series of law enforcement booklets, *Non-State Threats and Future Wars* (Frank Cass: 2003), and *Networks, Terrorism and Global Insurgency* (Routledge: 2005).

> Prophethood (meaning himself) will remain with you for as long as Allah wills it to remain, then Allah will raise it up wherever he wills to raise it up. Afterwards, there will be a Caliphate that follows the guidance of Prophethood remaining with you for as long as Allah wills it to remain. Then, He will raise it up whenever He wills to raise it up. Afterwards, there will be a reign of violently oppressive [The reign of Muslim kings who are partially unjust] rule and it will remain with you for as long as Allah wills it to remain. Then, there will be a reign of tyrannical rule and it will remain for as long as Allah wills it to remain. Then, Allah will raise it up whenever He wills to raise it up. Then, there will be a Caliphate that follows the guidance of Prophethood.[1]

On October 17, 2004, Al Zarqawi pledged allegiance to Al Qaeda and quoted from the above Hadiths (sayings of Muhammad), confirming Hazim's previous statements and writings on the role of eschatology and the five stages of Islam in terrorist doctrine.[2] The use of the above Hadiths by Al Zarqawi also support Bunker's view that a "war over social and political organization" is in effect.[3] Al Qaeda, within that context, can be viewed as a criminal-challenger to the nation-state form. The logical, sequential aims of Al Qaeda's jihad, and that of like-minded groups, are threefold:

- Establish a base of operation in a targeted nation.
- Enforce its version of sharia (a body of Islamic law) on the populace.
- Produce a caliphate candidate.[4]

Their version of jihad is perpetual and the continued rhetoric of terrorist leaders, coupled with missteps in American foreign policy, equals gasoline being thrown on burning hearts in the Islamic world. The US has failed to give proper emphasis to the role of eschatological expectation in terrorist doctrine.[5] Battlefield (tactical and operational) solutions to this struggle are insufficient; even if we wiped out all of the Jihadi fighters and suicide-bombers presently fielded, their ranks would be immediately replenished because there is no shortage of volunteers to take up the cause of jihad. We will attempt to explain this thesis, based on eschatological expectation, throughout this essay.

1. bin Al-Yaman, H. (nd) 'The Hadiths or Sayings of the Prophet', *As-Silsilah As-Sahihah*, vol. 1, no. 5.
2. Hazim, H. (2005) *American Realism Revisited, Lethal Minds & Latent Threats*, Iuniverse, Lincoln, pp. 73–75.
3. Bunker, R. J. (1997) 'Epochal Change: War Over Social and Political Organization', *Parameters*, vol. 27, no. 2, pp. 15–25.
4. ZarQawi, A. M. (2004) 'Pledge of Allegiance to Al Qaeda', originally published in Arabic, *Mu'asker al-Battar*, vol. 21, *Terrorism Monitor*, Jeffrey Pool, Trans. vol. 2, iss. 24, The Jamestown Foundation, Washington, DC. Available at: http://www.jamestown.org
5. This issue was echoed by Peters, R. (2006) 'Survival strategy: Middle Eastern Islam, Darwin and terrorism', *Armed Forces Journal International*, vol. 143, no. 7, pp. 42–44.

Jihadi Five Stages of Islam According to Several Hadiths

Zarqawi's quotation of the Hadiths is very revealing regarding the groupthink of emerging global criminal-soldiers who are willing to forfeit their lives for their cause. The radical Sunni network obviously believes that violence will begin the process toward a caliphate. In fact, many believe that they were ordained by God to do this. Droves of volunteers are weighing their options in life and signing up for suicide operations, most not acting out of desperation but in accordance with their own beliefs.

Their competitors, the Shiites, are even more ardent in their zeal for a caliphate. This belief is prevalent among radical Shiite sects and Shiite statesmen alike. They anxiously await the return of the Mahdi and a just imamate, the Shiite version of a caliphate. Iran remains a sponsor of terrorism and the leadership clings to a virulent form of eschatology that exalts the status of ayatollahs. Iran's ayatollahs believe they are duty-bound to rule in the Mahdi's place until his return, because their divinely given trust of shepherding the Islamic faithful is ordained by God and his prophet.

With these things in mind, researchers, statesmen, policy makers, and warriors should focus on how the ranks of terrorists ebb and flow along with their cultural and religious perceptions. In order to understand our enemies, and their growing numbers, we must understand their viewpoint and the eschatological aims fueling many of them. Many terrorists hold a deterministic and prophetic view of an inevitable collision between unbelievers and believers as stated in the Hadiths quoted by Zarqawi. Their motivation is based on their belief in a guarantee of eventual victory. Each life sacrificed is an arrow against the oppressor. Prophetically and providentially speaking, each of the five stages is destined to come about until Allah wills to bring about the fifth stage, a caliphate.

The issue before believers is how Allah will bring that about. Terrorists have already decided that violence is the only answer. The worldview and mindset constructed by terrorist leaders is firmly planted in their apocalyptic vision of the world. This view is not rooted in science but their interpretation of revelation. This not only proves formidable to overcome, but also hydradic in nature, meaning the cutting off of one head leads to several springing up in its place. It is absolutely essential to understand the worldview and mindset of terrorists when seeking to establish strategic insight into the Global War on Terror against Al Qaeda and others of a similar worldview. The current and emerging criminal-soldiers who adhere to this mindset have, and will continue to possess, a global, perpetual view of warfare. As a result, the war with Al Qaeda and affiliated groups is still in its opening phases and will be a generational conflict spanning decades.

Whereas the West has advanced based on its progress in science and technology, failure of modernization and political process in the Islamic nations of the Middle East spawned the current embracement of terrorism and its spread to other Islamic nations in Africa and Asia. Additionally, the current war did not spring from the ether. The genesis of American hatred began during the Sahwa (Awakening) period after the Six Day War of 1967. The careful listing of grievances against America, Israel, and the

West in general became normative for radical clerics and terrorist groups after the shame and humiliation Syria, Egypt, and Jordan experienced after that brief conflict.[6] Nations base their esteem on diverse measurements of power, chief among them military power. This war magnified the military ineptness of this coalition and the bankrupt nature of Nasser's political ideology based on his understanding of Arab unity. The failure of Nasserism, which promised progress for the Middle East through secular Arabism, caused the Sahwa among a demoralized Middle Eastern population.[7] Many Arabs turned to their religious identity after the crippling of their esteem during the Six Day War and soon being Arab became synonymous with being Islamic. It was argued that the war was Allah's judgment on the Arabs for abandoning Islam. Islam was again viewed in the early traditional way as being the answer for all of mankind's problems.[8]

Statesmen in the Middle East could no longer ignore the usefulness of Islamic thought in politics. The undercurrents of the Middle Eastern populous toward the Sahwa movement began to galvanize a new generation and Middle Eastern dictators used this to their political advantage. Leading people to Quranic truths would prove to be an indispensable part of a cleric's function, the impact of which was clear to statesmen. State appointed clerics were carefully selected to both mitigate the impact of radicalism and to solidify their standing in the eyes of the revived Muslims.[9] The Sahwa movement continued to build a foundation over the next several years and would soon be given a greater voice in the late seventies.

Two key events in Sunnism and Shiism took place in the same year, 1979, causing a revolutionary change in the Islamic world. Shiite and Sunni faithful interpreted the events of this year as signs of providence, giving rise to ummah (community) consciousness in the minds of believers. The two events were Russia's invasion of Afghanistan and the Iranian Revolution. Events in Afghanistan signaled to some Sunnis that warfighting was incumbent upon every able bodied believer. They poured into the conflict by the thousands. Just a few miles away, Shiites were beginning to gain significant political power in Iran and, for the first time in its history, a Shiite state emerged with clerics at the helm. Shiite emergence proved to be hostile toward America, manifesting itself in the hostage-taking incident. Sunni and Shiite revivals have proven to be thorns in the side of America, Israel, and in those countries that are witnessing an Islamic revival. The latter include Saudi Arabia, Yemen, and even the European countries of France and the Netherlands.

In order to understand the motivations of terrorists and the moral legitimacy they seek, researchers must take a look at how terrorists view Islamic history. Legitimacy is in the eye of the beholder and history is written by those who conquer others. Al Qaeda and those who share a similar view, ascribe the role of

6. Nasser, G. (1955) *Egypt's Liberation: The Philosophy of the Revolution*, Washington: Public Affairs Press, 1955, pp. 61–70.
7. Ibid.
8. Menahem, M. (2004) 'Reform vs. Islamism in the Arab World Today', *The Middle East Research Institute*, Special Report no. 34, Available at: http://www.memri.org.
9. Ibid.

conquerors to the early caliphs.[10] Therefore, terrorists hold all Western views of history as skewed. The entirety of the five stages of Islam begins with the prophet, is followed by a caliphate, endures a period of unjust rulers, followed by tyrannical rule (present) and culminates with the promised caliphate. Their understanding of legitimate history always includes Muhammad's reign and a caliph, which means "successor to the prophet". The brightest period of Islamic history began with Muhammad and his immediate successors, Abu Bakr, 'Umar, Uthman and Ali. All were chosen by other believers largely due to their close association with the prophet, their military and political successes, and their ability to stomp out apostasy. They were collectively called the Rashidun or the Rightly Guided Caliphs. All of the first four caliphs personally knew Muhammad before his death and succeeded him and each other in turn.[11]

The Caliphs were considered rightly guided because they followed Muhammad's teachings and the community was unified around them. Many terrorists believe the caliph was not just the answer for the Islamic community during that time but for all time. Terrorists seek to establish themselves on a historical basis by aligning themselves with the first caliphate. They seek to implement their own version of a true caliphate.

The expansion of Islam and its use of jihad were very effective after the death of Muhammad but this expansive role would also lead to greater dissension. Two factors contributed to the political and military origins of jihad: the death of Muhammad brought about a vacuum that needed to be filled by a competent leader while the military successes of the caliphs brought about a rapid conversion rate among Arabs. These two factors gave rise to a unity previously unthinkable. The expansive nature of the caliphs' approach was largely unchallenged. In their view, since Muhammad consolidated both spiritual and civil authority into his hands, there was no need to change this model; therefore, the title of Caliph Bakr was first given to Abu Bakr. He lived out the remainder of his life with the title. The last three caliphs, 'Umar, Uthman and Ali, were not so fortunate; they were all assassinated by internal or external enemies of the new empire. Terrorists see violence as a justifiable, even necessary, way of resolving issues that hinder their aims and the early caliphate was plagued by this thinking as well.

During the reign of the first four caliphs, other believers were consulted during conflict and resolution, although the caliph was not *required* to do so because he held the title of imam as well. The first four caliphs were supported because the ummah believed the caliph was the legitimate sole authority over the community and, thus he was revered as the embodiment of spiritual and political authority. One must keep in mind that the caliph was elected by consensus; therefore, consensus has always played a powerful role with Sunni imams.[12] Some Muslims

10. Hazim (2005), pp. 31–34.
11. Ibid.
12. Salmi, R. H., Majul, C. A. & Tanham, G. K. (eds) (1998) *Islam and Conflict Resolution*, University Press of America, Lanham, pp. 54–57.

yearn for the simplicity of that order today and they believe that a jihad against apostate regimes and unbelievers is necessary to return Islam to its former glory.

The Rashidun (Rightly Guided Caliphs) could declare jihad against unbelievers and believers alike for the purposes of self-defense, conquest, or to squash apostasy but, after the death of the last of the initial four, an even greater liberality of definition set in. Infighting among various tribes produced diverse claims upon the ummah and loyalties were deeply divided. The Shia, the party of Ali, split from the Sunnis, and gave birth to deep divisions and different Hadiths. This event furthered the rift between the Shia and Sunni because a Shia version of an Islamic successor, the imam, developed.[13] On the other hand, the Sunni's continuation of the caliph remained intact.

As the years passed, a pattern of diffusion of titles, Hadiths, and battles cemented the hostilities among Shiites and Sunnis, giving rise to various claimants of true successor to the prophet. Desire for political power gave rise to greater infighting in both Sunni and Shiite camps and the ummah was reeling and in search of leaders. Unity was gone and now any political leader could declare jihad as long as he had the support of an imam and such support was easily gained. This pattern continued throughout the centuries of Islamic dynasties and empires until the last caliphate fell.

The timeline for the caliphate ended on March 3rd 1924 when Turkish president Kemal Ataturk abolished the institution in favor of a new national Turkish identity.[14] Many terrorists point to the end of the Ottoman Empire as one of the most humiliating spectacles in Islamic history. This event was a symbol of Islamic humiliation at the hands of the West. A few spurious military attempts and religious calls to the faithful to reestablish the caliphate did take place but self-declared caliphs and movements towards a unified ummah ruled by a caliph fell on disenchanted and hardened hearts and thus to no avail.[15] Caliphate indicators did not surface again for several decades. This emergence came in the form of sermons and literature after the successes of the mujihadeen against Russia in Afghanistan. Soon, many mujihadeen would be wooed by Al Qaeda and America would become the next target when the soles of US soldier's feet tread upon the holy land.

The Gulf War brought further agitation into the region when American troops, rather than Bin Laden's mujihadeen/Al Qaeda network, were chosen by the Royal House of Saud to defend Saudi Arabia. The royal family infuriated many Muslims

13. Shiites believe that God gave them Twelve perfect imams and that the Twelfth will soon return. Al Mahdi is the Twelfth Imam. He was born in 868, is in a state of occultation (hidden), and will reveal himself on the Day of Resurrection.

14. Furnish, T. (2002) 'Bin Laden: The Man Who Would be Mahdi', *The Middle East Quarterly*, Spring. Available at: http://www.meforum.org. See also Robbins, J. (2001) National Defense University, 'Bin Laden's Vision Thing', *National Review Online*, October 8. Available at: http://www.nationalreview.com.

15. Ibid.

further by allowing the US to stay after hostilities ceased; this was viewed as an even greater sin by Bin Laden and others.[16] These actions were interpreted as provocations that fueled a smoldering rage in jihadists against the US and apostate regimes like the House of Saud. This rage was vented in several terrorism attacks by Al Qaeda over the next few years with some of the major events being those against embassies in Tanzania and Kenya and the US Cole in Yemen. These attacks signaled to the world that Al Qaeda was no longer an infant but rather growing swiftly and at an alarming rate. Al Qaeda reached full maturity on September 11, 2001. After this successful launch, Al Qaeda became more than a group; it became an idea with a voice, best expressed in violence.

Al Qaeda's doctrine departs from previous doctrines of jihad and borrows heavily from the ideological foundation of Abdullah Azzam's *Join the Caravan*. This work was central in formulating the ideology behind robust jihads that favored a supranational ummah that could lay claim to all believers, regardless of ethnicity. Azzam listed the following reasons for joining jihad:

- In order that the disbelievers do not dominate.
- Due to the scarcity of men.
- Fear of hellfire.
- Fulfilling the duty of jihad.
- Following the footsteps of the Pious Predecessors (Salafi: First three generations after the prophet).
- Establishing a solid foundation for the base of Islam.
- Protecting those who are oppressed in the land.
- Hoping for Martyrdom.[17]

Al Qaeda has used these tenets and added the classic terrorist's mantra that they can *legitimately target civilians* because enemy nations' civilians pay taxes to oppressive governments that seek to dominate the populations they are seeking to deliver.

Terrorists are fighting this type of jihad and drawing consistent motivation from militant religiosity, the oppression of tyrannical governments, and misguided American foreign policy. Recruits are taught about the currency of heaven and they are willing to pay the price. A suicide soldier's blood is hallowed in the minds of future recruits. Al Qaeda and other networks have learned how to replenish their ranks through the use of media campaigns, elaborate funerals, and vast community support. Devout jihadist leaders, in the mold of the now-deceased Al Zarqawi, view the world through the lens of the five stages of Islam listed in Table 1.

16. bin Laden, U. (1998) 'Jihad against Jews and Crusaders', World Islamic Front Statement, February 23; and 'The New Powder Keg in the Middle East', *Nida'ul Islam*, iss. 15, October-November. UBL repeatedly refers to the occupation of the Saudi peninsula in all of his released statements as a grievance against the US and proof of the House of Saud's unfitness to lead the ummah against infidels.
17. Azzam, A. (1987) *Join the Caravan*, available at http://www.al-haqq.org in December 2001.

The table deals with the progressive movements of the five prophetic stages of Islam as interpreted by many Sunnis and most Shiites. We will now give a brief description of how Al Qaeda and similar groups view history and the future:

1. The first stage is the represented by Muhammad's prophethood. He set up the foundation of Islam through receiving the revelations of the Quran and instructing the first believers around him on how they should live through the hadiths.
2. The second stage sees the expansion of Islam as a political dynasty in the Middle East and beyond. It was here that the rise of Islam was seen as unstoppable and in keeping with the prophet's instructions.
3. The third stage of Islam begins after the death of the Ali, the last rightly guided caliph according to the Sunnis. The Shiites differ, because they regard him and his progeny as the only legitimate heirs to Muhammad. This has created a schism in Islam that has continued to this day. Still, both parties agree that the ummah during this historical era is disjointed and in need of a shepherd. The pattern of oppression continues until the last caliphate falls in 1924.
4. At this point, the fourth stage of Islam commences and continues to the present. This stage is progressively worse than the previous. It is characterized by tyrannical oppression in which Islamic populations are held captive by infidels and their apostate, puppet leaders. They view this current time in history as a stage that was predicted by Muhammad, but also a stage that sets the tone for a new caliphate emerging.
5. The fifth stage, yet to come, is a period when a righteous caliphate emerges and brings about justice on the earth.

Caliphate Indicators and Concerns

> We only have ideas in so far as we are able to take the attitude of the community and then respond to it.
>
> George Herbert Meade

Ideas are powerful and conveyed through symbols. These symbols are in fact the anchors of ideas, languages, hopes, passions and human activity. Symbolic interactionism is a school of thought within sociology that seeks to explain behavior and social interaction through the study of symbols. In this context, every thought, word or action has some symbolic value that assigns meaning to self, community and outsiders. Once this pattern is established, the minds of the members are solidified and outsiders are usually shunned.[18] Al Qaeda has responded to the attitude of some within the Islamic community and created a

18. Mead, G. H. (1934) *Mind, Self, and Society*, University of Chicago Press, Chicago.

Table 1 Jihadi Stages of Islam[a]

Stage	*Name*	*Attributes*
Stage 1	Prophethood	**570 to 632**: The birth and rise of Muhammad in Arabia and the new religion of Islam.
Stage 2	Caliphate according to Sunnis and the beginning of the Imamate through Ali according to Shiites	**632 to 661**: The four successors of Muhammad or the Rightly Guided Caliphs ruled during this time period, and the Sunni's hold that this period was known as a righteous period that guided all of the believers appropriately. Shiites hold that Ali alone was rightly guided and the other caliphs were usurpers.
Stage 3a	Lesser Apostasy Commences Islamic Empires Begin	**661 to mid-1800s**: This period was characterized by apostasy and a general turning away of the faith. There were still periods of growth, revival, and stunning military accomplishments but Islamic piety did not approach the previous periods of Muhammad and the Rightly Guided Caliphs. The last caliphate fell in 1924 and this was merely symbolic; Jihadist refer to this frequently in their writing.
Stage 3b	Complete subjugation of Muslim Lands and ensuing rebellions from time to time. The most significant was led by a self appointed Mahdi in Sudan. Resistance begins with a Mahdi figure.	**1880-1899:** A member of the Sufi sect, the Mahdi, Muhammad Ahmad Abdallah and his followers waged successful military campaigns against the Turks and British, effectively uniting Sudan under his leadership until defeated by the British in 1899 at the Battle of Omdurman.
Stage 4a	The birth of Israel, Pan Arabism & Islamism and jihads in Afghanistan, Lebanon, the Iranian Revolution and Khomeiniism, Palestine and unrest in Chechnya and Bosnia as well	**1979:** Russia invades Aghanistan Abdullah Azzam and others called for supranational campaigns against apostates, oppressors and foreign military bases in Islamic lands. **1967:** Six Day War Israel defeats the Arab Alliance of Egypt, Syria and Jordan and the Sahwa, Islamic Awakening begins. The intellectual underpinnings were started by Sayyid Qutb. **1948:** Israel became a nation as well. **1932:** The unification of Saudi Arabia. **1924:** Fall of the Ottoman Empire and last recognizable caliphate.
Stage 4b	Al Qaeda and other terrorist groups become active on a global level	**1988 to 2006** (the present): The beginning of global upsurge in supranational propaganda and campaigns designed to bring about emirates. Provinces and territories such as Afghanistan have shariah as the foundation of law.

(continued)

Stage 5a (Future projections)	New Caliphate	**Yet to be fulfilled:** The caliphate is the womb from which the Mahdi will emerge. It is also the only true foundation of a just Islamic nation other than Muhammad's prophetic ministry.
Stage 5b (Future projections)	Mahdi	**Yet to be fulfilled:** The end of the world draws near with his emergence.

[a]Chart compiled from the following sources: Hijazi, (1995) 'Al-Mahdi, Muhammad ibn Abdullah and A Caliphate That Follows the Guidance of the Prophet sallallahu alayhi wa sallam', available at: http://www.witness-pioneer.org/vil/articles/aqeedah/al_mahdi.htm; Muslimheritage.com; Chronology of Major Events in Muslim Heritage; Salmi, R. H., et al. (1998). Ahmed, R. (2002) *Jihad: The Rise of Militant Islam in Central Asia*, Yale University Press, New Haven, pp. 223–224.

terrorist network shortly after the end of the Afghanistan jihad. There, the idea of global jihad gained traction and the symbol of a global caliphate emerged. The idea of targeting particular nations grew from this.

Al Qaeda has been very successful in terms of creating the symbols necessary to sustain its evolution and success within the global ummah and selected nations. Al Qaeda is an idea and a violent reform movement within Islam seeking volunteers that will take the lead role in reshaping the ummah. Other cult-like networks have embraced this ideology in terms of individual duties, collective duties, and fighting outsiders who are attempting to oppress the ummah. Individual members of these groups view themselves and their community as deliverers and America, its allies, Israel and anyone else against their cause as an outsider and deserving of death.

The idea of a ruling class of clerics was appealing to Ruhmallah Khomeini and he successfully applied it in Iran. His brand of Islam was deridingly called Khomeinism by his detractors but it ushered in a revolution.

> If you were to act correctly and fulfill your duties you would see that the conduct of affairs would be bound over to you. If the form of government willed by Islam were to come into being none of the governments now existing in the world would be able to resist it: they would all capitulate. But unfortunately we have failed to establish such a government.[19]

The Ayatollahs bolstered by Khomeiniism and the Iranian Revolution rose to a level of political prominence previously unknown in the Middle East to Shiite clerics and they, like all statesmen, will not surrender their new-found influence

19. Khomeini, R. (1970) *Velayate Faqeeh* (Governance of the Jurist) Islamic Government, Iran. Originally taken from lectures between January 21 and February 8, 1970. His lectures on Velayat-e faqeeh, the theory of governance and Islamic leadership were published and smuggled into Iran shortly afterward. Hamid Algar, trans., Institute for Compilation and Publication of Imam Khomeini's Works. International Affairs Division, 2001.

without a fight. They view themselves as an imamate leadership ruling in the absence of Mahdi and hope that a significant number of their citizens will continue to view them this way as well. So far, the results have been mixed but the ayatollahs are not against fusing nationalism and Shiism to their political advantage.

Nations that have more than three or more of the criteria listed below have caliphate potential insofar as Islamism has been acted upon in the past and can gain traction:

- A significant number of devout Muslims who demand an Islamic government.
- A significant number of clerics who espouse and justify violent theology.
- Political leadership that is anti-Western and is based on sharia law.
- Failing or disjointed state status.
- Significant numbers of terrorist operatives or sympathizers that have infiltrated or remain in the government and security forces.

Attempting to address the concerns of caliphate indicators is no small matter. Indicators of caliphate consciousness simply defined means this: a greater number of people are looking for a caliphate type leader who is able to galvanize the majority of zealots toward the common goal of Islamic dominance, not only as a religion, but as a political force. The Ayatollah Khomeini read the sentiment of his times and seized the moment among Persian Shiites, exhorting his fellow Shiites to form an Islamic government.

Tracking caliphate movements is not as difficult as some say. The primary thing to look for is the self-reported statements of those who are actively seeking to implement their version of sharia law upon every individual who claims to be Muslim. Every group that has this vision is taking steps toward implementing a caliphate. Al Qaeda's self-reported political objective of implementing an emirate in Iraq is only an intermediary step designed to bring about a caliphate.[20]

The caliphate and what it symbolizes is more than noteworthy; it is in fact the impetus behind the majority of militant cults and their rhetoric.[21] Militant cults and the new strain of Islam that endorses violence against civilians are not about self defense alone, it is angry and violent. Expressions of this extreme form of violence can be witnessed in the on-going suicide bombings and beheadings perpetrated by Islamic radicals. It is this way because of the following factors: oppression of the populace by the hands of Middle Eastern dictators, unwanted intervention by foreign governments, and the fact that there is often no other competing ideology. It is human nature for people, and ultimately the nations

20. ZarQawi, A. M. (2004) 'Pledge of Allegiance to Al Qaeda', *Mu'asker al-Battar*, iss. 21, October 17. Statement released on jihadi websites.
21. For more on Jihadi symbolism see Kennedy-Boudali, L. et al. (2006) *The Islamic Imagery Project: Visual Motifs in Jihadi Internet Propaganda*, West Point, Combating Terrorism Center, United States Military Academy.

they encompass, to actively seek to expand their role in the world. Jihadists do the same and, to date, militant Islam has become a legitimate political voice for many.[22] Al Qaeda and others desire a caliphate, not just a state. They define it as a nation led by a caliph who best upholds the traditions of Muhammad and actively adheres to the Quran. A true caliphate would be binding upon all Muslims. Jihadi acts of terrorism are the most palpable signs of activity toward a global caliphate.

The study of jihad was hotly debated by many in the field of security studies before September 11 but discussions concerning a global caliphate rarely came into consideration. Security experts were dismissive, opting instead to focus on regional jihads. The panorama of current events and historical data led agencies such as the CIA and FBI to one conclusion: regional jihads were the only legitimate concern for the international community. Jihadists were viewed as being bound only by regional concerns and the spillover from such conflicts would be limited to this realm. This proved false after 9/11 and the nightmare of terrorism within US borders became a reality. With these things in mind, the symbolism and function of a caliphate, both historically and currently, should now be weighed in terms of US security interests. The states and non-state movements listed in Table 2 could possibly seek to emulate caliphate status among Muslims.

Iran

The Iranian revolution that was launched by the Ayatollah Khomeini and his brand of Shia Islam became the dominant theology in Iran and has spread beyond. What was troubling about his systematic theology is the role it ascribed to clerics and that it advocated the violent overthrow of perceived apostates. Iraq's Shiites have been unleashed by the US and this will empower Shiites in many nations but primarily Iran. Sunni nations actively oppressing Shiite communities will be impacted as well. The revival of Shiites is both political and religious and is currently underway throughout the Middle East.[23] Khomeini's successors, the ayatollahs, have continued their rule in the ayatollahs' Regime of Iran. Khomeini's theology is captured best in *Valeyat Faqeeh* (Governance of the Jurist), and thereby, even in death, he speaks from this document.[24] To date, Iran is the best example of what a threatening Islamic government looks like. Although there is a strong reform movement within the country, it remains a stable state with considerable economic and military power firmly under the control of the ayatollahs.

Iran is currently the best possible candidate for an imamate (Shia version of caliphate). They are obviously concerned with some domestic issues, and Al Sistani's emerging quietist view of a cleric's role in politics, but US pressure for

22. Hazim (2005), p. 6.
23. Nasr, V. (2006) 'When the Shiites Rise', *Foreign Affairs*, July/August, 5 pp. Available at: http://www.foreignaffairs.org.
24. Khomeini, R. (1970).

Table 2 State and non-state caliphate candidates

Nations with Caliphate Potential	*Information and Details*
Iran (Shiite)	Iran continues with an Ayatollah led government that is striving to rule in the absence of the 12th Imam.
Iraq (Shiite)	Iraq has seen a revival in Shiism. Shiite militias are essentially running the prison system in Iraq.
Pakistan (Sunni)	Pakistan remains a target for extremists due to the fact it is the only Islamic country with nuclear weapons. There is also strong support for Al Qaeda and Taliban members among clerics, populace, military, and the ISI.
Afghanistan (Sunni)	Afghanistan instituted in 1996 - Ousted in late 2001. Karzai is facing more opposition from Afghans and has become more critical of US policy.
Somalia (Sunni)	Somalia, although small and torn by civil war, has proven to be a hot bed for extremists.
Less likely candidates: Nigeria (Sunni)	Nigeria has a large Islamic population but does not appear to be threatened by takeover by militants at this point.
Indonesia (Sunni)	Indonesia has the largest Muslim population in the world, but is primarily moderate.
Palestine (Sunni)	Palestine is in need of a political unification before any consideration can be given to it but the rise of Hamas, at the expense of Fatah, suggests that more extreme forms of radicalism are winning out. These forms of radicalism appear to be caliphate-seeking rather than state-seeking.
Non-State Movements	*Information and Details*
Virtual Ummah	Strong consensus among many internet savvy Muslims who have no strong ties to traditional leaders. This should be a concern because more are expressing the need for a caliphate.
Global Ummah	This will pose problems for states seeking to mitigate prophetic expectation confirmed through current events. Look for leaders to interpret the signs of the times for their followers.
Eschatological movements	This is simply a matter of interpretation that causes the masses of Islamic populations to look for acts of providence pointing to the Last Days. The interpretation of such events will cause some to act as harbingers of a new caliphate through acts of violence. They believe the more they act on God's behalf the more He will act on theirs.

ridding themselves of nuclear capability is their primary concern. The clerics are in the process of whipping up nationalism and religious solidarity in order to consolidate their hold on Iran's populace. The ayatollahs are using a front man like Mahmoud Ahmadinejad to advance their agenda. Iran's clerics have not taken a back seat to Ahmadinejad; they are pulling the strings, recently issuing a fatwa justifying the use of nuclear weapons against their enemies.[25] They are actively attempting to stave off US military force against them through various means of diplomacy and bellicose speech toward the US and Israel. One should view the nuclear issue in terms of realism. The unelected clergy truly fear US intentions and with good reason. They are doing what they think is necessary to ensure their survival and they are unwilling to forfeit their clandestine nuclear activity. The clergy view this as a legitimate deterrent and they view themselves as legitimate successors to the prophet and the ruling class in the absence of the Twelfth Imam. The Iranian president recently voiced such a prayer in public.[26]

Iran is doing what it views as consistent with sharia law in order to gain some parity with the West, in terms of WMDs. Although democratic movements are present in Iran, a renewed sense of national sovereignty is derailing the democratic movement the US is playing up. Currently, Iran is diametrically opposed to any US initiatives and has Russia supporting its position on nuclear technology. Mahmoud Ahmadinejad has secured an offer from the US to come to the table and have face to face meetings with his government, if he decides to follow through. This is truly a diplomatic victory for Iran, and the Shiite clergy in general, because it signals to many that a hawkish administration is willing to be dovish when facing an ascendant Iran. This reinforces the need for economic and military to be controlled by Iran's clergy when dealing with the West.

Iraq

Iraq is a laboratory in which several forces are vying to be the primary catalyst for change. If Iraq is the laboratory for democracy in the Middle East, it is also the laboratory for what happens when jihad ideology of resistance by any means necessary takes hold of a small percentage of the populace. The war in Iraq has produced a magnet for jihadists who are seeking to implement jihad toward a caliphate; they view themselves as deliverers, a term the US has reserved for itself.[27] Although Zarqawi was recently killed, his death will be useful to jihadists as well as to the US and Iraqi forces. One must remember how symbolic interactionism works, particularly in religious terms. The most important thing perverse religious movements and cults produce in people's minds is the sense that they are truly special and others are not. Zarqawi convinced himself and his

25. Freeman, C. (2006) 'Iran Clerics Back Nuclear Weapons', *The London Sunday Telegraph*, February 19, 2 pp. Available at: http://www.washtimes.com.
26. Daniszewski, J. (2006) 'Iran President's Call on Mahdi is Polarizing', *Los Angeles Times Sunday*, April 23, 2006.
27. Hazim (2005), pp. 139–140.

followers of this. This belief is a common thread that runs through all militant cults. The motivational psychology behind Al Zarqawi and those eagerly following his ideology is not that they live a significant life by worldly standards but that they die a significant death. He achieved this and now others of a similar mindset will follow this course in Iraq and beyond.

Here are five things to watch for in jihadist circles following Zarqawi's death in Iraq:

- He will now live beyond the grave and many idealistic jihadists will seek to emulate him.
- Unfortunately for Al Qaeda, their zeal will not be matched by his knowledge or charisma, and many will lack the discipline necessary to be effective jihadists.
- Unfortunately for the US, the movements will become more and more fragmented and disorganized, producing more violence on low level targets.
- The fragmentation will produce rivalries between jihadists who consider themselves purists versus those who are part timers and are using violence as a way of seeking attention from the media and potential recruits.
- A conglomeration of a new generation of terrorists in Iraq and elsewhere that include pragmatic jihadists, idealist jihadists, gangster jihadists and the like will emerge and begin to clash with one another and Iraqi/US forces more frequently.

Shiism in Iraq and a particular form of Shiism, quietism, is likely to rule the day in Iraq as long as Al Sistani remains healthy, significant, and active, but afterwards it's anyone's bet. Even if Al Sistani's approach remains after he is gone, it does not mean that the clerics will not have a role; it simply means that they will guide the political process and intervene when they deem it necessary. This does not bode well for US interests due to the fact that Al Sistani has emerged as the most powerful political figure in the post-Saddam era.[28] Iraq's likely course is to use US military involvement in hopes of becoming a stable, prosperous nation. Its hopes rest on the possibility of striving to use both Arab identity and Shia identity as a means to claiming greater legitimacy in the Islamic world. Iraq must become a stable state before it can claim any ascendancy to an imamate status and the Sunnis are unlikely to allow this to happen. Still, Iraq remains a candidate for such a status due to the nature of the current struggle within it and the fact that Shiites will not surrender their newly found political power, even if it means civil war.

Pakistan

Pakistan remains an enigma to most. Pakistan is responsible for training many of the jihadist elements in Kashmir and Afghanistan as well. The overwhelming pressure placed on Pervez Musharaf after September 11th caused him to make a

28. Cole, J. (2004) 'It Takes a Following to make an Ayatollah', *Washington Post*, August 15. Available at: http://www.washingtonpost.com.

decision, one that he had to make in order to avoid dire consequences. His immediate decision to join with the US should be viewed in terms of political realism but his choice has not eradicated the very real danger of a takeover by extremist elements within the country. He has been the target of many assassination attempts but remains in control.[29] The worse case scenario is a takeover by militants who will come into possession of nuclear weapons. This country is truly the envy of all serious jihadists and there is no doubt that many have infiltrated the military and intelligence ranks.[30]

Afghanistan

Afghanistan has experienced an increase of Taliban resurgence and an increase in US deaths. One aspect of this resurgence is the rise of 'Night Postings'—messages secretly placed on buildings that threaten those who cooperate with the government and stabilization forces with eventual death. The resurgence of the Taliban is a blight on the current path the US is treading. The US has not finished its work there, and what stands is a form of government that is weak, still largely controlled by warlords, and one that the masses of people do not buy into. Recently, Hamid Karzai was critical of the current approach of American policy and he even went so far as to call the Taliban "sons of this land."[31] Afghanistan is still open territory for a caliphate type government to emerge once again if the US chooses to leave the country and deploy its military sources elsewhere. The jihad is perpetual and the Taliban, still lead by their shadowy leader Mullah Muhammad Omar, are not leaving any time soon. The staying power of the Taliban is without question and a new generation will certainly emerge with its own view of history and their quest for a caliphate.

Somalia

Somalia has resurfaced once again as a legitimate threat to become a base for terrorism. The logic in the beginning is for The Supreme Islamic Courts Council (ICSC) to bring about an Islamic country. Its primary leader Sheik Hassan Dahir Aweys, whom US officials have branded a terrorist, claims that Somalia is Islamic, and therefore, sharia law is the natural course of action. The Islamic Courts Supreme Council is attempting to disassociate itself from terrorism and reach out to the international community; however, they cannot continue to hold onto an extreme form of Islam and not attract extremist elements. It is a well known fact that the new leadership frowns upon television, and in order to enforce this approach, two of their more zealous members killed a teen aged girl for ignoring their orders and continuing to watch a soccer game. To their credit, the ICSC

29. Benjamin, D. (2006) 'Why Pakistan's May be the West Best Bet for Peace', *Time Magazine*, April 30.
30. Risen, J & Judith, M. (2001) 'Pakistan's Intelligence had Links to Al Qaeda, U.S. says', *The New York Times*, October 29.
31. Tran, T. (2006) 'Karzai Criticizes US Led Coalition', Associated Press, June 23.

considered this too severe and arrested the men.[32] The ICSC will continue to draw this type of element into their militia as long as they attempt to establish an austere version of sharia governance in Somalia.

Other Countries

Al Qaeda has repeatedly made statements to the ummah to overthrow the leaders of several countries. Current caliphate concerns and indicators take on a new degree of needed vigilance since the historical data has proven that an increase in caliphate indicators correlates with an increase of terrorist events. The outcomes of caliphate strivings in the form of jihadist activity will result in several unpleasant manifestations for the US. Countries such as Indonesia and Nigeria do not have enough indicators to be considered caliphate candidates at this point and to make such statements one would have to lean toward alarmism. Palestine is an interesting case because the success of Hamas over Fatah has further radicalized the Arab dominated territories. These lands are poverty stricken and a new generation of terrorists, more agreeable to caliphate ideas, now control the government. However, given the fact the Fatah is still very much a political force, the likely outcome is ongoing civil strife between the competing factions.

Non-state Movements

In addition, to those state movements listed above, we have added non-state and transnational ones due to the fact that control of physical territory is not needed to build a significant movement. Terrorists are increasingly using media outlets and the internet (5th dimensional space) to wage havoc. Virtual jihadi training websites have replaced lost training camps in Afghanistan.[33] This has served to further fragment the global Islamic insurgency into smaller cells that are more difficult to identify. Three types of non-state movements may exist. The first is the virtual ummah. This is derived from a "leaderless resistance" model in which lone wolves (jihadi individuals and small cells) reach consensus on the internet. The second is the global ummah. Rather than being sub-national this movement is supra-national in scope. Non-contiguous enclaves of believers, the vast majority slum dwellers, become globally bound together via a charismatic figure. The basis of this movement would be the have-nots rising up against the haves. The final non-state movement is eschatological. This movement is derived from a Mahdi-

32. Hassan, M. O. (2006) 'Somalia Militants Arrest 2 in TV Killings', Associated Press, July 6, 2:43 pm. Available at: http://www.wtop.com.

33. For more on the network advantages of Al Qaeda see Bunker, R. J. & Begert, M. (2005) 'Operational Combat Analysis of the Al Qaeda Network', in *Networks, Terrorism and Global Insurgency*, ed. R. J. Bunker, Routledge, London, pp. 146–169.

like figure that effectively communicates an end of days message to his followers. More information and details on these movements can be found in Table 2.

Conclusion

There are four particular events that can be expected to take place in the next decade that will warrant great vigilance by any state seeking to reduce terrorism and insurgency within its borders, particularly those with a large Sunni population:

- There will be an increase in nations that are hostile toward the US, and they will use political Islam as a foundation for their citizens and a counterweight to democracy.
- There will be an increasingly strained relationship between the US and its Sunni and Shia allies. This has already taken place in some regions of Iraq where the liberators are now viewed as occupiers.
- Al Qaeda theology and ideas will become an even greater religious force that converts members of the ummah and turns them against the host nation to their cause, fueling more home grown terrorists.
- A latent function of the increase of terrorism will be the shock value of such tactics. These tactics will be copied by numerous secular and radical groups that have nothing to do with Al Qaeda. The recent beheadings in Colombia by the FARC and those in Mexico by the cartels represent a case in point.

The US is unprepared to deal with the threat of caliphate yearnings and the eschatology that spawns it. These yearnings will take on nationalist, religious, and sectarian clothing. The symbolism contained in these movements is powerful for both Sunnis and Shiites. Since there is no recognized figure for Sunnis, Al Qaeda's logical approach is to tap into the expectation of the Sunni masses. What the masses are looking for is representation from a leader who convinces them of his sincere concern for them. The oppression of political leaders and the random violence of terrorist organizers have disqualified both groups from being a legitimate voice for the masses, but the question remains as to what other voices will emerge in their place.

The 2006 Usama Bin Laden Tape: Interpreting an Adversary

Youssef Aboul-Enein

Youseff Aboul-Enein is a Lieutenant Commander commissioned in the Navy Medical Service Corps. He has served tours in Bosnia, Liberia and the Persian Gulf. He was raised in the Middle East and speaks two dialects of Arabic. In 1997 and 1999 he was tasked as Arabic linguist and Middle East Advisor during Exercise Bright Star in Egypt. Since 9/11 he has been detailed to the Washington DC area and is currently assigned as Country Director for the Arabian Peninsula at the Office of the Secretary of Defense for International Security Affairs and is Advisor on Islamic Militancy. At the OSD, he was Director for North Africa and Egypt (2003–2005), being involved in issues ranging from Libyan disarmament to military re-engagement with Algeria and the freedom of over 400 Moroccan Prisoners of War held by the POLISARIO Front. He has written on Islamic militancy and the Middle East for such journals as the Aerospace Power Chronicles, Military Review and Infantry. In collaboration with the Army Combined Arms Center, he has published essays translating excerpts of memoirs of Egyptian, Algerian and Syrian generals as well as a Hamas operative. He has a B.A. in Business Administration from the University of Mississippi, a M.A. in Health Services Administration and Business Administration from the University of Arkansas, Little Rock, and a M.S. in Strategic Intelligence from the Joint Military Intelligence College in Washington, D.C. He has also earned Non-Resident diplomas from the Naval War College, the Army War College Defense Strategy Course, and the Marine Corps Institute Amphibious Warfare School.

January 19, 2006 marked an end to a thirteen-month hiatus since the last tape of Usama Bin Laden was publicly broadcast on Al-Jazeera. It is important to examine this last tape not only in the context of Bin Laden's previous statements but also from the backdrop of the statements made by his more vocal deputy and strategist, Ayman Al-Zawahiri, and his on-the-ground commander in Iraq, Abu Musab Al-Zarqawi. This will unlock potential clues and theories as to why Bin Laden's tape aired last January and what he is attempting to accomplish with this latest public statement both on the ideological front and in terms of messages to Al-Qaeda supporters and leaders worldwide. This essay will postulate several theories as to why the tape was released and what it means in the context of the global Islamist radicalist agenda.

Why Release a Tape on or about January 2006?

Bin Laden probably made the tape months before its release and statements by various sources support that this is the case. Al-Jazeera first claimed it received the tape in December but then corrected itself, indicating it got it in January 2006.[1] Further, the text of Bin Laden's remarks in which he refers to former Deputy Defense Secretary Paul Wolfowitz and the current Defense Secretary Donald Rumsfeld in the same sentence is significant because Mr. Wolfowitz left the Defense Department in April 2005.[2] This probably provides the best indication of when the tape was made, likely between January and April 2005. The purpose of the tape was ostensibly to influence public anti-war sentiments in the United States and to respond to various pressures affecting Bin Laden as follows.

Reaching the Anti-war Movement in the United States

In his latest tape, Bin Laden obsesses about the anti-war movement and, although he has made appeals to the American people before, notoriously during the last Presidential election, this is the first statement in which he directly refers to public opinion polls, pronouncing "I say that the poll results please those of you who are wise and that Bush's rejection of the results is a mistake..." and that "...this is the essence of the poll results that favor troop withdrawal... "[3]

Bin Laden sees this as an opportunity to interject himself into the debate over Operation Iraqi Freedom and influence American public opinion. Signifying a new dimension in his public statements, Bin Laden's remarks for the first time urge audiences to read an American author, William Blum, stating:

1. Jordan, L. J. (2006) 'Analysts seek date, language of Bin Laden tape for clues', Associated Press Report, 21 January; Associated Press Military Writer Robert Burns contributed to the report.
2. Text of *Bin Laden Tape* released by Associated Press wire service 15:43 Eastern Standard Time; January 19, 2006.
3. Ibid.

> ...then it would be useful for you (Americans) to read the book *"Rogue States,"* which states in its introduction: If I were President, I would stop the attacks on the United States (by): First, I would give an apology to all the widows and orphans and those who were tortured. Then I would announce that American interference in the nations of the world has ended once and for all.[4]

Bin Laden understands that the American people are lost in his images and interpretation of *Takfiri* (those who declare apostasy) writers and his selective quotations from the Quran. It is expected that further Bin Laden remarks will also contain references to American authors who bolster his arguments and world vision.

Bin Laden's deputy Zawahiri looks to the war in Vietnam as a model for eroding US resolve to continue the war.[5] His views are shaped without a clear understanding of the radical differences in the objectives and nature between Vietnam and Operation Iraqi Freedom. Al-Qaeda leaders are influenced by images of Vietnam and not by an in-depth knowledge of American society and how it has changed in the last three decades since the end of the Vietnam conflict. This implied parallel with Vietnam, the first of two events both Bin Laden and Zawahiri see as models, has Bin Laden focusing on body counts saying:

> Pentagon figures show the number of your dead and wounded is increasing, not to mention massive material losses, the destruction of the soldier's morale and the rise in cases of suicide among them. So you can imagine the psychological breakdown that afflicts a soldier as he gathers the remains of his colleagues...[6]

The second seminal event that both view as a model was the May 2000 Israeli withdrawal from Lebanon, in which Hizbullah used a variety of tactics ranging from direct terrorist action against Israeli Defense Forces (IDF) to beaming images of suicide operations into Israel to impact public opinion. The most vocal group in Israel to protest the IDF presence in South Lebanon was composed of the mothers of reservists and active duty troops serving in that front. Zawahiri seizes on this in his January 30, 2006 tape on Al-Jazeera where he appeals directly to British and American mothers regarding the lives of their sons and daughters.[7]

Dominance of the Worldwide Jihadist Legacy

Bin Laden is under pressure to deliver another spectacular strike of the magnitude of 9/11 so he can maintain dominance over the jihadist legacy. Thirteen months represents the longest hiatus Bin Laden has taken from the public. The tape is designed to demonstrate that he is alive and in charge of the worldwide jihadist

4. Ibid.
5. *Zawahiri letter to Zarqawi*, July 9, 2005; Released and declassified by the Director for National Intelligence, October 25, 2005. Available at: http://www.dni.gov/release_letter_101105.html.
6. Associated Press (2006) *Text of Bin Laden Tape*, January 19.
7. *Al-Qaeda Deputy Ayman Al-Zawahiri's Latest Video on Al-Jazeera TV* aired on Al-Jazeera TV on January 30, 2006; Translated by The Middle East Media Research Institute (MEMRI).

agenda. He also mentions a major strike, not so much as to create fear within his enemies, but to fill his leaders with anticipation of another major strike against the West. The spectacular strikes like 9/11, the attack on USS Cole, and the African embassy bombings serve as recruiting tools. It is too early to tell what impact the cartoon crisis of February 2006, coupled with additional Abu Ghuraib photos released at the same time, will have on the ease for Al-Qaeda to find more willing recruits and for it to continue to create a bipolar atmosphere of intolerance and bigotry.

Management of Zarqawi Balanced Against the Centrality of Iraq

For the past thirteen months, the media has seen more of Zawahiri and Zarqawi in the airwaves. Zarqawi is seen as the central front for Al-Qaeda and with this centrality comes influence and donations for a person seen as a jihadist leader of action. There is always fear that Zarqawi will supplant Bin Laden, or at a minimum his deputy Zawahiri, as a leader of the jihadist movement. The video asserts to his worldwide operatives Bin Laden's dominance and control of the Al-Qaeda agenda. Bin Laden must also be weary of Zarqawi turning against him. Before Zarqawi pledged allegiance to Bin Laden, he disagreed with the tactic of attacking the far enemy (i.e. American soil) in favor of attacking Arab regimes and American interests in the Arab world. Bin Laden echoes Zawahiri's numerous statements in 2004 through 2006 regarding Iraq being the central front for their jihad. Bin Laden says in his recent video: "Iraq has become a point of attraction and restorer of (our) energies".[8] This is a dual message that emphasizes the importance of establishing a foothold in Iraq, in the heart of the Middle East, while at the same time admitting that successful jihadist operations against the Coalition and Iraqi security forces serve to rejuvenate the Al-Qaeda movement in terms of recruits and monetary donations.

Addressing Successful Democratic Elections in Islamic States

Successful elections in Iraq and Egypt have led Bin Laden's deputy to express frustration over Muslim Brotherhood participation in the 2005 parliamentary elections in Egypt. His criticism extends to Iraqi Sunnis who participated in greater numbers in the last elections. Zawahiri, on January 6, 2006, appeared on a videotape on Al-Jazeera in which he besieged Islamist parties to give up on the democratic process and wage jihad. He cites the past failures of the Muslim Brotherhood in Egypt and the Algerian Islamic Salvation Front (FIS) and refers to the book by Sheikh Salah Abu Ismail called "*The Testimony*," which is a collection of his court testimony in Egypt placed in book form that derides Islamist parties for participating in the democratic process.[9]

8. Associated Press (2006) *Text of Bin Laden Tape*, January 19.
9. Full text of Al-Zawahiri speech carried on the Al-Jazeera Arabic website on January 6, 2006. Available at: http://www.Al-Jazeera.net

Addressing Successful US Humanitarian Responses

In the last six months, Zawahiri has obsessed not only about successful elections but also laments the successful aid US forces have provided to victims of the 2005 Kashmiri earthquake. Zawahiri makes wild accusations that this is a front to infiltrate spies. He sees the humanitarian aid provided in Indonesia, southern Philippines and Pakistan as a threat to maintaining their bipolar vision of the West against Islam.[10]

Bin Laden's Threats

In Bin Laden's video, he threatens the United States and says that preparations are underway for another major attack.[11] This could be a plea for independent actors to carry out such an attack. The Madrid and Casablanca bombings were conducted by independent actors not directly affiliated with Al-Qaeda but sympathetic to its goals. One theory is that since Bin Laden can no longer maintain long-term camps, as he did under the Taliban, he must therefore rely more on independent actors. Before 9/11, Al-Qaeda training was several weeks. As they can no longer maintain a base of operations for any length of time, the qualitative edge of operatives will decrease as will the number of operatives and bombers who are under the direct control of Bin Laden.

As the United States successfully rid Afghanistan of effective Taliban control, Al-Qaeda has become more decentralized. Al-Qaeda now attempts to loosely export its methods and ideology to splinter groups around the world, most notably the Zarqawi group. But with this comes the risk for Bin Laden of marginalizing his core group, as the Zarqawi group is seen to be the more active fighting force against Coalition forces. In the July 2005 Zawahiri letter to Zarqawi, Al-Qaeda's deputy writes Zarqawi not only strategic and operational advice but a plea for funds.[12] In an intercepted communiqué to Zarqawi from Bin Laden dated February 25, 2005 and since declassified, he asks Zarqawi to help carry out an attack on America.[13] It is important to realize that delivering spectacular attacks keeps global jihadists motivated and serves as a recruiting tool for Bin Laden. But both Bin Laden and Zawahiri's pleas to Zarqawi for attacks and funds is an indication that Zarqawi is dominating the Al-Qaeda agenda. Constantly delivering such attacks places Bin Laden at the forefront as leading the response on behalf of what he consistently says is the victimized Muslim community but, in actuality, this position is being supplanted by Zarqawi. The current Bin Laden video can be

10. *Al-Zawahiri urges Pakistan quake aid*, carried on the English Al-Jazeera website on October 23, 2005. Available at: http://www.Al-Jazeera.net
11. Associated Press (2006) *Text of Bin Laden Tape*, January 19.
12. *Zawahiri letter to Zarqawi*, July 9, 2005.
13. 'Bin Laden Urges New U.S. Attacks', CBS News on-line story, Match 1, 2005,. Available at: http://www.cbsnews.com/stories/2005/03/01/world/main677194.shtml

seen as a desperate plea to keep the morale of the jihadist movement up, to hear reassuring words of victory from Bin Laden himself.

The Truce

Contrary to media translations, Bin Laden did not offer a truce but offered to consider upholding a truce if the United States offers it. This distinction is important as the United States attempts to understand why he mentions a truce and what this means in Bin Laden's thinking. Bin Laden is concerned about Muslim public opinion. He and Zawahiri are learning from the unpopularity of the Taliban and the repugnance of Zarqawi's tactics. They have evolved in their political thinking to realize that a grassroots level of support must be entrenched and composed of anti-American Islamist groups both Shiite and Sunni before an Amirate can be formed and from then a Caliphate. These political theories were clearly articulated in a strategic letter from Zawahiri to Zarqawi. Bin Laden is also sending a message to Al-Qaeda leaders that tactical truces with an enemy are acceptable.

When focusing on the tape, it is important to keep in mind that part of Bin Laden's thinking is grounded in seventh and eighth century AD Islamic precedents. Prophet Muhammad and his Meccan adversaries agreed to a truce after each exhausted one another in the Battle of Uhud. The Treaty of Hudaybiyah was agreed upon with the understanding that hostilities would resume when one or the other felt they had an advantage. Bin Laden views truces not as a form of lasting peace or compromise but rather as tactical vehicles to be used when in a position of weakness. Bin Laden's recent tape states this truce is to rebuild Afghanistan and Pakistan. We see the theme of rebuilding also appears in Zawahiri's October 2005 statement criticizing U.S. efforts at earthquake relief in Pakistan.

Conclusion and Recommendations

Bin Laden's concluding paragraph warns his enemies (primarily the United States) not to have our military might and modern arms fool us for, he says, "they win a few battles but lose the war." He then closes by reminding listeners that the Soviet-Afghan War lasted a decade and that patience and steadfastness are traits that will win the current conflict. In many ways, Bin Laden has summed up the multi-dimensional aspects of this war against Al-Qaeda. It will take not only the kinetic options that have decimated the Al-Qaeda leadership but also, more importantly, a robust public diplomacy campaign designed to seek out Muslim messages that can discredit Bin Laden's. It is also vital that policymakers take aspects of Bin Laden's remarks and highlight the message of weakness he portrays in mentioning a truce and exploit the contradictions in messages, tactics and strategies between Bin Laden and Zawahiri on the one hand and Zarqawi on the other. No doubt the April 2005 Amman Bombings were a strategic blunder by

Zarqawi that has led even Islamist parties to condemn his brutal tactics. Other recommendations for US policymakers and military planners include the need to:

- Perfect US humanitarian responses to disasters like the Pakistan earthquake and Asian Tsunami. Regular humanitarian and medical civil action programs (MEDCAPs) should be redoubled in underserved areas of the Arab and Muslim world (i.e. Southern Philippines, interior of Morocco and in Afghanistan). We are in a race to compete with jihadist humanitarian relief. Bin Laden's offer of honoring a truce to rebuild Afghanistan and Iraq is his way of saying he needs time to build a grassroots movement.
- Portray Bin Laden's mention of a truce as a sign Al-Qaeda is weakening and could be marginalized by other jihadist groups like Zarqawi.
- Stay with the message that, as democratic institutions and elections spread in Iraq, Egypt, and Algeria, this is empowering Muslims; and that Al-Qaeda's vision is a regression towards a totalitarian single-party rule of a diverse Muslim and Arab population.
- Zero in on the recent tape being designed to re-assert Bin Laden's slipping leadership after more than one year of constant Zarqawi publicity. It is vital to highlight divisions within the ranks of Al-Qaeda upper leadership.

Afterword

As of the writing of this essay, a Bin Laden audiotape was released to the public on February 20, 2006, appearing first on a jihadist web forum. In the 11-minute, 26-second tape, Bin Laden vows not to be captured alive saying, "I have sworn to only live free. Even if I find bitter the taste of death, I don't want to die humiliated or deceived".[14] Experts are aware of private accounts from Bin Laden's bodyguard Abu Jandal (aka Nasser Ahmed Nasser Al-Bahri and currently under restricted house arrest in the Yemeni capital Sana'a) who gave a series of extensive interviews in the Arabic Daily *Al-Quds Al-Arabi* from 2004–2005, as saying that he was given a pistol loaded with two bullets and was to kill Bin Laden if he was about to fall into enemy hands. According to Abu Jandal, he was the only one authorized to kill Bin Laden and recollects the Al-Qaeda leader saying: "Martyrdom rather then captivity".[15] This latest audio represents the first public admission from Bin Laden himself that he refuses to be captured alive and, taken in the context of the January 19, 2006 videotape in which he proposes to honor a truce, could signify the extreme pressure Bin Laden is under to stay alive and reconstitute his organization.

14. Hurst, S. R. (2006) 'Bin Laden Vows Never to Be Captured Alive', Associated Press, February 20.
15. Bergen, P. L. (2006) *The Osama Bin Laden I Know: An Oral History of al Qaeda's Leader*, Free Press, New York, pp. 260–261.

Acknowledgements

The author wishes to thank the Pentagon and George Wythe Libraries for providing material for this essay and CAPT Eugene Smallwood, MSC, USN, Special Assistant for Current Operations, Bureau of Medicine and Surgery, for his editorial comments and discussions that enhanced this piece. The ideas and assessments represent the author's sole opinion and are not indicative of any US Government position.

Hizballah's Global Criminal Operations

Michael P. Arena

Michael P. Arena is employed by a large state criminal justice agency where he is an analyst and trainer. Prior to serving in this position he was contracted through the University of California to evaluate federally funded multi- jurisdictional drug task forces for the California Governor's Office of Criminal Justice Planning. He holds an M.A. in Organizational Behavior and a Ph.D. in Forensic Psychology with an emphasis in the administration and management of criminal justice. He has published in a variety of behavioral and social science journals, including Deviant Behavior, Professional Psychology: Research and Practice, International Criminal Justice Review, Journal of Forensic Psychology Practice, and Behavioral Sciences and the Law. He is also the co-author (along with Bruce Arrigo) of The Terrorist Identity: Explaining the Terrorist Threat (NYU Press: 2006) which explores how self-concept combined with membership in a terrorist or extremist group shapes and sustains the identity of a terrorist as well as their subsequent justification for violence and the legitimacy of their actions. His major areas of interest include extremist behavior, domestic/international terrorism, security studies, and international policing. Please send correspondence to: PO Box 681, Sterling VA 20167, USA.

On July 12, 2006, Lebanese Hizballah militants attacked Israeli military outposts in the Shebaa Farms, kidnapping two Israeli soldiers and leaving at least eight dead.[1] The attack sparked a month long volley of Israeli air strikes in southern Lebanon and a barrage of Hizballah Katyusha rocket attacks on northern Israel. The crisis peaked with an Israeli ground assault before a ceasefire was finally reached in mid-August. The fighting caused hundreds of deaths and injuries, extensive damage to civilian infrastructure, and hundreds to become homeless.[2]

The Lebanese Hizballah (Party of God) first came onto the world stage in April 1983 when one of its operatives drove a van packed with explosives into the US Embassy in Beirut, killing 63 people. A second attack followed in October 1983 when an explosive-laden pickup was driven into the US Marine barracks also in Beirut and detonated, killing 241 Marines. Moments later, 58 French paratroopers were killed in the Beirut suburb of Jnah when another explosive-filled vehicle detonated in their barracks. Initially, an organization called the Islamic Jihad claimed responsibility for the attacks but it was soon determined that it was a front for Hizballah who was intent on expelling Western influence from the region. These attacks made Hizballah responsible for more American deaths than any other terrorist organization prior to September 11, 2001.

Hizballah evolved from a ragtag group of militants into a sophisticated organization with several thousand supporters and members and a multi-dimensional infrastructure complete with military, political, social welfare, and finance wings requiring a substantial amount of money to operate.[3] While Hizballah is often quoted as being allied with Syria, the organization's chief financial sponsor is Iran which is believed to provide somewhere between $60 to $100 million dollars a year to the group.[4] Iran has been a steady sponsor of Hizballah since its inception, however, its funding has fluctuated. Under the presidencies of Rafsanjani (1989–1997) and Khatami (1997–2005), Iran's financial support to Hizballah was cut by almost 70 percent.[5] This reduction may have been a key factor in Hizballah's reliance upon funding from business interests and external sources such as charitable donations from the Lebanese diaspora community.[6] Recently, it has also come to light that Hizballah receives a great deal of funding from a worldwide network of criminal enterprises.

Hizballah appears to be profiting from a variety of criminal enterprises, most notably, Intellectual Property Crime (IPC), drug smuggling, cigarette smuggling,

1. 'Out of control: The events that lead to the crisis', MSNBC.com, July 24, 2006, available at: http://www.msnbc.msn.com/id/13902569/site/newsweek/ (Retrieved 29 August 2006).
2. 'The draft resolution presented at the U.N.', CNN.com, August 11, 2006, available at: http://www.cnn.com/2006/WORLD/meast/08/11/un.draft/index.html (retrieved 29 August 2006).
3. US Department of State (2005) *Country reports on terrorism 2005*, Washington, DC, available at: http://www.state.gov/s/ct/rls/crt/c17689.htm (retrieved 2 May 2006).
4. Madani, B. (2002) 'Hezbollah's global finance network: The triple frontier', *Middle East Intelligence Bulletin*, vol. 4, No. 1. Available at: http://www.meib.org/articles/0201_12.htm (retrieved 1 November 2005).
5. Hamzeh, A. N. (2004) *In the path of Hizbullah*, Syracuse University Press, Syracuse.
6. US Department of State (2005).

and the exploitation of the African diamond trade. This essay aims to provide a brief description of these enterprises, instances in which Hizballah's members and supporters have been found to be involved in such crimes, and some indication as to how much money has been funneled to the Hizballah organization. However, it begins with a brief history of the Hizballah organization.

A Brief History of Hizballah

Lebanese Hizballah is a radical Shia organization which formed in 1982 as a result of an interaction of several disparate forces.[7] One of these forces was the political mobilization of the southern Shia community during the 1960s.[8] With Shia, Sunni, and Druze Muslims, Christian Maronites, and Greek Orthodox Christians, Lebanon utilizes a confessional system in which political offices and bureaucratic appointments are distributed along sectarian lines to govern its religiously divided population.[9] Inhabiting the rural regions of south Lebanon and the Biq'a Valley, Shia Muslims tended to be politically and economically marginalized until a charismatic Imam by the name of Musa al-Sadr began organizing the community and fighting for official representation in the late 1950s.[10]

The political awakening of the Shia community was also spurred by the growing power of the Palestinian refugee community who had escaped to Lebanon after the declaration of Israel in 1948 and whose population was growing after the violence of the Six Day War in 1967.[11] By the early 1970s, the Palestinian Liberation Organization (PLO) relocated its base of operations to Lebanon after King Hussein evicted the militants from Jordan. Once the PLO arrived, they proceeded to launch attacks on Israel's northern border and, subsequently, invite periodic incursions by the Israel Defense Force (IDF) into Lebanon. With tensions in the region at a peak, civil war erupted in 1975.[12] Intent on defending itself from the various armed forces in the region, Musa al-Sadr founded the Lebanese Resistance or what would come to be known as the Amal militia.[13]

A second force to influence the creation of Hizballah was the Iranian Revolution. The revolution had what Ahmad Hamzeh called a "demonstration effect" on the Lebanese Shia by showing them it was possible to create an Islamic

7. Goldberg, J. (2002) 'In the Party of God: Are terrorists in Lebanon preparing for a larger war?', *The New Yorker*, vol. 78, no. 31, pp. 180–195.
8. Saad-Ghorayeb, A. (2002) *Hizbu'llah: Politics and religion*, Pluto Press, Sterling.
9. Hajjar, S. G. (2002) *Hizballah: Terrorism, national liberation, or menace?* Strategic Studies Institute, US Army War College, Carlisle. Available at: http://www.carlisle.army.mil/ssi/pubs/2002/hizbala/hizbala.htm (retrieved 27 July 2006); Jaber, H. (1997) *Hezbollah: Born with a vengeance*, Columbia University Press, New York.
10. Jaber, H. (1997).
11. Becker, J. (1984) *The PLO: The rise and fall of the Palestinian Liberation Organization*, St. Martin's Press, New York.
12. Jaber, H. (1997).
13. Hajjar, S. G. (2002).

regime.[14] Heavily influenced by Khomeini, Hizballah became fiercely anti-Western, dedicated to destroying Israel, and committed to establishing an Islamic state in Lebanon in accordance with Islamic law.[15] The Iranian regime and its supreme leader Ayatollah Khamenei continue to be a source of inspiration for Hizballah.

The third and perhaps most influential force to contribute to the creation of Hizballah was the 1982 Israeli invasion of Lebanon dubbed Operation Peace for Galilee.[16] While Israel had made periodic incursions into Lebanon in the past, this large-scale invasion was aimed at permanently eliminating the PLO's threat to Israel's northern border. Israeli forces stormed the southern region with relative ease before moving north to Beirut and forcing the PLO leadership to flee to surrounding Arab states. At first, the Shia community welcomed the IDF hoping that, once the PLO was gone, Amal would be free to reign.[17] However, the Shia community soon realized Israeli officials had no intention of leaving Lebanon before implementing its own security plan. In response, small groups of Shia militants began attacking the Israeli troops who they viewed as occupiers. Anxious to spread its brand of Islamic revolution, Iran dispatched 1,500 members of its Revolutionary Guard to the Biq'a Valley to infiltrate organizations such as Amal and train Lebanese Shia militants.[18] Eventually, these militants gathered under one umbrella to form Hizballah. The IDF withdrew from Lebanon in 1985 but continued to occupy a 15 kilometer wide security zone on the Lebanese border to help prevent further cross-border attacks.[19] This strip of land would ultimately become Hizballah's proving ground in its resistance to Israel which finally made a complete withdrawal from the zone in 2000.

Since evolving from an underground movement into a bona fide political party, Hizballah's once guarded organizational structure has become more open to public view. Hizballah is organized into a hierarchical pyramid whose territorial divisions parallel Lebanon's governorates, more specifically, the regions of Beirut, Biq'a, and south Lebanon as they have the highest concentration of Shia Muslims.[20] The first administrative tier of this pyramid is Hizballah's seven-member council called the *Majlis al-Shura* or Consultative Council. It consists primarily of Shia clergy but also has some positions for laypersons. The Shura council's primary function is to oversee the second tier of the organization, the Executive Administrative Apparatus (*Shura Tanfiz*). This administrative body consists of the Politburo which oversees political activities, the Parliamentary Council which is made up of Hizballah members who have won seats in the Lebanese Parliament, the Judicial council which resolves conflict in the Hizballah

14. Hamzeh, A. N. (2004).
15. Jaber, H. (1997).
16. US Department of State (2005).
17. Jaber, H. (1997).
18. Hajjar, S. G. (2002).
19. Harik, J. P. (2004) *Hezbollah: The changing face of terrorism*, I.B. Tauris & Co Ltd, New York.
20. This organizational description of Hizballah relies upon that provided by Hamzeh as it is perhaps the most accurate and comprehensive available in open source literature. See Hamzeh, A. N. (2004).

controlled Shia community, and the Executive Council which handles the day-to-day activities of the organization through its eight units.

The eight units of the Executive Council can be viewed as the organization's third tier and is further subdivided into the Social Unit which oversees welfare services to members, supporters, and the families of martyrs; the Islamic Health Unit which provides health care; the Education Unit, which provides financial aid and scholarships; the Information Unit, which controls the organization's media outlets and propaganda campaigns; the Syndicate Unit, which oversees professional associations; the External Relations Unit, which acts as a liaison between Hizballah and the government; the Finance Unit, which is responsible for fundraising, expenditures, and budgeting; and the Engagement and Coordination Unit, which is responsible for general security and addressing threats against the organization. There are two additional components that fall outside the primary hierarchy and report solely to the Shura Council, the Islamic Resistance and the Security Apparatus. The Islamic Resistance is the closest entity Hizballah has to a standing army. The Security Apparatus is broken into two parts, the internal security, which polices the Hizballah membership, and the external security which is responsible for countering foreign intelligence services. The final components organized under the Executive Council and Military and Security Apparatus are the various geographic regions broken into Beirut, Biq'a, and South Lebanon and corresponding sectors, branches and groups. In whole, it is estimated that Hizballah has several thousand supporters and members and a few hundred terrorist operatives.[21]

Hizballah was designated as a Foreign Terrorist Organization by the US Department of State in 1997 based on the terror campaign it began in the 1980s. The bombings of the US Embassy and the Marine barracks were soon followed by the 1984 kidnapping and detention of seventeen Americans in Lebanon. The last hostage was finally released in December 1991. In June 1985, hijackers overtook TWA Flight 847 in route from Athens to Rome. One hundred and forty-three passengers and crew members were held hostage as they were shuttled back and forth from Beirut to Algiers over a four-day period.[22] During the ordeal, Robert D. Stethem, a Navy diver on board the aircraft, was murdered and dumped on the tarmac at Beirut International Airport prior to all of the remaining passengers eventually being released. During the 1990s, Hizballah was focused primarily on expelling Israel from southern Lebanon, however, working under a front organization, Hizballah is believed to have detonated a car bomb outside the Israeli embassy in Buenos Aires, Argentina, killing 32 people in 1992. Two years later, in 1994, a second attack in the form of another vehicle bomb was detonated outside the Israeli-Argentine Mutual Association (AMIA) in Buenos Aires, killing 86 people. As mentioned before, prior to the September 11, 2001 attacks Hizballah was responsible for killing more Americans than any other terrorist organization.

21. US Department of State (2005).
22. Testrake, J. (1987) *Triumph over terror on Flight 847*, Fleming H. Revell Company, Old Tappan.

Intellectual Property Crime

One criminal enterprise Hizballah has profited from is Intellectual Property Crime (IPC). According to Ronald K. Noble, Secretary General for the International Criminal Police Organization, intellectual property is defined as:

> [T]he legal rights that correspond to intellectual activity in the industrial, scientific, and artistic fields. These legal rights, most commonly in the form of patents, trademarks, and copyright, protect the moral and economic rights of the creators, in addition to the creativity and dissemination of their work, Industrial property, which is part of intellectual property, extends protection to inventions and industrial designs.[23]

Therefore, IPC refers to "...the counterfeiting or pirating of goods for sale where the consent of the rights holder has not been obtained".[24] The World Customs Organization reported there were over 4,000 cases in 2004 involving the seizure of more than 166 million counterfeit or pirated articles by customs officials.[25]

IPC is considered a low risk, high gain crime meaning it has the potential to provide considerable monetary rewards but does not carry substantial penalties if caught. As one suspect in an IPC investigation explained "It's better than the dope business, no one[']s going to prison for DVDs".[26] This makes IPC an attractive enterprise to organized crime, street gangs, and international terrorists associated with groups such as Hizballah. Terrorist groups typically take two types of roles in IPC.[27] The first type of role is direct involvement; where the group is implicated in the production, distribution, or sale of counterfeit goods and uses the money to fund its activities. The second is indirect involvement; where sympathizers or militants are involved in IPC and remit some of the profits back to the group through couriers or money wires via third parties. It appears Hizballah is indirectly involved in IPC as its members and supporters are committing the act of pirating intellectual property and then funneling the proceeds back to the group via third parties.

Hizballah's profiting from IPC was publicized in February 2000 when Paraguayan authorities arrested Khalil Mehri, a Lebanese businessman, at his apartment in Ciudad del Este.[28] Initially, authorities were interested in

23. *Intellectual property crimes: Are proceeds from counterfeited good funding terrorism?: Hearing before the Committee on International Relations, House of Representatives* (2003) 108th cong, 1st sess, GPO, Washington, DC. Available at: http://wwwc.house.gov/international_relations/108/nob0716.htm (retrieved 11 November 2005).
24. Ibid.
25. World Customs Organization (2006) 'The first review: Customs and Counterfeiting 2004', Press Release, August 18. Available at: http://www.wcoomd.org/ie/En/en.html (retrieved 27 August 2006).
26. *Counterfeit goods: Easy cash for criminals and terrorists: Hearing before the Committee on Homeland Security and Governmental Affairs, United States Senate* (2005) 109th cong, 1st sess, GPO, Washington, DC. Available at: http://hsgac.senate.gov/_files/TestimonyStedman.pdf (retrieved 16 July 2006).
27. *Intellectual property crimes* (2003).
28. Hudson, R. (2003) *Terrorist and organized crime groups in the Tri-Border Area (TBA) of South America*, Federal Research Division, Library of Congress, Washington, DC.

questioning him in the 1992 bombing of the Israeli embassy and the 1994 bombing of the Argentine Israelite Mutual Association but, instead, they found software with fund-raising propaganda for Hizballah's Al-Muqawamah (Islamic Resistance) and Al-Shahid, an organization dedicated to protecting the families of martyrs, along with money transfers to Canada, Chile, Lebanon, and the U.S. totaling over $700,000. Mehri was charged with piracy of computer software and compact disks, selling millions of dollars worth of counterfeit software, and funneling the profits to Hizballah. Mehri was soon released on bail and escaped to Syria via Sao Paulo, Brazil, and Paris, France before the court formally charged him with violating copyright laws and aiding a criminal enterprise.[29]

Paraguayan authorities soon discovered another link to IPC operations in the Tri-Border area (TBA) of Argentina, Brazil, and Paraguay—Assad Barakat. Barakat emigrated to Paraguay at the age of 17 with his father to escape the turmoil of the Lebanese civil war.[30] Assad worked as a street peddler before opening Casa Apollo, an electronics wholesale store in a stall at the Page shopping gallery in Ciudad del Este, and Barakat Ltd., an import-export business, which were used as front companies to operate a variety of illegal fund-raising operations.[31] Barakat has been described as the leader of Hizballah's financial network in the TBA and having connections to many high-ranking Hizballah officials.[32] He is reported to be the deputy to Hizballah financial director, Ali Kazan, and primary liaison in the TBA for Hizballah's Secretary General, Hassan Nasrallah. Barakat is also believed to have served as a treasurer for Hizballah and carried contributions to the organization in Lebanon. When Paraguayan authorities raided Barakat's shop in September 2001, they discovered a money remittance operation evidenced by monthly transfers to the Middle East totaling $250,000, bank drafts of $524,000 to Lebanon, two co-conspirators who sent half a million dollars to Canada, Chile, and the US, and a letter from a Hizballah commander congratulating Barakat for financing activities in the Middle East.[33]

In addition to engaging in drug smuggling, money laundering, fraud, currency counterfeiting, and extortion, Barakat used his shop in the Page gallery to sell huge quantities of pirated software smuggled into the region from Hong Kong.[34] When Paraguayan authorities seized 5,000 pirated Nintendo video games valued at $160,000 in the Chaco region of Bolivia and Paraguay, they learned Barkat had set up two shipment routes: one by sea and another by air. He used several businesses he owned in the Chilean port city of Iquique as a trans-shipment point to move the merchandise by land through the Chaco region to his shop in Ciudad del Este. In a second raid in October 2002 in Ciudad del Este, authorities seized

29. Madani, B. (2002).
30. Hudson, R. (2003).
31. Ibid; US Department of the Treasury (2004) 'Treasury designates Islamic Extremist, two companies supporting Hizballah in Tri-Border Area', Press Release, June 10. Available at: http://www.treas.gov/press/releases/js1720.htm (retrieved 26 July 2006).
32. US Department of the Treasury (2004).
33. Hudson, R. (2003).
34. Ibid.

4,600 falsified compact discs and 80 copy machines capable of cloning up to 20,000 compact discs per day in a clandestine lab located in the same building Mehri was arrested. Barakat is currently serving a six-and-a-half year sentence in Paraguay after Brazilian authorities detained him in June 2002.[35]

Hizballah may also be profiting from the commission of intellectual property theft in North America. During a recent hearing conducted by the US Senate Committee on Homeland Security and Governmental Affairs, Los Angeles County Sheriff's Department Lieutenant John C. Stedman[36] detailed two instances in which his investigative team encountered what he believed were indications that some associates of Hizballah may be involved in IPC in Los Angeles, California. The first instance was experienced while executing an IPC related search warrant of a suspect's home. During the search he saw small Hizballah flags displayed in the suspect's bedroom along with a photograph of Secretary General Hassan Nasrallah. The suspect's wife asked Lt. Stedman if he knew the individual in the portrait to which he responded in the affirmative. The wife explained, "We love him because he protects us from the Jews." The investigators also found dozens of audio tapes of Nasrallah's speeches and a locket which contained a picture of the male suspect on one side and a picture of Nasrallah on the other. The second instance involved the execution of a search warrant at a clothing store in which thousands of dollars in counterfeit clothing and two unregistered firearms were seized. The suspect revealed a tattoo of the Hizballah flag on his arm while being booked into custody.

Stedman explained that one of the biggest issues for those who commit IPC is how to disperse the money generated by the enterprise.[37] He identified one instance, not explicitly identified as being linked to Hizballah, in which a suspect who was arrested at Los Angeles International airport by US Customs officers had more than $230,000 strapped to her body. She told authorities that she was traveling to Lebanon for "vacation". The suspect was soon identified as the owner of a chain of cigarettes shops. Investigators seized more than 1,000 cartons of counterfeit cigarettes, an additional $70,000 in cash, and wire transfers to banks throughout the world.

Drug Trafficking

The illegal drug trade has proven to be another profitable enterprise for the Lebanese Hizballah. While testifying before a US Congressional Subcommittee, Ambassador-at-large for counterterrorism, Francis X. Taylor, stated that drug trafficking, in particular, is one illicit venture terrorist organizations have used to replace funding lost as a result of declining state sponsorship.[38] He went on to say that the terrorist organizations' role in the drug trade has taken several forms, ranging from protecting production operations to directly trafficking illicit drugs.

35. US Department of the Treasury (2004).
36. *Counterfeit goods*, 2005.
37. Ibid.
38. *Narco-terrorism: International drug trafficking and terrorism - A dangerous mix* (2002) Hearing before the Committee on the Judiciary United States Senate, 108th cong, 1st sess, GPO, Washington, DC.

Both drug traffickers and terrorist organizations have similar needs, such as covert funding sources, weapons, and operational security, and possess similar skill sets, such as the production of fraudulent documents, establishing front organizations, money laundering, and the clandestine movement of logistics and people. These similarities have made terrorist organizations a natural and effective fit for participation in the drug trade.

Hizballah's involvement in the drug trade may have begun with the smuggling of opiates out of the Bi'qa Valley, a Hizballah stronghold.[39] Lebanese and Syrian farmers have traditionally raised opium poppies and cannabis in the region to make hashish for local consumption.[40] However, the cultivation and processing of opium and cannabis has been largely suppressed since the Lebanese and Syrian governments joined international drug eradication initiatives in the early 1990s. According to the International Policy Institute for Counterterrorism, the success of the government-led eradication program prompted Hizballah to find an alternate drug supply, mainly from the Latin America route (Colombia, Peru, Brazil, etc.) and the Far East route (Pakistan, Afghanistan, Iran, Turkey, and Syria).[41] The Tri-Border area is believed to be a focal point for Hizballah's drug trafficking operations in Latin America as evidenced by several recent, highly publicized cases.

In January 2003, authorities in São Paulo, Brazil uncovered a Lebanese organized crime ring smuggling between 400 and 1,000 kilos of Colombian cocaine per month through Foz do Iguaçu and Ciudad del Este.[42] One of those arrested was Bassam Naboulsi, a Lebanese businessman living in the TBA whose brother, Hassan, owned Hassan International, located in Ciudad del Este's Page shopping gallery. The investigation revealed a link to another criminal network managed by the Naboulsi brothers' cousin, Assad Ahmad Barakat. The connection between the "Barakat clan" and drug trafficking emerged in May 2003 when Hassan Abdallah Dayoub, a Lebanese merchant living in Ciudad del Este and the cousin of Barakat, was arrested in Asuncion's Silvio Pettirossi Airport.[43] In his possession was an electric piano with 2.3 kilos of cocaine hidden inside. Hired by Barakat to act as a "mule," Dayoub is believed by authorities to have planned to sell the drugs in Damascus, Syria. Once in the Argentine capital, Dayoub intended to transfer to an Iberia Airlines flight to Madrid, where he would proceed on to his final destination of Damascus.

In June 2005, law enforcement officials dismantled an international drug ring in Quito, Ecuador, for trafficking cocaine to Europe, Asia, and other South American countries.[44] Initiated in September and dubbed Operation Damascus, the investigation resulted in the arrest of five male suspects from Lebanon, Syria, Nigeria, Algiers, and Turkey, and one Ecuadorian woman. It also resulted in the

39. Ibid.
40. Berry, L., Curtis, G. E., Hudson, R. A. & Kollars, N. A. (2002) *A global overview of narcotics-funded terrorist and other extremist groups*, Federal Research Division, Library of Congress, Washington, DC.
41. Ibid.
42. Hudson, R. (2003).
43. Ibid.
44. '"Hezbollah drugs ring" broken up', *BBC News*, June 22, 2005. Available at: http://news.bbc.co.uk/2/hi/americas/4117960.stm (retrieved 15 July 2005).

seizure of two automobiles, two motorcycles, two pistols, two shotguns, and US $174,115 in cash.[45] The ring was allegedly led by Rady Zaiter, a Lebanese man who used his restaurant in the capital city as a front for the operation. The cocaine which originated from Colombia was hidden in suitcases equipped with false bottoms and in the stomachs of drug couriers, and smuggled in shipments worth $1 million a piece.[46] According to an internal police report obtained by the Associated Press, evidence collected in the case indicated up to 70 percent of the drug ring's profits were funneled to Hizballah.[47]

The dismantling of the Ecuadorian drug ring is reported to have led to the arrest of a second drug ring consisting of 19 additional suspects in Brazil and the United States.[48] Fourteen Lebanese men and three locals were arrested in Sao Paulo, Brazil, for allegedly smuggling 120 kilograms (270 pounds) of cocaine a month to Europe and the Middle East.[49] Fake documents and approximately US $400,000 in cash were confiscated during the arrest. The ring employed about 20 Brazilian, African, Canadian, Dutch, and American drug couriers to transport the cocaine aboard flights bound for Germany, Portugal, Spain, and countries in the Middle East. In fact, the investigation was initiated when two American smugglers were arrested in Turkey in June 2004. Brazilian officials indicated that there was no evidence that profits from the scheme went to Hizballah. Instead, a majority of the money was reportedly invested in real estate in Lebanon.

Hizballah's involvement in the illicit drug trade is not limited to South America. In an interview with the Cable News Network's Wolf Blitzer, former Drug Enforcement Administration (DEA) director Asia Hutchinson stated that a 12 month long investigation concluded in 2001 provided the first instance in which millions of dollars in profits from the sale of pseudoephedrine in the US were being sent back to the Middle East and into the hands of terrorist organizations, particularly Hizballah.[50] The DEA initiated the investigation, dubbed Operation Mountain Express III, to reduce the availability of methamphetamine in the United States by cutting off the supply of pseudoephedrine, an essential ingredient in the manufacturing of the illicit drug.[51] While Operation Mountain Express I and II

45. 'Ecuador links drug bust, Hizb Allah', Al Jazeera.net, June 22, 2005. Available at: http://english.aljazeera.net/NR/exeres/CA2688EC-A3DB-400E-BCB1-E7BCE2AB6251.htm (retrieved 17 February 2006).

46. 'Police link Ecuador drug ring to Hezbollah: Authorities bust operation suspected of financing Muslim group', MSNBC.com, June 22, 2005. Available at: http://www.newsweek.co.uk/id/8312121/print/1/displaymode/1098/ (retrieved 17 July 2006).

47. 'Ecuador links drug bust, Hizb Allah', June 22, 2005.

48. '"Hezbollah drugs ring" broken up', June 22, 2005.

49. 'Brazilian police arrest 14 Lebanese and three locals in drug ring bust', Associated Press, June 17, 2005, *Terrorism Knowledge Base*, Memorial Institute for the Prevention of Terrorism, Oklahoma City. Available at: http://www.tkb.org/NewsStory.jsp?storyID = 71417 (retrieved 19 February 2006).

50. 'CNN Wolf Blitzer Reports: DEA investigates terrorist connection to drug trafficking in U.S.', CNN.com/Transcripts, September 2, 2002. Available at: http://cgi.cnn.com/TRANSCRIPTS/0209/02/wbr.00.html (retrieved 19 February 2006).

51. US Drug Enforcement Administration (2002) 'More than 100 arrested in nationwide methamphetamine investigation', News Release, January 10. Available at: http://www.dea.gov/pubs/pressrel/pr011002.html (retrieved 19 February 2006).

targeted the domestic supply of pseudoephedrine, Operation Mountain Express III focused on the pre-cursor's import from Canada.

The success of Operations Mountain Express I and II forced traffickers to begin smuggling the precursor chemical in from Canada via the Ambassador Bridge and into Detroit, Michigan.[52] The pseudoephedrine was smuggled into the US hidden in tractor trailers disguised as government and private parcel couriers. Shipments of the precursor chemical grew from 1,000 tablet bottles to 32,000 tablet bottles and eventually to huge barrels with tens of thousands of tablets. Detroit and Chicago, Illinois were used as distribution hubs before the precursor chemical was smuggled to California where it was distributed to meth "super labs" and converted into methamphetamine by Mexico-based drug traffickers. Operation Mountain Express III ended with the arrest of 371 individuals in 12 cities and the seizure of approximately $2 million in cash and close to 42 million pseudoephedrine tablets which, if used to manufacture methamphetamine, would have yielded close to 3,000 pounds with a street value of more than $19 million.

Cigarette Smuggling

Another US-based Hizballah criminal operation was revealed in July 2000 when federal authorities levied charges against 25 suspects for their involvement in racketeering, money laundering, immigration fraud, credit card fraud, marriage fraud, visa fraud, bribery, and providing material support to a terrorist organization.[53] Dubbed Operation Smokescreen, the investigation began in the mid-1990s after an off-duty sheriff, working as a security officer at a cigarette wholesaler in Statesville, North Carolina, watched three Arabic-speaking men enter the store, collect 299 cartons of cigarettes apiece, pay for the merchandise in cash, and load the goods into minivans before heading north.[54] With the passing of the Contraband Trafficking Act of 1978, it is a federal offense to transport more then 60,000 cigarettes or 300 cartons from one state to another without proof the appropriate state tax had been paid in each state. Realizing this, the off-duty deputy reported his suspicions to the Bureau of Alcohol, Tobacco, and Firearms (ATF) which initiated an investigation.

The ATF soon discovered a multimillion dollar cigarette smuggling ring which was using a classic organized crime scheme.[55] The ring purchased cigarettes in a

52. US Drug Enforcement Administration (2002) *DEA Update, 1 (01)*, January 23. Available at: http://www.Usdoj.gov/dea/pubs/update/012302.html (retrieved 19 February 2006).

53. US Federal Bureau of Investigation (nd) 'Operation 'Smokescreen': FBI dismantles terrorist financial support cell', Press Release, Washington, DC. Available at: http://www.fbi.gov/page2/smokescreen2.htm (retrieved 10 March 2003).

54. Bell, K. (2003) 'Hizballah fund raising in the American Heartland', *Policywatch*, no. 700, January 15. Available at: http://washingtoninstitute.org/templateC05.php?CID = 1578 (retrieved 23 July 2006).

55. Kaplan, D. E. (2003) 'Homegrown terrorists: How a Hezbollah cell made millions in sleepy Charlotte, N.C.', *U.S. News and World Report*, March 10. Available at: http://www.usnews.com?usnews/news/articles/030310/10hez.htm (retrieved 23 July 2006).

low tax state, in this case, North Carolina whose rate was 50 cents a carton, and transported them to Michigan, a high tax state which charged $7.50 a carton. The ring was also taking advantage of the fact that neither North Carolina nor Michigan marked cigarettes with a tax stamp making it difficult for authorities to determine if appropriate taxes were paid. By exploiting the discrepancy in tax rates, the smugglers stood to make roughly $13,000 per van load.[56] In all, the ring is estimated to have purchased $8 million in cigarettes making roughly $2 million in profit. As authorities began to make preparations to dismantle the ring, agents from the Federal Bureau of Investigation approached the federal prosecutor, informing him that they had stumbled onto a Hizballah cell operating out of Charlotte, North Carolina, and explained that they already had two of the cell members under electronic surveillance.[57]

The leader of the ring was Mohamad Youssef Hammoud who was born in September 1973 in the Beirut neighborhood of Bourj al-Barajneh.[58] By the age of 15, Hammoud had received combat training from Hizballah and was serving in its militia.[59] In 1992, Hammoud traveled to the Caribbean island of Margarita, 25 miles off the coast of Venezuela, after he was unable to acquire a visa to the US. Once there, he obtained a counterfeit visa and flew to New York where he was promptly detained. Hammoud had been well prepared on how to obtain asylum for entry into the US and spun a tale of having been kidnapped by the Israeli-sponsored South Lebanese Army and interrogated before being returned to the streets of Beirut. He was then met with suspicion from Hizballah who thought he may be collaborating with the Israelis. Caught between two opposing forces, Hammoud explained that he traveled to the US fearing for his life.[60] He eventually gained permanent status, as did other members of the cell, by paying a woman to enter into a sham marriage with him. Hammoud settled in Charlotte, North Carolina, where he began organizing the crime ring with his brothers, cousins, and friends from the old Beirut neighborhood.

Members of the cigarette smuggling ring became well versed in the art of criminal conspiracy. They opened multiple bank accounts, fraudulently obtained credit cards, and learned how to establish multiple identities by obtaining the names of departing international students by retrieving corresponding driver's licenses, social security numbers, and Immigration and Naturalization Service work authorizations and credit histories.[61] Many of the credit card scam and identity theft skills were taught by Said Mohamad Harb, one of the cell members who was described by authorities as "a one-man crime wave".[62] Through the assistance of the Canadian Security Intelligence Service, it was revealed that Harb was the key link in the cell's provision of material support to Hizballah. Harb was

56. Bell, K. (2003).
57. Ibid. Kaplan, D. E. (2003).
58. Diaz, T. & Newman, B. (2005) *Lightning out of Lebanon: Hezbollah terrorists on American soil*, Ballantine Books, New York.
59. Kaplan, D. E. (2003).
60. Diaz, T. & Newman, B. (2005).
61. Bell, K. (2003).
62. Kaplan, D. E. (2003).

childhood friends with Mohammud Dbouk who was sent to Canada from Lebanon by Hizballah's chief procurement officer to lead its North American Procurement Program which was charged with obtaining dual use military equipment from retail outlets in Canada and the US.[63] Through Dbouk, Harb arranged for the Charlotte cell members to fulfill equipment orders from Hizballah in Lebanon in exchange for a percentage of the purchase price. The Charlotte cell provided items such as night-vision goggles, cameras, global-positioning systems, metal-detection gear, video equipment, computers, and stun guns.

In July 2002, Mohammad Hammoud received 155 years in prison after being found guilty of cigarette smuggling, money laundering, immigration fraud, providing material support to a foreign terrorist organization, and violating the Racketeer Influenced and Corrupt Organizations (RICO) Act.[64] Mohammad's brother, Chawki, received 51 months of imprisonment. Three of the defendants pled guilty in exchange for their cooperation while prosecutors dropped the cases against two of the defendants for unspecified reasons. For their connection to the smuggling scheme, seven defendants received sentences ranging from 24 months probation to 46 months imprisonment. For the six connected to the marriage fraud aspect of the indictment, sentences ranged from 12 to 24 months probation. The five remaining defendants are still fugitives of justice.

In a related case, on March 29, 2006, a Federal Grand Jury in Detroit, Michigan, charged 19 defendants with operating a global racketeering conspiracy involved in trafficking contraband cigarettes, counterfeiting Zig Zag rolling papers and Viagra, producing counterfeit cigarette tax stamps, transporting stolen property, and laundering money from 1996 to 2002.[65] According to reports, Imad Hammoud and his partner Hassan Makki, who in 2003 pled guilty in federal court to racketeering and providing material support to Hizballah, obtained up to $500,000 worth of low-taxed or untaxed cigarettes a week in North Carolina, some of which were supplied by Mohamad Hammoud and the North Carolina cell, and on the Cattaraugus Indian Reservation near Irving, New York, and transported the cigarettes for resale in Michigan and New York.[66] Counterfeit cigarette tax stamps were applied to the packages to give the appearance that state taxes had been paid. Thousands of cartons were also sold after they were stolen from the R.J. Reynolds tobacco company in Kentucky.

63. Bell, S. (2004) *Cold Terror: How Canada nurtures and exports terrorism to the world*, John Wiley & Sons Inc., New York.
64. National Memorial Institute for the Prevention of Terrorism (2006) 'Legal case profiles: 00-CR-147', *Terrorism Knowledge Base*, July 11, Available at: http://www.tkb.org/CaseHome.jsp?caseid = 615 (retrieved 26 July 2006).
65. US Department of Justice, United States Attorney, Eastern District of Michigan (2006) 'Nineteen charged with racketeering to support terrorist organization', Press Release, March 29. Available at: http://www.usdoj.gov/usao/mie/press/mar_2006.pdf (retrieved 26 July 2006).
66. Egan, P. (2006) '18 charged in smuggling case', *Detroit News*, March 30. Available at: http://www.detnews.com/apps/pbcs.dll/article?AID = /20060330/METRO/603300338/1003 (retrieved 26 July 2006); LaFaive, M. D. (2006) 'Terrorists profit from smuggling', *Budget & Tax News*, June 1. Available at: http://www.heartland.org/Article.cfm?artid = 19067 (retrieved 26 July 2006).

The indictment alleged that the enterprise operated from Lebanon, Canada, Brazil, Paraguay, China, North Carolina, Florida, and Dearborn, Michigan and perpetrated crimes in the states of Michigan, California, Florida, Georgia, Illinois, North Carolina, and West Virginia.[67] A portion of the illicit profits were funneled to Hizballah. Funds were also collected in the form of a "Resistance Tax" above the black market price per carton which customers were told would go to Hizballah and charitable donations to benefit Hizballah's orphans and martyrs program in Southern Lebanon. In July 2006, two of the defendants pled guilty to their involvement in violating the RICO statute and face a maximum penalty of 20 years in prison and a $250,000 fine, eight of the other defendants will face trial in January, and the remaining defendants are wanted as fugitives.[68]

Exploiting the African Diamond Trade

The link between the diamond trade and international terrorism was publicized in November 2001 when the *Washington Post* published an article claiming international terrorist groups, namely al Qaeda and Hizballah, had made millions of dollars from the illicit sale of diamonds mined by rebel groups in Sierra Leone.[69] The topic of international terrorists profiting from the illicit diamond trade received a more comprehensive treatment when the Global Witness, a British non-governmental organization dedicated to exposing the relationship between natural resource exploitation and human rights abuses, published "For a few dollars more: How al Qaeda moved into the diamond trade".[70] The report detailed how international terrorists had infiltrated West African diamond networks by taking advantage of illicit trading structures, weak governments, and lax trade regulations.

The US General Accounting Office (GAO) identified the illegal trafficking of precious metals and stones as one means by which terrorist groups raise funds, explaining that illicit diamond dealing is an attractive criminal enterprise for several reasons.[71] Diamonds serve as a form of currency that can be used for money

67. Egan, P. (2006).
68. US Department of Justice, United States Attorney, Eastern District of Michigan (2006), 'Two men plead guilty to racketeering', Press Release, July 7. Available at: http://www.usdoj.gov/usao/mie/press/2006/2006-07-10_ihamadeh.pdf (retrieved 26 July 2006).
69. Farah, D. (2001) 'Al Qaeda cash tied to diamond trade: Sale of gems from Sierra Leone rebels raised millions, sources say', *Washington Post*, November 2, Available at: http://www.washingtonpost.com/ac2/wp-dyn?pagename = article&node = &contentId = A27281-2001Nov1 (retrieved 1 November 2005).
70. Global Witness (2003) *For a few dollars more: How al Qaeda moved into the diamond trade*. Available at: http://www.globalwitness.org/reports/show.php/en.00041.html (retrieved 1 November 2005).
71. US Government Accounting Office (2003) 'Terrorist financing: U.S. agencies should systematically assess terrorists' use of alternative financing mechanisms', Washington, DC. Available at: http://www.gao.gov/new.items/d04163.pdf (retrieved 1 November 2005); FBI investigation did not reveal any evidence to suggest this link. The Global Witness quickly rebutted that the scope of the FBI investigation was far too limited to adequately investigate the issue. See Donahue, P. J. (2003) 'Treasury Department disputes diamonds and terrorism report', December 19. Available at: http://www.professionaljeweler.com/archives/news/2003/121903story.html (retrieved 1 November 2005). As a result, terrorists and the diamond trade, as a whole, remains a contentious issue.

laundering, exchanged for cash, or to purchase an array of illicit goods such as arms or drugs. The international diamond industry is fragmented and there is limited scrutiny of the flow of diamond from mine to consumer. In addition, there are numerous small mining operations across Africa which has porous borders and little rule of law, making it less complicated for traders to acquire and smuggle diamonds. Areas such as Sierra Leone became notorious for the sale and export of conflict diamonds, the name given to diamonds mined in a war zone and used to finance armed conflicts. The Revolutionary United Front used the proceeds of the sales to drive their failed attempt to overthrow the government of Sierra Leone, during which they committed countless human rights abuses.[72] Diamonds are conducive to smuggling because of their low weight, lack of odor, and untraceable origins. Additionally, they can be easily sold on the black market. Authorities report that in Antwerp, the world's largest diamond trading center, a substantial number of diamonds are sold on the black market with no transaction records.[73]

Hizballah has been profiting off the African diamond market since the 1980s when it first began establishing networks of operatives in the region.[74] In the Congo, Hizballah is reported to take a direct role in the market by purchasing diamonds from miners and local merchants at a fraction of the market value and selling them in Antwerp, Bombay, and Dubai.[75] In West Africa, Hizballah is reported to be siphoning off profits from the region's diamond trade through the extortion of Lebanese merchants.[76] As the Deputy Chief of mission for the US Embassy in Sierra Leone explained, "One thing is incontrovertible is the financing of Hizballah... It's not even an open secret, there is no secret. There's a lot of social pressure and extortionate pressure brought to bear: 'You had better support our cause, or we'll visit your people back home'".[77]

With roughly 100,000 Lebanese living in Côte D'Ivoire (formerly the Ivory Coast), 20,000 in Senegal, and 6,000 in Sierra Leone, West Africa plays host to a substantial Lebanese community.[78] Their history in West Africa began around the turn of the century as immigrants moved to the region in an effort to escape the economic and population problems of Lebanon. The British colonial authorities welcomed the immigrants and provided them with loans and other incentives in hopes that they would displace local merchants in the commodities market with the African interior. The Lebanese Shia merchants took on a major role in the

72. Farah, D. (2004) *Blood from stones: The secret financial network of terror*, Broadway Books, New York.
73. US Government Accounting Office (2003).
74. Farah, D. (2001).
75. Farah, D. (2001) 'Digging up Congo's dirty gems', *Washington Post*, December 30. Available at: http://www.globalpolicy.org/security/issues/diamond/2001/1230hezbol.htm (retrieved 1 November 2005).
76. Global Witness (2003).
77. 'Hizballah extorts diamond profits from Lebanese, U.S. says', *Rapaport News*, June 30, 2004, Available at: http://www.rap.net.news/newsitem.asp?num = 9852&type = all&topic = conflict (retrieved 11 November 2005).
78. 'Hezbollah and the West African diamond trade', *Middle East Intelligence Bulletin*, vol. 6, 2004. Available at: http://www.meib.org/articles/0407_12.htm (retrieved 1 November 2005).

diamond market when the precious gems were discovered in eastern Sierra Leone in 1930. Their success in the lucrative diamond market has enabled them to move into other positions of influence such as the government.[79]

It is unclear exactly how much revenue Hizballah could be generating from this illicit enterprise but the figures may be substantial. A Union Transport Africaines Flight bound for Beirut crashed in December 2003 upon take-off from Contonou, Benin, in West Africa. According to media reports, a foreign relations official of the African branch of Hizballah was onboard the aircraft couriering $2 million to the group in Beirut.[80] The money is said to have been contributions from wealthy Lebanese nationals living in Africa, although there was no distinction between money that may have been voluntary giving and that which was extorted.

Conclusion

The gradual decrease in state sponsorship for terrorism has forced many terrorist organizations to seek alternative sources of funding. The Lebanese Hizballah is no exception. It has come to rely upon a worldwide network of members and supporters who engage in various forms of criminal enterprise and remand a portion of its illicit profits back to the group. Regardless if the Hizballah leadership is completely witting of the source, it is presumed that generating its own funding has enabled the organization to become less dependant upon Iran, whose funding has fluctuated over the years, and more self-sufficient. Furthermore, this source of funding may prove vital in the aftermath of recent fighting between Hizballah and the IDF. The group will desperately need money to rebuild its weapon and equipment stockpiles and infrastructure. It will also need money to rebuild goodwill among the Lebanese Shia population. In mid-August, its Secretary General pledged to pay for rent and furniture to those Lebanese Shia whose homes were destroyed.[81]

It is anticipated that Hizballah's criminal networks will remain dynamic and adaptable in the face of law enforcement initiatives to cut off terrorism funding. According to the FBI, terrorists will switch to another commodity or industry once they realize authorities have become aware of their illegal activities.[82] With this utilitarian aim, these networks may become active in any number of illegal enterprises in an effort to meet the organization's financial needs. The enterprise may have been around for a while, like cigarette smuggling and trafficking in stolen automobiles, or it may yet to be contrived. The only limit is that the enterprise is lucrative and relatively undetected.

79. Farah, D. (2004).
80. 'Hezbollah profiting from African diamonds', *Washington Post*, June 29, 2004. Available at: http://www.washingtonpost.com/wp-dyn/articles/A15153-2004Jun29_2.html (retrieved 1 November 2005).
81. 'Hezbollah pays out $12K in U.S. cash to Lebanese who lost their homes', FoxNews.com, August 18, 2005. Available at: http://www.foxnews.com/story/0,2933,209340,00.html (retrieved 19 August 2006).
82. US Government Accounting Office (2003).

One final observation is warranted when assessing Hizballah's global criminal operations. There is concern that those who are participating in illicit enterprises worldwide could be tasked with committing an act of terrorism on behalf of Hizballah or at the behest of Iran.[83] As stated earlier, Argentine authorities were first interested in questioning Ali Mehri in connection to the Buenos Aires bombings before he was arrested for IPC related crimes. Authorities determined that Assad Barakat played a crucial role in financing the AMIA bombing by creating a cell to arrange for the import of the materials into the TBA to be used in the attack.[84] Videotapes seized from the home of Mohamad Hammoud's in Charlotte, North Carolina, featured Hizballah members with explosives strapped to their waists pledging "...to detonate ourselves to shake the ground under the feet of our enemies, America and Israel".[85] A confidential source stated that Hammoud would not have hesitated in carrying out a terrorist attack in the US had Hizballah issued an authorization.[86] With an intimate knowledge of the inner workings of smuggling routes, clandestine money transfers, and illicit materials procurement, Hizballah may be well positioned to perpetrate a terrorist attack almost anywhere in the world.

83. Ephron, D. & Isikoff, M. (2006) 'Nasrallah's men inside America', MSNBC.com, August 14. Available at: http://www.msnbc.msn.com/id/14208386 (retrieved 19 August 2006).
84. Hudson, R. (2003).
85. Burger, T. J. & Shannon, E. (2003) 'Hizballah Is Moving Up the Threat Chart', Time.com, February 25. Available at: http://www.time.com/time/world/article/0,8599,426711,00.html (retrieved 23 July 2006).
86. Ibid.

The Criminalisation of Russian State Security

Mark Galeotti

In 2004, as part of its campaign to revive public support for the armed forces (and to stem the tide of draft-dodging), the Russian ministry of defence issued a series of posters including one which sought to highlight soldiers' roles in fighting crime. In garish tones and simple lines reminiscent of Soviet-era propaganda, the poster shows lantern-jawed soldiers holding at gunpoint swarthy criminals while a female police officer pulls contraband from their car. Vignettes in the background show masked commandoes taking out a terrorist and a Border Guard helicopter buzzing a smugglers' boat, as the smugglers desperately dump their illegal cargo into the sea.

What difference a decade makes. After all, in the 1990s, politicians and observers alike were often characterising the security apparatus as a threat rather than an asset to law and order. The parliamentarian Alexander Gurov, for example, one of

Dr Mark Galeotti is the Director of the Organised Russian and Eurasian Crime Research Unit at Keele University, UK, and Senior Lecturer in International History. His research concentrates on Russian and post-Soviet organised crime and security affairs in general. His most recent books are Global Crime Today (Routledge, 2005) and Soviet and Post-Soviet Organised Crime (Ashgate, 2002). He writes a monthly column in Jane's Intelligence Review and served a secondment as an advisor to the British Foreign Office 1997-98. He continues to work with a variety of government, law enforcement and commercial agencies.

the first Russian police (militia) officers seriously to look at organised crime, warned that police officers were becoming dominant forces in the country's underworld.[1] In 1994, investigative journalist Dmitri Kholodov wrote 'our Russian army is sliding down into a world of organised crime'.[2] Shortly thereafter, he was killed by a booby trap bomb, while investigating claims that commandos from the elite 16th Spetsnaz Brigade were training organised crime hitmen.[3] Meanwhile, Chechen rebels were buying their guns not just from individual soldiers but by the case-load direct from the military armouries and manufacturing plants of their enemies. In short, the 1990s saw not just a criminalisation of much of the Russian security forces but also their growing interpenetration with the wider 'civilian' underworld.

All elements of the security apparatus have played a role in fighting organised crime both within their own ranks but also society as a whole, from military units deployed to assist the police, to the way the espionage and counter-intelligence agencies - especially the Federal Security Service (FSB - *Federalnaya sluzhba bezopasnosti*) - now have fighting organised crime as one of their primary missions. The regular police of the Ministry of Internal Affairs (MVD - *Ministerstvo vnutrennykh del*) are, of course, at the front line. While there are dedicated investigation units at the local, regional[4] and national level, the pervasiveness of organised crime within the Russian economy and society means that few elements of the police do not have regular contact with it. Even the traffic police patrols have become used to waving past expensive foreign cars, which could contain a senior politician, a business leader or a successful criminal - none of whom any sensible Russian cop wants to cross. Thus, they operate in an environment in which the '*mafiya*' is at once ubiquitous but also often hard to distinguish from other powerful communities. Combined with the way that the '*mafiya*' is much more diffuse and networked than such counterparts[5] as the Japanese yakuza or Cosa Nostra crime families, this may explain why the Russian police concentrate much more on seeking to solve specific crimes instead of directly attacking the main groupings and their kingpins. In this, they buck the trend towards the intelligence-led and enterprise policing prevailing in much of the world. In part this reflects their problems in establishing positive relations in a society which still largely sees them an ineffective at best, corrupt at worst. It is also a by-product of a trend towards paramilitarisation dating back to the early 1990s,[6] and the

1. *Novaya gazeta*, January 30, 2001.
2. *Moskovskii komsomolets*, June 20, 1994.
3. *Radio Russia*, October 18, 1994, cited in *BBC Summary of World Broadcasts: former USSR* (henceforth *BBC SWB*), October 20, 1994; *Newsweek*, October 31, 1994; *The European*, November 4-10,1994.
4. The Russian Federation is a confederation of 21 republics and 67 other constituent units, including the metropola of Moscow and St. Petersburg, each of which has its own Interior Ministry or police command, responsible to the central MVD.
5. For further discussion of the networked nature of Russian organised crime, see Galeotti, M. (ed.) (2002) *Russian and Post-Soviet Organised Crime*, Ashgate, London; Varese, F. (2001) *The Russian Mafia*, OUP, Oxford.
6. Galeotti, M. (2003) 'Russian police reform: centralisation, modernisation and paramilitarisation', *Crime & Justice International*, no. 70.

common vice of agencies to stick with what they are comfortable with rather than taking an objective look as to whether it works.

However, while there has been real progress, ranging from anti-corruption campaigns within the police through to efforts to combat a culture of embezzlement and exploitation within the military, nonetheless the picture is actually rather less appealing than the poster might suggest. A culture of criminality is still widespread within the Russian security apparatus and for every arrest, many more crimes go unsolved or even unreported. Six soldiers were eventually charged with Kholodov's murder but cleared of any charges, for example, and the case is still open.[7] Initial admissions from Air Assault Force intelligence chief Colonel Pavel Popovskhikh that then-defence minister Pavel Grachev was furious about Kholodov's articles and demanded that he be 'dealt with' and 'have his mouth shut' have since been brushed aside.[8]

The Security Forces and Organised Crime

While understandably the Kremlin is most concerned about the rise of organised crime groupings within the security forces, in many ways the wider and more serious problem is the way that criminalised elements within them have become allies and service providers for the country's underworld.

The roots of this thriving relationship between the putative protectors of the state and the criminals are found in the culture of lawlessness, indiscipline, desperation and demoralisation within the security forces. In the Soviet era, corruption was endemic, but also kept within certain bounds, both by the KGB (which remained relatively 'clean') and also a widely-shared notion of the 'etiquette' of illegality. In this respect, the members of the security forces were simply observing an age-old Russian moral economy which distinguished between what was *prestuplenie*, a crime in the eyes of the law and what was *zlodeyanie*, morally wrong.[9] Historically, judicious bribe-taking was considered a perk of a police officer's job, counterbalancing the low official salary, but there was also a sense of the limits of such behaviour. As one retired officer told the author, the general rule of thumb was that the kind of misdemeanour which could be punished by a fine was fair game for a bribe - "after all, the criminal still gets to pay for his crime" - but that crimes for which the law stipulated a custodial sentence were deemed off-limits.[10] This may not have been as widely-accepted as he claimed, and there certainly were those police officers who were prepared to go much further, but nonetheless this does illustrate the implicit moral economy of police corruption

7. *Moscow Times*, June 27, 2002; *Interfax news agency*, June 10, 2004.
8. *Interfax news agency*, June 10, 2004; *Moscow Times*, June 11, 2004.
9. For further discussion of this, see Frank, S. (1999) *Crime, Cultural Conflict, and Justice in Rural Russia, 1856-1914*, University of California Press, Berkeley; Frierson, C. (1987) 'Crime and punishment in the Russian village', *Slavic Review*, vol. 46, no. 1; Galeotti, M. (2001) '"Who's the boss, us or the law?" The corrupt art of governing Russia', in *Bribery and Blat in Russia*, eds. Stephen Lovell *et al.*, Macmillan, Basingstoke.
10. Conversation, April 2001.

in the late Soviet era. Likewise, while it was accepted that a senior officer would rely on his rank to secure preferential accommodation and consumer goods for himself and his family, until the mid-1980s, there was a tacit 'sliding scale' as to just how far they could go. Above all, the understanding was that their perks were linked with their and their family's immediate lifestyles, and to use military office as a means to acquiring goods for sale or otherwise turning it into an illicit business was beyond the pale and fair game for the investigations of the KGB's Third Main Directorate, responsible for political control of the armed forces.

Criminality in the Ranks

However, from the twilight years of the Soviet Union through the 1990s to today's Russia, the security apparatus has suffered a steady decline in effectiveness, discipline and morale, and crime within the ranks has continued to grow.[11] Within the army, in part, this is a product of *dedovshchina*, 'grandfatherism', a tradition of hazing and exploitation, originally encouraged precisely as a means of keeping a large conscript army in control given the absence of an adequate cadre of professional non-commissioned officers.[12] Successive Human Rights Commissioners have highlighted the problem and the proportion of serious hazing-related crimes being prosecuted has begun to rise, but even so, the official figures - which are widely accepted as serious understatements - are that 6,000 servicemen suffered hazing in 2005 - of whom 16 died and 256 committed suicide.[13] It also reflects the poor conditions of service; through the 1990s wages continually failed to keep pace with inflation and were typically paid months in arrears, but even now, 165,000 officers - almost one in three career soldiers - still lack apartments.[14] The two Chechen wars have only served to exacerbate the problem, both by exposing soldiers to opportunities for looting and abuse of their powers but also by worsening the problem of draft-dodging, such that in many regions courts are offering petty offenders the choice of conscription instead of prison. In 2006, Defence Minister Sergei Ivanov admitted that over 20,000 crimes had been reported within the military in 2005,[15]

11. For general discussion of this problem, see Turbiville, G. (1995) 'Organized crime and the Russian armed forces', *Transnational Organized Crime*, vol. 1, no. 4; Staar, R. (1998) 'Russia's military: corruption in the higher ranks', *Perspective*, vol. 9, no. 2; Galeotti, M. (2001) 'The challenge of "soft security": crime, corruption and chaos', in *Securing Europe's East: new security challenges in postcommunist Europe*, eds. D. Averre & A. Cottey, Manchester University Press, Manchester.

12. See, for background, Human Rights Watch, *The Wrongs of Passage: Inhuman and Degrading Treatment of New Recruits in the Russian Armed Forces*, 2004, available at: http://hrw.org/reports/2004/russia1004/index.htm (accessed 10 October 2006) and the special issue on the subject of *The Journal of Power Institutions in Post-Soviet Societies*, iss. 1, 2004, available at: http://www.pipss.org/sommaire190.html (accessed 10 October 2006).

13. *Jurist*, February 3, 2006, available at: http://jurist.law.pitt.edu/paperchase/2006/02/russian-military-court-convicts.php (accessed 28 September 2006).

14. *RIA-Novosti* news agency, August 25, 2004.

15. *Interfax* news agency, February 15, 2006.

while the Main Military Prosecutor noted that the crime rate within the ranks continues to rise.[16]

Corruption and theft are rife. This was already becoming a problem as the USSR collapsed but reached epic proportions in the 1990s, especially thanks to the opportunities provided by force reductions (which allowed assets to be lost from the books and passed into private hands or sold at bargain prices[17]) and the withdrawal of forces from Germany (which was supported by German funds for rehousing, providing a lucrative target for embezzlement[18]). In 2003, Colonel General Georgy Oliynik, head of the defence ministry's finance department and thus senior auditor, was convicted with working with three other generals to siphon off up to $450 million of military funds in the mid-1990s.[19] The defence minister of the time, Pavel Grachev, even acquired the popular (if unfavourable) nickname 'Pasha Mercedes' following widespread allegations that he acquired one of a series of brand new luxury German cars bought with embezzled funds.[20]

The mid-1990s were a period of extraordinary and almost uncontrolled entrepreneurialism within the armed forces, almost all of which was criminal to a greater or lesser extent.[21] At the very least, army personnel, time and facilities were put to unsanctioned business use in order to raise funds to allow their units to survive. In some cases, after all, regiments and bases found their power supplies cut off or their rations restricted because the central defence ministry could not or would not pay bills on time. More often, though, was that what the military sociologist Yury Deryugin described as the 'alarming tendency' towards the 'commercialisation' of the armed forces was geared towards private profit and often exploited either other soldiers or the state.[22] With so many officers involved, it also contributed to a tradition of *krugovaya poruka* or 'circular guarantee' of mutual cover and a culture of intolerance towards whistle-blowers – indeed, Lt. Colonel Alexander Zhilin, editor of the defence ministry's own newspaper *Armiya Rossii*, was sacked personally by Grachev after he began

16. *RIA-Novosti*, August 4, 2006.

17. For instance, *dachas*, country houses, owned by the defence ministry, were sold to senior army officers in 1992 at 1991 valuations – despite the collapse in the value of the ruble in the intervening year, which meant that they went for around one-tenth their market value. *Ostankino-1 TV*, January 15, 1993, in *BBC SWB*, January 18, 1993; *Sovietskaya Rossiya*, May 22, 1993.

18. This became a particular bête noire for then-Vice President Alexander Rutskoi. See, for example, his press conference of 18 June 1993, reported in *BBC SWB*, June 21, 1993. This was also a topic Kholodov was investigating before his murder, which took place before he was able to testify on the matter before a Duma [lower house of parliament] committee; *ITAR-TASS* news agency, October 18, 1994.

19. *Jamestown Foundation Monitor*, December 14, 2000; *Nezavisimoe Voennoe Obozrenie*, May 11, 2006.

20. See, for example, *Moskovskii Komsomolets*, October 20, 1994.

21. This is best explored in Turbiville, *op cit.*

22. *Nezavisimaya gazeta*, August 24, 1994; see also Galeotti, M. (1994) 'RUSSIA: Entrepreneurial army', *Oxford Analytica Daily Brief*, October 26.

highlighting corruption within the military.[23] By 1999, Military Prosecutor Yury Demin had to admit that economic crime within the military was 'endangering national security'.[24]

There has been some progress since Yeltsin was replaced by Vladimir Putin in 2000, but this is still a serious problem. According to Chief Military Procurator Alexander Savenkov, 500 million rubles (US$ 17 million) were embezzled in the first half of 2004 – equivalent to the cost of converting an entire infantry division of conscripts into one manned by professional soldiers.[25] Especially worrisome is the trade in weapons; with tightened security at weapons manufacturing facilities, military stocks have become the main source of illegal weapons in Russia[26] and many of the guns used by Chechen rebels have turned out to have been bought from the very Russian soldiers against whom they are turned.[27] Even those who do not have access to goods to sell can instead sell their own or their subordinates' labour.[28] After all, the most serious problem is precisely within the officer corps; according to Main Military Prosecutor Colonel General Savenkov 46.9% of crimes are committed by senior commanders,[29] while a leaked General Staff report on corruption within the Defence Ministry listed an array of senior figures under investigation or forced to make restitutions, including not only Grachev and his predecessor as defence minister, Air Marshal Shaposhnikov, but also three deputy defence ministers (Generals Kobets, Burlakov and Churanov) and 22 generals.[30] Prosecutor-General Yuri Skuratov seems to have had good reason for alleging, as he did in 1997, that the armed forces had become the most heavily corrupted element of the state apparatus.[31]

Military facilities and transports are also largely exempted from regular police and other controls, in the absence of a specific warrant and some often time-consuming negotiations between civilian and military authorities. In the 1990s, this was often exploited on an essentially ad hoc basis; the commander of a Far

23. *Ostankino-1 TV*, February 12, 1993, in *BBC SWB*, February 17, 1993; *Moskovskie Novosti*, February 14, 1993.

24. *Reuters*, October 8, 1999.

25. *Moscow Times*, July 28, 2004.

26. Pyadushkin, M. with Haug, M. & Matveeva, A. (2003) *Beyond the Kalashnikov: small arms production, exports and stockpiles in the Russian Federation*, CAST/SaferWorld, Geneva, pp. 18, 30–31; see also *Jamestown Foundation Prism*, December 22, 1995.

27. In 1995, Presidential Advisers Emil Pain and Arkady Popov wrote in a report to President Yeltsin that the Chechens were buying guns from "smart traders in military uniforms." *OMRI Daily Digest*, February 8, 1995 and April 5, 1995.

28. This is a common activity, as officers hire out their soldiers for manual labour and pocket the proceeds. See, for example, *The Guardian*, February 4, 2006; *BBC News online*, February 2, 2006, available at: http://news.bbc.co.uk/2/hi/europe/4674366.stm (accessed 20 September 2006); *UPI*, January 22, 2002, available at: http://www.cdi.org/russia/johnson/6035-11.cfm (accessed 20 September 2006).

29. *RosBalt* news agency, May 24, 2005; for an excellent overview of the problem, see Staar, R. (1998) 'Russia's military: corruption in the higher ranks', *ISCIP Perspective*, vol. 9, No. 2, available at: http://www.bu.edu/iscip/vol9/Staar.html (accessed 20 September 2006).

30. Cited in Zhilin, A. (1995) 'Corruption keeps generals in line', *Jamestown Foundation Prism*, September 22.

31. *St. Petersburg Times*, June 2–8, 1997.

Eastern Long-Range Aviation regiment, for example, was caught using his bombers to move goods into neighbouring Central Asian states.[32] This was essentially a 'grey market' operation, in that the goods were licit, but their transport by military aircraft was an illegal use of state assets. Given the risks in such operations, it is hardly surprising that officers seeking to carry them out looked instead to more lucrative markets, just as the opportunities for inspection-free transport made such 'businesses' of interest to the criminals. In particular, the 1990s saw military and Border Troop aircraft and land transport being used to ship drugs from Central Asia, originally simply on a contract basis for organised crime but later – as will be explored below – in their own right.[33] The presence of a large Russian deployment in Tajikistan, a country both with a strong domestic opiate industry and on the border of Afghanistan, did much to encourage this trade.

On a more personal level, in 2002 it came to light that special executive jets run by the air forces to provide secure transport and airborne command facilities for senior defence ministry officials were instead being chartered illegally by senior members of the Izmailovo-Golyanovskaya *mafiya* gang.[34] Even more striking are the cases in which military facilities have been used to provide safe havens for criminal operations, typically storing illegal goods or else as small workshops engaged in such activities as refining narcotics or repainting stolen vehicles and otherwise rendering them untraceable. This appears to have become much more widespread. Industry sources have linked military compounds in Vladikavkaz and Mozdok with major operations counterfeiting branded cigarettes, for example, while chemical weapons bases in the St. Petersburg regions have since around 1998 been used to manufacture synthetic drugs, many for export westwards.

Police Gone Bad

The law enforcement agencies, while mercifully lacking the tradition of *dedovshchina*, still suffered a decline in their relative prestige, resourcing and remuneration through the 1990s, albeit one which has begun to be addressed under President Putin. Even so, if anything they are regarded as even more corrupt than the military, perhaps because of the greater opportunities facing them. After all, corruption is for many Russian police officers both an economic necessity and a way of life. A major survey of police officers produced in 2002 revealed that more than half also carried out extra work, ranging from moonlighting as security guards or drivers through to running rackets.[35] In some cases, they may even end up guarding mobsters. When alleged organised crime boss Vasili Naumov was assassinated in 1997, for example, it emerged that his

32. *Moscow News*, January 11, 1993.
33. See, for example, *Moscow News*, September 10, 1993; *Trud*, June 19, 1994.
34. *Interfax* news agency, April 22, 2002.
35. This was a private survey carried out for the MVD and not published; the author has seen the executive summary produced by the polling company.

bodyguards were members of *Saturn*, an elite police unit.[36] They were apparently engaged legitimately through a front company. More serious is outright corruption, though. President Putin has himself admitted that 'the law enforcement bodies, unfortunately, are still afflicted with corruption and inefficiency,' from the lowest level to 'the highest, where we are talking about [bribes of] hundreds, tens of thousands, perhaps millions' of dollars.[37] This culture of corruption even infected those agencies meant to combat it, such as the MVD's Internal Security Department, infamous for blackmailing rather than prosecuting corrupt officers. Indeed, so notorious did the Tax Police become for abusing their powers to extort money from businesses - in one reported case, a team demanded $200,000 from a company to avoid a full audit[38] - that this led to their being disbanded in 2003.

Worse, though, is the evidence that corrupt police officers at every level not only take bribes to turn a blind eye to organised crime, but actively demand payments in return for facilitating illegal activities. The Russian investigative journalist Yuri Spirin explored the role of this so-called 'police mafia' on the drug-trafficking routes from Central Asia and the Caucasus, and charted the rising figures demanded, from the equivalent of $200 per kilo of heroin demanded by Tajik border guards as it leaves Afghanistan through to the $2000 on average paid to ensure safe passage into Moscow or St. Petersburg.[39] Likewise, Border Troops at Moscow's Sheremetyevo-2 airport have been charged with running a service smuggling wanted criminals out of the country on false passports while, in the Urals region, police licensing services, responsible for registering private security agencies, have been found to be facilitating the establishment of such firms for criminal gangs as covers for their protection racketeering.

Demob Unhappy

Much has been made of the presence of former soldiers and police within the *mafiya*. In many ways this has been overplayed, as they represent no more than a small proportion of the total membership - sportsmen, for example, appear much more heavily represented. One reason for this exaggeration is that, as a country with conscription, many young men who might end up as criminals will have served a term within the armed forces. They will often then be described in newspaper accounts as 'ex-soldiers.' The other is that such individuals may well have abilities making them disproportionately effective and newsworthy.

36. *Kommersant-daily*, March 13, 1997; Moskovsky Komsomolets, June 1, 2003.
37. *New York Times*, August 13, 2005.
38. *NTV* news, April 5, 1996, reported in the *OMRI Daily Digest*, April 9, 1996.
39. Spirin, Y. (2002) 'Heroin Heroes', report of Stringer News Agency [Moscow], *February 12, cited in Library of Congress,* Involvement of Russian Organized Crime Syndicates, Criminal Elements in the Russian Military, and Regional Terrorist Groups in Narcotics Trafficking in *Central Asia, the Caucasus, and Chechnya,* Library of Congress Federal Research Division, Washington, DC, p. 21.

One example would be Alexander Solonik, a notorious mob assassin, formerly a special service sniper, himself killed in Greece in 1997.[40] But there are specialists of every kind available, from computer hackers (former employees of FAPSI, the Federal Government Communications and Information Agency are regarded as the best) to cryptographers.

This is also a demobilisation problem. The armed forces have been cut from around three million to an official strength of 1.2 million but in practice less than a million, largely in a haphazard and under-funded way, while the police force was also allowed to shrink through much of the 1990s, through a failure to fund recruitment. For many career soldiers, demobilisation meant the loss of subsidised housing, food from the canteen and, least tangible but no less important, a sense of purpose and identity. Former soldiers, police, and security officers have a limited and often unsatisfactory range of legal employment options. Although the dramatic growth in the private security industry has at least provided one source of jobs, for others, having become used to a culture of criminality and corruption while in service, crime can become a logical, even attractive career prospect, and one in which their skills can actually be an asset. In the 1990s, for instance, the notorious *Uralmash* gang in Ekaterinburg reportedly hired former commando instructors to train up their enforcers.[41] They may also have an array of contacts which are often extremely valuable. For example in 2002, a cashiered soldier was arrested in Tver and charged with heading a small but influential gang responsible for wholesale heroin imports into the city. It transpired that his success was due to his contacts within the military, allowing him to arrange direct imports from Tajikistan, tapping major 'military mafia' import routes discussed below.[42] This helps explain the attention given to retraining former officers by such agencies as the OECD, NATO and Western defence ministries.[43]

The Security Forces in Organised Crime

Although there is ample evidence of the collusion of serving or retired members of the security and intelligence community in organised crime, this is either largely as individuals or else within their professional duties. After all, there is considerable suspicion that some Russian-based or -originated organised crime groups have been granted a degree of latitude or simply paid in order to assist intelligence operations. To uncover substantive cases in which specific organised crime gangs have emerged within the security apparatus, one must look to the police and the military.

40. *Pravda.ru*, January 24, 2003; Karyshev, V. (2003) *Aleksandr Solonik: killer zhiv'?*, EKSMO, Moscow.
41. Finckenauer, J. & Voronin, Y. (2001) *The Threat of Russian Organized Crime*, US Department of Justice, National Institute of Justice, Washington, DC, p. 15.
42. *Nezavisimaya gazeta*, April 6, 2002.
43. See, for example, the OECD's *Russian Officer Conversion Programmes: Overview and Future*, document OCDE/GD, 1996.

'Werewolves' within the Police

Organised crime groups within the police forces are such a problem that they even have their own nickname in common parlance: 'werewolves' (in part a play on the criminals' use of the word 'wolves' to describe especially effective or dangerous police officers). Gangs which form within the police tend to be defined by their duties, in that they specialise in crimes for which their official roles are especially helpful.

Given their wide-ranging powers and the relatively weak control and scrutiny placed on their operations, it is perhaps not surprising that several police units moved quickly from collecting the odd bribe to a more methodical business of protection racketeering, joining the expanding range of providers of what the Russians call *krysha*, a 'roof'. According to Interior Minister Gryzlov, the Main Directorate for Combating Organised Crime (GUBOP – *Glavnoe upravlenie po bor'be s organizovannoi prestupnost'yu*) was the worst source of such 'werewolves'.[44] Nonetheless, from the early 1990s, organised groups of protection racketeers have been present in police commands across the country[45] and, by 1997, a reported 30% of police officers maintained a *krysha* of some kind, commensurate with their rank, duties, connections and capabilities.[46]

However, extortion can also be directed against individuals. In the most infamous recent example, six senior policemen from the élite Moscow Criminal Investigations Directorate (MUR – *Moskovskii ugolovny rozysk*) were arrested in 2003, including three colonels and three lieutenant colonels, as well as Lt. General Vladimir Ganeev, head of the Emergency Situations Ministry's security department.[47] At least $3 million in cash were seized in more than 40 raids carried out around the capital, as well as two kilograms of gold, antiques, a 'large number' of rubles, and plastic explosives, while $60,000 in cash was discovered in Ganeev's office.[48] They were accused of operating as an organised criminal gang, which since 1999 had specialised in planting drugs and weapons on victims in order to blackmail them. So lucrative was this business that five of them had together built a $3.5 million housing complex with its own football pitch, while on official

44. This is discussed in Kaliyev, R. (2002) 'Can "power ministries" be transformed?', *ISCIP Perspective*, vol. 13, no. 1, available at: http://www.bu.edu/iscip/vol13/kaliyev.html (accessed 20 September 2006). Of course, from the entrepreneurs' point of view, the 'worst' *kryshas* can also be the best, if they are the most effective and dangerous to other potential predators, and the GUBOP certainly meet these criteria; see Yurchak, A. (2002) 'Entrepreneurial governmentality in post-socialist Russia', in *The New Entrepreneurs of Europe and Asia*, eds. V. Bonnell & T. Gold, M. E. Sharpe, Armonk.

45. *Washington Post*, May 12, 1997; Library of Congress, *Involvement of Russian Organized Crime Syndicates, Criminal Elements in the Russian Military, and Regional Terrorist Groups in Narcotics Trafficking in Central Asia, the Caucasus, and Chechnya*, Washington, DC: Library of Congress Federal Research Division, 2002, p. 27.

46. Webster, W. et al. (1997) *Russian Organized Crime*, CSIS, Washington, DC, p. 30.

47. *Pravda.ru*, June 24, 2003; *Izvestiya*, June 30, 2003; *Pravda.ru*, July 2, 2003; *Gazeta.ru*, July 16, 2003, available at: http://www.gazeta.ru/2003/07/16/Interiormini.shtml (accessed 10 October 2006); *Moscow Times*, September 7, 2006.

48. *ORT*, June 23, 2003.

salaries of about $300 a month.[49] Ganeev was eventually sentenced to 20 years in prison, the others for terms of 15–20 years, all in hard-labour camps.[50]

'Gangsters in Shoulder-Boards'

Criminal groupings within the military will usually have links with corrupt local politicians and other gangs operating in their vicinity, but are organisationally separate. They tend to be rather more specialised than 'civilian' gangs, exploiting particular assets at their disposal.

The first of these is their access to weapons and lethal expertise. Kholodov's suspicions that elements within the 16th Spetsnaz Brigade were training hitmen, for example, has never been proved or disproved, but appears widely held within Moscow police circles. More often, though, it is former soldiers, bound by ties of loyalty and shared experiences, who form their own organised crime gangs, such as the group which kidnapped oil executive Sergei Kukura in 2002, which was drawn largely from ex-paratroopers.[51]

The second specific asset which such gangs can exploit is their access to particular opportunities for embezzling state resources, which may bring them into partnership with 'civilian' criminals who can then make use of the stolen goods. Cases of fuel supplies, spare parts, and even weapons being diverted by gangs of officers and then sold on to other groups are commonplace and, in some instances, even military vehicles have been written off as destroyed and then sold on to criminals for resale, including two helicopters which reportedly ended up in the hands of the Colombian Cali drug cartel[52] and fully 34 trucks written up as casualties of the fighting in Chechnya then sold on to companies in the North Caucasus.[53]

Thirdly, military gangs rely on their relative impunity and control over their own vehicles and facilities to provide safe havens for criminal enterprises and secure smuggling routes. As noted above, the army, air forces, and Border Troops have all harboured gangs involved in the trafficking of drugs, contraband, and even people on contract to organised crime gangs. What has changed in recent years is that increasingly they operate as players in their own right, rather than simply providing a specific service to other gangs. For example, Spirin has also explored the way that opiates, swapped for weapons by Tajik soldiers with Afghan warlords, are then sold on to Russian officers based in Tajikistan. They then use their own aircraft – which are subject neither to Russian not Tajik customs controls – to move the drugs back home, not least through Moscow's Chkalovskiy

49. *RFE/RL Russian Foreign Policy & Security Watch*, July 1, 2003.
50. *Rian.ru* news agency, September 8, 2006; *Argumenty i fakty*, September 13, 2006.
51. *Gazeta.ru*, October 7, 2002, available at: http://www.gazeta.ru/2002/10/01/Searchforkid.shtml, (accessed 20 September 2006); *Moscow Times*, October 2, 2002; *New York Times*, September 18, 2002.
52. *Washington Post*, September 29, 1997.
53. *Kommersant-deily*, July 17, 1997.

military airfield, for resale to local 'civilian' gangs who handle street distribution.[54] A similar process took place at the Vaziani air base in Georgia, which was held by Russian forces until it was handed over to the Georgians in 2001. By 1996, it had become infamous as a 'customs-free' hub for not just military but also civilian flights eager to move goods in, from, and through Georgia without having to worry about either Russian or Georgian controls.[55] By 1999/2000, local military commanders were apparently involved in running sophisticated smuggling operations, whereby they sourced weapons in Russia, flew them to Vaziani and then moved them by land or air to buyers in conflict zones such as Chechnya and Nagorno-Karabakh in Azerbaijan.[56]

Likewise, there is growing evidence that military bases and secure compounds which for years have offered a degree of 'extraterritorial' sanctuary to *mafiya* operations have also become the incubator for 'in-house' criminal ventures, such as workshops creating counterfeit goods and drug refineries. For example, bases in the North Caucasus appear to have become home to plants manufacturing counterfeit cigarettes, such as the 1.9 million packs seized as they were being loaded on a military transport aircraft at the Mozdok base in Northern Ossetia.[57] In this way, these bases are following the trail blazed by the militarised, impoverished, and thoroughly criminalised exclave of Kaliningrad. First, the region became a haven for criminals operating both in St. Petersburg (with which it is linked by regular military transports) and the neighbouring Baltic states.[58] Then, officers based there began supplying specific goods and services to criminals, including guns and a transport route to take cars stolen in Europe into St. Petersburg and drugs back the other way.[59] As crime became comprehensively entrenched within the region – some estimates suggest that fully half its income comes from such 'informal activity'[60] – these gangs instead became active participants in the regional underworld, diversifying into new activities (such as the smuggling of counterfeit goods) and taking on the financial risks of the deals themselves. In the process, they also had to develop direct relations with 'civilian' gangs, most notably the St. Petersburg-based *Tambovskaya* network.

54. Yuriy Spirin, 'Heroin Heroes', *op cit*.
55. *Iprinda news agency*, September 4, 1996, in *BBC SWB*, September 7, 1996.
56. *Caucasus Reporting Service*, December 3, 1999, available at: http://www.iwpr.net/?p = crs&s = f&o = 158944&apc_state = henicrs1999 (accessed 10 October 2006); *Caucasus Reporting Service*, January 14, 2000, available at: http://www.iwpr.net/?p = crs&s = f&o = 162030&apc_state = henicrs2000 (accessed 10 October 2006); *Army & Society in Georgia*, January 2000.
57. See the Coalition for Intellectual Property Rights' *Special 301 Filing to the Office of the US Trade Representative*, February 16, 2001, available at: http://www.cipr.org/activities/articles/special_filing_301.htm (accessed 10 October 2006).
58. See Galeotti, M. (2002) 'Kaliningrad at the Crossroads', *Jane's Intelligence Review*, vol. 14, no. 8.
59. *AFP*, May 18, 1999; US Library of Congress Federal Research Division (2003) *Nations Hospitable to Organized Crime and Terrorism*, Library of Congress, Washington, DC, p. 53.
60. *The Guardian*, April 7, 2001.

As a result, while clearly still very much a minority within the armed forces, organised crime rings are emerging which are not simply providing a specific professional service to 'civilian' gangs but operating in their own right, often diversifying and in the process establishing for themselves secure and distinctive niches within the Russian underworld. In some cases this also results in conflicts with 'civilian' gangs, as the soldiers begin to try to control or participate fully in criminal industries they previously merely facilitated.

Prospects for Change

Under Boris Yeltsin, the Kremlin spoke much about the need to combat corruption, but did little. It was left to individuals to introduce measures, such as former Interior Minister Anatoly Kulikov, who created the 'Clean Hands' anti-corruption campaign in 1995.[61] However, without any enthusiasm at the top of this very presidential political system, such measures lacked any overall coherence and tended to lose momentum as soon as their particular patron had been promoted or - more often - replaced, as Yeltsin had little patience for crusaders. Within the police, Kulikov's reforms failed to deal with the cultural roots of the problem, and his own enthusiasm for militarising the service - he was himself a former commander of the MVD's Interior Troops and appointed many of his former comrades to key police positions - distracted him from thoroughgoing reform.[62] As noted above, the police's own internal affairs sections have often simply become the '*krysha*'s *krysha*', shaking down corrupt officers rather than prosecuting them. Kulikov was dismissed in 1998 and replaced by Sergei Stepashin, a former political officer who seems to have understood more clearly the importance of changing the culture of the force, but spent only 13 months in post before being made acting prime minister, without having had any real chance to make his mark. He, in turn, was succeeded by a career police officer, Vladimir Rushaylo, whose efforts were heavily concentrated on the war in Chechnya and consequent terrorist threat.

Within the armed forces, the 'special sections' of the KGB, which had had some successes in controlling the most egregious examples of corruption and criminality, were incorporated into the new Federal Counter-Intelligence Service, later renamed the FSB. However, they were made up of soldiers in the same plight as their comrades and often proved as susceptible to the same temptations. Furthermore, combating corruption was and remains an unpopular and dangerous pursuit, so these sections largely seem to concentrate on the counter-intelligence dimension of their role. Beyond this, law-enforcement within the military is handled by the military procuracy and the Commandant's Service. The former is a relatively very small service, whose investigators generally respond to appeals for

61. *Komsomolskaya Pravda*, November 9, 1995; *Ekspert*, June 24, 1996.
62. *Moskovsky komsomolets*, January 23, 1998; Bennett, G. (2000) *The Ministry of Internal Affairs of the Russian Federation*, Camberley: CSRC, p. 6.

assistance from local commands, while the latter is specifically subordinated to those local commands.[63] Thus, military law enforcement is largely controlled by those same commanders who are also responsible for the majority of serious crimes. This is clearly problematic. Even in the late Soviet era, more far-sighted members of the officer corps were proposing the creation of a separate, dedicated military police force. In 1994, President Yeltsin's *Federal Programme for Stepping Up the Struggle Against Organised Crime* envisaged their creation and in 1996, the Defence Ministry drafted a bill on establishing a 10,000–12,000-strong force.[64] However, as with so many initiatives of the Yeltsin era, this was never assigned the resources and political muscle necessary to turn rhetoric into reality. Despite having been revisited periodically, as of writing, ten years later, there is still no such force, so even the Main Military Procuracy must often rely on local officers to investigate their own units, causing particular problems in trying to uncover and prosecute the kind of close-knit and well-connected conspiracies behind military organised crime.

Putin's position is rather more ambiguous than Yeltsin's. On the one hand, he has had good working relations with many of the most corrupt figures within post-Soviet Russia. On the other, he is much more sharply aware of the security implications of organised crime and its overlap with the security structures. Although, during his time in office, there has undoubtedly been an increase in the attention given the problem, he appears to regard loyalty as more valuable than honesty, and those who have fallen to investigations have tended to be associated with his political rivals. To a considerable extent, corruption allegations have become part of the toolkit used by the new regime to demote, displace and promote in order to create the police and military structures that it wants.[65]

In February 2003, for example, Putin used one of his regular meetings with the *kollegium*, or governing board, of the MVD to criticise the level of corruption within the force and the extent to which they were not just involved in bribe-taking but even becoming drawn into 'corporate wars and economic disputes'.[66] Then-Interior Minister Boris Gryzlov, a political appointee of creature of Putin's, agreed that the police were not doing enough to tackle corruption and demanded an intensification of the struggle against it at 'all levels' of the law-enforcement system, following which came the purge of MUR and other high-profile arrests and operations. However, it did not take long before allegations began to arise that this was simply a piece of political theatre in the run-up to the 2004 presidential elections, especially as it was followed by an uncharacteristic flurry of successes by the MVD, which over just two months apparently solved most of Russia's high-profile murders of recent years. Besides which, many of those charged proved to

63. *ITAR-TASS*, June 19, 1997.
64. See *Krasnaya zvezda*, November 2,1990; *Izvestiya*, May 26, 1994; *Interfax*, October 30, 1996, cited in *BBC SWB*, October 31, 1996; *ITAR-TASS*, June 19, 1997.
65. The way in which Putin's kremlin has sought to reshape the so-called 'power ministries' and its success, is very effectively explored in N. Petrov, 'Siloviki in Russian Regions: new dogs, old tricks', *The Journal of Power Institutions in Post-Soviet Societies*, February 2005.
66. *Moscow Times*, February 7, 2003.

be of rival political opinions. In a poll following the MUR case, a majority of respondents (63%) actually doubted the suspects were guilty, presumably as a result of this widespread belief that such campaigns are essentially pieces of political theatre and factional in-fighting.[67]

While there certainly has been a decrease in the more extreme and overt manifestations of organised criminality, what has happened is largely that the gangs have instead adapted to the new 'rules of the game' and work with a lower profile and more discrimination. This does mean that Russia's streets are a little safer for innocent bystanders, but does not represent a major step forward.

The prospects are thus gloomy. Russian organised crime has not only benefited immensely from the protection, weapons, and skills it can buy from corrupted members of the security forces, it has also infected it. Actual organised crime groups within the police and military are still relatively small and few, and the main relationship of criminalised members of the security apparatus with the underworld is as facilitators, suppliers, and consumers. However, while they represent only a small fraction of the '*mafiya*', organised criminal groupings within the police and security apparatus are disproportionately important in the way they further undermine public confidence in the state, create alternative chains of command, and have access to specialised and dangerous powers, weapons and skills. Polled in 2005, only 2% of respondents said that there was no problem of lawlessness and the abuse of office by Russian police, while 83% characterised it as one of the country's biggest problems.[68]

Putin is more energetic than his predecessor and does appear to be becoming increasingly aware of the political challenge posed. That said, his room for manoeuvre on some issues is limited – the threadbare state budget does not, for example, allow for major increases in salaries to reduce the pressure to take bribes. His perspective is also limited: rather than appreciating that the strongest foundation for a genuinely law-based state is for the leadership itself to observe the laws, he appears to believe that he can purge those aspects of criminality and corruption which pose a threat to his rule, but turn a blind eye to others. This will seriously hinder efforts to cleanse the security apparatus, and will ensure that this remains a problem for the foreseeable future. Nonetheless, there are some slight glimmers of hope. Gryzlov – who was widely derided as out of his depth in this position – returned to party politics in 2004, to be succeeded by a former police investigator, Rashid Nurgaliev. Arguably the most well-respected and -qualified interior minister of post-Soviet times, Nurgaliev may be able to make some inroads into the culture of corruption within the police if he is given the time and freedom this requires. While the situation within the armed forces is more complex, Putin's growing concern at the extent to which criminality within the

67. The poll was held in June and July 2003; a summary of the results is available at: http://bd.english.fom.ru/report/cat/az/U/werewolf_epaulet/eof032601 (accessed 10 October 2006).
68. *Russkii kurier*, March 2, 2005.

ranks is undermining the effectiveness and discipline of the military may mean that at last political will is put behind efforts to cleanse the 'power ministries.' In the meantime, though, and for the immediate future, the Russian security agencies will remain comprehensively infected, too often not so much 'sliding into a world of organised crime' as Kholodov wrote, but enthusiastically plunging into its depths.

Maras Morphing: Revisiting Third Generation Gangs

John P. Sullivan

> In the future, war will not be waged by armies but by groups whom today we call terrorists, guerillas, bandits and robbers, but who will undoubtedly hit upon more formal titles to describe themselves.
>
> Martin van Creveld[1]

> Netwar is about Hamas more than the PLO, Mexico's Zapastistas more than Cuba's Fidelistas, the Christian Identity Movement more than the Ku Klux Klan, the Asian

John P. Sullivan is a Lieutenant with the Los Angeles Sheriff's Department, where he serves as Director of the National TEW Resource Center. He previously served as Officer-in-Charge of the Los Angeles Terrorism Early Warning Group. He has managed intelligence, emergency operations and terrorism response activities and is a researcher specializing in terrorism, intelligence, urban operations, and police studies. He is author or co-author of four books and over 60 chapters, papers, articles or monographs on these and relatd topics. He is co-editor (along with Peter Katona and Michael D. Intriligator) of *Countering Terrorism and WMD: Creating a Global Counter-Terrorism Network* (Routledge, 2006). His recent research focus includes suicide bombings, civil-military interaction in peace operations and counterinsurgency. He holds a M.A. Urban Affairs and Policy Analysis from the New School for Social Research, New York, NY, and a B.S. in Government from the College of William and Mary in Virginia.

1. van Creveld, M. (1991) *The Transformation of War*, The Free Press, New York, p. 197.

> Triads more than the Sicilian Mafia, and Chicago's Gangsta Disciples more than the Al Capone Gang.
>
> John Arquilla and David Ronfeldt[2]

Third generation gangs reside at the intersection between crime and war. They are a byproduct of the significant changes in societal organization that result from the confluence of globalization and technological advances that alter the nature of conflict and crime, favor small, agile groups, and fuel the privatization of violence.[3] While street gangs are generally viewed as minor criminal nuisances with varying degrees of sophistication and reach, some gangs have evolved or morphed into potentially more dangerous entities. In many of the world's cities, especially in the 'lawless zones' of mega-slums where civil governance is weak and insecurity and instability dominate, organized armed groups in the guise of gangs, *maras* or *pandillas* reign. This essay recounts the evolution of third generation street gangs, typically described simply as third generation gangs (3 GEN Gangs), over the past decade and updates my prior research and writing about this phenomenon.

The Model Revisited: Defining Third Generation Gangs (3 GEN Gangs)

I defined the organizational framework for understanding contemporary gang evolution in a series of papers starting with my 1997 article "Third Generation Street Gangs: Turf, Cartels, and Net-warriors."[4] I then expanded the details of the 'Third Generation Street Gang Model' in an expanded paper, "Third Generation Street Gangs: Turf, Cartels, and Net Warriors,"[5] and refined the model in my 2000 *Small Wars and Insurgencies* paper "Urban Gangs Evolving as Criminal Netwar Actors."[6] In these works, I noted that the prospect for street gang evolution was satisfied—at least for some gangs—with the potential reach offered by new technologies (such as the Internet and mobile digital communication). These technologies allowed some gangs to move beyond their traditional turf (or prison)

2. Arquilla, J. & Ronfeldt, D. (1997) 'The Advent of Netwar,' in *In Athena's Camp: Preparing for Conflict in the Information Age*, eds. J. Arquilla & D. Ronfeldt, RAND, Santa Monica, CA, p. 227.
3. See Sullivan, J. P. (2001) 'Gangs, Hooligans, and Anarchists—The Vanguard of Netwar in the Streets' in *Networks and Netwars: The Future of Terror, Crime, and Militancy*, eds. J. Arquilla & D. Ronfeldt, RAND, Santa Monica, CA, Chapter Four, pp. 99–126 for a discussion of factors that influence the current shift in the nature of crime and conflict to favor gangs. A detailed discussion of the privatization of violence, and the roles gangs play in that respect is found in my essay Sullivan, J. P. (2002) 'Terrorism, Crime and Private Armies', *Low Intensity Conflict & Law Enforcement*, vol. 11, no. 2/3, pp. 239–253. See also Bunker, R. J. (ed) (2005) *Networks, Terrorism and Global Insurgency*, Routledge, New York, pp. 69–83.
4. Sullivan, J. P. (1997) 'Third Generation Street Gangs: Turf, Cartels and NetWarriors', *Crime & Justice International*, vol. 13, no. 10, Article 688, Available at: http://158.135.23.21/cjcweb/college/cji/index.cfm?ID = 688.
5. Sullivan, J. P. (1997) 'Third Generation Street Gangs: Turf, Cartels, and NetWarriors', *Transnational Organized Crime*, vol. 3, no. 2, pp. 95–108.
6. Sullivan, J. P. (2000) 'Urban Gangs Evolving as Criminal Netwar Actors', *Small Wars and Insurgencies*, vol. 11, no. 1, pp. 82–96.

and later drugs-market orientations to engage in more sophisticated activities. At that time, some gangs appeared ready to move into a third generation.

Examples of gangs with third generation attributes described in these works included the Chicago-based "El-Rukn" gang, San Diego's "*Calle Trienta*," and Cape area gangs or vigilantes in South Africa including "Hard Livings" and "Pagad." For example, five members of the El-Rukn's were convicted for conspiring to conduct terrorist activity as a mercenary proxy for Libya; *Calle Trienta* was used as a proxy by the Arellano-Felix cartel and was involved in the 1993 assassination of Cardinal Juan Jesus Posadas Ocampo in Guadalajara. In South Africa, both Hard Livings and Pagad (an Islamist vigilante group), respectively radicalized by civil war and jihadists, engaged in bombings and assassinations, as well as conventional political activity. Subsequently, endemic high-intensity gang violence in Brazil demonstrates third generation potential in many of Brazil's cities, including Rio de Janeiro and São Paulo.

Briefly, I observed that gangs could progress through three generations. A close analysis of urban street gangs (as well as their prison based cousins) shows that some of these criminal enterprises have transitioned from traditional turf gangs, to market-oriented drug gangs, to a new third generation that combines political and mercenary aims. As gangs transverse this generational shift, their progress can be charted by the interaction of three factors: *politicization*, *internationalization*, and *sophistication*. The resulting 'third generation' gang possesses many of the organizational and operational attributes found with net-based triads, cartels and terrorist entities.

The progress of gangs along this 'generational' continuum is a consequence of technological and organizational changes that enhance the power of relatively small groups particularly where the information revolution enables small groups to extend their reach. These actors can expand their influence in seconds, across vast distances, enabling a shift from hierarchies to network forms of organization. Some of these small groups—urban criminal gangs in particular—embrace network forms and utilize advanced information technology to wage netwar.[7]

Netwar, as defined by its theorists, is "an emerging mode of conflict (and crime) at societal levels, involving measures short of war, in which the protagonists use—indeed, depend upon using—network forms of organization, doctrine, strategy and communication."[8]

These three gang generations can be summarized as follows:

- *First Generation Gangs* are traditional street (or prison) gangs with a turf orientation. When they engage in criminal enterprise, it is largely opportunistic

7. Ibid; See also Sullivan, J. P. (2000) 'Gangs, Hooligans, and Anarchists—The Vanguard of Netwar', *Small Wars and Insurgencies*, vol. 11, no. 1, pp. 99-100.
8. Arquilla, J. & Ronfeldt, D. (eds) (1997) *In Athena's Camp: Preparing for Conflict in the Information Age*, RAND, Santa Monica, CA, p. 227.

and local in scope. These turf gangs are limited in political scope and sophistication.

- *Second Generation Gangs* are engaged in business. They are entrepreneurial and drug-centered. Their tendency for centralized leadership and sophisticated operations for market protection places them in the center of the range of politicization, internationalization, and sophistication.

- *Third Generation Gangs* have evolved political aims and are the most complex gangs. To date, most 3 GEN Gangs have been primarily mercenary in orientation; in some instances however, they have sought to further their own political and social objectives.

The characteristics differentiating the three generations of street gangs are summarized in Figure 1. A more detailed discussion of these three generations follows.

First Generation Gangs

Traditional street gangs are almost exclusively turf-oriented. They operate at the lower threshold of extreme societal violence, possess loose leadership and concentrate their attention on turf protection and gang loyalty within their immediate environs (often a few blocks, a cell-block, or a neighborhood). When they engage in criminal activity, it is largely opportunistic and individual in scope. Turf gangs are limited in political scope, and are unsophisticated in tactics, means, and outlook. When they engage in rivalry with competing gangs, it is localized. Despite their limited spatial influence, these gangs, due to their informal network-like attributes, can be viewed as proto-netwarriors. Local criminal organizations can evolve into armed bands of non-state soldiers should they gain in sophistication within failed communities with disintegrating social

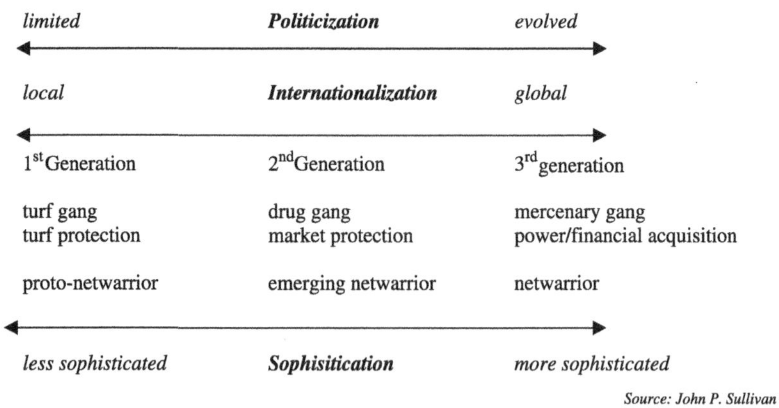

Figure 1 Characteristics of street gang generations

structure. While most gangs will stay firmly in the first generation, a few (e.g., some 'Crip' and 'Blood' sets and some Hispanic gangs like '18th Street') span both the first and second (nascent organized crime groups with a drug focus).

Second Generation Gangs

Second generation gangs are essentially criminal businesses. They are entrepreneurial in outlook and generally drug-centered. They use violence to protect their markets and limit or control their competition. They seek a broader, market-focused, occasionally overt political, agenda and often operate in a broader spatial or geographic area. Their operations sometimes involve multi-state, cross-border, or international reach. They tend to embrace centralized leadership and conduct sophisticated operations for market protection. As such, they occupy the center of the range of politicization, internationalization, and sophistication. Second generation gangs sometimes use violence as political interference to incapacitate enforcement efforts by police and security organs. Generally, this instrumental violence occurs in failed states, but clearly occurs when gangs dominate community life within 'failed communities.' Further evolution of these gangs is a danger when they link with and provide services to transnational criminal organizations or collaborate within narcotics trafficking and distribution networks and other criminal ventures. Because of their attributes, second generation gangs can be considered emerging netwarriors.

Third Generation Gangs

The overwhelming majority of street or prison gangs remain firmly in the first or second generations; however, a small number in the United States, Canada, Central and South America, as well as South Africa have acquired third generation characteristics. Third generation gangs have evolved political aims, operate or seek to operate at the global end of the spectrum, and employ their sophistication to acquire power, money, and engage in mercenary or political activities. To date, these gangs have been primarily mercenary in orientation; yet, in some cases they seek political and social objectives. Examples of third generation gangs can be seen in Chicago, San Diego, Los Angeles, and Cape Town, South Africa. Chicago witnessed the first third generation incursion when in 1986 the 'El Rukn' gang (later known as the 'Black P Stone Nation'), under the leadership of Jeff Fort, sought to carry out terrorist attacks on behalf of Libyan President Gaddafi.

The political dimension of the third generation also first emerged in Chicago, where gang 'empowerment' and political objectives manifest themselves in '21st Century Vote' and 'United Concerned Voters' League,' the political arms of the 'Gangster Disciples' and 'Unknown Conservative Vice Lords,' respectively. These gangs have evolved from turf-based entities, to drug-oriented enterprises operating in up to 35 states, to complex organizations controlling entire housing projects, schools, and blocks, that conduct overt political activity while actively seeking to infiltrate and co-opt local police and contract security forces. South Africa also experiences third generation activity, with Cape area gangs—such as 'Hard Livings'—engaged in both political action and a long-standing terrorist or quasi-terrorist near-war with the vigilante group Pagad (People Against Gangsterism and Drugs). These activities demonstrate the often-subtle interaction of gangs and politics. "Gangs, as organizations of the street and participants in the drug economy, play an important role in the global era," where "non-state actors, among them gangs...often exercise effective political control over urban and rural territories of weakened states."[9] This shift from simple market protection to power acquisition is characteristic of third generation activity.

Internationalization is the final indicator of gang evolution. Gangs in Los Angeles and San Diego have been notable in this regard, with Los Angeles gangs having outposts in Tijuana, Mexico, Nicaragua, El Salvador, and Belize, and San Diego gangs linking with Baja cartels. The mercenary foray of San Diego's 'Calle Treinta' ('30th St.'/'Logan Heights') gang into the bi-national orbit of the Arellano-Felix (Tijuana) cartel is notable for assassinations, drive-by shootings, and other enforcement slayings. The impact of international and cross-border gang reach is aptly illustrated in the *Calle Trienta* example found in "Gangs, Hooligans and Anarchists:"[10]

> During their heyday, Calle Trienta's international gang combat left a trail of over 200 bodies from San Francisco to Tijuana to Venezuela.[11] Notorious activities include a 1993 San Diego shootout killing 26 and the 1993 slaying of Cardinal Juan Jesús Posadas Ocampo in Guadalajara. Calle Trienta members have been linked to assassinations, drive-by shootings, and torture slayings on both sides of the border. In November 1997, a Mexican judge issued an arrest warrant for seven "Logan 30s" members believed to be in San Diego, for the Tijuana assassination attempt of J. Jesús Blancornelas, publisher of the Tijuana paper *Zeta*.[12] Blancornelas observes that the cross-fertilization of street gangs and drug traffickers results in a "binational army of killers working in both Mexico and America."[13]

Because of their attributes, third generation gangs can be considered netwarriors. Networked organizational forms are a key factor contributing to the rise of non-state- or criminal-soldiers. According to analyst Robert J. Bunker, sophisticated informal, network-like organization combined with failed communities with disintegrating social structure fuel the rise of societal warfare by

9. Hagedorn, J. M. (n.d.) 'Gangs and Politics', in *Youth Activism: An International Encyclopedia*, ed. Lonnie R. Sherrod. Available at: http://gangresearch.net/GangResearch/Policy/gangsinpolitics_files/youthact_files/gangsinpolitics.htm.
10. Sullivan, J. P. (2000) 'Gangs, Hooligans, and Anarchists—The Vanguard of Netwar', *Small Wars and Insurgencies*, vol. 11, no. 1, p. 115.
11. Rotella, S. (1997) *Twilight on the Line: Underworlds and Politics at the U.S.-Mexico Border*, W.W. Norton & Company, New York, p. 152.
12. '7 San Diego Gang Members Sought in Tijuana Ambush' (1998) *Los Angeles Times*, August 9.
13. Blancornelas, J. J. (1998) 'The Drug Crisis Isn't Just in Mexico', *Los Angeles Times*, September 27.

"armed nonstate actors intent on legitimizing forms of behavior that current societies consider to be criminal or morally corrupt."[14]

Figure 2 MS-13 Gang Member Tattoos. FBI Photo

Maras Morphing: Continuing Evidence for the Model

Since the initial publications describing third generation gangs, both operational experience and the literature confirm continued trends in gangs evolution and their potential (multi) national security implications.[15] The case of Mara Salvatrucha (MS-13) and Eighteenth Street (*Calle* 18 or M-18) spreading from Los Angeles across North and Central America saliently illustrate the potential impact of third generation gangs with *clicas* (cliques or cells) of both gangs demonstrating elaborate, flexible, and redundant organization and leadership, functioning as networks with extensive transnational linkages.[16]

These *maras* have their own internal culture (symbols, tattoos, graffiti) (Figure 2), recruit, perform internal logistics functions, conduct attacks, collect intelligence, perform information operations (websites), and arm their members with heavier small arms (AK-47s, M-16s, and grenades).[17] Bruneau, paraphrased

14. See Bunker, R. J. (1997) 'Epochal Change: War over Social and Political Organization', *Parameters*, vol. 27, no. 2, Summer; and Bunker, R. J. (1996) 'Street Gangs—Future Paramilitary Groups,' *The Police Chief*, pp. 54–59 for discussion of the emergence of non-state (criminal) soldiers as new warmaking entities.
15. See for example Bruneau, T. C. (2005) 'The Maras and National Security in Central America', *Strategic Insights*, vol. 4, iss. 5. Available at: http://www.ccc.npps.navy.mil/si/2005/May/bruneauMay05.pdf.
16. Ibid.
17. Ibid.

below, describes five (multi) national security threats or challenges associated with transnational *maras*:[18]

- They *strain government capacity* by overwhelming police and legal systems through sheer audacity, violence, and numbers. For example in El Salvador, 49 percent of murders committed in January 2005 were attributed to gang violence.
- They *challenge the legitimacy of the state*, particularly in regions where the culture of democracy is challenged by corruption and reinforced by the inability of political systems to function well enough to provide public goods and services.
- They *act as surrogate or alternate governments*. For example in some regions (i.e., El Salvador and Guatemala) the "governments have all but given up in some areas of the capitals, and the maras extract taxes on individuals and businesses."
- They *dominate the informal economic sector*, establishing small businesses and using violence and coercion to unfairly compete with legitimate businesses while avoiding taxes and co-opting government regulators.
- They *infiltrate police and non-governmental organizations* to further their goals and in doing so demonstrate latent political aims.

Journalist Ana Arana describes how MS-13 and M-18 morphed into substantial transnational security threats as a consequence of the cross-fertilization of criminal actors that results from internationalization. In her *Foreign Affairs* essay "How the Street Gangs Took Central America," Arana recounts a December 2004 action in Honduras:

> [A] bus driving through the northern city of Chamalecon in Honduras was stopped by gunmen. The assailants quickly surrounded the bus and opened fire with their AK-47s, killing 28 passengers. The attackers, police later revealed, had been members of the notorious street gang known as Mara Salvatrucha (or MS-13) and had chosen their victims at random. The slaughter had nothing to do with the identities of the people onboard; it was meant as a protest and a warning against the government's crackdown on gang activities in the country.[19]

The mastermind behind this symbolic attack (a tactic employed elsewhere—particularly in Brazil by 3 GEN Gangs as discussed later in this essay), Ebner Anibal Rivera-Paz, was arrested two months later in Falfurrias, Texas, demonstrating how these "[u]ltraviolent youth gangs, spawned in the ghettos of Los Angeles and other US cities, have slowly migrated south to Central America, where they have transformed themselves into powerful cross-border crime networks."[20] Arana describes how the *maras*' were dispersed from Los

18. Ibid.
19. Arana, A. (2005) 'How the Street Gangs Took Central America', *Foreign Affairs*, vol. 84, no. 3, p. 98.
20. Ibid.

Angeles in the aftermath of the 1992 riots, after police determined that local gangs perpetrated much of the riot's looting and violence. When changes in US immigration law allowed felons (both non-citizens and naturalized citizens—who could be stripped of citizenship) to be repatriated to their countries of origin and expelled once they completed their prison terms, significant numbers of LA gang members were deported south.[21] As a result, gangs now "battle each other and the police for control of working-class neighborhoods and even entire cities."[22] The depth of impact can be extrapolated from Arana's finding that El Salvador, with a population of 6.5 million, now has at least 10,000 hard core gangsters with an additional 20,000 associates; while Honduras, with a population of 6.8 million, has an estimated gang population of 40,000. In addition, *maras* effectively rule at least fifteen Salvadoran municipalities.[23]

In 2005, it was estimated that during the past 12 years, "US immigration authorities have logged more than 50,000 deportations of immigrants with criminal records to Central America."[24] Such deportations are credited with creating "an 'unending chain' of gang members moving between the US and Central America."[25] The effect of this gang migration through deportation combines with recruitment to spread MS-13 "across El Salvador to places like San Miguel, an agricultural hub and the country's third-largest city. The area has become a base of the gang's strength and a pivot point in the group's spread to the Washington, DC area."[26]

MS-13 and its rival M-18 embody the downward spiral of immigration, gang membership, and deportation resulting in a state of unofficial war and reciprocal brutalization between gang members and the police that challenges cities from Texas to Tegucigalpa.[27] Currently, Salvadoran gangs with California ancestry have between 60,000 to 300,000 members spread across nine countries, turning their "neighborhoods and towns into urban guerilla strongholds."[28] These *maras* recruit from the slums of San Salvador, Guatemala City, Tegucigalpa, and elsewhere and have morphed into an "international network which extends from the tiny isthmus to the United States and Spain. They traffic in arms and smuggle drugs, control prostitution, and make millions by collecting protection money from truck-

21. Arana estimates that between 2000 and 2004, 20,000 gangsters were deported to Central America. Ibid, p. 100.
22. Ibid.
23. Ibid.
24. Lopez, R. J., Connell, R. & Kraul, C. (2005) 'MS-13: An International Franchise: Gang Uses Deportation to its Advantage to Flourish in U.S.,' *Los Angeles Times*, October 30. Available at: http://www.latimes.com/news/local/la-me-gang/30Oct30,0,6717943.story?coll = la-home-headlines.
25. Ibid.
26. Ibid.Ibid; Currently MS-13 membership is estimated at 5,000 in the greater Washington, DC area including Northern Virginia and Maryland. That is twice the estimated MS-13 membership in Los Angeles the gang's origin. While LA-based MS-13 members established outposts in the National Capitol Region in the early 1990s many now trace their gang roots to Central America.
27. Logan, S. & Bain, B. (2006) 'Street gangs, a transnational security threat,' *ISN Security Watch*, February 8. Available at: http://www.isn.ethz.ch/news/sw/details.cfm?id = 14715.
28. 'MEDIAWATCH: El Salvador's gangs' (2006) *AlertNet*, Reuters Foundation, September 18.

drivers, shopkeepers, and even private households in their barrios and shantytowns."[29]

The attraction to gang life is a feature of slums and a lack of opportunity in the globalized economy. It is also amplified by the power of global networks and communications. "Street gangs create systems of social networks. These networks rely on crime to finance what is essentially a lifestyle that allows youths to survive in a world where there are limited opportunities, a lack of parental presence, and little hope for a chance at a better life."[30] This 'need' is found throughout the regions where the *maras* and their counterparts flourish. A consequence of this networked criminal social bonding is the spread of criminal norms and increasingly the 'barbarization' of criminal conflict. For example, recent gang violence in Mexico demonstrates the transmission of virulent criminal soldier norms embodied by their shared TTP—tactics, techniques and procedures:

> TIJUANA—The caller painted an ominous scene: A convoy of 40 vehicles carrying 70 heavily armed and masked men was prowling the streets of Rosarito on Tuesday evening. The three police officers who arrived were quickly abducted. The next morning their mutilated bodies turned up in an empty lot. Their heads were found in the Tijuana River later that day.[31]

Such barbaric tactics accompany increased tactical prowess as evidenced in gang and cartel employment of precisely executed paramilitary operations in their quest to control key smuggling routes.[32] According to Jose Luis Santiago Vasconcelos, a member of the Prosecutor General of the Republic (PGR) investigative team for the beheadings, "the abductions and beheadings were characteristic of the brutal Central American-based Mara Salvatrucha gang...Acts like the ones we have just seen are manifestations of groups related to the maras."[33]

MS-13 currently plays significant roles in smuggling drugs, contraband and people across Central America, Mexico, and the US having "set up shop in seven Mexican states, from Chiapas, in the south, all the way to Tamaulipas, on the US border."[34] In addition, they have embarked upon a return to the US, appearing in nontraditional metropolitan areas ranging from New York, Washington, DC, Charlotte, NC, Massachusetts, and several Canadian cities. This bi-directional flow and spread raises several interrelated issues. Arana summarizes these succinctly:

> MS-13 may have originated in the United States during the early 1980s, but the gang that has recently returned to the country is much more dangerous than its original incarnation. The group has grown more sophisticated and developed a taste for (and skills with) more high-powered weaponry (AK-47s, left over from

29. Ibid.
30. Logan, S. & Bain, B. (2006) 'Recruitment, redemption in the MS-13', *ISN Security Watch*, February 14. Available at: http://www.isn.ethz.ch/news/sw/details.cfm?id = 14778.
31. Marosi, R. (2006) 'Mexico's Cartels Escalate Drug War,' *Los Angeles Times*, June 23. Available at: http://www.latimes.com/news/printedition/front/la-fg-behead23jun23,1,4156759,print.story?coll = la-headlines-frontpage.
32. Ibid.
33. Ibid.
34. Arana, A. 'How the Street Gangs Took Central America,' p. 103.

> recent civil wars, are easily obtained in Central America). At the same time, in the Washington, D.C. area, where MS-13 now has an estimated 5,000 members, it has begun using machetes (the traditional weapon of the Central American peasant) as a favorite killing tool.[35]

In addition to a spread in criminal reach, barbaric tactics, and sophisticated doctrine, "the *maras* have recently raised other more specific security threats. In September 2004, US officials grew concerned when a Honduran authorities reported sighting in Tegucigalpa a known al Qaeda operative named Adnan G. El Shukrijumah, and rumors circulated of a meeting between the jihadists and the *maras*."[36] While this incident remains unvetted, the potential alliance of convenience between third generation gangs and jihadi global insurgents remains a chilling potential.

'Gangsta U.'—Prisons: The Crucible for Gang Evolution

Prisons play a pivotal role in the evolution of gangs. Prison-gang interaction is key to solidifying gang culture, recruiting new members, establishing a base of operations for indoctrination and communications. Prisons can become a key node in a gang's internal network or as a key node in inter-gang connectivity. In El Salvador, a prison near San Miguel is such a node where "some of the connections between the Salvadoran branches of the gang [MS-13] and their extensions in the US flow through the Ciudad Barrios prison."[37] Close to 1,800 MS-13 gangsters are incarcerated in Salvadoran prisons, with 60% of such gang members deportees from the US. Salvadoran officials have isolated MS-13 members in order to avoid conflict with rival gangs, but this concentration "has created opportunities for deported Los Angeles leaders to turn the gang into a more potent organization."[38]

MS-13's name itself is demonstrative of the influence prisons and prison gangs have over the broader gang milieu. The number 13, which corresponds to the letter 'm' or 'eme' "is a nod to their allegiance to the Mexican Mafia, which maintains a dominant presence in southern California prisons, where gang rival lines are split between northern California gangs, known as Nordenos, and southern California gangs, known as Surdenos."[39] This connection with the prison-based Mexican Mafia, an umbrella for gang interaction is an important element of gang evolution. "Such close ties to the Mexican mafia, particularly the Tijuana Cartel, helps explain how the MS-13 grew beyond the streets of Los Angeles into a loosely tied organization of members across the US."[40]

Prisons serve as important sources of gang socialization into the criminal domain. In addition, they solidify group identity and identification of individuals with their gang and gang culture. Equally important, prisons serve as a

35. Ibid, p. 104.
36. Ibid.
37. Lopez, R. J., Connell, R. & Kraul, C. (2005) 'MS-13: An International Franchise: Gang Uses Deportation to its Advantage to Flourish in U.S.'
38. Ibid.
39. Logan, S. & Bain, B. (2006) 'Street gangs, a transnational security threat.'
40. Ibid.

'school house' where gang members can refine their skills, meet new associates, and build their social network. Prisons can also provide a stable base of refuge from enforcement efforts and their rivals by leveraging the protection of corrupt or co-opted prison officials to shield and further their activities. From this 'safe haven,' gangs can extend their reach into the streets to orchestrate gang action beyond prison walls. This scenario has been dramatically played out in Brazil where the *Primeiro Comando da Capital* (PCC or First Capital Command) a prison-based gang is engaged in active open conflict with the state.

The PCC exemplifies the destabilizing potentials of 3 GEN Gangs. In a recent PCC campaign conducted in May 2006, São Paulo was paralyzed in the face of gang violence. The PCC's raw power was demonstrated in the face of more than 150 murders, prison riots in nearly100 prisons, and terrorist-style attacks against police and transit infrastructure in a gang coordinated 'megarebellion' spanning from 12–19 May.[41] The PCC controls more than 140,000 prisoners in São Paulo state along with 500,000 supporters and affiliates outside the prison system throughout Brazil.[42] In addition to São Paulo, the PCC operates in Matto Grosso do Sul, Parana, Bahia, Rio Grande do Sul, and Brasilia. It has demonstrated the ability to co-ordinate simultaneous prison riots, destabilize cities, manipulate judicial, political and security systems, and dominate the informal economy. Its network is "held together by a criminal financial system that finances education, facilitates crime and engages in killings."[43]

The PCC's May sequence involved at least 180 acts of violence directed against police and fire stations, buses, banks and a shopping center; at least 39 police were killed and 3 million commuters stranded in the violent crime spree which "looks more like a guerilla offensive with multiple fronts in a war between the state and a powerful prison-based gang."[44] The PCC dominates Brazil's drugs trade, and uses violence to protect its profits and retain its political influence inside the prisons and in the *favelas* of Brazil's megacities. The transfer of PCC leaders within the prison system triggered the audacious May attacks. The resulting prison riots spread from São Paulo to the states of Parana and Mato Grosso do Sul. These were augmented by attacks outside prison walls to demonstrate that the PCC has the means to confront the state. These means included combined arms attacks (grenades and machine guns) against police, bombings, ambushes and drive-by shootings.[45]

41. Logan, S. (2006) 'Brazil's P.C.C.: True Power Behind the Violence', *PINR: Power and Internet Report*, May 24. Available at: http://www.pinr.com/report.php?ac + view_printable&report_id = 495&language_id = 1.
42. Ibid.
43. Ibid.
44. Soares, M. & McDonnell, P. J. (2006) 'Inmates Unleash a Torrent of Violence on Brazilian City', *Los Angeles Times*, May 16. Available at: http://ww.latimes.com/news/nationworld/la-fg-brazil16may 16,0,4259050.story? = collla-home-headlines.
45. Downie, A. (2006) 'Brazil gang takes on state', *Christian Science Monitor*, May 16. Available at: http://www.csmonitor.com/2006/0516/p06s01-woam.html.

Gangs and Broader Conflict

While Brazil's PCC provides an extreme example of a 3 GEN Gang's capacity to challenge a state, other examples of the potential for gangs to foster instability and insecurity can also be found. Max Manwaring highlights the gravity of gang challenges to the state:

> When linked with or working for transnational criminal organizations, insurgents, drug barons, or warlords, the gangs' activities further reduce police and military authorities' abilities to maintain stability and, in doing so, challenge the sovereignty within and between which they move.[46]

Gang involvement or connections to terrorism are another variation of this challenge. Consider the potential for prisoner radicalization when jihadis and gangsters converge. This potential was realized in a plot to attack Southern California synagogues, National Guard recruitment centers, and other sites conceived by Islamist extremists and gang members who came together in a group known as *Jamiyyat Ul Islam Is Sahheeh* (JIS) in Folsom prison, part of California's vast penal system.[47] The potential for prison radicalization and gang convergence was also seen in the case of Jose Padilla who was arrested in 2002 for an alleged plot to conduct a 'dirty bomb' attack in the US.[48]

Gang connections to terrorism can also be nurtured outside of prisons and jails as seen with Tamil and Punjabi gangs in Canada. Violent Canadian street gangs appear to have links to terrorist groups in South Asia, with the strongest links seen between Toronto's Tamil gangs and the Tamil Tigers (the Liberation Tigers of Tamil Eelam or LTTE). According to recent research, Tamil gangs such as the VVT (Valvetlithurai) are linked through key players and tactics. One Toronto car bombing believed to be conducted by the gang used the same explosive mix as LTTE bombs.[49] The VVT is known to operate in Toronto, Montreal, and the UK.

The potential for street gangs to morph into Islamist terrorist movements has not yet been realized, but the Fall 2005 French Riots where "Youth gangs, overwhelmingly French-born and Muslim, have engaged in a nation-wide rampage that by November 8 had burned 5,000 vehicles, a few schools, kindergartens, police stations, shopping malls, and post offices. Police officers have been wounded and an older man beaten to death. Some 800 individuals have been arrested and a curfew locally imposed to stem this anomic wave of gang violence that is spreading all over France—and beyond. But the riots increasingly and

46. Manwaring, M. G. (2005) *Street Gangs: The New Urban Insurgency*, Strategic Studies Institute, US Army War College, Carlisle, p. 11.
47. Krikorian, G. & Warren, J. (2005) 'Terror Probe Targets Prison in Folsom', *Los Angeles Times*, August 17.
48. See Cilluffo, F. et al. (2006) 'Out of the Shadows: Getting Ahead of Prisoner Radicalization,' *Prisoner Radicalization Task Force*, George Washington University Homeland Security Policy Institute and University of Virginia Critical Incident Analysis Group, Washington, DC for a detailed exploration of the potentials for radicalization in correctional facilities.
49. Bell, S. (2002) 'Gangs Linked to Terrorism, Study Finds Members, Tactics Overlap,' *National Post*, March 5. Available at: http://www.canada.com/national/story.asp?id = {83782BE7-A841-4B62-B18F-E9CC8826BAC2.

alarmingly suggest that Islamist radicals see criminality as an opportunity for recruitment, while the criminals see Islam as a legitimizer."[50]

While the Islamist capture of gangs in the *banlieue* has yet to be realized, the destabilizing impact of mass gang rioting has. The 2005 unrest spanned 21 nights and resulted in 2,921 arrests; a year later, after a gang attacked police in Epinay and youths set fire to a bus in Grigny and then stoned responding police and firefighters, French police and intelligence are concerned that new violence can erupt. Interior ministry intelligence reported in October 2006 noted the potential for renewed riots stating "coming violence could be less spontaneous but 'more structured, and targeting representatives from the last institution remaining in some neighborhoods—the police.'"[51]

Lawless Zones: The Human and Spatial Terrain of Gangs

Gangs reign when instruments of social control are weak or nonexistent. Historically, while transnational organized crime groups exploited the seams between states, they benefited from the existence of a stable state. Traditional criminal enterprises, including gangs, did not seek to challenge the state; rather, they exploited corruption and political influence to further their activities. This appears to be changing as a new range of transnational gangsters exploit shadow economies, the absence of effective states, and endemic corruption.[52] Louise Shelley observes that the "newer crime groups most often linked to terrorism have no interest in a secure state."[53] They promote and exploit grievances at local levels and through the globalization of conflict maneuvering to capture profit. These terrorist-transnational criminal relationships are particularly poignant in 'global cities' and sub-national or cross-border enclaves or 'lawless zones.'[54]

Lawless zones can be found in the *barrios*, *favelas*, *gecekondas*, *chawls*, ghettos and mega-slums of global cities; in rural enclaves or frontiers; or in the *desakotas* (urban villages) where sprawl has blurred the distinction between urban and rural, center and periphery. They are regions ranging from a few small blocks to large uncontested areas and failed states where state institutions such as the police and traditional government services hold minimal or no traction. Gangs fill the political void and seek to further their ends through violence:

> Crime and violence often blur when criminal enterprises seek to incapacitate enforcement efforts by the state, its police, and security forces. The use of violence as political interference has traditionally been a phenomenon of failed

50. Radu, M. (2005) 'Europe, Fall 2005: Gangs in Search of an Ideology,' *Watch on the West*, vol. 6, no. 7. Available at: http://www.fpri.org/ww/0607.200511.radu.eurpopegangs.html.
51. 'Riot warning for France suburbs' (2006) BBC News, October 23. Available at: http://news.bbc.co.uk/2/hi/europe/6078738.stm.
52. Shelley, L. (2005) 'The Unholy Trinity: Transnational Crime, Corruption, and Terrorism', *Brown Journal of World Affairs*, vol. 11, iss. 2, p. 102.
53. Ibid.
54. See Sullivan, J. P. & Bunker, R. J. (2002) 'Drugs Cartels, Street Gangs, and Warlords', in *Non-State Threat and Future Wars*, ed. R. J. Bunker, pp. 40–53 for a discussion of lawless zones, such as *Ciudad del Este* and the Tri-Border Region and their impact on the crime-terrorism nexus and state erosion.

states, but a similar phenomenon occurs when street gangs exploit 'failed Communities' and dominate community life.[55]

Lawless zones are synonymous with the global cities of discord described in Mike Davis's recent book *Planet of Slums*. In the slums and mega-slums described there in, the informal sector reigns and is fraught with conflict. Such conflict "is usually transmuted into ethnoreligious or racial violence. The godfathers and landlords of the informal sector (invisible in most of the literature) intelligently use coercion, even chronic violence to regulate competition and protect their investments."[56] Sectarian violence is also a prominent feature of such areas. Politically, slum life with its informal political and economic structure "is a semifeudal realm of kickbacks, bribes, tribal loyalties, and ethnic exclusion. Urban space is never free. A place on the pavement, the rental of a rickshaw, a day's labor on a construction site, or a domestic's reference to a new employer: all of these require patronage or membership in some closed network, often an ethnic militia or a street gang."[57]

Mega-slums with their subsistence economies can trigger a wide variety of responses to structural failure, deprivation and neglect. These can be positive NGOs, church or social movements, or predatory groups: *maras*, street gangs, militias, or, as is seen in the 'edge cities' surrounding Istanbul, Cairo, Casablanca, London, or Paris, *al Salifia Jihadia*.[58] "Failed states and 'lawless zones' fuel a bazaar of violence where warlords and martial entrepreneurs fuel the convergence of crime and war."[59] The endless conflict in such zones is fueled by and exploits gang members and child soldiers.

Child Soldiers or Participants in Organized Armed Violence

In many ways, the exploitation of children as warriors and terrorists in contemporary conflict zones[60] is similar to the dynamics of street gang violence "where bands of youths seeking turf, belonging and power use violence as a salve for their powerlessness to intimidate and dominate 'failed communities'."[61] This is occurring worldwide. Gangs like the Sexy Boys and Hard Livings in Cape Town's poor sections are growing in sophistication and brutality, and they increasingly seek children as members.[62]

55. Sullivan, J. P. (2000) 'Gangs, Hooligans, and Anarchists—The Vanguard of Netwar', *Small Wars and Insurgencies*, vol. 11, no. 1, p. 108.
56. Davis, M. (2006) *Planet of Slums*, Verso, New York, p. 185.
57. Ibid.
58. Ibid., pp. 201-202.
59. Sullivan, J. P. (2005) 'Child Soldiers: Warriors of Despair,' *Small Wars Journal*, vol. 2, July. Available at: http://www.smallwarsjournal.com/documents/swjmag/v2/sullivan.htm.
60. See Singer, P. W. (2005) *Children at War*, Pantheon Books, New York, for a detailed review of child soldiers involved in insurgency and terrorism worldwide.
61. Sullivan, J. P. 'Child Soldiers: Warriors of Despair'.
62. Dixon, R. (2006) 'Cape Town Gangs Seek Out Children,' *Los Angeles Times*, September 25. Available at: http://www.latimes.com/news/nationworld/world/la-fg-gangs25sep25,1,186603.story?coll = la-headlines-world.

Gangs are a form of organized armed group that incubate in 'failed communities' or 'lawless zones.' Although dangerous, they possess a number of "positive attributes for those that belong to them and, in some cases, even those that don't. Often they fulfill social, political or economic functions in the communities they dominate."[63] Rio de Janeiro's *favelas* provide an important case study of children engaged in armed violence.[64] More people (especially children) die from small arms fire in Rio than in many conventional armed conflicts. Although not politically oriented armed groups, "Rio's drug factions are a territorial and openly armed paramilitary presence in most of the city's *favelas*."[65] Many similarities between child soldiers and Rio's 'youth drug faction workers' have been observed. These include voluntary recruitment, weapons use, and participation in armed confrontation. Since Rio is not in a conventional war and drug factions have no stated intent of supplanting the state, many child rights activists feel the term 'child soldiers' is imprecise, yet, due to the level of armed confrontation, territorial domination, and power of local populations, the term 'juvenile delinquent' is also inaccurate. In order to bridge this gap, they have termed them as 'Children and Youths in Organised Armed Violence' (COAV) in order to avoid legitimizing already high levels of lethal state force deployed against them.[66]

The working definition of children and youths engaged in armed groups—such as institutionalized street gangs in the US and South Africa, Central American *maras* and *pandillos*, Jamaican area and corner gangs, Brazilian drug factions, and similar groups elsewhere—has been articulated as:

> Children and Youth in Organised Armed Violence (COAV)—Children and youth employed or otherwise participating in Organised Armed Violence where there are elements of a command structure and power over territory, local population or resources.[67]

Conclusion: Global Gangs and a New Feudalism

Gangs are a significant global phenomenon, "with millions of members and a voice of those marginalized by processes of globalization."[68] As networks and technology influence economic processes, new forms of social, political and criminal opportunity arise. Saskia Sassen, a sociologist at the University of Chicago and London School of Economics describes the rise of 'global cities' in this context.[69]

63. Dowdney, L. (2005) *neither War nor Peace: international comparisons of children and youth in organised armed violence*, COAV, Rio de Janeiro. Available at: http://www.coav.org.br.
64. See Dowdney, L. (2003) *Children of the Drug Trade: A Case Study of Organized Armed Violence in Rio de Janeiro*, Viva Rio/ISER, Letras 7, Rio de Janeiro, p. 11.
65. Ibid., p. 12.
66. Ibid. p. 12–13.
67. Ibid, p. 13.
68. Hagedorn, J. M. (2005) 'The Global Impact of Gangs,' *Journal of Contemporary Criminal Justice*, vol. 21, no. 2, p. 153.
69. See Sassen, S. (2005) *Denationalization: Territory, Authority and Rights in a Global Digital Age*, Princeton University Press, Princeton for a powerful seminal view of the re-emergence of cities in the global political order.

Sassen observes that the flow of capital, labor, goods, and people—all cross-border economic processes—have traditionally occurred within the context of an inter-state arrangement of nation-states. Yet as the result of privatization, deregulation, transnational firms, and technology enabling the participation of national economic actors in the global market, this has changed. The result is the redistribution of strategic economic territories, where national units are no longer the primary spatial focus of transnational economic transactions. Sub-national or non-state actors are the principal beneficiaries of this economic restructuring.[70] Cities, sub-national regions, cross-border hubs, and supra national markets and trade blocs are among those impacted (as are transnational criminal and terrorist actors).[71] Hagedorn describes several reasons why understanding gangs in a global rather than local context is crucial, three of these are directly quoted below:

- Globalization's valorization of some areas and marginalization of others has meant a flourishing of an underground economy for survival and as profitable, internationally connected enterprises run by gangs, cartels, and similar groups.
- The wealth of the global economy has led to the redivision of space within cities all across the globe...These spatial changes have influenced the nature and activity of gangs.
- Some gangs institutionalize and become permanent social actors in communities, cities, and nations rather than fading away after a generation. These gangs often replace or rival demoralized political groups and play important albeit often destructive, social, economic, and political roles in cities around the world.[72]

As such, gangs are more than a crime problem. "Many are deeply involved with politics, real estate, religion, and community organizations...Gangs are thus social actors...As social actors within poor communities with weak mechanisms of social control, gangs militias, factions, and cartels have the capacity not only to wage war but also to rein it in."[73] John Rapley describes this 'power' in a section entitled 'Gangster's Paradise' in his essay "The New Middle Ages."[74] In this section, he describes the situation in Kingston's gangland where "The local gang maintains its own system of law and order...It 'taxes' local businesses in return for protecting them, punishing those who refuse to pay with attacks on property and people. It provides a rudimentary welfare safety net by helping locals with school fees, lunch money, and employment—a function the Jamaican government used to perform...As one kind of authority has withdrawn, another has advanced."[75]

This situation, which is replicated in mega-slums worldwide, reflects an emerging power structure—that of criminal-states, where lawlessness, micro-

70. Sassen, S. (2005) 'The Global City: Introducing a Concept,' *Brown Journal of World Affairs*, vol. 9, iss. 2, p. 27.
71. Ibid.
72. Hagedorn, J. M. (2005) 'The Global Impact of Gangs,' *Journal of Contemporary Criminal Justice*, vol. 21, no. 2, p. 154.
73. Ibid, p. 163.
74. Rapley, J. (2006) 'The New Middle Ages', *Foreign Affairs*, vol. 85, no. 3, pp. 95–103.
75. Ibid., p. 95.

politics, and private actors rise to the forefront. These swaths of gang turf—private 'statelets'-exist in a "delicate, often symbiotic relationship with the larger state."[76] These reflect not only the lot of 'failed states' but also that of *changing states*, where reconfiguration rather than overt collapse prevails. That is because not all private actors that have assumed state-like functions engender chaos or failure. As seen in Jamaica's gang areas, some gang-dominated communities are among the safest in their respective countries.[77]

This political situation may or may not entail overt violence with the state but gangs dominate the political stage and, while they don't seek to secede from the state, they can dictate the terms of that sovereignty.[78] As such, this emerging political landscape resembles an evolution in "Back to the Future," where "variegated informal and quasi-informal state-like activities will continue to expand, as will the power and reach of those who live by them."[79] This situation harks back to the medieval era, as well as to the situation in classic Rome. Violence and the fruits of violence—political control— once again seem to be devolving to small, private actors. This is a challenge to existing order and requires state security organs and global security policymakers to closely examine the dimensions of gang evolution and the relationship of third generation gangs to human security and political stability. The continued morphing and evolution of gangs into the third generation is thus an important indicator in the evolution of the state.

76. Ibid, p. 96.
77. Ibid.
78. Ibid., p. 100.
79. Ibid., p. 103.

Gangs and *Coups D' Streets* in the New World Disorder: Protean Insurgents in Post-modern War

Max G. Manwaring

Max G. Manwaring holds the General Douglas MacArthur Chair and is Professor of Military Strategy at the U.S. Army War College. He is a retired U.S. Army colonel and an Adjunct Professor of International Politics at Dickinson College. He has served in various civilian and military positions, including the Strategic Studies Institute at the U.S. Army War College, the U.S. Southern Command, and the Defense Intelligence Agency. Dr. Manwaring is the author and co-author of several articles, chapters, and reports dealing with political-military affairs, democratization and global ungovernability, and Latin American security affairs. His most recent publication is Uncomfortable Wars Revisited, University of Oklahoma Press, 2006. Dr. Manwaring holds a B.S. in Economics, a B.S. in Political Science, and M.A. in Political Science, and a Ph.D. in Political Science from the University of Illinois.

A new kind of war is being waged in various parts of the Americas, Africa, Asia, Europe, the Middle East, and everywhere around the world today.[1] Some of the main protagonists are those who have come to be designated as first-, second-, and third-generation street gangs. In this war, gangs are not sending conventional military units across national borders or building an industrial capability in an attempt to "filch some province" from some country.[2] These nonstate actors are more interested in commercial profit and controlling territory (that is, turf) to allow maximum freedom of movement and action. That freedom within countries and across national frontiers ensures commercial market share and revenues as well as secure bases for market expansion. Rather than trying to depose a government in a major strike (*golpe* or *coup*), as some insurgents have attempted, gangs take control of turf one street or neighborhood at a time (*coup d' street*). In addition to drug smuggling, these gangs are known to have expanded their activities to smuggling people, body parts, weapons, and cars, along with associated murder, kidnapping, and robbery; home and community invasion; and other lucrative societal destabilization activities. What makes all of this into a new kind of war—Post-Modern War—is that the security and sovereignty of affected countries is being impinged every day, and gangs' illicit commercial motives are, in fact, becoming an ominous political agenda.[3]

This challenge to rethink contemporary asymmetric conflict, as conducted by "irregular" forces, takes us to the direct linkage between gangs and insurgents. Although gangs and insurgents may differ somewhat in terms of motives and modes of operation, both types of nonstate actors must eventually seize political power to guarantee the freedom of action as well as the ideological or commercial enrichment environments they want. Additionally, the protean nature of the gang phenomenon and contemporary insurgency does not accommodate conformity to any prescribed definition. Thus, this author maintains the position taken in 2005—that is, the common denominator that defines gangs as mutations of insurgents is the irrevocable need to depose or control an incumbent government. As a consequence, the "Duck Analogy" applies. When third-generation gangs look like, walk like, and act like insurgents, while they may be a peculiar breed, they are, nevertheless, insurgents.[4]

To help leaders and opinion makers come to grips analytically with the most salient strategic aspects that dominate contemporary asymmetric gang-related conflict, this essay does three things. First, it clarifies the causal context of the

1. For early discussions of these phenomena, see Huntington, S. (1996) *The Clash of Civilizations and the Remaking of World Order*, Simon & Schuster, New York; and Kaplan, R. D. (2000) *The Coming Anarchy*, Random House, New York.

2. von Clausewitz, C. (1976) *On War*, Princeton University Press, New Brunswick, p. 596 [trans. Michael Howard & Peter Paret].

3. Sullivan, J. P. (2002) 'Terrorism, Crime and Private Armies', *Low Intensity Conflict & Law Enforcement*, Winter, pp. 239–253; Sullivan, J. P. & Bunker, R. J. (2003) 'Drug Cartels, Street Gangs, and Warlords', in *Non-State Threats and Future Wars*, ed. R. J. Bunker, Frank Cass, London, pp. 40–53; Manwaring, M. G. (2005) *Street Gangs: The New Urban Insurgency*, Strategic Studies Institute, Carlisle.

4. Manwaring (2005).

worldwide gang phenomenon. It starts with the general context of this type of conflict. The contextual part of the chapter ends with the logical conclusion that poor, insensitive, misguided, and/or corrupt governance—the central strategic problem—exacerbated by the blending of crime and violence with the political motivations of gang-related and other nonstate actors has led to the ultimate threat, that is, "the steady unraveling of many putative sovereign nation-states..." and an explosion of failing or failed states over much of the globe.[5] With this as background, we can answer the fundamental "Why?" question and begin to understand the adversary and the type of conflict we face.

Second, the essay moves from cause to effect. It outlines the ways, means, and ends that make up the strategic architecture of selected gang activities. That is, motives and vision, organization, programs of action, and results. To further elaborate causes and consequences, we examine selected cases or vignettes from Central America, the Caribbean, and South America that demonstrate how differing types of gang activities contribute to the instabilities that lead to the erosion of nation-state sovereignty and the processes of state failure are examined. One set of examples will suffice—territorial and commercial enrichment activities with subtle political motives. With these as background, we can answer the necessary "Who, What, and How?" questions. With these answers, we can advance our understanding of the political-psychological and military-police elements that lead to strategic success or failure in Post-Modern War—that is, the outcome.

Third, the remainder of the chapter is devoted to an explanation of the outcome or result of the sample of cases. This includes an analysis of the strategies that have contributed best to the success of the gang-related activities and the failure of counter-gang efforts in Central America, Jamaica, and Brazil. The explanation of the outcome will also answer the "So what?" question and will lead to generalizations, insights, and recommendations. In these terms, this essay moves from the author's 2005 introductory discussion of the gang phenomenon to a more advanced examination.[6] All this is designed to lead to the broad strategic vision necessary to understand and win a counter-gang war—not only the battles, but the war itself.

Context

It is this author's observation and experience that in dealing with the gang phenomenon—as in any kind of insurgency—a strategic approach is absolutely necessary to achieve success. Battles may be won at the tactical and operational levels of war, but wars are won or lost at the strategic level. The French and US military victories and political defeats in Algeria and Vietnam, respectively, are cases in point. The following commentary is an exploration of the strategic context

5. Olson, W. J. (1997) 'International Organized Crime: The Silent Threat to Sovereignty', *The Fletcher Forum*, Summer-Fall, p. 69.
6. Manwaring (2005).

within which the gang phenomenon operates. This contextual base explains the central strategic governance problem and the threat of state failure in the global security arena. Additionally, the context explains the most salient causes and effects of the phenomenon. In doing this, we address the Clausewitzian admonition that the most fundamental judgment that the statesman and commander have to take is to establish "the kind of war on which they are embarking; neither mistaking it for, nor trying to turn it into, something that is alien to its nature."[7] Clausewitz also reminds us: "It is possible to increase the likelihood of success without defeating the enemy's forces."[8] The problem is to understand that "war is a true political instrument. . . ."[9] "[T]he political object is the goal. . . and means can never be considered in isolation from their purpose."[10] With this kind of strategic approach to conflict, we can better understand how the desired outcome might or might not be achieved—and the most or least effective ways and means (that is, strategies or practices) for conducting the overall effort.

The Global Threat Situation and the Central Strategic Problem

With the ending of the Cold War and the beginning of the Post-Modern Era, many new challenges at home and abroad demand world leaders' attention and action at a time when what should be done remains unclear. The confusion in the current security environment stems in part from the quixotic hope that the disappearance of the Soviet Union would automatically move the world from war to peace. It did not. Instead, the world changed in unexpected ways, and the promise of a peace dividend degenerated into a "new world disorder." The contemporary chaotic strategic situation described by Samuel Huntington as a "clash of civilizations" reflects a lack of legitimate governance in many parts of the world, as well as the global chaos and instability that thrive under those conditions.[11] Hard evidence over time and throughout the world, however, shows that destabilizers and instabilities related to the clash of nationalities and the resultant political disorder are the general consequences of misguided, corrupt, insensitive, and incompetent governance. Thus, this author argues that governance is the central strategic problem in the contemporary unstable global security environment.[12]

7. Clausewitz (1976), p. 88.
8. Ibid, p. 92.
9. Ibid, p. 88.
10. Ibid, p. 87.
11. Huntington (1996); and Kaplan (2000).
12. These and subsequent assertions are consensus statements, based on a series of interviews conducted by the author with more than 300 senior US and Latin American officials and journalists. These interviews took place from October 1989 through July 1994, September 1996, December 1998, November 2000, February 2001, March 2002, February 2003, March and August 2004, February 2005, and March through May 2006. To allow anonymity for these who have an objection to their names being made public, these are cited hereafter as Author Interviews. Also see Fishel J. T. & Manwaring, M. G. 'The Central Political Challenge in the Global Security Environment: Governance and Legitimacy', *Uncomfortable Wars Revisited*, University of Oklahoma Press, Norman, pp. 55–70.

The General Threat to Governance

The general threat to the United States and the rest of the global community is the widespread violent challenge to incumbent governments' moral right to govern. It can be direct, as in the case of the highly organized and politicized terrorism conducted by the Red Brigades and experienced in Italy during the late 1970s and early 1980s, or it can be indirect, as in the case of roving bands of government-controlled thugs operating in Zimbabwe in the late 1990s and early 2000s, and the mercenary "infiltrators" currently working in that country.[13] At the same time, it can also involve "proxies" or "pseudo-paramilitaries," like those now operating in Colombia.[14] In any case, the basis of the challenge is the growing perception that many governing regimes—"democratic" or not—do not or cannot provide the necessary balance among political freedom, economic and social development, and physical security that results in peace, stability, and well-being.[15] In that context, a challenger's proposed explicit or implicit alternative political structure or philosophy—even if it is as extreme as that of Che Guevara fanatics, jihad, or gangsterism and warlordism—represents a different (and supposedly better) way of attaining that balance. Thus, we have the privilege of contemplating a world that is increasingly divided by the pathological claims of opposed ideologies, nationalisms, and commercial motivations.[16]

The cumulative result of the various activities discussed above is the story of failed and failing governments covering much of the globe. Even in cases where failure is not explicitly manifest, many countries have only the trappings of government and little of the reality. In all these cases, governments lack the resources and/or the will to enforce their own laws, provide security to their citizens, sustain healthy economies, and maintain their own sovereignty. It is in this context that criminal organizations flourish. Nevertheless, the threat from crime is hardly new. What is new is the profitability of criminal activities in a world where governments are weak and opportunities for crime have grown exponentially. In this environment, the ability of national and transnational criminal organizations to challenge the security and sovereignty of individual states has become a reality.[17]

13. See Lewis, A. (2001) 'A Regime of Thugs', *New York Times*, May 5; Manwaring, M. G. (1998) 'Italian Terrorism, 1968–1982: Strategic Lessons That Should Have Been Learned', *Low Intensity Conflict & Law Enforcement*, Summer, pp. 121–135; Jackson, P. (2004) 'Legacy of Bitterness: Insurgency in North West Rwanda', *Small Wars & Insurgencies*, Spring, pp. 19–37.

14. Cariboni, D. (2006) 'New Breed of Paramilitaries Infiltrate Urban 'Refuges'', Inter-Press Service (IPS), June 27. Available at: http://p.7.newes.re2.yahoo.com/s/oneworld/20060626/.

15. Aravena, F. R. (2003) 'Nuevo contexto de seguridad internacional: nuevos desafíos, nuevas oportunidades?', in *La seguridad en América Latina pos 11 de Septiembre*, ed. F. R. Aravena, FLACSO-Chile, pp. 23–43; Polgatti, A. C. (2004) *Conflicto y Guerra en la Post Modernidad*, Mago Editores, Santiago.

16. Maritain, J. (1951) *Man and the State*, University of Chicago Press, Chicago.

17. Olson (1997) 'International Organized Crime', pp. 70–71.

The Threat to Authority, Security, and National Stability

In this context, the organizations and activities of the most sophisticated of the gang phenomena (third-generation gangs) reflect expertise in communications, marketing, transportation, banking, and negotiations with other organizations.[18] Senior US and Latin American officials have noted that gangs and their criminal allies function as a consortium in much the same way as virtually any multinational Fortune 500 company. Thus, the gang phenomenon is a business organization striving to control the price of commodities, such as cocaine, arms, microchips, automobiles, and/or human body parts. In performing its business tasks with super efficiency and for maximum profit, the classical flat organization employs its chief executive officers and boards of directors, councils, systems of internal justice, public affairs officers, negotiators, and project managers. And, of course, the gang/criminal company has a security division—though somewhat more ruthless than its counterparts in legitimate Fortune 500 corporations.[19]

The annual net profit from gang-related activities is estimated to be in the billions of dollars. Precise numbers are not important. However, the enormity of the amount of money involved is important. The benefits these financial resources can generate when linked to utter ruthlessness of purpose and no moral or legal constraints are formidable. In this connection, a third-generation gang can afford the best talent—whether accountants, computer specialists, extortionists, or murderers—and the best equipment and technologies. With such extensive resources, a gang and its criminal allies can bribe government officials, hire thugs to intimidate those who cannot be bought, and kill those who cannot be intimidated. Third-generation gangs with bottomless pockets and no ethical compunctions, other than survival and self-enrichment at any cost, can move, shift, diversify, and promote operations at will—and, most significantly, they can outspend most of the legal political jurisdictions in the world.[20] All these means of generating freedom of movement and action include deliberate acts of violence and terror against key individuals and institutions associated with governance, economic development, and security. Gangs and drug cartels operating in Latin America and elsewhere call these activities "business incentives." Insurgents call these same types of activities "armed propaganda." Regardless of what they are called or where they take place, such activities are aimed at lessening regime authority—and replacing it with their own.[21]

18. Sullivan (2002).

19. Aguilar, S. (2004) Vice Minister of Justice, El Salvador, 'New Security Threats in the Western Hemisphere', USAWC Strategic Studies Institute-Florida International University conference, Center for Strategic and International Studies (CSIS), Washington, DC: 2004; Ambassador Jordan D. C. (1999) *Drug Politics: Dirty Money and Democracies*, University of Oklahoma Press, Norman; Bonilla, O. (2004) 'Current Situation of Gangs in El Salvador', Unpublished paper for the Consejo Nacional de Seguridad Pública, El Salvador, November.

20. Ibid.

21. Author Interviews. Also see Bejarano A. M. & Pizarro, E. (2003) 'Colombia: A Failing State?', *ReVista: Harvard Review of Latin America*, Spring, pp. 1–6.

Citizens' fears of cartels and gangs are exacerbated—particularly in Central America, the Caribbean Basin, and Brazil—because of regional gangs' apparent immunity from effective law enforcement efforts and the populace's lack of personal and collective security. This has created a dangerous synergy between organized criminality and terror that is blurring the traditional line between criminal and political violence. In that context, the greatest fear haunting many Latin American officials and citizens is that criminal violence is about to spiral completely out of control and acquire a political agenda.[22]

The Threat to State Sovereignty

As gangs have evolved from first- and second-generation criminal groups, they have gone from small street, turf-oriented, petty-cash entities to larger, internationalized, commercial-political organizations. In that evolutionary *coup d' street* process, gang violence moves from the first-generation level of "protection," extortion, gangsterism, and brigandage to a second-generation level of drug trafficking and other national and regional criminal activities. Gangs tend to continue first- and second-generation activities as they evolve to the third-generation phenomenon. They achieve third-generation status as they develop into more sophisticated organizations with broader markets and transnational alliances and more ambitious economic and political agendas.[23]

While third-generation illegal organizations become more powerful, the societies they prey upon become increasingly unstable, with more widespread social violence, serious degradation of the economy, and further governmental inability to provide personal and collective security and to guarantee the rule of law throughout the national territory. The West Indian Commission made this point in the Caribbean context as early as 1989: "... nothing exemplifies the powerlessness of regional governments more... than the sheer enormity of the inducements of the illegal drug trade.... On top of all this lie the implications for governance itself—at the hands of the 'dons' [gang leaders and drug traffickers]... who threaten governance from within."[24]

A government's failure to extend a sovereign presence throughout its national territory—Colombia is one example—leaves a vacuum in which gangs, drug cartels, leftist insurgents, the political and narco-Right, and the government itself may all compete for power. In that regard, ample evidence clearly demonstrates that Central American and Caribbean governments' authority and presence have diminished over large geographical portions of

22. Ibid. Also see Aguilar (2004); Jordan (1999); Bonilla (2004).

23. Sullivan (2002).

24. The fifteen-member commission was formed by Commonwealth Caribbean leaders in 1989 to help chart a course for the English-speaking Caribbean community into the twenty-first century. See Griffith, I. L. (1997) *Drugs and Security in the Caribbean: Sovereignty Under Siege*, Pennsylvania State University Press, University Park, p. 1.

those regions. However, contrary to popular perceptions, such areas are not "lawless" or "ungoverned." These territories are governed by the gangs, insurgents, warlords, and/or drug barons who operate where there is an absence or only partial presence of state institutions. In this sense, gangs' activities are not simply criminal and commercial in nature. They are much more far reaching. For their own preservation and expansion, the third-generation gangs and their leadership have little choice but to challenge the legitimate state monopoly on the exercise of control and use of violence and to take control of parts of states. A gang leader, then, acts in much the same way as any warlord or drug baron. At the same time, that status takes the gang into another, different level of conflict—intrastate war. This unconventional type of conflict pits nonstate actors (such as gangs, warlords, drug barons, and/or insurgents) directly against nation-states and requires a relatively effective war-making capability.[25] That, in turn, takes us back to the relationship between gangs and insurgents.

The Concomitant Attempt to Control or Depose Governments

We infer that street gangs are a mutated form of urban insurgency. Differentiating whether a third-generation gang is a criminal or an insurgent organization is irrelevant. Its putative objective is to control the state—or enough of it—to ensure its own ends. That is a real and substantive threat to national security and sovereignty and should be addressed as such. The common denominator that clearly defines gangs as mutations of urban insurgents is the irrevocable need to depose or control an incumbent government. Interestingly, it has been observed that other common denominators relate gangs and insurgents. First, there is not much difference between the alienated and marginalized youth recruited by gangs and those recruited by the Revolutionary Armed Forces of Colombia (FARC). Also, there is not much difference between the strategies used by gangs and insurgents.[26] Thus, it must be reiterated that if third-generation gangs look like, walk like, and act like insurgents, they probably are related to insurgents.[27]

The gang challenge to governance, the associated threat to national security and stability, the "silent challenge" to sovereignty, and the attempt either to control or depose governments are the most salient lessons that should have been learned by affected countries' involvement in the contemporary global security arena. The consistency of these lessons derived from relatively recent experience—from Asia's Golden Triangle to the Middle East, to Mexico, and from Central America to Haiti and the rest of the Caribbean Basin, and to the

25. Mackinlay, J. (2002) *Globalisation and Insurgency*, The International Institute for Strategic Studies, Pennsylvania State University Press.
26. Marks, T. A. (2003) 'Urban Insurgency', *Small Wars & Insurgencies*, Autumn, p. 141.
27. Author Interviews.

White Triangle coca-producing countries of South America's Andean region—inspires confidence that the lessons are valid.[28]

It is within this context that the phenomenon of gangs plays much more than a bit part on the world stage. Sendero Luminoso's founder, Abimael Guzmán, would likely warn: "These are the realities of the contemporary global security environment. All else is illusion."[29]

From Cause to Effect: Finding Order in Chaos

In this global security environment, governments, military and police forces, and other agencies responsible for various aspects of national security have little choice but to rethink security as it applies to "new" unconventional threats that many political and military leaders have tended to ignore or wish away. Probably the most significant "new" unconventional threats facing leaders today are those generated by the gang phenomenon. First-, second-, and third-generation gangs are engaged in perpetrating destabilizing and devastating violence all over the world, but contemporary leaders are confused regarding what this phenomenon is and what it is not. Their confusion is demonstrated by the various names being attached to such violence. Some call it "terrorism," others call it "criminal anarchy," "narco-terrorism," or "complex emergency situations." Widespread confusion is also shown by the various names that have been attached to the perpetrators of gang violence. They have been and are called "technicals" in Somalia, "soldiers" in Sierra Leone, "Tontons Macoutes" in Haiti, and "pseudo-militaries" in Colombia. Regardless of the names of these groups, political, military, and police leaders would be well advised to take an important step toward understanding and dealing with the gang phenomenon by following the advice of Sun Tzu. He explained, "What is of supreme importance in war is to attack the enemy's strategy."[30]

Even though no standardized organizational charts or well-thought-out published statements of purpose and strategy for mutating gangs exist, some very instructive common patterns of behavior have been observed. Thus, moving from broader to more specific examples, this part of the chapter examines the strategic architecture of selected first- and second-generation gang activities that are not explicitly political in Central and South America and the Caribbean. That architecture focuses on ways, means, and ends—synonymously, motives and

28. Author Interviews. Also see Griffith (1997); Lee III, R. W. (1990) *The White Labyrinth*, Transaction, New Brunswick; and Belaunde, L. B. (1990) 'Corrupción y discomposición del Estado', in *Pasta Basic de Cocaina, abuso de drogas*, eds. F. R. Leon & R. C. de la Mata, Peru, Lima, pp. 301-321; and Flynn, S. E. (1993) *The Transnational Drug Challenge and the New World Order*, Center for Strategic and International Studies, Washington, DC.

29. See Guzmán, A. (1985) 'El Discurso del Dr. Guzmán', in *Los partidos políticos en el Perú*, ed. R. Mercado, Ediciones Latinoamericanos, Lima; Comité Central del Partido Comunista del Perú (1986) *Desarrollar la guerra popular sirviendo a la revolución mundial*, Comité Central del Partido Comunista del Perú, Lima.

30. Tzu, S. (1977) *The Art of War*, Oxford University Press, London, p. 77 [trans Samuel B. Griffith]

vision, organization and leadership and programs of action, and results. The cases and architecture further center on specific territorial and commercial enrichment activities with subtle political implications.

The Basics of the Situation in Central America

The consensus among those who study this phenomenon is that many transnational gangs in Central America originated in Los Angeles, California, during the early 1990s. They were formed by young immigrants whose parents had come to the United States to avoid the ongoing instability and insurgencies in Central America during the 1980s. Once in the United States, many of the young immigrants were exposed to and became involved with gangs in the rough neighborhoods where they grew up. The gangs began moving into all five Central American republics in the 1990s, primarily because convicted felons were being sent from prisons in the United States back to the countries of their parents' origins. These gangs include the famed *Mara Salvatrucha* (MS-13), *Mara*-18, other smaller gangs in El Salvador, and an estimated 63,700 kindred spirits in Guatemala, Honduras, and Nicaragua.[31] It is noteworthy that the word *mara* is a slang term for "gang" and is derived from the name of a type of ant known for its ferocity. Literally, *trucha* means "trout" and is also a slang term for "shrewd Salvadoran." Thus, *Mara Salvatrucha* means a gang of shrewd Salvadorans. Additionally, *Mara*-18 is the designation for the 18th Street Gang.

What the Maras Do

Even though gangs in each country have some unique characteristics and can be bitter rivals for control of neighborhoods and other disputed territory or "turf," their origins, motives, and patterns of action are similar. These similarities begin with the various Central American gangs and their activities being intricately linked across international borders. Virtually all of them have flourished under the protection and mercenary income provided by larger and older transnational organized criminal networks. The basis for those alliances is the illegal drug trade that is credited with the transshipment of up to 75 percent of the cocaine that enters the United States. In addition to trafficking in drugs, Central American gangs are engaged in trafficking in human beings and weapons and are responsible for kidnappings, robberies, extortion, assassinations, and other illicit profit-generating activities.[32]

31. *'Central America and Mexico Gang Assessment'* (2006) USAID Bureau for Latin America and Caribbean Affairs, Washington, DC, April; Hereinafter referred to as AID Paper (2006).

32. Arana, A. (2001) 'The New Battle for Central America', *Foreign Affairs*, November/December, pp. 88-101; Arana, A. (2005) 'How the Street Gangs Took Central America', *Foreign Affairs*, May/June, pp. 98-110; Bonilla, O. (2004) 'Current Situation of Gangs in El Salvador', Unpublished paper written for the Consejo Nacional de Seguridad Pública del Salvador, November.

The root causes of gang activity in Central American countries and Mexico are also similar. They include gang members growing up in marginal areas with minimal access to basic social services; high levels of youth unemployment, compounded by insufficient access to educational and other public benefits; overwhelmed, ineffective, and often corrupt justice systems; easy access to weapons; dysfunctional families; and high levels of intra-familial and intra-community violence. It must be remembered, however, that it is not poverty, injustice, or misery that willfully kill, maim, and destroy. It is individual men and women—and, sometimes, boys and girls—who are prepared to implement all kinds of horrible and coercive "intimidations" and "instabilities" in their search for status and well-being.[33]

Thanks to the activities of disaffected youth gangs, overall crime rates have increased dramatically throughout the Central American region. Honduras has a murder rate of 154 per 100,000 population—double that of Colombia, even though that country is fighting three different insurgencies as well as its various drug cartels. In El Salvador, the homicide rate is about 40 per 100,000 inhabitants; Guatemala's murder rate has risen 40 percent from 2001 to 2004 and is now approximately 50 per 100,000; and the murder rate in Mexico is estimated to be about 14 per 100,000. The Mexican figure is low by Central American standards but is considered "epidemic" by the World Health Organization (WHO). Additionally, as if these statistics were not grim enough, Mexico has the highest incidence of kidnapping in the entire world—with an estimated 3,000 kidnappings in 2004.[34]

The General Results of Gang Activity

The impact of gang violence on regional economies is significant. The Inter-American Development Bank (IDB) estimates the cost of violence throughout all of Latin America to be 14.2 percent of gross domestic product (GDP).[35] Despite the fact that the data required to calculate these costs is admittedly vague and inconsistent, the governments of all five Central American countries and Mexico have expressed serious concerns. For example, Belize, Guatemala, and Mexico recently signed a multilateral agreement committing their governments to combating "narco-terrorism" and criminal gangs.[36] In the meantime, El Salvador and Honduras unilaterally continue to pursue hard-line anti-gang policies. They include stronger law enforcement efforts and longer prison sentences.

Clearly, Central American gangs, their activities, and impacts are linked across borders. An instability threat is definitely spilling out of the region into neighboring countries—including the United States. This is a regional problem that

33. AID Paper (2006); see also, Manwaring (2005).
34. See www.seguridadpublicaenmexico.org.mx
35. Londono, J. & Guerrero, R. (2006) 'Violencia en América Latina: epidemiología y costos', IADB Working Paper, no. R-375, p. 22; Also see AID Paper (2006).
36. AID Paper (2006).

requires regional solutions, but for further analytical clarity we will take a closer look at the situation by briefly examining the two major gangs in El Salvador.

El Salvador

As noted above, the roots of the *maras'* presence in El Salvador are traced to Southern California in the 1980s and 1990s. In the aftermath of the 1992 Los Angeles riots, police determined that local gangs—including a little-known group of Salvadoran immigrant youth known as the *Mara Salvatrucha*—had carried out most of the looting and violence. In response, California passed strict, new anti-gang laws. Then, with the subsequent "three strikes and you're out" legislation of 1994, the prison population in that state increased dramatically. Additionally, in 1996, the US Congress passed a "get tough" approach to immigration law. As a result of these successive pieces of legislation, thousands of convicted felons have been deported to El Salvador over the past several years. Significantly, until very recently, the Immigration and Naturalization Service's rules prohibited US officials from informing El Salvadoran officials of the deportees' backgrounds.[37]

The results were disastrous for El Salvador. The deportees, also called "returnees," many of whom had no childhood memories of ever living in El Salvador, arrived with their outlandish tattoos, their "Spanglish" language, and their arrogant attitudes. They quickly introduced the California gang culture, illegal drugs with their related "crack dens" and "crack babies," extortions, car-theft rings, burglaries, and contract killings. At first, Salvadoran officials had no idea what was happening—and when they began to understand the depth and seriousness of the problems brought by the gangs, they did not have the knowledge, experience, organization, or resources to deal with them. Given its momentum, the gang problem in El Salvador is thought to have escalated faster that in any other Central American country, and that country now "is captive to the growing influence and violence of gangs."[38]

Organization

The two main gangs, MS-13 and MS-18, boast 10,000 to 20,000 members. The Salvadoran National Council on Public Security calculates 39,000 members—22,000 in MS-13, 12,000 in MS-18, and another 5,000 in other gangs.[39] However, regardless of the lack of precise figures, both of those estimates are foreboding numbers in a country with a population of 6.5 million. Like the estimated membership numbers, gang organization is not perfectly clear. Nevertheless, there appears to be a hierarchical pyramid structure that is common among Central American, Caribbean, and South American gangs.

37. Ibid; Arana (2005).
38. Ibid.
39. Bonilla (2004).

At the top of the pyramid are the international bosses. Then, a second layer of international/transnational gang leadership exists. These second-level individuals oversee well-connected cells that are engaged primarily in trafficking global arms, drugs, and human beings. At the third level, gang cell members are involved in lower-level national vs. international trafficking of all kinds. Despite their national orientation, third-level members are in touch with upper-level as well as second-level members. This third level of gang membership contains centralized command and control elements that manage operational planning, finances, strategy, and provide some administrative support to the higher and lower echelons. Thus, they may be considered parts of a "Hollow Corporate Model." Additionally, national third-level gang cell members may manage geographically distributed "project teams."[40]

The fourth level of the generalized gang pyramid comprises the "neighborhood" gang members. This is a series of decentralized cliques (*clickas*) or cells that are responsible for specific neighborhoods or areas. Fourth-level individuals are not full-fledged MS-13 or MS-18 members. They make up three distinct levels at the lowest level of the gang pyramid—"sympathizers," "aspirants," and "nobodies," who do the drudge work in the *barrios* (neighborhoods/slums). They also act as "soldiers" for higher-level cells and project teams, or they may act as contracted mercenaries for other criminal organizations. As might be expected, this fourth-level group represents the largest segment of the total gang population, and their ages range from 8 to 18.[41]

Program of Action to Maximize Profits

The gangs' multi-level organization indicates a substantial enterprise, designed especially for conducting large-scale and small-scale business all the way from the transnational (global) level down to specific streets in specific *barrios*. This type of organization is also designed for quick and effective decision making and implementation of decisions. In short, the first priority of the Salvadoran MS-13 and MS-18 gang organizations is operating a successful business, along with its promotion and protection. More specifically, this type of organization permits continuous, protean operations over time. It allows for diversification of activities, diffusion of risk, and flexibility, in that quick adjustments to correct mistakes or to exploit developing opportunities may be made. The organization also provides a coherent mechanism for enforcing discipline and safeguarding operations at all levels. Additionally, it provides a planning facility that can deliberately expand operations and increase profits.[42]

Regarding expansion of operations, the Salvadoran gangs are situated to negotiate the establishment of their own trafficking corridors through Central

40. AID Paper (2006); Author Interviews.
41. Ibid.
42. Ibid.

America and Mexico. They are positioned to organize friendly or unfriendly takeovers of small cartels. They have also become sophisticated enough to begin to prohibit members from getting new tattoos and to discipline severely (execute) members who break rules related to the consumption of crack and cocaine. All this indicates an evolution from first-generation well into second-generation gang status. Nevertheless, the current organization of MS-13 and MS-18 also reflects that these gangs maintain a first-generation focus on turf. The gang members at that level of development operate under loose leadership, engage in a broad range of opportunistic, petty cash-type criminal activity, and are involved in serious inter-gang rivalry.[43]

The second-generation part of the organization is interested in market protection and expansion and focuses its illegal activities on drugs as a business. As the generalized pyramid organization suggests, the upper echelons are more cohesive, and leadership is more centralized. This second-generation group does not retain a specific turf orientation. Drug selling becomes a group rather than an individual activity, and the gangs exploit both violence and technology to control their competition and absorb new markets. Thus, both generations of gang members currently exist within the overall organization. The turf part of the gang is more prevalent, but the "marketers" are more productive and powerful.[44] As MS-13 and MS-18 continue to evolve in their internationalization and sophistication and span the second and third generation divide, they are more and more likely to develop explicit political aims that would truly challenge nation-states. This cautionary corollary takes us to the "Sullivan-Bunker Cocktail."

Results of Salvadoran Gang Activities

John Sullivan and Robert Bunker outline a pragmatic "cocktail mix" of nonmilitary methods by which a transnational nonstate actor, such as a second-generation gang, can challenge the *de jure* security and sovereignty of a given nation. This "Sullivan-Bunker Cocktail" has proved to be the case in no less than fifteen municipalities in El Salvador and in other political jurisdictions in neighboring Central American republics, Mexico, and Brazil.[45] Here is how it works:

> If the irregular attacker—criminal gangs, terrorists, insurgents, drug cartels, militant environmentalists, or a combination of the above—blends crime, terrorism, and war, he can extend his already significant influence. After embracing advanced technology weaponry, including weapons of mass destruction (including chemical and biological agents), radio frequency weapons, and advanced intelligence gathering technology, along with more common weapons systems, the attacker can transcend drug running, robbery, kidnapping, and murder and pose a significant challenge to the nation-state and its institutions.

43. Sullivan & Bunker (2003), pp. 48–49.
44. Ibid; Manwaring (2005), pp. 9–10.
45. Arana (2005), p. 101; Sullivan & Bunker (2003), pp. 45–53.

> Then, using complicity, intimidation, corruption, and indifference, the irregular attacker can quietly and subtly co-opt individual politicians and bureaucrats and gain political control of a given geographical or political enclave. Such corruption and distortion can potentially lead to the emergence of a network of government protection of illicit activities, and the emergence of a virtual criminal state or political entity. A series of networked enclaves could, then, become a dominant political actor within a state or group of states. Thus, rather than violently competing with a nation-state, an irregular attacker can criminally co-opt and seize control of the state.[46]

This is an example of a second-generation gang developing secure support bases through the application of coercive physical-psychological-political measures. In creating those secure support bases, gangs dominate local populations and erode the will of the system to resist their commercial enrichment efforts. This kind of "mix" of nontraditional activities is also a good example of the gang phenomenon expanding its role while staying under the threshold of state concern and counter-action. Even though there may be no explicit political agenda, control of territory (turf) and the people in it are keys to the achievement of minimal goals. In these terms, gangs must eventually take or control political power to guarantee the kind of environment they want.

As a consequence, the gang nonstate actor represents a triple threat to the authority and sovereignty of a government and those of its neighbors. First, murder, kidnapping, intimidation, corruption, and impunity from punishment undermine the ability of the state to perform its legitimizing security and public service functions. Second, by violently imposing their power over bureaucrats and elected officials of the state, gangs and their allies compromise the exercise of state authority and replace it with their own. Third, by taking control of portions of a given national territory and performing the tasks of government, the gang phenomenon can *de facto* transform itself into states within a state.

Response to the Gangs

In 2003, El Salvador's Flores administration passed hard-line (*mano dura*) legislation aimed at making it easier to jail gang members involved in criminal activity. However, that law was not strong enough. As a result, in 2004, legislation was passed approving the new president's anti-gang program, called Super Mano Dura (Super Firm Hand/or super hard line). This law provided steeper penalties for gang membership—up to five years in jail for gang membership and up to nine years for gang leadership. President Saco's government reported that this "get tough" program reduced the number of murders that year by 14 percent. The following year, in 2005, new legislation tightened gun ownership laws and began a complementary effort of prevention and rehabilitation called Mano Amiga (Friendly Hand).[47]

46. Ibid.
47. Fishel, J. T. & Grizzard, M. (2005) 'Countering Ideological Support to Terrorism in the Circum-Caribbean', *CSRC Discussion Paper 05/52*, September, p. 4; AID Paper (2006); Author Interviews.

Unfortunately, the hard-line approach sent the message to the Salvadoran public that law enforcement is the only effective way to deal with the gang problem; thus, prevention and intervention programs have received much less attention and fewer resources than necessary to make them effective. Then, unanticipated second- and third-order consequences resulted in straining the capacities of the already overcrowded prison system. Moreover, the judicial and police systems became saturated; there were not enough properly trained personnel in those systems to manage the gang problem. By the end of 2005, a total of 12,073 prisoners were held in 24 prison facilities with a combined design capacity of 7,312. Unfortunately, the gang problem has worsened significantly, and the only thing Salvadoran leaders agree on is that something must be done.[48] In sum, neither the Salvadoran government nor the United States has officially raised the level of the gang threat to the level of a threat to national security. To date, the Maras are viewed simply as a problem for law enforcement and the judicial system.

Jamaica

Similar to other countries in the Circum-Caribbean and elsewhere in the world, Jamaican posses (gangs) are the byproducts of high levels of poverty and unemployment rates as well as lack of upward social mobility. Among other things, the posses also represent the consequences of US deportation of Jamaican criminals back to the island, and—significantly—of regressive politics in Jamaica.[49] Unemployment and criminal deportation speak for themselves, but the political situation in Jamaica requires some elaboration.

Given the shift from the production of commodities toward knowledge-based products and the reduction of the costs of transport, goods, and labor under "globalization," the Jamaican government has experienced a loosening of control of its traditional resource bases. As a result, the government no longer has the income to provide public services in a welfare-type state. If anything, the Jamaican government has tended to "outsource" delivery of services to private and semi-private organizations. Under these conditions, local posses have taken on "social investment" in the areas they control. An important part of posses' programs of action is what is called "shared government, with a welfare aspect."[50] As a result, gang-controlled communities in Jamaica are considered to

48. Ibid.

49. An estimated 13,000 criminals have been deported from the United States since 1999. See: 'Buba, Bobo, Zambo and Zeeks—Domestic and International Issues Fuel Gang Violence in the Caribbean', *The Economist*, November 4, 2004; Fishel & Grizzard (2005); Griffith, I. L. (1997) *Drugs and Security in the Caribbean: Sovereignty under Siege*, Pennsylvania State University Press, University Park; Author Interviews.

50. Ibid; also see Olson, W. J. (1997) 'International Organized Crime: The Silent Threat to Sovereignty', *The Fletcher Forum*, Summer-Fall; and Rapley, J. (2006) 'The New Middle Ages', *Foreign Affairs*, May/June, pp. 95-103.

be among the safest in the country, and the posses are helping the people in their "jurisdictions" with education, public health, and employment problems. Thus, as the state has reduced its traditional security and service functions, posses have stepped in to fill the vacuum.[51]

Organization

The posses are Jamaican in origin and composed primarily of members of Jamaican descent. It is estimated that there are at least 85 different posses operating on the island with anywhere between 2,500 to 20,000 members. Each posse operates within a clearly defined territory or neighborhood. The basic structure of a Jamaican posse is fluid but cohesive. It comprises the all-powerful "don" or "area leader" at the apex of the organization, an upper echelon, a middle echelon, and the "workers" at the bottom of the social ladder. The upper echelon coordinates the posse's overall drug, arms, and human trafficking efforts. The middle group manages daily operational activities. The lower echelon performs street-level sales, purchases, protection, and acts of violence as assigned. When posses need additional workers, they prefer to use other Jamaicans. However, as posses have expanded their markets, they have been known to recruit "outsiders" as mules and street-level dealers. African-Americans, Trinidadians, Guyanese, and even Chinese immigrants are given tasks at the worker-level. They are kept ignorant of gang structure and members' identities. If outsiders are caught, the posse is not compromised; if they are not, the revenue continues to come in.[52]

Program

The Jamaican posses are considered to be extremely self-reliant and self-contained. They have their own aircraft, watercraft, and crews for "pick up and delivery" and their own personnel to run legitimate businesses and conduct money-laundering tasks. In that connection, posses have expanded their operations into the entire Caribbean Basin, the United States, Canada, and Europe. The general reputation of Jamaican posses is one of high efficiency and absolute ruthlessness in pursuit of their territorial and commercial interests. Examples of swift and brutal violence include—but are not limited to—fire bombing, throat slashing, and dismemberment of victims and their families. As such, Jamaican posses are credited with the highest level of violence in the English-speaking Caribbean and 60 percent of the crime in the entire region.[53]

This example of the gang phenomenon fits very well into the typology description of second-generation gangs. They are organized for business and

51. Ibid.
52. 'Out of the Underworld', *The Economist*, January 27, 2006, p. 26.
53. Ibid; also see Fishel & Grizzard (2005); Griffith (1997); and Rapley (2006).

commercial gains. They have a more hierarchical leadership structure than more politically oriented and security-conscious third-generation gangs. Members tend to focus on drug trafficking and market protection first and on market expansion second. They use the level of violence necessary to protect their markets and control their competition. They also use violence as political interface to negate law-enforcement efforts directed against them by police and other security organizations. And, as they seek to control or incapacitate national and international security institutions, they dominate community life and territory. In this environment, posses are almost forced to link with and provide services to other posses and to other transnational criminal organizations from time to time.[54]

Domination of posses' respective turf in the confined area that is Jamaica generates a stability based on constant cooperation and negotiation with other gangs and transnational criminal organizations, as well as with the state. That kind of cooperation was demonstrated in May 2006 with a month-long series of civic activities called a "Safe Communities Campaign," a government initiative to assist selected communities—including the posses in them—to think and act in terms of reggae icon Bob Marley's message of "love, peace, and unity."[55] When these kinds of efforts fail, as this one did, the result is conflict and a level of violence commensurate with the level of importance of the issue(s) involved. In that context, one can see the rise of private, "don"-controlled, enclaves that coexist in delicate—often symbiotic—relationships with the Jamaican government and its security institutions. That, in turn, blurs the line between criminal and political violence and makes the posses increasingly immune to state intervention.[56] As a further consequence, the effective sovereignty of the state and the personal security of citizens are being impinged every day, and the posses' commercial motives for controlling people and territory are, in fact, an implicit political agenda.[57]

This, again, is an almost classic example of first- and second-generation gang activity and development. The generic evolution of urban street gangs illustrates that this is a compound-complex issue that has implications at three different levels of analysis. First, all three generations of gangs generate serious domestic instability and insecurity. Of course, as gangs evolve, they generate more and more violence and instability over wider and wider sections of the political map and create regional instability and insecurity. Second, because of their internal (intrastate) criminal activities and their international (transnational) commercial and political alliances and actions, they exacerbate the confusion regarding the traditional distinctions between police law enforcement functions and military national security functions—to the extent that very little that is effective or lasting has been done to control or eliminate them. Third, thus, first- and

54. Manwaring (2005), p. 10.
55. 'Anti-crime community initiative to be launched', *Jamaica Gleaner*, February 6, 2006.
56. Rapley (2006).
57. Ibid; Author Interviews.

second-generation gangs inadvertently erode the effective sovereignty of the nation-states within which they operate.

Within the context of that frustration, some contemporary civilian, military, and police leaders appear to recognize that this modern global world is much too interrelated, complicated, and dangerous for them to advocate a strictly law-enforcement solution—or even a strictly military solution—to provide any viable response to contemporary security, stability, and sovereignty threats. What is required is a unified civil-military effort to apply the full human and physical resources of the nation-state—and the international community—to generate effective multilateral solutions to transnational issues.[58] This type of unified international effort has not been forthcoming.

Response

The Organization of American States (OAS), the United States, and the various Caribbean governments have been unable or unwilling to deal effectively with the gangs that permeate the region. The OAS affirmed in 2003 that gang-related "threats, concerns, and other challenges are cross-cutting problems that may require hemispheric cooperation" and that "the traditional concept and approach [to security threats] should be expanded to encompass new and non-traditional threats...." The final result of this affirmation was the *condemnation* of "transnational organized crime, since it constitutes an assault on institutions in our states and negatively affects our societies."[59] Nevertheless, the OAS has been reluctant to go beyond its diplomatic "condemnation." The United States has not done a great deal more. To be fair, however, it must be noted that for 2006, the United States allocated $10 million for the ongoing antidrug and anticrime efforts outlined in the "Third Border Initiative" and is providing other benefits under the Caribbean Basin Initiative.[60] Given the entire scope of the issue, however, this clearly is not enough.

The democratically elected governments in the Caribbean argue that criminal gangs, such as the Jamaican posses, have been able to profit from their globalized operations to the point where they have succeeded in putting themselves beyond the capability of most countries in the region to destroy them or even seriously disrupt their operations. Today, as only one example, it is estimated that the Colombian drug cartel earns more money in one year from its activities than most of the countries in Latin America and the Caribbean generate in taxes in a year. Thus, most governments in the region are simply outmatched by the gang

58. 'Draft Declaration on Security in the Americas', Approved by the Permanent Council of the Organization of American States at its regular session, held on October 22, 2003, in Mexico City, pp. 1, 3, 8.

59. US-CARICOM Update, 'Secretary Rice Meets with Caribbean Officials to Discuss Democracy, Trade, and Security', March 24, 2006.

60. Olson (1997); Author Interviews.

phenomenon. The gangs have more money, better arms, and more effective organizations than the states.

Additionally, gangs are gradually supplementing the brute violence of previous generations with the brainpower of a new generation of members who are computer savvy and MBA business-school trained. Many of this new generation—like the older generations—are also recipients of "graduate educations" from North American and other prison systems. In all, increasing gang effectiveness, violence, and impunity have fueled doubts in the citizenry about the problem-solving ability of their elected leaders.[61] As a consequence, elected governments in the Caribbean in general and Jamaica in particular are not doing much more than the OAS or the United States to deal with the gangs.

The Brazilian PCC (Primeiro Comando da Capital)

The great city of São Paulo, Brazil—the proverbial industrial "locomotive" that pulls the "train" of the world's eighth largest economy—was paralyzed for five days in mid-May 2006. Virtually nothing moved. Transportation, businesses, factories, offices, banks, schools, and shopping centers were shut down. Additionally, hundreds of people were killed and wounded, buses were torched, banks were robbed, police stations were attacked, and rebellions broke out in 82 prisons within the state of São Paulo's penal system. The city of São Paulo was a frightening place during those five days in May. Beyond the severe limitations of the state government's security forces—which were reportedly as involved in extra-judicial killings as the criminal perpetrators of the chaos—conditions in São Paulo made any effort to assert governmental authority or conduct essential public services problematic.[62]

Organization and Motives

Ostensibly, this turmoil and retribution was triggered by prisoners in the São Paulo prison system who were being transferred to a "maximum security prison" that was not equipped to allow the inmates to watch the much anticipated World Cup soccer matches on TV. Thus, probably, an ambitious prisoner-initiated "prison rights" agenda was a part of the motive for the rebellion. The consensus is that at its base, the "surprise May explosion" in São Paulo was a show of force by the largest criminal gang in the Western Hemisphere.[63] That organization, called the PCC (Primeiro Comando da Capital) has an estimated 65,000 to 125,000 full- and part-time dues-paying members and is led by a brilliant and uncompromising

61. Ibid.
62. Chang, J. (2006) 'Gang Kicks Around Political Clout', *Miami Herald*, May 31; 'The Mob Takes on the State', *The Economist*, May 20, 2006; and Cirino, J. A. (2006) 'Marcola, el jefe del arena urbana fuera de Control', *Investigación*, May 24.
63. Ibid.

38-year-old career criminal called "Marcola" (Marcos Williams Herbas Comapcho). And, although, it is thought that there are no more than 6,000 active PCC members in Brazil's prison system, it is known that the PCC has extended its influence into the *favelas* ("ungoverned" slums)[64] of São Paulo, Rio de Janeiro, and the other major cities of the country. This has been accomplished through a long series of carefully negotiated, and sometimes forced, alliances with other gangs, and *favela* chiefs (*jefes da favela*).[65] As a result, at any given time, Marcola controls at least 60,000 PCC members. Consequently, the May explosion in São Paulo was initiated, orchestrated, and terminated by Marcola—from a "maximum security prison" with his mobile telephone.[66]

It is argued that the purpose of the subliminal message in Marcola's "show of force" was to announce to the state and federal governments that the PCC and its allies in the *favelas* are strong enough to compel the negotiation of terms of sovereignty.[67] Given that Marcola got everything he wanted out of the negotiations to end the chaos in São Paulo, it is probably safe to say that the PCC and the *jefes* or barons of the *favelas* have grown more powerful, while the state has lost a measure of its authority and has become more constrained.[68]

Program of Action

Favelas are the base of the PCC's extended power. In the *favela*, "traffic" is everything, and "territory controlled" is critical. The PCC, like other criminal gangs throughout the Western Hemisphere and the world, is deeply involved in drug trafficking, arms trafficking, kidnapping, robberies, and extortion. To maintain its momentum and expand its markets, the organization has increasingly adopted an offensive mode with tactics appropriate to urban guerrilla war in which it looks for confrontations with rival gangs and police and military forces. PCC members and temporary-hire "soldiers" from the *favelas* carry out their violent tasks armed with automatic weapons, machine guns, hand grenades, rocket propelled grenades, antipersonnel mines, and crudely armored vehicles. Command and Control (C2) is provided primarily through a very efficient communication network based on mobile telephones. This takes us back to Marcola and his cell phone. In areas controlled by the PCC, or in areas that might be "invaded" by PCC units, one has a choice of submitting and contributing or *subir al cielo* (go up to heaven).[69]

In addition to its violent turf-controlling effects and related trafficking activities, the PCC appears to have more than a casual self-serving criminal rights

64. Abandoned by the state, *favelas* are city-states within the major cities of Brazil. They are feudal in nature and structure and are noted as such by Rapley (2006).
65. A *jefe da favela* may be considered roughly equivalent to a feudal baron.
66. Chang (2006); *The Economist* (2006); Cirino (2006).
67. Ibid.
68. Ibid.
69. Cirino (2006); Author Interviews.

agenda. The organization hires 18 to 20 full-time lawyers, who not only act as advocates for gang members, but also act as mentors for young people. One of the great successes of the PCC has been to infiltrate or "colonize" the governmental organization that administers the entrance examinations required for entry into Brazilian public service. The job of the PCC mentor is to ensure that young gang members who have the ability and the desire to enter into public service obtain the necessary education and pass the appropriate examinations. As a consequence, the PCC is putting its own people into bureaucratic positions it considers important in the Brazilian system. Thus, in addition to controlling "ungoverned" slums in the major cities of the country, the PCC appears to be steadily extending its influence into the public service. A logical conclusion to draw from this effort would simply be that Marcola is deliberately developing a parallel state within the state.[70]

Response

It would appear that the São Paulo state government and the Brazilian federal government were not particularly concerned with the specific issues that brought on the May crisis in São Paulo. The official state of São Paulo response to the May violence and chaos was simply: "I say to our people the police are still in the streets, they [the people] can go out and have fun this weekend."[71] This "business (or fun) as usual" approach to the gang problem and to the ungoverned territory issue is similar to that expressed not too long ago when a high-ranking civilian official said, "Not to worry. Brazil will grow out of this."[72]

On the positive side of this situation, the São Paulo "explosion" brought to light socioeconomic-political-psychological problems—poverty, corruption, penetration of the political system, and impunity—that probably will be debated in upcoming elections. Hopefully, that will result in more than just "tough talk." On the negative side of the problem, this unfortunate episode demonstrates that loosely governed states and ungoverned territories within them are attractive venues for gangs and other nonstate actors seeking to avoid the reach of criminal justice systems and to evade surveillance and sanctions. At the same time, this well-planned and carefully implemented incident in São Paulo vividly illustrates a real and significant threat to the security, stability, and effective sovereignty of the Brazilian state.

In this connection, the PCC provides a good example of a second-generation gang moving strongly toward third-generation status. The PCC is using a variety of illegal and legal approaches to power and illustrating the increasing lack of differentiation among gangs and insurgents in contemporary urban insurgency.

70. Ibid.

71. Police Colonel Elizeu Éclair, reported by *BBC News*, May 20, 2006. Available at: http://news.bbc.co.uk/go/pr/fr/-/2/hi/Americas/49999906.stan.

72. Author Interviews.

Additionally and importantly, the May incident in São Paulo is a prime example of a "new jungle" within which gangs and their warlord and insurgent cousins can find space from which to conduct their illicit, commercial, enrichment trafficking. At the same time, they have the place from which to initiate serious political attacks directed toward the achievement of control of the state and its governing apparatus.

Implications

In the Western Hemisphere's "new wars," it appears that commercial enrichment remains the primary motivation for the various destabilizing gangs and their criminal allies. The gangs are not yet directly challenging governments for control of the state—and they are not sending conventional military forces across national borders. As a consequence, most political leaders are still thinking in traditional terms and have not caught up with reality. They do not appreciate the extent and nature of the challenge to political order and competent government being raised by the gang phenomenon.[73] In the meantime, gangs are moving to ensure that they have maximum freedom of movement and action within and between national territories. Significantly, it must be understood that this is the purview of legitimate sovereign governance.

Solutions to the problems of stability, security, and illegitimate sovereign governance take us back to state failure. State failure is a process—not an outcome. It is a process by which the state loses the capacity and/or the will to perform its legitimizing security and governance functions. It may also be a process by which the state is responding to the fact that it had never developed those capabilities in the first place. In any event, there is ample evidence to show that gangs develop out of and prosper in "ungoverned" or poorly governed areas, and it follows that gangs and post-modern war are the products of the state failure processes.[74] Thus, the ultimate threat of destabilizing gang activities is not instability or even violence. Instead, it is either state failure or the coerced imposition of a radical socioeconomic-political restructuring of the state and its governance. In either case, failed states simply do not go away. They tend to linger and to go from bad to worse. The longer they persist, the more they and their spillover effects endanger regional peace and security. Failing and failed states become dysfunctional states, rogue states, divided states (governed by rival warlords), criminal states, or narco states.[75] For example, Haiti comes immediately to mind, as do Liberia, Sierra Leone, and Somalia.

73. Olson (1997).
74. Sullivan & Bunker (2003).
75. Esty, D. C. et al. (1998) 'The State Failure Project: Early Warning Research for U.S. Foreign Policy Planning', in *Preventive Measures: Building Risk Assessment and Crisis Early Warning Systems*, eds. J. L. Davies & T. R. Gurr, Rowman & Littlefield, New York; Dorff, R. H. (2003) 'Strategy, Grand Strategy, and the Search for Strategy', in *The Search for Security: A U.S. Grand Strategy for the Twenty-First Century*, eds. M. G. Manwaring, E. G. Corr & R. H. Dorff, Praeger, Westport, pp. 127-240.

Key Points and Lessons

What makes the above cases or situations and their implications significant beyond their own domestic political context is that they are situations from which contemporary lessons of irregular urban political warfare can be learned. Additionally, these cases are harbingers and results of much of the ongoing political chaos of the Post-Modern Era of the twenty-first century. They stress the following:

- Gangs contribute significantly to national, regional, and global instability. As they evolve, they generate more and more terror, violence, and instability over wider and wider sections of the political map.
- Gangs, far from being apolitical and unique, are becoming more and more similar to their politicized insurgent and warlord cousins. They maintain a political logic that is a continuation of regional politics by other means.
- Gangs use highly political-psychological, as well as purely violent, ways and means to achieve their objectives.
- The primary characteristics of a gang and its leadership are individual and group survival and personal gain. Beyond this there are no rules.
- Gangs tend not to be considered as serious challenges to national security and sovereignty. Rather, they are treated as low-level law-enforcement problems.

The gang phenomenon has been with us for several years. In that time, violence and instability have varied from acute to tolerable and back through the cycle again and again. However, just because a situation becomes tolerable does not mean that it will go away or should be ignored. Sun Tzu reminds us: "There has never been a protracted war from which a country has benefited."[76]

From Failure to Success? More Lessons

The current threat from the gang phenomenon is different in nature and method from that of past conflicts. In the past, what mattered most were military bases, preserving access to sea lines of communication, choke points, raw materials, and territory—and denying those assets to one's enemies. And, in the past, the enemy was a clearly discernable military force, backed by a nation-state's industrial capability to create and then maintain that military force outside its own borders. Now, adversaries are aiming directly at achieving or controlling palpable political power. And, the enemy is not a traditional recognizable military entity with a "fixed address" and clearly defined, traditional military maneuver methods. Rather, the enemy now becomes an illusive state, nonstate, or individual political actor who prefers unconventional and indirect confrontational methods.

This "new" kind of confrontation cannot be dealt with by infantry, tanks, and aircraft attacking specific territory or destroying buildings, neighborhoods, or

76. Tzu (1971), p. 73.

cities, although that may be important in a given discrete tactical context. More than anything else, strategic success in contemporary conflict is based on the sophisticated political-psychological application of all instruments of power. In short, this kind of war relies mostly on words, images, and ideas—and a certain disregard for convention. We have seen those new asymmetric elements of gang strategy being applied, at will and with impunity, by the weak against the strong. Thus, we do not need a further explanation of past counter-gang failures. What we need is a forward-looking discussion of past and future counter-gang successes. That discussion centers on the strategies that contributed to the failure of gang strategy and the success of counter-gang strategy in one seminal situation—the Italian case of the late 1960s through the early 1980s.

The Italian Experience with the Gang Phenomenon, 1968–1983

In post-Napoleonic Europe, Italy was defined simply as a "geographic expression." In post-World War II Europe, Italy had only advanced to the status of "the sick man of Europe." That "sick" country was experiencing virtually every symptom of "failing state" status. Productivity was down; gross domestic product (GDP) was down. The Italian currency was down and moving further downward. The only statistics moving upward on the charts were labor strife, poverty, crime, and immigration. In that socioeconomic milieu, chronic political instability was illustrated by the succession of 39 governments over the 35 years between the promulgation of the 1948 Constitution and 1983. This state of affairs adversely affected societal relations and increased Italy's vulnerability to criminal and subversive designs. As a result, from 1968 through 1983, literally 297 different "leftist" groups, along with several additional militant separatist, pacifist, anarchist, and monarchist organizations, mobilized and conducted a "terror" campaign to overthrow the Italian state.[77]

The so-called "Red Brigades" were at the forefront of that campaign and proved to be the most practical, calculating, and cynical of all the Italian "terrorist" organizations at conducting political war. Additionally, these Red Brigades were the theoretical equivalent to a highly politicized third-generation gang supported by outside forces.[78] One can quibble about the difference between the support of the Soviet Union to the Red Brigades vs. the support of illegal drug trafficking organizations to Latin American and Caribbean gangs, but support is support. And, again, the common denominator in this equation is that both of the "outside forces" were or are dedicated to the overthrow or control of the state. As a consequence, we concentrate our attention on the Red Brigades, rather than the more than 300 additional organizations that made up the Italian

77. Pisano, V. S. (1987) *The Dynamics of Subversion and Violence in Contemporary Italy*, Stanford University, Hoover Institution Press, Stanford, pp. 5–37.

78. A third-generation gang is a mercenary-type group with goals of power and a set of fully developed political aims. See Sullivan & Bunker (2003); Manwaring (2005).

gang phenomenon during the 1968–1983 time period. This is a good example from which to learn how governments might ultimately control—or succumb to—the strategic challenges of the gang phenomenon.

Additional Contextual Background

Italian "terrorism" not taken very seriously through the 1970s and was allowed to fester and grow. It was not until after the highly publicized 1978 kidnapping, people's trial, and execution of five-time Prime Minister Aldo Moro that the Italian government directly addressed the instability and violence issue. The murder of Prime Minister Moro marked the first time in more than 10 years of kidnappings, murders, maimings, and bombings that the Italian government decided that the violent gang phenomenon was, in fact, more than a complex law enforcement problem. The various gangs or gang equivalents through the use of terrorism were challenging the integrity of the country's political institutions and creating an unacceptable level of internal instability. Decision makers began to understand that the intent of every one of the 300 or more leftist, rightist, and separatist antigovernment organizations, including the Red Brigades, was to "destroy the political equilibrium of Italy and give impetus to the conquest of political power...."[79] As a consequence, the increasing violence and criminality of that 10-year period from 1968 to 1978 were finally defined as a national security problem.

Significantly, Italy's planning and coordination of the response to the terrorist challenge essentially fell to the paramilitary Carabinieri. At the same time, the mandate given to those political, economic, informational, and security instruments of the state that would implement the counter-terrorist (counter-gang) effort was two-fold. First, there would be no "Dirty War" in Italy. Second, there would be no strategic ambiguity—that is, the various political-security instruments of the Italian state would integrate all their actions under the direction of a Carabinieri General. The intent was straightforward: together, these unifying and legitimizing efforts would reestablish the kind of stability that was derived from popular Italian perceptions that the authority of the state was genuine and effective and that it used morally correct means for reasonable and fair purposes. In that context, the Italian experience illustrates the effective "best practices" through which to reverse the impetus toward failing or failed state status.[80]

Objectives and Vision of the Red Brigades

The Italian gang phenomenon emerged from the prolonged protest cycle of the late 1960s. During those years, demands for political, economic, and social

79. Pisano (1987). Also see Testimony of Red Brigadist Antonio Savasta, quoted in Richard Drake (1995) *The Aldo Moro Murder Case*, Harvard University Press, Cambridge, MA, p. 50; Declaration of Red Brigades sent to *L'Expresso* and published as 'Le due anime delle Br', March 1, 1987.
80. Ibid; Author Interviews.

reforms were widespread and included elements of the entire society. Extreme left-wing fringe elements, ranging from white-collar workers to industrial workers to university students, organized and became a political force when workers and students expressed their grievances in mass demonstrations that often were confronted violently by police. Thus, the Red Brigades evolved from demonstrators favoring socioeconomic reforms into militants defending themselves against police repression. As time moved on, the violence of the Red Brigades changed from self-protection to proactive and aggressive actions. Those actions increasingly shifted from demonstrations, sit-ins, and passing out propaganda to direct violence against individuals and property. All these efforts were considered to be part of the war against the state because "the State, it juristic ideology, and its law are nothing other than instruments through which the elites exercise their control over the people."[81]

For the Red Brigadists, these political crimes quickly became acts of justice. At first, they were acts of retribution and vengeance against perceived attackers. For example, Aldo Moro had to be eliminated because he embodied "all that was the most intelligent and the most dangerous in the [governing] regime." Then, progressively, more ordinary individuals were singled out—depending on the "bureaucratic need."[82] "You make a political analysis, but then you need a victim. When you have singled out your victim... he is the one to be blamed for everything. In that moment, there is already the logic of a trial in which you have already decided that he is guilty; you only have to decide about his punishment.... [Y]ou punish him not only for what he has done but also for all the rest."[83] From that point, together with adventure, action became an objective, a motive, and a reward in itself.[84]

Basic Organization of the Red Brigades

The Red Brigades were founded in Milan by members of a militant leftist group called the Metropolitan Political Collective (CPM). Some of the organizers came from Marxist-Leninist backgrounds, and others from the more traditional Italian left. The CPM quickly spread to Turin, where workers of that major industrial city increasingly became more violently involved with the police. Subsequent organizational splintering, reorganization, ideology, and actions were adapted to the needs of the organizers' militant orientation. In that connection, similar to the MS-13 gangs in Central America and the Jamaican posses, only people who were able to pass a rigorous vetting process and initiatory rights were accepted into the ranks of the Red Brigades. That process carefully evaluated an individual's military courage and group loyalty. Successful recruits were divided

81. Ibid.
82. Testimony of Antonio Savasta, quoted in Drake (1995), p. 51.
83. Savasta, quoted in della Porta, D. (1995) 'Left-Wing Terrorism in Italy', in *Terrorism in Context*, ed. Martha Crenshaw, Pennsylvania State University Press, University Park, p. 150.
84. Ibid; Author Interviews.

into regular and irregular forces. Regulars were the only members who were allowed into the vertical command structure and were required to go "underground" and work for the organization full time. Irregulars kept their jobs and lived with their families. Their primary tasks were to recruit sympathizers and to help generate support for the movement. At the same time, like their counterparts in Latin America and the Caribbean, rules on centralization and vertical hierarchy were enforced strictly, and disagreements with authoritative decisions were not tolerated.[85]

The organizational structure of the so-called Red Brigades included a strategic directorate, an executive committee, several "columns," and a number of "fronts." The column was the basic self-sustaining unit of the movement. It was composed of regulars and was given a specific geographic area of responsibility, such as Genoa, or certain neighborhoods of Milan, Turin, or Rome. The columns controlled subordinate brigades, termed logistical or mass, depending on the mission. The logistical brigades provided support, and the mass brigades were responsible for intelligence and operations. Thus, the primary orientation of all recruits was either specifically military or to provide support for the military actions of the group. Because of that political culture, again—like Western Hemisphere gangs—the Red Brigades attracted those individual men and women who understood discipline and were prone to violence.[86]

The Program to Destroy the "Moribund Italian State"

At the height of Italian "terrorism" in the late 1970s, when people were asked about the program of the Red Brigades, most citizens would describe their "terrorism" as *ad hoc* and arbitrary. Arbitrary perhaps, but *ad hoc* it was not. Red Brigade leadership opposed the idea of spontaneity, and all actions of the organization were carefully planned, organized, and implemented.[87] The primary means of attacking the state and the intent of any action conducted by the Red Brigades was simply to disrupt and destroy symbols of (1) whatever the leadership defined as "bad" or as a "threat" to organizational security and (2) whatever would accrue to the progressive discrediting of public institutions that, in turn, would erode the basic public trust in the Italian government.[88]

Typical human targets for the mass brigades included representatives of the capitalist system of production, political figures, and members of the judiciary and security agencies. Typical material targets included property in any way related to the types of individuals noted above. Attacks on property either were complementary to attacks on persons or served for the training and testing of recruits. Targeting tactics involved close, long-term observation of targets and

85. Ibid.
86. Ibid.
87. Ibid.
88. Ibid; testimony of Red Brigadist Patrizio Peci, recorded in Moran, S. E. (ed.) (1986) *A Rand Note: Court Depositions of Three Red Brigadists*, Santa Monica: RAND, February, p. 47.

the use of explosives, individual weapons, and ambush, raid, or abduction—depending on the difficulty of attacking a specific individual and his prescribed punishment.[89] As only a very few examples, major attacks included: (1) the wounding of Gavino Manca in Milan, an executive at Pirelli, and the murder of Pietro Coggiola in Turin, an executive with Lancia; (2) the abduction and murder of the President of the Christian Democratic Party and former Prime Minister Aldo Moro in Rome; (3) the murder of Supreme Court Judge Ricardo Palma in Rome; and (4) the murder of Assistant Deputy Police Commissioner Antonio Esposito in Genoa.[90]

Interestingly, the degree of public tolerance for terrorist violence did not allow the murder of the five escorts accompanying Aldo Moro to be classified as murder—that is, only "major murders," such as that of Mr. Moro, were counted as murders. In any event, the ratio of woundings to murders generally was consistent over the late 1970s and early 1980s at about 2:1. And, the ratio of abductions/kidnappings to murders over the same period was about 3 to 4:1.[91]

Thus, the program of the Red Brigades was straightforward, transparent, and unchanged from the organization's beginnings in 1969 through the early 1980s. The leadership stressed terrorism as a tactic and a strategy in an irregular urban war. It assumed that terrorism would challenge the integrity of Italy's political and socioeconomic institutions and create an unacceptable level of instability. In turn, the resultant instability was expected to erode the basic public trust that must underlie the legitimate functioning of the state.[92]

Response to Red Brigades' Strategy

The Italian experience with urban irregular war was the transition point toward a new age of unconventional conflict, in which the definition of 'enemy' became elusive and the use of 'power' against that foe became diffuse. Underlying these ambiguous issues was the fact that this war was an intrastate affair. It was Italians versus Italians. All these ambiguities intruded on the traditional Italian and world vision of war and required a new paradigm that would address the addition of a number of political-social-psychological-moral dimensions designed to attack the strategy of the Italian gang phenomenon.

Thinking about the New Paradigm

Italian planners generally understood that an ambiguous antigang urban political war, in fact, was a series of 'wars' within the general war. These wars would include (1) the more traditional police-military war against the gangs; (2) a 'war'

89. Ibid; della Porta (1995), p. 130.
90. Ibid; these data may also be found in Pisano (1987), pp. 157-167.
91. Ibid.
92. Ibid.

for legitimacy and the moral right of the incumbent democratically elected regime to exist; (3) a 'war' to unify a multi-dimensional political-social-psychological-police effort within the fragmented Italian bureaucracy; (4) an information 'war' to convince the Italian people of the moral rectitude of the counter-gang campaign; (5) a 'war' to isolate the gangs from their internal support; (6) a 'war" to isolate the gangs from their external support; and (7) an intelligence 'war' to locate and neutralize the men and women who lead, plan, and execute violent destabilizing actions.[93] These wars represent the major strategic dimensions that determine the outcome of the general war and take into account the so-called "forgotten" Clausewitzian political-psychological-socio-economic-moral dimensions of conflict. According to one of Clausewitz's translators, Michael Howard, these crucial "forgotten" dimensions make the difference between winning the battles or winning the war itself.[94]

Because of the continuing absence of a homogenous parliamentary majority and the resultant political instability, the Italian government could not micro-manage the paradigm. It, fortunately for Italy, was limited to the promulgation of fundamental measures that would facilitate the conduct of a counter-terrorist strategy at the national security level. Thus, at the national security level, it was understood that the concept of "wars within the war" would be the basis for the new paradigm. This concept was further reinforced by the fact that it is very close to the ideas that both Carl von Clausewitz and Niccolò Machiavelli addressed in their treatises on war and on gaining control of a state. Machiavelli, for example, argues that good laws and good arms allow the leader with *virtu* to master *fortuna* to take—or maintain—effective control of a state.

Superior *virtu* consists of six related elements: (1) a well-disciplined and trained security force; (2) careful planning for the application of that force before and after power is achieved; (3) the skillful use of spies (intelligence); (4) isolation of the enemy from the various sources of his support; (5) *unison* (unity) of political-military effort; and (6) perceived prudence (*prudenza*, that is, moral rectitude, self-restraint, and justice).[95] Italian strategic leaders also understood that this particular conflict was a situation in which countrymen were pitted against each other. As a result, there was no way this confrontation could be allowed to degenerate into a simple military or "Dirty War." This intrastate war would have to be fought with *prudenza*, so as to avoid, as much as possible, damage to the future state of peace, prosperity, stability, and security of the country.[96]

93. Author Interviews; SWORD Papers, See note 100, this essay.

94. Howard, M. (1981) 'The Forgotten Dimensions of Strategy', *The Causes of War*, Temple-Smith, London, p. 109.

95. Machiavelli, N. (1965) *The Art of War*, DaCapo Press, New York, pp. liv-livi, 7-8, 34, 36, 46, 77-78, 171, 179, 202-204.

96. Ibid.

Implementing Some Fundamental Support Measures

At the national security level, it was understood that the conduct of the diverse wars within the general war could not be left to the discordant elements of the Italian state bureaucracy working separately and pursuing their own agendas. An organization would have to be created that was designed to achieve an adequate level of governmental "unity of effort" (*unison*) and that could be made more effective with the addition of a centralized intelligence capability. As a consequence, the government created a temporary Counter-Terrorism Task Force. That organization was given the primary responsibility for (1) intelligence collection and (2) counter-terrorist operations. Thus, intelligence, operational planning, and multi-organizational civil-military coordination fell to the unifying Counter-Terrorism Task Force.[97] And, in that context, the prescribed mode of operations for the task force was the subtle use of soft power supported by relevant information warfare, careful intelligence work, and surgical precision in removing specific individual men and women terrorists or gang members from the general populace.[98]

Then, at the legislative level, it was agreed that the moral legitimacy of the republic that emerged out of World War II was strong enough to allow the planning, public dissemination, and implementation of a coordinated and legitimized counter-terrorist (counter-gang) policy. State legitimacy also was strong enough to allow the promulgation of a modern criminal code and "hard law" legislation directed specifically against the gang phenomenon. This legislation brought the pre-World War II Criminal Code of 1930 up to date and specifically addressed conspiracy and violent actions taken for the purposes of subverting the democratic order.[99] As a consequence, the concept of national security was expanded to allow the Italian government to confront, morally as well as physically, the nontraditional strategy of the gang phenomenon.

The More Traditional Police-military War

Experience shows that a successful war against an asymmetric, irregular enemy must be conducted by a highly professional, well-disciplined, motivated security force that is capable of discrete, rapid, decisive surgical action anywhere in a given battlespace. Moreover, that action must be designed to achieve political and psychological as well as police-military objectives. These research findings were published in what is known as the SWORD papers.[100] In Italy, there was a

97. Author Interviews.
98. Author Interviews.
99. Ibid.; Pisano (1987), pp. 144–151; della Porta (1995), pp. 118–119.
100. This assertion is derived from statistical tests based on interviews with several hundred civilian and military officials and scholars with direct experience in 60 "low intensity conflicts." The results of this research were first published in Manwaring, M. G. & Fishel, J. T. (1992) 'Insurgency and Counterinsurgency: Toward a New Analytical Approach', *Small Wars & Insurgencies*, Winter, pp. 272–305. Hereafter cited as SWORD Papers.

certain reluctance to take the broadened definition of national security to its logical conclusion and correspondingly broaden the role of the military to a controversial internal protection mission. Planners understood that legitimacy considerations required that the role of the regular armed forces should be limited to supporting the major police organizations. As a result, the ever present but relatively unobtrusive paramilitary Carabinieri was given the mission of conducting the more traditional "police-military war," and Carabinieri general Carlo Alberto della Chiesa was given the mandate to direct that effort.[101]

As an example of this prudent *unison* approach to "the police-military war," the regular Italian armed forces generally assumed routine, inconspicuous, and unobtrusive police functions to allow the State Police, other police forces, and the national Carabinieri freedom to concentrate on the counter-gang mission. The Carabinieri metaphorically replaced the smart bomb aimed at an apartment in downtown Milan with a discrete knock on the door. In doing that, they were able to destroy a Red Brigade cell without destroying the apartment building or displacing its residents. Within the short to mid-term, the Carabinieri gained the approval and admiration of the community and contributed directly to the enhancement of the popular perception that government action was used for reasonable and legitimate purposes. That, in turn, generated positive implications for future social peace in Italy. Under General della Chiesa's leadership, long-term and short-term mutually supportive objectives were determined and pursued, and the war was discreetly brought under control as early as 1981–1982.[102]

The Legitimacy War

The SWORD data show that the moral right of a regime to govern is the most important single dimension in a war against any adversary. The thrust of a program to take down a government relies on grievances such as political, economic, and social injustices as the means through which government is attacked.[103]

Once the Italian parliament had provided the legislation that would allow the prosecution of a serious Anti-Terrorist War, it was recognized that legitimacy would be key to the success or failure for the terrorist gang phenomenon or for the government. The Red Brigades, for example, identified legitimacy as the primary center of gravity in their strategy to destroy the incumbent regime.[104] The Italian bureaucracy understood that popular perceptions of various injustices tended to limit the right—and the ability—of the government to conduct the business of the state. It countered with programs designed to preempt the terrorist strategy.

101. Author Interviews.
102. Ibid.
103. SWORD Papers.
104. Author Interviews.

The coordination task was to ensure that every policy, program, and action—political, economic, social, opinion-making, and security—would contribute directly to enhancing the popular perception that governmental authority did, in fact, serve public needs and was applied in a morally correct manner.[105]

The War for Unity of Effort (Unison)

This dimension of an irregular—or unconventional—war involves overcoming parochial bureaucratic interests, fighting "turf battles," and ensuring that all governmental efforts are focused on the ultimate common goal, survival. That is to say, the government must have the necessary organization to coordinate and implement an effective unity of political-diplomatic, socioeconomic, psychological-moral, and security-stability efforts against those who would destroy the government. And, it had to have the ability to accomplish these tasks in a manner acceptable to the Italian people—which equates back to legitimacy. Without an organization at the highest level to establish, enforce, and continually refine a national plan, authority is fragmented and ineffective in resolving the myriad problems endemic to an asymmetric/irregular assault on the state—thus, it will be a failure.[106]

The Italian government understood that lack of *unison* was a major deficiency in the conduct of the business of the state and in the conduct of the anti-terrorist campaign. As noted above, in 1978–1979, the parliament passed an emergency national security measure that created a temporary task force composed of state police, finance guard, and Carabinieri personnel. As a consequence, planning and coordination, to the extent that it was achieved in Italy, essentially fell to that task force. Although not perfect or all-encompassing, it was adequate to the task at hand, achieved its objectives, and was responsible for bringing the Red Brigades and the rest of the gang phenomenon under control within just over two years.[107]

The Information War

When the vast majority of the people are willing to support the state and government forces implement well-motivated counter-terrorist actions, a cooperative synergism of trust is created, which makes the state's informational and public diplomacy efforts effective. The ultimate center of gravity of a country (that is, the hub of all power and movement on which everything depends) is made up of its people and their views or public opinion. People are the country's primary sources of physical, psychological, and moral strength. Legitimate long-term military and other power depend on the proverbial "hearts and minds" of the citizenry. Thus, the climate of opinion that might ultimately lead to support

105. Ibid.
106. SWORD Papers.
107. Author Interviews; Pisano (1987), p. 146.

rather than hostility or indifference toward the political institutions of the state must be carefully channeled by a legal, democratic, and moral orientation.[108]

In the Italian case, the state and the media embarked on a strong counter-terrorist, public diplomacy campaign. The objectives were to expose and exploit the fact that the various left-wing, right-wing, separatists, pacifist, and other groups making up the terrorist gang phenomenon were not popular organizations representing the masses. Rather, these groups were self-appointed elites whose goals were not in line with what the people wanted or needed. In the final analysis, the government's antiterrorist information war demonstrated that the Red Brigadists viewed Italians who were not ideological "true believers" as not being really people. As an example, the 2,384 victims who had been murdered, maimed, or kidnapped by any one of the gang phenomena in 1979 were not considered to be human beings deserving of personal dignity, according to the public diplomacy campaign. Instead, the victims were considered "tools of the system," "pigs," and "watch dogs."[109] Moreover, the campaign pointed out that Red Brigadists considered everyone else—even other comrades on the left—to be merely "shit."[110] As a result, terrorist violence, regardless of political orientation, began to be perceived by the Italian public as more and more as wanton and completely beyond what might be necessary to make a political statement.

The Wars to Isolate the Terrorists from Internal and External Sources of Support

The problem here is to isolate politically, psychologically, and militarily the violent irregular and asymmetric opposition from their primary sources of aid—whoever and wherever they may be.[111]

Internally, the Italian gang phenomenon was isolated from the rest of the society as a result of the effect of the legitimacy war, the information war, and the physical paramilitary war. As the terrorists withdrew more and more into their own highly secretive and compartmentalized organizational structure, they nearly completely isolated themselves from the rest of the Italian community. That separation from the outside world further restricted access to external reality, the capability to recruit new members, and the ability to organize significant actions.[112]

Support for the Italian terrorists, however, was not necessarily localized within the borders of the country. Italian terrorist groups, especially the Red Brigades, were known to be supported from within the Soviet Union; Soviet surrogates such

108. SWORD Papers.
109. Interview with militant quoted in della Porta, p. 150.
110. Quoted in Fenzi, E. (1987) *Armi e bagagli: un diario dalle Brigate Rosse*, Costa & Nolan Genoa, p. 76.
111. SWORD Papers.
112. Author Interviews; della Porta (1995), pp. 157–159.

as Bulgaria and Czechoslovakia; and Middle Eastern and North African states, including Iraq, Iran, and Libya.[113] More specifically, this aid included "Energia bombs" as part of the materials provided by Palestinians and "revolutionary training" as part of the aid provided by Cuba, Libya, and the Soviet Union.[114]

Support for the Italian government's antiterrorist program on the part of external powers, such as the United States and other Western countries, proved to be relatively ineffective. If credit is given where it is due, the Italian state deserves most, if not all, of the credit for effectively bringing the gang phenomenon under control. It is important to note that governmental success was at least partially based on a certain level of failure and internal isolation on the part of the various terrorist organizations.[115]

The Intelligence War

Individual men and women lead, plan, execute, and support any given conflict. As a result, a major concern in any kind of war must be individuals. As a key part of the attack against an irregular enemy's strategy, the state's intelligence apparatus must be in place or be created so that it can locate, isolate, and neutralize the adversary's organizational and leadership structure. The SWORD data show clearly that the best police or paramilitary forces are of little consequence unless they know exactly who the enemy is and precisely where enemy forces are located.[116]

The Italian government's efforts to find, discredit, and neutralize the Red Brigades and their leadership focused on the activities of General dalla Chiesa's counter-terrorism task force and the Ministry of the Interior's Central Directorate for Crime Prevention.[117] The Central Directorate for Crime Prevention coordinated the operations of the counter-terrorism branch offices organic to the state police in every province of Italy. Dalla Chiesa's task force coordinated the entire intelligence collection effort as well as police operations. Thus, an intelligence orientation or mind set as well as an organization that had the capability to strike at times, places, and in ways that took the terrorist gangs by surprise were established. The short-term effect was to neutralize a given group. The long-term effect was to shift the balance of power decidedly toward the legitimate organs of Italian government.[118]

113. For only a few examples, see *Rand Note* (1986), pp. 36, 59-60; Pisano (1987), pp. 119-143; della Porta (1995), p. 120; *Panorama*, September 15, 1980, p. 45; Federico Orlando (ed.) (1980) *Siamo en Guerra*, Armando, Rome, pp. 195-196; Pisano, V. S. (1982) 'Libya's Foothold in Italy', *The Washington Quarterly*, Spring, pp. 179-182.
114. Ibid.
115. Author Interviews.
116. SWORD Papers.
117. Author Interviews.
118. Ibid.

A specific example from this situation is instructive. Because of the self-imposed isolation of the Italian terrorist organizations, they had only little intelligence with which to work. On the other hand, the state developed a large and increasingly effective intelligence network. Nevertheless, it was probably the role of the legal Italian Communist Party (PCI) that was decisive in destroying the Red Brigades and their various political allies. The PCI's capillary structure—strengthened by a large number of efficient ancillary organizations that had been collecting information on the entire political organizational spectrum for years—was able to identify and locate specific organizations, leaders, and members relatively easily and quickly. The PCI furnished a great deal of this kind of intelligence to the state security organizations and made them appear to be much more efficient and effective that they really were. In any event, timely and accurate human intelligence provided by the PCI considerably enhanced the Italian government's ability to attack the organization and leadership architecture of the Red Brigade's and other terrorists' strategies.[119]

Implications

Analysis of the central strategic problem in Italy resulted in the identification of three levels of threat—cause, effect, and response. By 1978 and beyond, however, analysts recognized that the greatest single threat to Italian security and stability (closely related to cause, effect, and response) was actually a void, a failure of the government. The terrorist threat was indeed caused, exacerbated, and allowed to intensify because the elected political institutions of the Italian government had failed to provide responsible governance and had failed to recognize and respond to the associated challenge posed by the terrorist gang phenomenon.[120]

The telling points of the above implication focus on the fact that the thrust of any given terrorist, insurgent, or other asymmetric program to depose a government relies heavily on grievances such as political, economic, and social injustices. Moreover, these are the primary means through which a government is attacked and destroyed. A counter-terrorism campaign that fails to understand its citizens' legitimate grievances and fails to adapt its strategy to deal with public opinion as the key center of gravity in conventional and unconventional conflict is likely to fail.

For Italians, terrorism was the most important political phenomenon of the 1970s and 1980s. For the rest of the world, terrorism is likely to be the most important political phenomenon of the twenty-first century. Precisely how an array or combination of threats might be accomplished now and in the future is limited only by the imagination, but the Italian experience dictates that a minimum of two possibilities must be taken into consideration.

119. Ibid.
120. Ibid.

First, the Red Brigades and their 300 or more allies demonstrated to the world how the weak could attack the strong. Literally hundreds of violent nonstate actors, gangs, and, even perhaps individual loonies, have learned that they can easily and cheaply hold whole nations at ransom. Whether the irregular attackers are sincerely trying to achieve specific political objectives or only trying to gain some monetary or visceral satisfaction for carrying out violent acts is irrelevant. Second, nonstate and other political actors in the global security arena are almost certain to use nuclear weapons, chemical and biological weapons, and cyber weapons in current and future conflicts as "equalizers." Given the asymmetry between challengers and the challenged, only the foolish will fight conventionally. These are the realities of power and politics in the contemporary "clash of civilizations" and world chaos.

Finally, the Italian case demonstrates that success in countering terrorism and asymmetric war of all kinds in the "new world disorder" will be constructed on the same theoretical bases that supported favorable results in the past. Even though every conflict is situation specific, it is not completely unique. Throughout the universe, there are analytical commonalities at the strategic and high operational levels. Seven dimensions or dependent variables, each composed of multiple independent variables, determine the success or failure of an asymmetric, irregular intrastate war. In essence, they may be considered "wars within the general war," as noted in the section above, entitled *Thinking about the New Paradigm*. In that connection, it should be emphasized that the new paradigm has power and virtue in part because of the symmetry of its application—both for a besieged government and its allies, and for a violent internal challenger and its allies. That is to say, no successful strategy—on either side of the conflict spectrum—has been formulated over the past 50 years that has not explicitly or implicitly taken into account all of those strategic dimensions, or "wars within the war."

Key Points and Lessons

As demonstrated in the Italian counter-terrorism campaign, the conscious positive or negative choices that a government makes about how to conduct national security and stability efforts will define the future of the state. There is very little glamour, only a few sound bites, and not many career enhancement possibilities inherent in making and implementing those positive choices. But, they do have potential for directing progress toward national and global stability, democracy, and sustainable peace.

- In 1978–1983, the Italian gang phenomenon included over 300 politically diverse organizations motivated to the violent replacement of a "moribund" state. The resultant anti-government campaign relied on internal urban terrorist tactics and strategies from which to develop a support base and to act as an ideological substitute for conventional war.

- The primary "terrorist" organization, the Red Brigades, utilized a vigorous, broad, and violent set of terrorist tactics to implement its objective of bringing down the Italian state. The Red Brigades were a theoretical equivalent to a third-generation gang, and illustrated the increasing lack of differentiation between insurgents, "terrorists", international criminals, and gangs.
- The Italian government—once it made the political decision to treat the increasing levels of violence and instability generated by the Red Brigades and their militant allies as a national security problem—planned, organized, and implemented a soft multilayered political-paramilitary response. That approach to attacking the violent opposition's terrorist strategy was successful, and brought "terrorism" under control within a surprisingly short two to three year period.
- As a corollary, it was recognized that the unwillingness or inability of a government to develop a long-term, multi-dimensional, and morally acceptable strategy to confront violent internal nonstate actors is a threat to the stability and sovereignty to the state itself. In these terms, the state has the clear responsibility to take legitimate measures to confront such violent political actors and avoid the intended destruction of the state.

These hard-won lessons learned from the Italian experience with the gang phenomenon are all too relevant to the "new" political powers of the twenty-first century. Sun Tzu maintained, "Those skilled in war subdue the enemy's army without battle."[121] In that context, he also argues that "the reason the enlightened prince and the wise general conquer the enemy whenever they move and their achievements surpass [and surprise] those of ordinary men is foreknowledge.... What is called 'foreknowledge' cannot be elicited from spirits, nor from gods, nor by analogy with past events, nor from calculations. It must be obtained from men to know the enemy situation [and strategy]."[122]

The Challenge, Threat, and Main Task for Now and the Future

A multi-polar world in which one or 100 non-state (criminal) actors are exerting differing types and levels of asymmetric power within a set of cross-cutting alliances is extremely volatile and dangerous. The security and stability of the global community is threatened, and the benefits of globalism could be denied to all. Thus, it is incumbent on the United States, the West, and the rest of the international community to understand and cope with the governance challenges exacerbated by the destabilizing and devastating political violence generated by the gang phenomenon. The ultimate threat is that, unless and until leaders at the highest levels recognize what is happening strategically, reorient thinking and actions appropriately, and are able to educate and lead their various

121. Tzu (1971), p. 77.
122. Ibid, pp. 144–145.

constituencies into the realities of the Post-Modern World, it is only a matter of time before the destabilizing problems associated with the gang phenomenon will cause the failure of one vitally important legitimate state actor or another.

The challenge, then, is to come to terms with the fact that contemporary security, at whatever level, is at its base a holistic political-diplomatic, socio-economic, psychological-moral, and military-police effort. The corollary is to change from a singular military or law-enforcement approach to a multi-dimensional, multiorganizational, multicultural, and multinational paradigm. The main tasks in the search for security now and for the future are to construct national and international stability and well-being based upon the lessons—negative and positive—learned from present and past cases. The consistency of those lessons is impressive. That consistency warrants confidence that success in countering a gang phenomenon and its associated terrorism in its various protean forms will be achieved as a result of understanding successful results that have been achieved in the past. They are encompassed in the "wars within the war" of Italian experience and include: (1) a realistic strategic vision to counter an irregular/unconventional challenge to the state; (2) a management structure to plan, unify, and implement that vision; and (3) the use of appropriate instruments of state and international power the conduct the multidimensional wars within the general war. This is nothing radical. It is basic security strategy and national asset management.

Trafficking in Nuclear Materials: Criminals and Terrorists

Louise I. Shelley

Criminals and terrorists are part of an integrated network that includes those that secure nuclear material and transport it to terrorist purchasers. The main trajectory of this route is from Russia, through the Caucasus on to Turkey. Georgia, in particular, has been the epicenter of the smuggling with 300 reported incidents in recent years.[1] Research conducted along the smuggling route by the author, with colleagues from the region, suggests that the links between the

Louise I. Shelley is a Professor in the School of International Service and the founder and Director of the Terrorism, Transnational Crime and Corruption Center (TraCCC), American University. Her present research focuses on human smuggling and trafficking, the role of non-state actors in the proliferation of nuclear materials and the relationship between crime and terrorism. Recipient of numerous awards including the Guggenheim, Fulbright, NEH, and Kennan Institute, she is an active scholar having published three books as well as approximately 100 articles and book chapters. Since the mid-1990s, she has worked closely with scholars in Russia, Ukraine, and Georgia where TraCCC has established centers to study the problems of organized crime and corruption. She is also active in communicating the policy implications of her research and has testified repeatedly before the U.S. Congress, presented her findings at international fora and in the mass media.

1. 'Radioactive Sources Recovered', *UNA-Georgia Online Magazine*, July 28, 2006. Available at: http://www.civil.ge/eng/article.php?id = 13210 (accessed 13 August 2006).

criminals and the terrorists are not random even though the connections between these two kinds of non-state actors are not readily apparent. Both groups of non-state actors are specialists in subterfuge. They manage to mask their interactions which occur in prisons, uncontrolled territories, or diaspora communities where they are not readily observable to outsiders.

The states of the former Soviet Union, with abundant and lightly guarded medical facilities and research institutes with radioactive materials, have been the source of many of the detected cases of nuclear smuggling. Less often has the smuggling of highly enriched uranium, plutonium, and cesium been detected. Although some of the smuggling, especially of the less radioactive materials, has been done by opportunists, some of the cases of the smuggling of the most highly radioactive materials has been linked to criminals.[2]

One of the unfortunate legacies of the former USSR are the strong crime networks that developed over decades. These crime networks can facilitate the movement of nuclear materials long distances before they reach the perimeter of the former USSR. In contrast to the unified state control structures that collapsed along with the USSR, the crime networks that cross the borders of the Soviet successor states survived. The criminals' bonds, often formed in the labor camps of the Soviet era, endured beyond the state that sought to control them.

The collapse of the USSR left many nuclear facilities and sites without adequate protections.[3]Despite the increased threat of the proliferation of weapons of mass destruction, particularly involving nuclear materials and biological weapons, effective cooperation among governments of the Soviet successor states never developed. Hostilities among many Soviet successor states combined with the proliferation of uncontrolled borders facilitated the diversion and movement of these dangerous materials. Pre-existing smuggling routes were already in place across the vast territory of the former USSR to move drugs, people, and arms, and these routes could be adapted for the transport of nuclear materials

The illicit networks of the Soviet era have adapted to the global economy. As post-Soviet crime groups have globalized, their networks have expanded beyond the former USSR and Eastern Europe to émigré communities overseas and to prisons in western Europe where these criminals are often incarcerated with terrorists. Increased international transport, communications, and mobility have given smaller groups increased access to international markets and the possibility of being the transporters of nuclear materials.

With a huge stockpile of nuclear materials, often badly guarded, and with enormous quantities of abandoned radiological materials, the criminals of the former USSR have had access, often through disgruntled scientists or corrupt

2. Zaitseva, L. & Hand, K. (2003) 'Nuclear Smuggling Chains Suppliers, Intermediaries, and End Users', *American Behavioral Scientist*, vol. 46, no. 6, pp. 822–844; Rensselaer, W. L. (1998) *Smuggling Armageddon: The Nuclear Black Market in the Former Soviet Union and Europe*, St. Martin's Press: New York.

3. For an early warning about this see Potter, W. C. (1995) *Before the Deluge? Assessing the Threat of Nuclear Leakage from the Post-Soviet States*, Frontline. PBS.org, October. Available at: http:/www.pbs.org/wgbh/pages/frontline/shows/nukes/readings/potterarticle.html. (accessed 14 August 2006).

insiders, to a commodity that has many potential buyers internationally. Some of the material being moved now appears to have been removed from facilities in the 1990s. The American intelligence community acknowledges that a certain amount of material was probably diverted from nuclear facilities.[4] This material currently being smuggled was probably removed when inadequate attention was paid by the Russian state and the international community to the difficult lives of the scientists and employees of the nuclear facilities.[5]

Western programs to secure nuclear materials and provide protection along the borders of the former Soviet Union have made only moderate headway. At present, only 40% of the borders that have been evaluated as being high risk have been equipped with nuclear detection equipment and only six of the megaports that ship millions of shipping containers to the United States have been equipped with detectors.[6]

The international community is presently facing the legacy of a post-Soviet transition with unforeseen difficulties. The existence of poorly guarded weapons of mass destruction (WMD) facilities, the persistence and proliferation of post-Soviet crime groups, and the continued lack of effective border controls on the perimeters of the former Soviet Union provide a significant challenge to international security in the face of an increasing demand for nuclear materials by terrorists and states such as Iran and North Korea who likely already have nuclear weapons programs.[7]

Research Method and Data

The analysis herein is based on a wide variety of interviews and published sources. These include extensive reading of the local press in Russia and Georgia. The location of relevant and insightful articles was facilitated by research collaborators from the region. The author also read the scholarly literature on organized crime and its regional variations as well as the emerging literature on the problems of terrorism in Russia. Research sponsored by the Terrorism, Transnational Crime and Corruption Center (TraCCC) with scholars from Russia, Azerbaijan, Kazakhstan, and Georgia facilitated the understanding of such relevant issues as illicit cross-border flows, illegal migration, and the growth of drug trafficking.[8] Research on the tangible impact of corruption in closed cities

4. Bunn, M. (2006) 'Cooperation to Secure Nuclear Stockpiles A Case of Constrained Innovation', *Innovations*, Winter, pp. 115-137; Bunn, M. & Wier, A. (2006) *Securing the Bomb 2006*, Project on Managing the Atom, Belfer Center for Science and International Affairs, John F. Kennedy School of Government, Harvard University, July, p. 27. Available at: http://www.nti.org/e_research/stb06webfull.pdf (accessed August 13, 2006).

5. Rensselaer, W. L. (1998).

6. Bunn & Wier (2006), p. 30.

7. For a discussion of the threat posed by Iran and North Korea, see Ibid., p. 34.

8. S. Golunov (nd) *Transngranichnaia prestupnost' v zone iuzhnykh postsovetskikh rubezhei rossii: Sotsialnye i politicheskie aspekty problemy*, Transnational Crime and Corruption Center (TraCCC) at American University, pp. 1–95. Available at: http://www.american.edu/traccc/resources/publications/goluno02.pdf (accessed 14 August 2006).

and on borders was essential to understanding the mechanisms facilitating this smuggling.

Little attention was paid to the data in the database of the International Atomic Energy Agency (IAEA) and other databases on nuclear smuggling. My research, and that conducted with my colleagues, determined that important information is unreported to the IAEA or that information is not full or entirely accurate. There are many reasons for the failure to report cases to the IAEA including the desire not to disturb the citizens of the country or that reports of nuclear seizures may discourage tourism and foreign investment. Apart from these rational disincentives for reporting incidents of nuclear smuggling, many law enforcement officials in the countries of the former USSR who have the responsibility to report or uncover the smuggling are corrupt. Therefore, it is not in their interest to find this material as they are bribed not to examine cross-border contraband. Moreover, incidents of organized crime involvement in nuclear smuggling that appear in the IAEA database may be an artifact of the police clamping down on a rival crime group to that which pays them off.

Other problems of relying on the IAEA database and other such databases is that they include a significant number of cases that could be called "random noise", low levels movement of illicit nuclear materials by opportunists who do not have established supply or demand chains. These obscure the patterns associated with the transport of the most dangerous material such as highly enriched uranium (HEU), cesium, or plutonium. The suppliers and potential buyers for these materials are hard to trace because they are moved by professionals who are specialists in moving high value and prohibited goods. Therefore, this analysis focused exclusively on understanding the actors involved in moving only the most dangerous materials.[9]

To analyze the networks associated with the most dangerous materials, the research focused on sources other than official reports and databases. Instead, this study relied on sources of information that would make it possible to understand the networks that facilitate smuggling across vast territories of the former USSR and beyond.

Most analyses of nuclear smuggling examine the problem only at a particular locale—the facility that might be the source of the material, the border crossing at which the material is detected, or the country in which loose material has been found. By examining these separate data points, it is not possible to understand how the crime network operates. Instead, this research has attempted to reconstruct the entire network, by looking at nodes in which the nuclear smuggling is concentrated. This led the research to focus on the movement between Russia and Georgia and to understand this movement as part of a larger international network.

9. See for example 'Georgia Reports Four New Cases of HEU Seizures', *NIS Export Control Observer*, July 2005, p. 5.

The Criminal Actors

A range of actors moves nuclear materials. Some of those who move nuclear materials consciously move the materials, even at risk to themselves, because they believe that something this dangerous must have worth.[10]These opportunists move materials that are often of little potential danger to the larger society because they have low radiation content and could not be used for making a dirty bomb let alone a full scale bomb. Of much greater concern is the HEU that, when properly encased, will not be picked up by radioactive detectors presently in place.[11]Individual smugglers may unknowingly carry this dangerous cargo. As a recruited mule (or low level transporter), such as those in drug trafficking organizations, the actual transporter of the materials is isolated from the larger organization and lacks knowledge of the full operations of its network. Upon arrest, the carrier of the materials can disclose little concerning those who hired him or the intended destination of his cargo.

The interaction of criminals and terrorists is often not apparent in nuclear smuggling. Close analysis of the reported data of the IAEA does not reveal a crime-terror link and only ten percent of reported cases reveal the presence of an organized crime group involved in the smuggling.[12] The absence of this link in the data does not indicate that the problem itself is absent, as the earlier cited problems with IAEA data reveal.[13]

Therefore, while the criminals and terrorists manage to establish trust across ethnic groups and borders, the law enforcement and intelligence community that seeks to apprehend them is fragmented. The mistrust and inability to share information among government ministries within countries and among different countries is easily exploited by the smugglers of these potentially deadly materials. The imbalance between the trust established between criminals and terrorists and the mistrust that exists among those who seek to control them creates ample opportunities for the smuggling networks to continue.

How Do We Know that the Criminals and Terrorists Interact?

The absence of available reports in official data does not negate the fact that criminals and terrorists interact in the smuggling of nuclear materials. There are a variety of locales in which these groups can interact, including immigrant communities overseas, uncontrolled territories, and in prisons. Many of these

10. Based on interviews by the TraCCC team in Georgia concerning individuals who have been caught transporting low level radiation sources.
11. Lee, R. (2006) 'Nuclear Smuggling, Rogue States and Terrorists', *The China and Eurasia Forum Quarterly*, vol. 4, no. 2, May, p. 30.
12. Zaitseva, L. (2006) University of Salzburg, 'Organized Crime, Terrorism and Nuclear Trafficking', *Terrorism, Transnational Networks and WMD Proliferation: Indications and Warning in an Era of Globalization Conference*, Sponsored by the Defense Threat Reduction Agency's Advanced System Concepts Office, Naval Postgraduate School, Monterey, CA, July 25–27.
13. For an example of a case that is known but not reported in the IAEA database see Baran, Z. (2006) 'Kosovo precedent no solution for Caucasus region', Letter to the Editor, *Financial Times*, May 17.

immigrant communities in western Europe are outside the control of law enforcement and intelligence authorities. Even more dangerous are the uncontrolled territories, of which there are many, close to the perimeters of the former Soviet Union including Transdniester, Abkhazia, Ossetia and Nagorno-Karabagh and the former Pankisi Gorge area of Georgia. Criminals and terrorists have been documented to interact in the Pankisi Gorge area.[14] Another major area of interaction is inside prisons. Prisons are no longer merely schools of crime but the corporate headquarters of crime groups. It is in prisons that relationships are formed and orders are entered for supplies of all varieties of illicit commodities, including weapons and nuclear materials.[15]

The clearest example of this crime-terror interaction is evident in Spanish prisons prior to the Madrid bombings, where the ringleaders of the plot were ordinary criminals recruited by terrorists. As a result of the role of the prison as an incubator of criminal-terrorist interactions, the Spanish authorities in the aftermath of the March 11th bombing developed recommendations to identify and limit the possibilities of terrorist recruitment among prisoners.[16] Unfortunately, the Spanish experience is not an isolated case but a pattern observed in many penal institutions in western Europe, Russia and elsewhere.[17]

The criminals and terrorists establish relationships in prison because of their proximity and the intensity of association. As the great American criminologist, Edwin Sutherland explained in his theory of "differential association," the extent of involvement in crime is explained by the intensity and duration of the relationship.[18] In prisons, especially the moderate regimes that exist in many western European prisons, allow interaction among criminals in the various cell blocks. The criminals and the terrorists have the possibility to interact over a long time with limited other activity to serve as a distraction.

How is it that prison authorities allow criminals and terrorists to interact? In theory, prison administrations should separate out criminals from terrorists. Terrorists should be isolated in maximum security facilities, away from petty and professional criminals. But the present nature of terrorist operations makes this

14. The man arrested in the planned ricin attack in London had been arrested in Pankisi where he interacted with criminals and terrorists. See Segell, G. (2006) 'The London Ricin Cell: Implications for the Future', *Terrorism, Transnational Networks and WMD Proliferation: Indications and Warning in an Era of Globalization Conference*, Sponsored by the Defense Threat Reduction Agency's Advanced System Concepts Office, Naval Postgraduate School, Monterey, CA, July 25–27.

15. Cuthbertson, I. (2004) 'Prisons and the Education of Terrorists', *World Policy Journal*, vol. 21, pp. 15-22; Daniel, A. (2006) 'Terrorism as a Business and the Business of Terrorism', *Understanding and Responding to Terrorism: A Multi-dimensional Approach Conference*, North Atlantic Treaty Organization (NATO) & Turkish Institute for Police Studies (TIPS) Terrorism Project, Washington, DC, September 8–9.

16. 'Conclusiones de la Comision', 11-M Masacre en Madrid, *elmundo.es*. nd, pp. 248–250. Available at: http://www.elmundo.es/documentos/2004/03/espana/atentados11m/documentos.html (accessed 13 August 2006).

17. For Russian discussion of the rise of Islam in prison see 'Islam na zone, Beseda s aktivistom dav'ata v mestakh zakliucheniia'. Available at: www.islam.ru/pressclub/gost/zona/ (accessed 14 August 2006).

18. 'Differential Association', n.d. Available at: http://en.wikipedia.org/wiki/Differential_association (accessed 12 August 2006).

impossible to do because the true identities of the terrorists are masked from the state authorities. The terrorists in prison are often there under false names, with new identities constructed either by their skillful operatives or as a result of their interaction with criminals.

Terrorists commit criminal acts to survive. These criminal acts are not merely financial in nature but consist of a wide range of supporting activities including document fraud, illegal cross-border transport of people, and money laundering.[19]With such a variety of criminal activity, there is increased likelihood that terrorists will be arrested for one of their many criminal activities.

Prison authorities, without adequate knowledge of who they have confined in their prisons, cannot isolate criminals from terrorists because they do not know that they have arrested terrorists.[20]Unless they engage in undercover work in prisons—introducing informants and monitoring conversations and visitors, they may be entirely ignorant as to the actual identity of those they have in their custody. Therefore, the incarcerated terrorists are often merely "criminals", petty or otherwise, who are free to recruit other prisoners to their terrorist cause or to establish long-term relationships with criminals. The criminals are, therefore, usually unaware that the individuals with whom they interact are terrorists because they believe they are merely their fellow criminals who are incarcerated for car theft, petty crimes, and even drug charges.

The interaction of the criminals and the terrorists can proceed without the knowledge of the prison authorities or even the knowledge of the criminals who enter into business relationships to provide services for the terrorists. The criminals market themselves to the terrorists as transporters, movers of people and providers of fraudulent documents.

Will Criminals Knowingly Engage with Terrorists?

Traditional organized crime groups such as the mafia and the yakuza need the state and the global economic system.[21]They thrive on obtaining government contracts and depend on the international financial system to retain its value and thereby retain their wealth. These organized crime groups have little in common with the newer transnational crime groups, often originating in post-conflict situations, who thrive on chaos and ongoing conflict. Some of the crime groups of the Soviet successor states fit the model of the newer transnational criminals who possess neither large resources nor loyalty to the state. Their services are merely available to the highest bidder. The risk calculations of these newer crime groups are entirely different from those of the crime groups

19. Laqueur, W. (1999) *The New Terrorism*, Oxford University Press, Oxford, pp. 210–225.
20. For an indication of this problem, see the Swiss acknowledgement of their confinement of a major terrorist but his short term in prison indicates that he was confined as an ordinary criminal. Whitlock, C. (2006) 'In Neutral Switzerland, A Rising Radicalism', *Washington Post*, June 20, pp. A14–A15.
21. Shelley, L. (2005) 'Unraveling the New Criminal Nexus', *Georgetown Journal of International Affairs*. Winter/Spring, pp. 5–13; Shelley, L. (2005) 'The Unholy Trinity: Transnational Crime, Corruption and Terrorism', *Brown Journal of International Affairs*, vol. 11, iss. 2, pp. 101–111.

of more established societies where law enforcement functions better and association with terrorists enhances risk.

The newer crime groups in ungovernable regions are now forging alliances with terrorist organizations because the crime groups and terrorist organizations do not possess long-term financial strategies or long-term political horizons. In such regions as the uncontrolled territories of Georgia, South Ossetia, and Abkhazia, through which smuggled materials flow, neither the criminals nor the terrorists need fear state bodies of control.[22] Corrupt and ineffective law enforcement in conflict regions makes attempts at control almost futile.

Newer transnational crime groups have proliferated in both number and membership since the end of the Cold War. The wars in the former Yugoslavia, the regional conflicts in Central Asia, the Caucasus, and in Trandniester of Moldova, Sri Lanka and contemporary post-Taliban Afghanistan have led to many new crime groups not known internationally before the 1990s. Now these crime groups operate transnationally, selling drugs, arms, people, and contraband. In their illicit activities, these newer crime groups differ little from the more established ones. But they do differ in their willingness to cooperate with terrorists. In their home countries, these new transnational crime groups are masked within the large shadow economy. The years of war and conflict have destroyed and impoverished families and undermined community values. These groups thrive on the surrounding poverty and demoralized populations, their operations facilitated by the absence of an effective state.

They capitalize on state-based legal controls by exploiting differences in legal norms and procedures among jurisdictions. Often embedded in the host society, this crime is not family-based, nor is it hierarchically and rigidly structured like the mafia. Instead, it draws on different levels of society that contribute in different ways to the perpetuation of the crime activity. This pattern has been observed in the Balkans and the Caucasus as well as in Afghanistan.

The newer crime groups may not share the ideological motivations of the terrorists but they too do not want a secure state. In fact, the crime groups may promote grievances, because it is through the prolongation of conflict that they enhance their profits.[23] The milieu in which transnational crime, terrorism, and corruption merge is extremely threatening to the international order. The embedded nature of network crime structures in local communities and the inability of both domestic and international militaries, as well as law enforcement agencies, to control their activities make them a growing danger. The failure of the international community to recognize the centrality of this unholy trinity allowed this nexus to flourish in the 1990s and the beginning of this century.[24]The

22. Kukhianidze, A. *et al.* (2004) *Smuggling Through Abkhazia and Tskinvali Region of Georgia*, TraCCC, American University, Tbilsi, Georgia: Polygraph, Ltd, p. 5. Available at: http://www.traccc.cdn.ge/publications/index.html (accessed 17 May 2006).
23. Berdal, M. & Malone, D. M. (2000) *Greed & Grievance: Economic Agendas in Civil Wars*, Lynne Rienner Publishers, Boulder.
24. Shelley, L. (2005) 'The Unholy Trinity', Winter-Spring.

relationship of this nexus to the proliferation of weapons of mass destruction is poorly understood by many.

The links between transnational crime and terrorism are most evident in the case of Islamic-based terrorism but they are not exclusive to jihadist groups. They also exist in other regions such as Sri Lanka, Russia, and Northern Ireland that have had their own long term conflicts.[25]Often, in conflict regions or ones with frozen conflicts, crime groups do not look to the future but instead need the profits from their illicit trade for their immediate military objectives. In some cases, they use the profits generated from their illegal activities to fund insurgencies or terrorism such as those in contemporary Afghanistan, Nepal, and Sri Lanka.[26]

Tracing the Network

The network of nuclear smuggling goes from the facilities that house the materials, across vast territories of the former Soviet Union, to the perimeter of its territory.[27] The majority of detections of serious nuclear materials have occurred in the Caucasus and Turkey, particularly Georgia. The absence of available data does not preclude the transport of material from the Russian border through Kazakhstan and on to the countries of Central Asia. Neither is the transport of material from the highly criminalized Far East to North Korea excluded. Available data on the latter two possible smuggling routes is not available to this researcher although criminal actors are known to operate from these areas within Russian territory according to research done by TraCCC's centers in the Russian Far East and in the border areas of Siberia.

The routes have changed from what was observed in the early 1990s. No longer are materials transiting to Western Europe. Instead, the materials are increasingly following a Southern route to the Caucasus and towards Turkey.[28] There is no indication that there are unique smuggling routes for nuclear materials. Rather, it seems that it is safer and easier to use established smuggling routes that already move a wide variety of materials. The increasing smuggling of drugs from Afghanistan through Central Asia is taking the same route across Russia as the nuclear material.[29]

25. Section on Chechnya by Nabi Abdallaev in Shelley, L. *et al.* (2005) *Methods and Motives: Exploring Links Between Transnational Crime and International Terrorism*, National Institute of Justice, US Department of Justice, June 23; Richardson, J. (2005) *Paradise Poisoned: Learning about Conflict, Terrorism and Development from Sri Lanka's Civil Wars*, International Centre for Ethnic Studies, Colombo; Horgan, J. & Taylor, M. (1999) 'Playing the Green Card: Financing the Provisional IRA, Part 1', *Terrorism and Political Violence*, vol. 11, no. 2, pp. 1-36.

26. Cornell, S. E. (2006) 'The Narcotics Threat In Greater Central Asia: From Crime-Terror Nexus to State Infiltration?', *China and Eurasia Forum Quarterly*, vol. 4, no. 1, pp. 37-67; US Department of State (2005) *Trafficking in Persons Report 2004*, Washington, DC, p. 216; Richardson (1999).

27. See write up of talk by Shelley, L. & Orttung, R. (2006) *The links between Organized Crime and Terrorism in Eurasian Nuclear Smuggling*, Kennan Institute Meeting Report, vol. 28, no. 7.

28. Zaitseva, L. (2002) 'Illicit Trafficking in the Southern Tier and Southern Turkey Since 1999: A Shift from Europe?', *The Nonproliferation Review*, Fall-Winter. Available at: http://cns.miis.edu/pubs/npr/vol09/93/93zait.pdf (accessed 14 August 2006).

29. Fenopetov, V. (2006) *Afganski opiaty i ikh negativnoe vliianie na strany, SNG*, May 16. Available at: http://srtracc.sgap.ru/ (accessed 14 August 2006).

In addition, there is significant smuggling of human beings, not only from the former Soviet Union but of individuals from the Indian subcontinent, and Afghanistan, who transit the former Soviet Union on the way to Turkey with the intention of moving on to Western Europe. Valuable textiles and rugs also travel from Central Asia through the Black Sea region winding up in Istanbul.

Some crime organizations specialize in one particular commodity but increasingly these crime organizations are diversified and will move different commodities on demand. The officials they have bought off at the border crossings allow any commodity to cross. In the special case of nuclear smuggling, the intelligence capacity of the crime groups allows them to know where the detectors are located and where they can bypass the controls.[30]

The movement of nuclear materials from Russia through the Caucasus is not random. The proximity of the Caucasus to the markets with existing demand for the nuclear materials—Turkey, Western Europe and the Middle East—makes this region a crucial part of the nuclear smuggling route.

The presence of uncontrolled separatist zones is key to moving the material from Russia to the Caucasus, where it can be moved to its ultimate destination by sea or land. Facilitating this contraband trade has been the enhanced dispersion of Georgian crime groups since the Rose Revolution in late 2003, when they realized that the Georgian state under President Saakashvili would actually attempt to control their activities. Therefore, members of these crime groups joined their colleagues already abroad whose network extends across Russia to Western Europe and even as far as South America.[31]Despite their distance, they still maintain important ties to their homeland, facilitating their ability to provide an integrated network across a vast territory.

The nuclear materials being seized in Georgia are found on the basis of operative information. The detectors, as previously mentioned, do not have the capacity to detect well shielded uranium. Operative information is hard to obtain in such a highly secretive arena where there is an absence of cooperation among law enforcement and intelligence on a regional basis.

There are many indications that only a fraction of the materials that move through the Caucasus are actually detected. The separatist regions of Abkhazia and North Ossetia, through which some of the seized material has transited, are black holes where no effective law enforcement of any kind exists. The extensive reform of Georgian law enforcement has deprived the police of any experienced personnel. Some of the dismissed police personnel have joined the ranks of the criminals with whom they were previously associated.[32]Arrests of dismissed police personnel involved in car theft rings reveal that some of them are even facilitating cross-border smuggling into Western Europe. With inadequate technical capacity, the absence of effective law enforcement, and the absence

30. Lee, May (2006).

31. Interview by the author with Bacho Akhalaia, Head of Georgian penitentiary system. Tbilisi, Georgia, January 2006.

32. Kupatadze, A. *et al.* (2007) 'Policing and Police Reform in Georgia', in *Organised Crime and Corruption in Georgia*, ed. L. I. Shelley et.al, Routledge, London.

of cooperation among regional law enforcement, the possibilities of moving nuclear materials undetected remain high.

Problems at the Source

There is extensive high-level corruption in Russia's nuclear facilities. This high-level corruption is important because it creates an atmosphere in which low-level workers and insiders will be in a position to steal nuclear material. Previous research suggests that the low-level employees are the ones most likely to be engaged in theft. This problem existed not only in the difficult years of the 1990s, when those working in the nuclear facilities were poorly paid, but endures as a serious problem today even after economic conditions have improved. Therefore, the nuclear materials detected since 2000 may have been removed earlier from facilities and stored outside. There also may be smuggled materials that have more recently disappeared from storage facilities.

The most obvious case of corruption in the Russian nuclear sector is the former Russian Minister of Atomic Energy (MinAtom), Yevgeny Adamov, who is awaiting trial in Russia for allegedly misusing funds received from the United States to safeguard the nuclear facilities. He was extradited to Russia from Switzerland even though he was wanted by the United States for money laundering and other charges.[33]

The Russian expression that "the fish rots from the head" appears to characterize the Russian nuclear industry. With Adamov, a figure known to be corrupt at the helm, there was no incentive for those under his command to maintain institutional integrity. His predecessor Viktor Mikhailov was ousted, possibly in connection with technology transfers to Iran and Iraq.[34]

Anatolii Kalinovskii, the director of the isotope factory at Mayak, misused his office in the late 1990s and falsified documents to repeatedly carry out contraband transfers of valuable non-nuclear substances.[35] The customs authorities filed 9 cases against him for violating customs regimes by improperly declaring goods, and he received a suspended sentence. More recently in Novosibirsk, the director of the Novosibirsk Chemical Concentrate Plant, Yurii Vladimirovich Zabelin, was removed from his job on January 28, 2005 after criminal cases were filed against him for using plant money for his own private purposes, and for paying a consulting firm that apparently gave him sophisticated advice on manipulating plant finances to his benefit.[36]The high level corruption at the plant created an atmosphere in which low-level workers were able to steal

33. 'UPDATE: Moscow court upholds decision to prolong Adamov's arrest', *RIA Novosti*, September 5, 2005. Available at: http://www.ransac.org/Projects (accessed 14 August 2006); 'Russian former nuclear energy minister released from prison on bail', *Regnum news Agency*, July 24, 2006. Available at: http://www.nuclearno.com/text.asp?11016 (accessed 24 August 2006).

34. 'Viktor Mikhailov leaves MinAtom.' Available at: http://www.bu.edu/iscip/digest/vol3/ed0304.html (accessed 14 August 2006).

35. Lee, R. (2006) *Reappraising Nuclear Security Strategy, Policy Analysis*, Cato Institute, no. 571, June 14, p. 7. Available at: http://www.cato.org/pubs/pas/pa571.pdf (accessed 24 August 2006).

36. Kuznetsov, A. & Zvereva, I. (2005) 'Kadrovye resheniya bez rezkikh dvizhenii', *Novaya Sibir*, February 4; Kuznetsov, A. (2004) 'Amortizatsiya s ekspropriatsiei', *Novaya Sibir*, October 8.

material. According to Yury Vishnevsky, the former head of the monitoring agency Gozatomnadzor, the Novosibirsk plant lost "grams of weapons grade or kilograms of low enriched uranium" in 2002.[37]

Existing literature outlines aborted cases of nuclear smuggling from facilities where corruption and insiders facilitated these illicit activities.[38] What recent research indicates is that the problems of corruption have not ended but the security of the material is made more precarious by the crime problems associated with the nuclear facilities, a consequence of both organized crime penetration into the construction sector and service industries as well as the rise of the drug trade in Russia.

The Links between Nuclear Facilities and Organized Crime[39]

There are several ways in which organized crime groups have links to the nuclear facilities. First is the growing drug trade within the closed cities near Chelyabinsk, for example in Ozersk and Snezhinsk. In 1999, the closed city of Ozersk had the most drug users per capita in Russia. They abused mainly heroin and marijuana, according to Andrei Glukhov, deputy head of the Ozersk federal anti-drug agency.[40]This problem even spread to workers of the nuclear facility of Mayak who were dismissed once their drug addiction was discovered. The problem of drugs in the closed cities was still growing in March 2005, according to head of the Snezhinsk police force. In contrast, the capacity of the state to address this problem has not kept pace with its growth.

Large numbers of released convicts are now returning to Ozersk. In Soviet times, such people were banned from the closed cities but are now able to live there because they are seeking to return to their families who can give them homes in the absence of housing, employment, or social benefits to sustain them. Between 2003 and 2005, there has been a three-fold rise in the number of returning convicts.[41] These individuals, who have been incarcerated with serious criminals from around Russia and the Soviet successor states, are part of a criminal network that can expedite the movement of illicit commodities beyond the community of the closed nuclear cities.

Undermining security further is the fact that the number of illegal entrants into the closed cities has also increased. According to official statistics, the number of illegal entries into Ozersk rose to 224 in 2003 and 138 for the first five months of 2004, making this problem a major concern.[42]These registered illegal entries are probably only a small fraction of the overall number of those people who enter

37. Press Conference with Gosatamnadzor head Yurii Vishnevskii, November 14, 2002. Transcribed by *Federal News Service* (2002) November 14.
38. Lee (2006); Zaitseva & Hand, February 6 (2003).
39. The author wants to acknowledge the research done in the field by Robert Orttung.
40. 'Shkval'nyi veter', *Ozerskii vestnik*, March 26, 2005; According to the speech of Lynov, S. K. (2000) head of the central medical-sanitary unit in the city of Ozersk at a meeting with Mayak workers on the results of 1999 and signing a new collective bargaining agreement, February 24.
41. *Ozerskii vestnik*, July 10, 2004.
42. Ibid.

closed cities illegally. Trespassers can enter into the closed cities for an extremely small amount of money, according to some reports for as little as $5. Residents of nearby villages develop relationships with individual soldiers and use them as a channel to get in and out of the city. One smuggler explained the process in the following way: "I pick one guard and get to know him, giving him cigarettes and candy. After a month of our 'friendship,' I can bring in anyone I want. Of course, I have to agree with the solider about the exact time of entry and exit."[43]

People found guilty of smuggling workers face meaningless penalties that do not deter them. One consequence of these entries is the expanded drug trade. Another unfortunate consequence may be the ability to move nuclear materials.

Russian nuclear facilities depend on a network of construction companies and retail goods suppliers that are often run by organized crime groups. In Russia, as in other countries with serious organized crime problems such as Japan, Italy and the United States, construction companies are frequently associated with or controlled by organized crime groups. In Russia, through these companies, crime groups can gain access to the nuclear facilities. In one interview conducted by the author with an American defense contractor working on a nuclear site in the Russian Far East, his construction manager refused to comply with the demands of organized crime. The Russian manager was murdered. The new manager retained by the American had no such problems. The American project manager presumed that organized crime had gotten to the new manager of this project on what was supposed to be a project to secure a high priority nuclear site.

The proximity of the criminal actors to the nuclear facilities as residents of the closed cities, drug suppliers, and as part of the construction firms in the closed cities, all provide opportunities for the crime groups to become transporters of nuclear materials.

Crime Groups Facilitating Nuclear Smuggling

Nuclear smuggling is not confined to one single crime group. Rather, smuggling networks are comprised of different post-Soviet crime groups which interact together to move goods across borders. Nuclear materials are just one of many illicit commodities that the smugglers move both wittingly and unwittingly across the largely unpoliced and unmonitored borders of former Soviet territory.

There is not a uniform structure or a single type of group that dominates post-Soviet organized crime. When Russian officials cite statistics stating that they have 6,000 to 8,000 crime groups operating on their territory, they are describing a very diverse phenomenon.[44]These groups can range from just a few individuals who engage in repeated acts of banditry to large scale organizations that traffic in drugs, arms, and people. They consist of ethnic Russian groups, ethnically distinct groups (i.e. Armenians, Azeris, Chechens, Georgians) or larger organizations such

43. 'Prizrak Usamy brodit po 'zapretke' (2004) *Chelyabinskii rabochii*, August 12.

44. Shelley, L. (1994) 'Post-Soviet Organized Crime', *Demokratizatsiya*, vol. 2, no. 3, Summer, pp. 341–358.

as Solntsevo in Moscow within whose organizations work criminals of many different ethnic groups. At the height of the traditional criminal world of the USSR were the thieves-in-law (*Vory v zakone*), a group of criminals that eschewed any form of cooperation with the state. At the time of the collapse of the USSR, Georgians represented 40% of this total and other Caucasian groups contributed to the majority of non-Russian participants. This institution still exists but the thieves have transformed themselves and cooperate actively with state officials.

Not included in these official statistics of crime groups released by the Russian Ministry of Interior are the corrupt groups which have emerged from the former Party structures who meet the criteria of the Palermo Convention of Transnational Crime which defines crime in the following way. An "'organized criminal group' is a structured group of three or more persons, existing for a period of time acting in concert with the aim of committing one or more serious crimes or offences established in order with this Convention, in order to obtain directly or indirectly, a financial or other material benefit".[45] These latter groups are never viewed by the Russian state as organized crime groups because they are often Slavs who have high level political connections.

Also, Russian law enforcement knows little about the many international crime groups who are now operating on their territory. This includes groups not only from the Soviet successor states but also emanating from such Asian countries as China, Mongolia, Korea as well as groups from Western and Eastern Europe.

The involvement of these diverse groups in nuclear smuggling has been shown by previous cases. In the mid-1990s, "60 Minutes" and "US News and World Report" did a well documented expose of the involvement of the sports mafia, tied to high ranking officials in Ekaterinburg, in the movement of large quantities of beryllium, a restricted substance that was contaminated with .1 kilograms of highly enriched uranium, outside of Russia to Lithuania.[46]

In the late 1990s as well, security officials discussed a case of nuclear smuggling with a Russian researcher known to the author. That case involved the unusual combination of Russian, Mongolian, and Chinese criminals. This combination suggests that Russian groups will cooperate with outsiders to perpetrate a theft even in this high risk area.

The detection of materials, emanating from Russia, on Georgian territory suggests the involvement of Georgian criminals who link with their Russian colleagues who secure the materials. Georgian criminals specialize in the transport of illicit commodities, especially stolen cars. Because of this expertise, they have the capacity to move contraband long distances. Russian newspapers identify the presence of Georgian thieves-in-law near the nuclear facilities in the Southern Urals and Siberia. Cell raids conducted within Georgian prisons in

45. UN General Assembly (2000) *Crime prevention and criminal justice*, November 2, article 2, section A.Available at: http://www.uncjin.org/Documents/Conventions/dcatoc/final_documents/383e.pdf (accessed 14 August 2006). Article 2, Section A.

46. For technical information on this case see: http://www.atomicarchive.com/Almanac/Smuggling_details.shtml (accessed 14 August 2006); for media reports see: http://www.nti.org/db/nistraff/1995/19951960.htm (accessed 14 August 2006).

January 2006 by the reformist prison administration reveal that the imprisoned criminals in Georgia were in daily contact with their entire network ranging from the Russian Far East to Western Europe through the cell phones that they possessed within their prison cells. With their control of the prison through large monthly payoffs to the prison administrator, they were able to use the prison as their corporate headquarters. Using encoded messages, they could arrange the logistics for all their illicit operations.[47]Therefore, Georgian criminals may be, either knowingly or unknowingly, facilitating the movement of these dangerous commodities.

Separatist Regions and Smuggling

The separatist conflicts of the early 1990s that created the breakaway territories of Abkhazia and Ossetia have resulted in regions on Russia's southern border with the Caucasus that are criminalized and corrupted. In Abkhazia and South Ossetia, well established smuggling networks emerged, particularly since 1998, which are comprised of corrupt officials, members of law enforcement bodies and criminal groups from both sides of the conflict (Georgian-Abkhazian and Georgian-Ossetian), Georgian guerrillas, and the impoverished and marginalized parts of the population.[48]These impoverished participants include first of all internally displaced people (IDPs), refugees, and people residing in the conflict zones. The peacekeepers introduced by Russia into the region have not proved to be a force for stability but merely provide one additional group to participate and benefit from the cross-border smuggling.[49]

The breakaway region of Adjara on the Georgian border of Turkey was the locale of extensive sponsored smuggling, particularly of drugs, under the leadership of Aslan Abashidze. It was also the locus of one very important seizure of nuclear materials as well as other lesser ones.[50] The territory of Adjara was brought back under the control of the Georgian central state after the Rose Revolution and the self-exile of Abashidze to Moscow. Despite efforts by the Georgian government to regain control of the separatist territories of S. Ossetia and Abkhazia, they remain, as before, territories outside the control of any central state. There is an enormous variety of commodities which are smuggled through these territories including: fuel and cigarettes, scrap iron, drugs, timber, cash, alcohol, arms, stolen cars. Small quantities of serious radioactive materials are also believed to have traversed from Russia into Georgia through South Ossetia and possibly Abkazia.[51]

47. See note 31.
48. Kukianidze *et al.* (2004).
49. Kukianidze *et al.* (2004)
50. Available at: http://www.atomicarchive.com/Almanac/Smuggling_details.shtml (accessed 14 August 2006).
51. Data provided by the Ministry of State Security to TraCCC office in Georgia. Tbilisi, December 11, 2004; See also Baran, May 17, 2006 who cites this as a continuing problem.

To give an idea of the volume of illicit trade and movement, in 2002 before the Rose Revolution, 2.3 million individuals and 500,000 transport vehicles passed through the border checkpoints of the North Caucasus Regional Administration of Russia; more than 800 illegal entrants were detained and around 70 firearms, 55,000 cartridges, 19 kg of explosives, 10 kg of drugs, and $140,000 worth of contraband goods were confiscated; nearly 26,000 individuals were refused border crossing privileges because of absent, fraudulent, or false documents; and border guards seized around 20 members of illegal armed groups.[52]

Important changes have occurred in smuggling in the conflict zones as a result of the Rose Revolution. As the latest report of smuggling from 2006 indicates, control has not been established over these important border areas even though many guerillas lost their influential protectors in the Georgian central and regional government. Senior police who are holdovers from the Shevardnadze era are still protectors of criminal businesses tied to the conflict zones.

Conclusion

The smuggling network to move nuclear materials combines intended purchasers with the criminals who have the logistical capabilities to move materials. A well developed criminal network extends from Siberia and the Urals where nuclear facilities exist to Western Europe where Post-Soviet criminals meet terrorists in prison. Contrary to the view that the nuclear trade is chaotic and disorganized, there is a well organized transport network that moves a large variety of illicit commodities. Nuclear materials are just one of the commodities being moved along this network.

Since the late 1990s, analysts of nuclear smuggling have noted the increasing movement of nuclear smuggling to the southern tier of the former Soviet Union. This trend has continued because the crime networks that survived from the former USSR are linked strongly to the Caucasus. The absence of effective controls on the border regions of the North Caucasus, exacerbated by the enduring conflicts in the separatist conflicts, makes this region a prime locale for the departure of nuclear materials from Russia to its intended market.

The problem of nuclear smuggling into Turkey has been a long term reality. Eighteen trafficking incidents were identified between 1993 and 1999.[53] The problem has continued since then. There is great current concern on the part of Turkish authorities that with the on-going conflict in Iraq, and the more recent conflict in Lebanon, there is increasing incentive for terrorists in the region to obtain nuclear materials through Turkey. Terrorists, with their need to escalate violence for ever greater effect, are more likely to seek nuclear materials than in the past.

52. Olianchuk, V. (2002) 'Na rossisko-gruzinskoi granitse zaderzhan grazhdanin Gruzii', *Ria Novosti*, August 30.

53. Center for Nonproliferation Studies, *Overview of Reported Nuclear Trafficking Incidents Involving Turkey, 1993-1999*, Monterey Institute of International Studies, Monterey. Available at: www.cns.miis.edu/research/wmdme/flow/turkey/index.htm (accessed 14 August 2006).

The long borders, absence of legal protections, and absence of cooperation among law enforcement and intelligence in the Caucasus, Turkey, and neighboring countries, means that criminals and terrorists enjoy a strategic advantage. They can cooperate undetected by the agencies responsible for their control.

The existence of a crime-terror link in nuclear smuggling enhances the threat posed by the dispersion of nuclear materials. Thankfully, it does not guarantee the effective utilization of these materials either to create a dirty bomb or a nuclear weapon. Much more is needed in terms of human manpower, optimal working conditions and well trained scientists or engineers. Yet the threat of their effective deployment increases with the continuing departure of the materials from the former Soviet Union and the enhanced motivation of terrorists to obtain these materials.

The existence of crime-terror networks requires much more attention and analysis by the international community. Only those who have ignored the role of prisons in the incubation of terrorism, can deny that there is a link between criminals and terrorists. Technological solutions to safeguard against the diversion and transport of nuclear materials provide only part of the answer. Much more attention needs to be paid to the human component of the nuclear smuggling.

Note

This research was supported by IREX's Policy Connect Collaborative Research Program and Ploughshares.

Outlaw Private Security Firms: Criminal and Terrorist Agendas Undermine Private Security Alternatives

Graham Hall Turbiville, Jr.

In November 1999, Russian officials and private citizens were still bemused by the spectacular, decade-long growth and activities of private security firms around

Graham Hall Turbiville, Jr is a Senior Fellow with the Strategic Studies Department, Joint Special Operations University (JSOU), Hurlburt Field, FL, a component of the US Special Operations Command. Dr. Turbiville also serves as a senior consultant and researcher for a DoD/Intelligence Community program dealing with geographic and cultural intelligence in several areas of the world, and producing history-based assessments of tribal/clan societies in contemporary war and conflict. Dr. Turbiville earlier served 30 years in intelligence community analytical and leadership positions at the Defense Intelligence Agency and the Department of the Army. These included as director/chief of long-range and current intelligence offices and directorates, director of a Joint Reserve Intelligence Center, and other assignments dealing with foreign combined arms, security, and special operations forces. He has authored many monographs and studies for military, law enforcement, and intelligence venues. His articles have appeared in Special Warfare, Military Review, Marine Corps Gazette, Infantry, Army, International Defense Review, The Military Engineer, ALOG: Army Logistician, Low Intensity Conflict and Law Enforcement, Transnational Organized Crime, Crime and Justice International, Strategic Review, RUSI: Journal of the Royal United Service Institute, Journal of Soviet Military Studies, National Guard, among others. Edited works include Global Dimensions of High Intensity Crime and Low Intensity Conflict and the three-volume National Defense University Press series, The Voroshilov Lectures.

the country. The existence of these security businesses—dubbed by the Russians as "private protection organizations" (*chastnoye okhrannoye predpriyatiye*—ChOP)—had, of course, been unknown in Soviet times when the state controlled all dimensions of public and national security. But, by the end of 1999, the disarray in former Soviet law enforcement institutions and the rise of the most disparate, pernicious, and violent forms of organized crime, had seen the establishment of all manner of ChOP regimens to fill a law enforcement vacuum, buttress business agendas, and provide personal protection for those who needed and could afford it. Legislation intended to oversee and monitor ChOP activity, promulgated in 1992, scarcely reflected the coming pace and diversity of development. The Russian Ministry of Internal Affairs (MVD)—specifically the Main Directorate for the Maintenance of Public Order—estimated at the time (late 1999) that there were some 11,000 ChOP's Russia-wide employing more than 165,000 personnel and possessing about 71,000 weapons.[1] Legislation and MVD oversight mechanisms that had been created in an effort to oversee their activities were universally recognized as ineffective or worse. The association of ChOPs with activities that challenged the bounds of legality and, not infrequently, were judged blatantly criminal had become part of the public safety environment.

Still, it was more than a surprise when the Russian newspaper *Moskovskiy Komsomolets* reported the surfacing of a ChOP that would be difficult to surpass as the ultimate "outlaw private security" enterprise. Its existence came to light through efforts to insure some 1,500 personnel of a firm named "Islamic Order" (*Islamskiy Poryadok*). Islamic Order, it was reported, was duly registered, held a license, had a bank account, and was listed at a street address in Grozny, the capital of Chechnya. But it turned out to be a cover organization for the notorious Chechen guerrilla and terrorist leader, Shamil Basayev, and its stated "liberation of hostages" mission at least suggested that the perpetrators of this deceit had a well-developed and black sense of humor. According to *Moskovskiy Komsomolets*, the Chechen guerrilla employees, and the now-deceased Basayev himself, were to be insured for $10,000 each, an amount totaling $15 million.[2] The newspaper noted the differential between this amount and the one million dollars that at the time was offered by the Russian military commander in Chechnya, General Gennady Troshin, for the elimination of Shamil Basayev.[3]

This episode appears to have been confirmed in part, at least, by an MVD spokesman.[4] Whatever its total accuracy, the information highlighted an issue that already was plaguing not only Russia but a number of states around the world, that is, the problem of regulating private security organizations and insuring that criminality

1. Luk'yanov, I. & Kazanskaya, O. (1999) 'Kakiye lyudi bez okhrany', (What Kind of People Are Without Protection?) *Profile*, vol. 45, no. 167. Available at: http://www.profile.ru

2. Shamil Basayev died on July 10, 2006 in the explosion of a vehicle in Ingushetia. The circumstances surrounding the explosion are far from clear, but the large, Russian-initiated or accidental blast killed Basayev and several fellow guerrillas. It is supposed that no insurance payment was forthcoming.

3. Khinshteyn, A. (1991) '15,000,000 $ dlya Basayeva' ($15,000,000 for Basayev), *Moskovskiy Komsomolets*, November 20.

4. Luk'yanov & Kazanskaya (1999).

or terrorism were not a part—or the centerpiece—of their business model. The terrorist dimension of this issue has become even more acute in the global war on terrorism—the Long War—as the "Islamic Order" model above is shown to be a broader phenomenon. Before addressing this, a brief word about context is in order.

The ways in which conflict, weakened government institutions, and societal disarray contribute to rising levels of criminality and armed violence have been productively examined by historians, political scientists, and security specialists over the last several decades. When an old order dies, weakens or loses legitimacy—and when war and ethnic or religious antagonisms become acute—organized crime, "banditry", and the creation of environments suitable for the growth of terrorism and insurgency appear in a variety of forms.[5] A phenomenon that has more recently become of interest to scholars and security planners, is that these same kinds of conditions, also spark the intensified growth and employment of private security (or military) organizations, businesses, and regimens in various forms.[6] Whether formed to fill critical gaps in a government's ability to deal with dangerous or complex security environments, or to provide value-added services for government, large corporations, or other enterprises, they are businesses mainly formed to earn money and operate in accord with business models designed to accomplish that end. Around the world, these have been created with active government support and oversight because of perceived value; with grudging governmental acquiescence because of pressing need and a lack of alternatives; with general government indifference because of preoccupation with other problems; and sometimes with strong but ineffective opposition from severely weakened regimes.

Private security organizations worldwide have been formed for a variety of sanctioned purposes that include public safety, national security, regional stability, and even international security missions and activities. Control, oversight, and performance by government bodies set up to monitor private security activities have varied widely in quality, and like the regular government police and security establishments themselves, shoddy performance, poor personnel selection criteria or vetting, criminality, and corruption have been a part of the record along with the provision of essential security services. This essay, focuses not on those private security establishments that have strayed or fallen short, as many institutions do from time to time, but rather on those that were either formed for the express

5. Historian E. J. Hobsbawm's review of "social banditry" over the centuries in his still pertinent study *Bandits*, Weidenfeld & Nicolson, London, 1969, pp. 17–18, made this point well. While Hobsbawm focused principally on one form of banditry, his observations and arguments are extremely useful for assessing more modern forms of outlaw, guerrilla, or criminal.

6. These range in character, size, and composition–as well as real or ostensible mission–from firms akin to the fictional *No. 1 Ladies' Detective Agency*, http://www.randomhouse.com/features/mccallsmith/books.html, to Colombian or private militias; from a "Wheat Stalker" investigative firm in western Kansas (available at: http://www.kapi.org/) 'Who knows what evil lurks in the heart of the Great Plains', to the paramilitary Blackwater Security Consulting, http://www.blackwaterusa.com/securityconsulting/, or the former Sandline International, http://www.sandline.com/site/index.html, closed in April 2004; and many, many variants in between and on the periphery.

purpose of criminality or terrorism using the cover of legitimate security firms, as well as those that otherwise turned to criminal or terrorist agendas. It also focuses on the many disparate private security businesses and enterprises abroad, rather than the larger, regularized and generally well-regulated US and Western firms that have been so well treated in the growing body of "privatized security" literature. While the above Russian anecdote illustrates the potential, it also clearly illustrates more than rare happenstance or an occasional scheme. There are enough examples from around the world to illustrate the advantages that criminal and terrorist groups see in using a "private security cover", and in the active plans by such groups to use private security venues them for their own purposes.

For example, pointing to the existence of a defined current and future planning tenet, and as a suggestion of what has already transpired in the past, is the advice offered in the recently translated 2005 al-Qaeda and "*jihadi* strategy" document by Abu Bakr Naji entitled *Management of Savagery*. The work, among other things, describes how al-Qaeda may consider approaches for defeating the US and its allies. Of note as regards this chapter, is the *jihadi* imperative set out to infiltrate institutions over the course of a long struggle and the theoretical framework for actions that have already been undertaken not only by al-Qaeda but by various terrorist (and criminal) groups. Specifically, Abu Bakr Naji indicates:

> Our battle is long and still in its beginning.... Its length provides an opportunity for infiltrating the adversaries and their fellow travelers and establishing a strong security apparatus that is more supportive of the security of the movement now, and later the state. (We) should infiltrate the police forces, the armies, the different political parties, the newspapers, the Islamic groups, the petroleum companies (as an employee or as an engineer), *private security companies*, sensitive civil institutions, etc. That actually began several decades ago, but we need to increase it in light of recent developments.[7]

These targets vary in their vulnerability and potential payoff and it may be that private security establishments offer some of the greatest payoffs, combined with effective cover and reduced risks. In this regard, it is instructive to review the kinds of lawlessness and criminality that have become associated with foreign private security establishments around the world to frame the challenges and then address how private security establishments have sometimes facilitated—or have otherwise been linked with—terrorism and insurgency abroad.

Private Security: Incentives for Penetration and Cover

The antecedents, legislation, and imperatives shaping the creation of private security and paramilitary enterprises in the first decade of the 21st Century—

7. Naji, A. B. (2006) *Management of Savagery: The Most Critical Stage Through Which the Umma Must Pass*, sponsored by the John M. Olin, Institute for Strategic Studies, Harvard University, [trans William McCants], May 23, as presented by the US Military Academy Counterterrorism Center at West Point, p. 121. Available at: http://www.ctc.usma.edu/Management_of_Savagery.pdf.

including their intensified formation in the wake of the September 2001 attacks on the US and other major terrorist events elsewhere—have been ably addressed in a number of instructive articles and books.[8] There is a spectrum of public policy debates and views on the propriety of using non-government security and military establishments, and the dangers this global development poses to everything from national sovereignty to economic health. In the West, at least, their roles are generally understood amidst the uneasiness, and internal and external oversight is present in varying levels of effectiveness.

This is far from the case in other areas of the world, where the numbers and diversity of large and small security "enterprises" have rapidly expanded, oversight is uneven, and the impact on local, national and regional security and stability may be substantial. For criminals, and groups with terrorist agendas as well, the advantages of a "private security firm cover" became quickly evident in many parts of the world. The perception was, as one frustrated Russian senior police general official put it in late 2002, why not "just call your 'gang' a private security firm, purchase a license for weapons, and provide 'protection' until your heart's content?"[9] Criminal penetration of private security, while instructive and important itself, also illustrates the vulnerability of these business to a level of infiltration that present a more dangerous threat to national security and public safety.

In general, the pretense of operating a security firm provides a measure of legitimacy, even if a shallow one, and obscures or makes tacitly acceptable activities that might otherwise be suspect. Among the many benefits evident in actual experience are the plausible maintenance of a high level of privacy or secrecy; frequent comings and goings; surveillance and other information acquisition; firearms possession; and association with a broad spectrum of less-than-upright individuals. Collaboration with police through bribery or other incentives has proven commonplace and safer for the police and the private firm. This has included the use of police databases, communications, uniforms, credentials, and other resources and sometimes those of the military as well. Indeed, the targeted recruitment of ill-paid former and serving police, other government security, and sometimes military personnel is a common practice, with far higher compensation, even if criminal, a proven incentive in many places. The practice by regular law enforcement bodies of using private security organizations to carry out extra-legal "justice" operations has been far from infrequent in some countries.

8. Singer, P. W. (2004) *Corporate Warriors: The Rise of the Privatized Military Industry*, Cornell University Press, Ithaca; Bunker, R. J. (2006) 'Combatants or Non-Combatants? Where Private Military Companies Fit in Modern, Classical and Legal Definitions', *Journal of International Peace Operations*, vol. 2, no. 1, pp. 17–18; Nemeth, C. P. (2004) *Private Security and the Law*, Butterworth-Heinemann, Boston; Avant, D. D. (2005) *The Market for Force: The Consequences of Privatizing Security*, Cambridge University Press, New York; Adams, T. K. (1999) 'The New Mercenaries and the Privatization of Conflict', *Parameters*, vol. 24, Summer, pp. 103–116; and many others.

9. Falaleyev, M. (2002) 'To What Trenches Have the Private Security Firms Been Called? Thousands of Private Security Firms Have Been Set Up in Russia', *Komsomolskaya Pravda*, December 10, translated in CEP20021209000330.

Private security firms in many areas of the world are a primary vector for the legal or gray market acquisition of weapons—sometimes in huge quantities—and including far more than the side arms sometimes specified in private security oversight regulations. Criminal groups well understand that the mere existence of an armed group with seemingly legal status or protection serves as a means of coercion for a variety of shakedown and extortion rackets. Certainly, however, among the major factors in the successful use of security firms by criminals or terrorists have been the sheer proliferation of such companies, which provides a near anonymous sea in which to swim; the low threshold for establishing security companies; the subsequent weak and haphazard oversight so often exercised; and the increased technological sophistication of even near-street thugs inclined to create a more legitimate visible face.

Private Security and Criminal Conduct in Specific Regions

To provide some insight into what the generalizations above have meant in the real world, it is instructive to look at how specific criminal activities have become associated with private security companies in various countries and regions. The intent is not to provide a comprehensive survey, but to underscore the diversity and commonality of private security problems and the relative ease with many of them have turned—or been turned—to illegality and crime in various forms. This easy vulnerability to penetration marks private security as a potential cover or vector of terrorism as discussed further below. Certainly, there are few better examples than the states of the former Soviet Union and the former Communist regimes of Eastern Europe, where crime and turmoil have led to remarkable growth in private security organizations.

The Russian private security enterprises on the eve of the millennium that had proliferated in the years following the USSR's dissolution, constituted, in part at least, a perceived, legitimate social requirement stemming from Russia's "collapsed system of public security". Already by the mid-1990s, some 6,605 Russian "private security enterprises and security services" had been officially registered, with some 26,000 individuals—many former military or security-service personnel—acquiring private investigative licenses. By the fall of 2003, Russian specialists estimated that there were 16,000 registered firms employing about 350,000 people (up from 11,000 firms and 165,000 employees in 1999).[10] By early 2005, the number of firms estimated had risen to 21,000 employing perhaps 500,000 security officers and other personnel.[11] Two years later, as one Russian observer put it, "somehow without noticing it ourselves, we have created a well-armed and trained parallel army, whose numbers exceed those of the Federal Security Service and the Federal Border Service taken together."[12] A number of

10. *Vedmosti*, September 24, 2003.
11. ITAR-TASS Information Agency, February 2, 2005, translated in CEP20050202000389.
12. Falaleyev (2002).

these firms and individuals were deeply involved in organized criminal activity or had turned into small private armies for individuals or organizations whose goals by and large did not corresponded with public interest.

As noted earlier, Russians use the acronym ChOP as a catch-all to describe the spectrum of private protection organizations. To this, reflecting the practice in the West, they have also added the term "private military organization" (*chastnaya voyennaya organizatsiya*—ChVO). The term can refer to well-organized and regulated Western style paramilitary companies; to private militias such as Moscow-allied Chechen prime minister Ramzan Kadyrov's armed groups ("American uniforms, Russian weapons, Islamic beliefs and a Chechen spirit" as he characterized them); or it may reflect the plethora of private protection organizations whose armament and focus became more militarized than earlier organizations.[13] Such groups, who might wear military-looking camouflage and be manned by former special police or military personnel, soon began to carry out what was described as "the combat application of 'personal detachments' for purposes that are by no means oriented on security."[14]

Racketeering, extortion and coercion, property crimes, the forced seizure of assets and even whole businesses, armed clashes, and assassinations are reported with some frequency. While private security weapons were supposed to be limited to side arms for protection, an array of Kalashnikov automatic weapons, assault shotguns, Dragunov sniper rifles, and other arms or explosives are among them. As early as 2002 in the Moscow *Oblast'* (Region), there were more than 600 private security firms possessing 4,300 known firearms. Criminals made a conscious effort to infiltrate these firms for the arms acquisition opportunities they provided. In a one month period, the MVD conducted a counter-terrorist operation and stripped seven of these firms of their arms licenses for violations.[15] Despite occasional crackdowns, some ChOP's are so wealthy that, in return for mutual support and legal cover, they "sponsor" government special units, buying them equipment and new materiel that they would otherwise be unable to afford.[16] They are, in short, a source of revenue for some government law enforcement and security services, not to mention well-paid post-government employment.

Criminalized private security groups were perfectly aware of the need to have everything administratively in order regarding their legal status and activities. An excellent example of this was the notably murderous Orekhovo-Medvedkovo criminal group in Moscow, personnel of which were convicted in the spring of 2004 after a trial whose phases went on for some years. The criminal grouping involved in a spectrum of often-violent criminal activity and killed enumerable rivals as they pretended to conduct legitimate security business. The "paper" cover of their real activities was detailed in information coming out of their marathon trial:

13. Liss, A. (2005) 'Chechnya's gun-toting strongman', BBC World News, November 26. Available at: http://news.bbc.co.uk/.
14. Falaleyev (2002).
15. ITAR-TASS Information Agency, October 11, 2002, translated in CEP20021017000200.
16. Ibid.

> They almost all had licenses to act as security guards. Private security enterprises were created so that they had the right to carry weapons legally and officially provide protection for companies—they set up security contracts with them openly and aboveboard. The visible part of the gangsters' life was reflected in the private security enterprises' documents: work records, route sheets, post numbers, who had which weapons, what establishments were being guarded—all the documents were in order, everything was perfect.[17]

Raiding and seizure of assets by armed security companies affiliated or hired by rival financial, manufacturing, and other corporate enterprises became an issue for the Russian corporate and financial world. Leonid Vedenov, the head of the MVD Directorate for the Protection of Public Order's assessment and licensing component, indicated that from 2000-2005, some 1,000 business and enterprises had private security groups use physical force to seize assets, sometimes with unsanctioned police support.[18] This kind of assertive and often illegal role of ChOP's in Russian business dealings also had an impact on the activities of police enforcement including the employment of units in the family of "special designation" (*spetsnaz* and *osnaz*) police components. One type of unit—formerly designated as Rapid Reaction Militia Detachments (SOBR) and now called Militia Detachments of Special Designation (OMSN)—is a case in point. A senior Russian officer noted that:

> Virtually no major operation is conducted without the involvement of *spetsnaz* personnel. Even routine searches of offices are frequently conducted with OMSN backup, *because there is a strong probability that the efforts of investigators and operatives will be opposed by security guards and private security services.*[19]

A situation analogous to that in Russia existed in Eastern Europe soon after the dissolution of Communist regimes and their police establishments. In the 1990s, for example, a burgeoning number of Bulgarian firms were notoriously known as "wrestler companies" because of their practice of hiring athletes for strong-arm work in extortion and racketeering. "Wrestler",[20] in fact, became a synonym for gangster. Similarly, Romanian firms carried out a range of intelligence gathering, bribery, and coercion on behalf of their clients, which appalled even the befuddled and reorganizing Romanian law enforcement establishment of the time. Among the illegal activities credited to Romanian private security have been conducting a range of illegal intelligence gathering activities to include industrial espionage; seizing property and extorting "taxes" through blackmail, coercion and violence; bribing, blackmailing, or otherwise subverting government officials; and creating

17. Mokhel, R. (2005) 'All Stranglers Together', *Moskovskiy Komsomolets*, January 11, translated in CEP20050111000182.
18. ITAR-TASS, February 2, 2005.
19. Il'ya Zubko (interview with General Major Vladimir Gorshukov, MVD Deputy Chief of the Main Directorate for Combating Organized Crime), 'Spetsnaz prikhodit po zayavkam' (Spetsnaz Can Be Requisitioned), *Rossiyskaya Gazeta*, November 10, 2004. Available at: http://www.rg.ru/ (archives).
20. 'Interior Minister Declares War on 'Wrestler' Companies', BTA broadcast in English, 1835 GMT, March 7, 1997, translated in FTS19970307000876.

intelligence and police style secret databases for private use (a practice facilitated by the security service background of the "detective" employees).[21]

As in many other areas around the world, the number of Eastern European firms has continued to grow in the 21st Century. By the fall of 2005, there were 130,000 private security personnel in Bulgaria and about 37,000 (more than double the number of 2001) in neighboring Romania, although the latter appeared to suffer more from private firms engaging in criminal and other illegal activity.[22] While the same kinds of problems still surface—and there remain a number of unregistered security firms—problems generally are more limited than in the mid-1990s due to the increased association of these countries with European professional, legislative, and oversight regimens.

Some concerns remain about other security businesses in southeastern Europe as a recent study pointed out.[23] The work considered private security businesses that, in addition to Bulgaria and Romania, addressed Albania, Bosnia and Herzegovina, Croatia, the Former Yugoslav Republic of Macedonia, Moldova, Serbia and Montenegro (as it then existed), and the territory of Kosovo. Specifically, this concerned the potential for mischief stemming from the affiliation of private security firms with other entities and their access to arms. As regards the former issue—evident in some way in every country— worries centered on links (sometimes multiple) to political parties, criminal groups, paramilitary groups or ethnic groups. As regards, arms, every southeastern European country examined (excepting the Kosovo territory) allowed private firms to possess personal weapons and in the case of Albania, Serbia, and perhaps some other countries, to have automatic arms.[24] Loosely controlled armories and worrisome affiliations and linkages constituted a potential danger for misuse and, given the area's volatility and background in smuggling of all types (including to terrorist groups), perhaps constituted a continuing, working mechanism for arms diversions or other misuse.

In Turkey, as elsewhere in parts of Europe, crime, the enduring terrorist potential of the Kurdish Workers Party (PKK), and the new specter of al-Qaeda and Islamic extremist groups have generated a wholesale increase in private security establishments. As of mid-2005, there were some 4,000 companies with various security missions that were estimated to employ about 130,000 personnel. While many of these were ostensibly targeted against criminal activities such as street crime, burglary, and other typical public safety threats, some were formed in response to a rise in "terrorist" bombing incidents. The immediate suspicion arose that some of these companies were perpetrating crimes themselves, perhaps in an effort to foster new business. These doubts were not allayed by the questionable

21. Stefan, G. (2001) 'Over 1,600 Firms Coordinated by Former Securitate People Compete With Police, Intelligence Services', *Adevarul*, March 30, translated in EUP20010330000066.
22. The statistics were published in the Bulgarian *Monitor*, September 15, 2005 and appeared originally on September 15, 2005. Available at: http://www.csd.bg/artShow.php?id = 6325.
23. South Eastern Europe Small Arms Clearinghouse (SEESAC) (2005) *SALW [Small Arms and Light Weapons] and Private Security Companies in South Eastern Europe: A Cause or Effect of Insecurity?* SEESAC, Belgrade, August. Available at: http://www.seesac.org/reports/psc.pdf
24. Ibid.

background of some of the often-prominent ex-officials who set up security businesses. The concern prompted increased calls in the Turkish Parliament for better regulation and oversight. They also highlighted the uncomfortable possibility that, despite legislation promulgated earlier that year, the Interior Ministry may not really know how many companies actually exist, how many were only paper entities, how many and what kind of people were actually employed, and what training and preparation they received. The concern was encapsulated by a Republican People's Party Deputy for Izmir, who echoed concerns heard elsewhere around the world, that unless "a sound structure is formed it is inevitable that private security companies will first become gangs, then armies of looters and finally mafia organizations."[25]

Moving to the far different region of Latin America, private armed groups affiliated with wealthy landowners, political parties, and businesses have had a long history. However, this precedent has been dwarfed by the currently increasing number of private security establishments—indigenous, foreign national and international—that operate in behalf of businesses, civil institutions and individuals. As elsewhere, private security firm growth has been spurred by the pressing need to provide some measure of institutional and personal protection amidst the violent spillover or aftermath of wars and insurgency; the presence of uncontrolled weapons; soaring crime rates; random and political violence; corrupt and ineffective Latin American police and justice establishments; and a host of political, ethnic, and criminal agendas. However, private security firms from Mexico to the tip of South America, formed to address these problems, have had at best spotty performances and have been subject to criminalization, misconduct, and illegal activities in many forms. While extensive documentation along with innumerable anecdotal accounts of corrupted private security regimens have been compiled by government and human rights groups alike, a few examples from several countries can serve to illustrate the kinds of issues in the region.

Mexico is a good case in point. The excellent scholar of Mexican history and conflict, Paul J. Vanderwood, devoted a chapter in his book *Disorder and Progress* to what he called "Bandits into Police—and Vice Versa". He describes the sometimes effortless transition of late 19th and early 20th Century Mexican bandits into law enforcement personnel; the ease with which that transition was reversed; and the difficulty sometimes in telling the difference.[26] Mexican private security companies and personnel have certainly maintained that tradition in 21st Century Mexico, which is much plagued by high rates of street and organized crime and policed by often corrupt law enforcement and judicial establishments. High crime rates and unreliable police spurred both the creation of Mexican private security businesses of various types as well as the migration of foreign

25. See the Turkish newspaper recap in 'Security or Mafia?', *Nokta*, June 19, 2005, pp. 44–45, translated in GMP2005080702200.

26. Vanderwood, P. J. 'Bandits Into Police–and Vice Versa', *Disorder and Progress: Bandits, Police, and Mexican Development*, Scholarly Resources Books, Wilmington, 1992, pp. 53–60.

security branches from the larger firms in the US and elsewhere. Between 1998 and 1999 alone, private security companies reportedly increased by about 40 percent, resulting at the turn of the millennium to more than an estimated 10,000 ill-monitored private security firms, only 20% of which—2,984—were registered, with 153,885 personnel.

As in most parts of the world, substantial numbers of private security personnel were former or moonlighting police officers.[27] The competence and trustworthiness of such businesses have been problematic at best, illustrated by informed assessments from outside security specialists. In Guadalajara in 2006, for example, the US Overseas Advisory Council—citing the Regional Security Office and most local Mexican officials—judged that *all* firms were mediocre at best, and indicated that not a single outfit could be recommended. If possible, local companies performed security using their own employees rather than the poorly paid, trained, and mistrusted alternatives.[28]

Kidnapping, robbery, extortion, and coercion on behalf of various criminal, economic and political agendas have been associated with Mexican private security, just as they have been with the often-complicit serving federal, state and local serving police officers. To cite some examples from a long, dreary, and continuing mosaic of corruption (and while numerous serving police were also arrested apace in 2005 for similar crimes), three private security officers operating in Ciudad Juarez (directly across the Rio Grande from El Paso, Texas) were arrested for kidnapping a businessman and demanding a ransom. These were determined to be employees of a Sinaloa-based company ("Private Alarms Protection") that had a deployed component in Ciudad Juarez. At about the same time, three additional private guards were arrested on suspicion of murdering two women. In fact, among the most notorious crimes in the US-Mexican border has been the murder of scores of young women, cases steeped in mystery, believed motivated by everything from drug-trafficking to kidnapping to devil-worship and, so far, resulting in few plausible law enforcement successes. The countless private security and guard organizations located in Ciudad Juarez have been widely suspect in these murders, along with the police, and the three arrested were said to be from the private firm "Border Eagles". Private security like this typically patrols the kind of residential and business areas where young women have been killed. While estimates vary, one source judged that there were 107 "known" security business operating in the border city, with a combined employee total (some 6,000) that exceeded the active police officers several-fold. As elsewhere in Mexico, training for private officers is often negligible in the fly-by-night firms, the pay small, and benefits slight or non-existent. Only half of

27. Reames, B. (2004) 'Police Forces in Mexico: A Profile', Mexico Policing Project—Lawyers Committee for Human Rights, USMEX 2003-04 Working Paper Series, La Jolla. Available at: http://repositories.cdlib.org/cgi/viewcontent.cgi?article = 1025&context = usmex.
28. US Department of State (2006) *Guadalajara, Mexico: 2006 Crime and Safety Report*, Overseas Advisory Council, Washington, DC, April 20. Available at: http://www.osac.gov/Reports/report.cfm?contentID = 45279.

the known firms were legally registered, though that requirement in reality seems to mean little.[29]

Documented and undocumented immigrants play an important role in private security firm recruitment in some parts of Central America. In Costa Rica, a Dutch anthropologist and researcher indicated that "most" private security guards there are Nicaraguan and that private security is more in evidence than in some Colombians cities, despite Costa Rica's relative peacefulness. The influx of Nicaraguans began with the Sandinista and civil war violence and has continued because of economic incentives. With perhaps 10% of the Costa Rican population estimated to be from Nicaragua now, there is a large base for low-income jobs. Street-level private security falls into that category.[30] According to a UN official stationed in Costa Rica, the number of private security personnel more than doubled from 2004 to 2005, i.e., from 8,000 to 19,000, which includes only the personnel registered with the Ministerio de Gobernación, Policía y Seguridad Pública. However, the formal requirement for training, education, and emotional stability was totally lacking.[31] While Costa Rica is a relatively well-off and stable country, there is some concern that the new private security company growth—relying on poorly trained and undocumented personnel—may have the potential for future trouble.

Public impatience with violent criminals has generated formal local and neighborhood organizations and informal vigilante groups that have taken police indifference or ineffectiveness into their own hands. This has been true in other areas of Central America as well. In Honduras, for example, the most recent US State Department human rights report pointed to the proliferation of "unlicensed security guard services and vigilante groups" as well as so-called Citizen Security Councils and private security companies with ties to the police. While the ostensible purpose of these non-government groups is to prevent crime and violence, they have been widely accused of violent vigilantism and acting as death squads—with police acquiescence or encouragement—in so-called "social cleansing". According to some reporting, said to be based on Honduran government sources from 1999–2005, nearly 1,000 suspected criminals, gang members, street children, and others were killed in extrajudicial actions perpetrated at least in part by security groups.[32]

29. See Frontera NorteSur (FNS), 'More Baddies With Badges', Frontera NorteSur Center for Latin American and Border Studies, New Mexico State University, Las Cruces, October 16, 2005.Original sources cited include articles from El Universal, Proceso/Apro, Frontera, and others. See also Frontera NorteSur (FNS), 'Private Security Firms Questioned as a Bloody Week Unfolds', September 18, 2005, available at: Email: fnsnews@nmsu.edu. Original sources cited by Frontera NorteSur include articles from *Norte*, *El Universal*, *El Diario de Juarez*, and others. Frontera NorteSur is archived at http://www.nmsu.edu/ ~ frontera/.

30. The Dutch -anthropologist-researcher was Marije Van Lidthe de Jeude. See Patterson, K. (2006) 'Remittances Driving Central American Economies', Frontera NorteSur Center for Latin American and Border Studies, New Mexico State University, Las Cruces, April 17.

31. 'Better PR needed to stem crime fears, U.N. aide says', *A.M. Costa Rica*, July 8, 2006. Available at: http://www.amcostarica.com/070706.htm.

32. US Department of State (2006), *Honduras: Country Reports on Human Rights Practices-2005*, Bureau of Democracy, Human Rights and Labor, Washington, DC, March 8.

In Guatemala, a similar phenomenon exists, where city, village, and other private protection organizations are suspected of extra-judicial killings, disappearances, and various forms of organized crime to include arms and drug trafficking. By 2000, the money spent nationally for private security exceeded the public security budget by about 20 percent. The rapidly increasing number of firms produced a range of estimates, the most authoritative indicating that, by 2006, there were some 180 private security companies employing 180,000 people. This number compared to only 18,500 police, a bare 10 percent. With only eight police officers exercising oversight of private security firms, real monitoring was non-existent.[33] Salvadoran private security firms paralleled this disparity in private and public security—and effective oversight—where the presence of 158 companies with 18,244 "guards" in 2004 compared with a National Police force that had only 5,000 of its 16,800 total police officers serving actively at any given time.[34]

Colombia's decades of conflict and terrorism have made it one of the best known centers of *autodefensas* and other well-armed private militias, the most famous/notorious being the United Self-Defense Forces of Colombia (*Autodefensas Unidas de Colombia*—AUC). Linked crime and conflict—and the presence of huge arms supplies and trained fighters—have generated professed private security organizations of all types, a number so well know for human rights abuses and criminal involvement that it need not be addressed in any detail here.[35] Oversight of the countless formal and informal security entities is scarcely conceivable amidst the other problems. Nevertheless, the need—and government ineffectiveness—continue to generate attention, as security firms' involvement in "money laundering, drug trafficking, and paramilitarism" continue to function and grow. One of the most recent examples is the 2006 capture and arrest of Emilse del Rosario Lopez Romero, known as La Gata (The Cat). Lopez had formed a security force of some 180 "bodyguards", many armed with automatic weapons as well as the usual array of pistols and shotguns. Ostensibly a businesswoman, she claimed the need for private security to protect her lottery businesses and her son, a city mayor. However, she was soon discovered to be linked with criminal activities to include influencing elections and extorting businesses. Even her capture and arrest, however, did not change

33. United States Agency for International Development (2006) *Central America and Mexico Gang Assessment*, by R. Loudis et al., Bureau for Latin American and Caribbean Affairs, Office of Regional Sustainable Development, Washington, DC, April. For earlier estimates, see Waszink, C. (2000) *Security and Development Brief: Guatemala*, Program on Security and Development, Monterrey, pp. 6–7, available at: http://sand.miis.edu/research/2000/may2000/guatebrief.pdf; and US Department of State (2002) *Guatemala: Country Reports on Human Rights Practices - 2005*, Bureau of Democracy, Human Rights, and Labor, Washington, DC, March 31; and Replogle, J. (2005) 'In Guatemala, a rise in vigilante justice', *Christian Science Monitor*, October 6.

34. United States Agency for International Development (2006), *Central America and Mexico Gang Assessment*, Bureau for Latin American and Caribbean Affairs, Office of Regional Sustainable Development, Washington, DC, April.

35. For an excellent short treatment see Spencer, D. (2001) *Colombia's Paramilitaries: Criminals or Political Force?* US Army Strategic Studies Institute, Washington, DC, December.

the status of her security force, which remained legal due to its association with a still functioning lottery business.[36]

By spring 2006 in Paraguay, the National Police authorities in Asuncion reported that there were 280 private security firms operating throughout the country, employing a total of more than 13,000 officers and personnel. Only 30 of the companies were termed to be legal, leaving some 250 businesses (with 7,000 personnel) classified as "irregular". There was no national legislation governing their activities and there seemed to be no immediate prospect of getting it. As elsewhere in parts of Latin America, this total number of private security personnel exceeded the 25,000-officer National Police force.[37] Further, the private companies were said in a number of cases to be better equipped, organized, trained, and paid than the government law enforcement establishment, contributing negatively to police retention.[38] Criminal activity attributed to private firms was widely reported, ranging from extortion, to property seizures, to political intimidation, to murder. In the latter category was the notorious ambush-assassination in Asuncion of Vice President Luis Maria Argana in March 1999. While Paraguay eventually judged that there was political and army complicity in the murder, and while two individuals were convicted, reports at the time suspected the involvement of seven members of a "commando" style private security team that had attracted the attention of authorities with their paramilitary training, use of high-powered and automatic weapons, and instruction in special tactics.[39] At a minimum, the presence of unregulated companies and firearms made such suspicions plausible, if difficult to prove.

In Brazil, control of weapons in the hands of the 2,800 private security firms is a major issue. In less than a decade, some 56,800 firearms "disappeared from the companies, and the Brazilian police are attempting to set up an electronic inventory system to track such weapons in the future".[40] In Sao Paulo—likely reflecting the situation nationwide—it was estimated by the "Sao Paulo State Private Security Companies' Union" that 80% of the private security companies there are "clandestine" and in substantial measure both unauthorized and untrained for security work. Recognizing that the union has an agenda of its own in its desire to exercise control over professional standards (and collect dues), there are clearly many unregistered companies that by some estimates could be as high

36. 'Hay Gata encerrada', *Semana*, no. 1241, February 27-March 5, 2006, http://www.semana.com.co/; and 'Gobierno ordena desarmar en la Costa el ejército de Emilse del Rosario López Romero, 'La Gata', *El Tiempo*, November 12, http://www.eltiempo.com/

37. 'La seguridad privada tiene más efectivos que la Policía' (2006) *Ultima Hora*, April 30, http://www.ultimahora.com/default.asp.

38. 'Los guardias privados están mejor preparados que policías' (2006) *Ultima Hora*, May 5, http://www.ultimahora.com/default.asp.

39. Bureau of Democracy, Human Rights, and Labor (2005) *Paraguay: Country Reports on Human Rights Practices*-2004, U.S. Department of State, Washington, DC, February 28.

40. 'Federal Police Establish Register of Weapons Owned by Security Firms' (2006) *Istoe*, July 12, translated in LAP20060711340001.

as 500,000 personnel in this area with a population in excess of 10 million people.[41] Criminality involving some of these firms spanned the usual crimes against property and persons. They included also the use of private armed security groups by landowners to eliminate landless squatters—many of the latter organized by the Landless Workers' Movement—through coercion and sometimes fatal violence. Among the most notorious and continuing practice, going back at least a decade, is the social cleansing by death squads who execute vagrants, street youths, and beggars in Sao Paulo and Rio in particular. This elimination of groupings deemed socially undesirable involved police personnel and those moonlighting as private "security" in the employ of local businesses.[42]

African private security growth has paralleled that in other areas of the world reviewed above. It has been characterized by the widespread creation of smaller indigenous companies, the establishment of larger businesses (some of which now export their business regionally), and the influx of foreign, mostly Western-owned firms, offering an array of services in individual countries and regionally. Of passing interest only—reflecting the reputation for "gray market", legally questionable, or downright illegal private security initiatives in some African states—was the frequent role unnamed private security firms played in the Nigerian get-rich-quick scams. Very often the imaginary stolen money, gemstones, diamonds, valuable documents, and the like were said to reside safely with a private security firm.[43]

South Africa, in particular, saw rapid privatized security increases in the 1990s. By the turn of the millennium, there were an estimated 3,200 security companies employing 200,000 personnel in the Republic of South Africa, most of these being guards of various types and, collectively, well-outnumbering the South African Police Service. Criminal activity then and today has ranged from minor offenses to major crimes, despite efforts to exercise control with limited personnel and inadequate legislation—problems present in many African states as every survey makes clear.[44] Among the unusual variants that private security regimens may take is illustrated by Cote d'Ivoire.

In Cote d'Ivoire, it was estimated that some 300 private security firms with more than 20,000 employees were present in 2005, though the number may have been substantially higher than that. In addition to the large or better known companies—said to include "Wackenhutt, Delta Assistance, BIP, BGSP, Omeifra,

41. Flosi, C. (2005) 'Clandestine Security Companies Proliferate in Sao Paulo', *O Estado de Sao Paulo*, February 16, available at: http://www.estado.com.br/.
42. See, for example, 'Mass murder. Death squads. Roadside executions... the truth about policing Brazilian-style', *The Daily Mail*, August 25, 2005; and Altieri, A. (2004) 'Brazil's homeless visible through death', *BBC News*, September 29, available at: http://news.bbc.co.uk/1/hi/programmes/3694092.stm.
43. See the 'Nigerian Scam Overview', available at: http://www.rickmcginnis.com/scam/overview.htm, among other sites addressing the phenomenon.
44. Irish, J. (1999) *Policing for Profit: The future of South Africa's Private Security Industry*, ed. M. Schönteich, Monograph no. 39, Institute for Security Studies, August, http://www.iss.co.za/Pubs/Monographs/No39/Contents.html.

ASP," and others—there are additional local security businesses as well. One of the consequences of socio-political tensions there following the civil war and unresolved issues of land reform and other problems, was a perceived effort to politicize or leverage existing or newly forming "private security groups" in behalf of one agenda or another. It is widely judged that a number of these firms have become, in effect, partisan intelligence-gathering entities, with at least the potential for direct action. They constitute, essentially, "militias with official seals" as one observer described them. The alignment of some companies in terms of tribe or clan adds additional complexity (there are at least 60 ethnic groups in Cote d'Ivoire), contributing as it does to undermining efforts to promote national cohesiveness, disarmament and reconciliation, while at the same time forming small or larger armed groups that can be mobilized.[45] One observer stated the perceived danger this way:

> As in Iraq, private military companies are flourishing. Thanks to their carrying of weapons, they offer more "strong-arm" services, ranging from personal body-guarding to military training. They are made up of former soldiers, often French. According to the local leader of one of these groups, some *Licorne* soldiers [deployed French "Unicorn Force" peacekeepers], once their four-month commission is up, come knocking at their door. The state has entrusted the surveillance of several of its industrial sites to this company....Should the situation get worse, these companies, which operate on the borderline of legality, could cross the narrow line separating them from mercenary activity and hire their services out to the highest bidder.[46]

But one security development is particularly notable and concerns the presence of a strong Lebanese minority (estimated at from 50,000 to more than 100,000 people), part of the Lebanese diaspora that has seen Lebanese expatriates buying businesses and other properties from the French who departed amidst earlier violence. As public safety and larger security concerns have emerged in recent years, and when the aftermath of the 2004 civil war led to increased insecurity and crime, the Lebanese formed one of the most powerful private security establishments in Abidjan, so strong that it is characterized in some reporting as a militia. Remaining French settlers—the "old Whites" as they're called, who were targeted in most intense 2004 violence by President Laurent Gbago's rampaging "Young Patriots" thugs—have formed an alliance with the Lebanese. According to one of the several thousand remaining, uneasy French settlers, the Lebanese "are determined to stay here at any price" and "have the heavy materiel - grenades and rocket launchers" that promise an opportunity to do so and protect their substantial investments.[47]

45. Traore, A. (2005) 'Private Security Firms: The Dangers Facing Ivorians', *Le Jour Plus*, March 21, translated in AFP20050321000094.
46. 'M.B.', 'The Flourishing Security Business in Abidjan', *Le Figaro*, July 5, 2005.
47. Peyrard, M. (2005) 'Cote D'Ivoire: Fear Mounts', *Paris Match*, September 22, pp. 78-81, translated in EUP20050926029020.

Moreover, it was judged that members of the Lebanon-based terrorist group Hezbollah had been imported to buttress the Lebanese security establishment. This was reported to include some veterans of urban combat in Beirut. Given Hezbollah's establishment of cells in Europe, North and South America, Asia, and other parts of Africa, the reports are not implausible, and the US warned about the potential for Hezbollah trouble-making in Cote d'Ivoire.[48] More broadly, a parallel may seen in remote locations like the Brazil-Argentina-Paraguay Tri-Border area or Iquique, Chile, where Lebanese and other Arab expatriates (including a strong Hezbollah presence) run all kinds of businesses (at least some with private security). On Hezbollah's part, a variety of businesses and financial institutions there are used to launder money or raise revenues. This activity that highlights the analogous value-added of a port like Cote d'Ivoire's Abidjan (the source of much speculation along these lines).[49] This is one of the kinds of issue that suggests the association of private security and terrorism deserves some attention.[50]

Private Security and Terrorism

Private security firms have been held up as both a potential counter-terrorism asset and also as a potential way for terrorists to disguise and facilitate their agendas in some of the same ways that organized criminals have used these security firma as umbrellas. As regards the former possibilities, by the mid-1990s Russian specialists were quick to seek some way of harnessing private security to the interests of the state and make a little money at the same time, amidst the wreckage of the USSR and the burgeoning growth of commercial security companies. At a security conference in Moscow in 1997—where former KGB and MVD "counterterrorists-turned-private operators" were well represented—Russian Interpol chief Yevgeniy V. Malyshenko suggested a role for Russian firms in infrastructure protection based on foreign experience.[51] Such early efforts have been made more precise and introduced formally into Russian counterterrorism programs, apparently gaining some momentum in the wake of many spectacular Chechen attacks including the Beslan school massacre in September 2004. Particular interest was directed towards the protection of facilities and government and commercial infrastructure using

48. 'Cote d'Ivoire: Islamist Risk?', *Jeune Afrique-L'Intelligent*, December 25, 2001 - January 7, 2002, translated in AFP20020105000119.

49. Geslin, J.-D. (2002) 'Diamond Connection', *Jeune Afrique-L'Intelligent*, March 18, 2002, pp. 34-36, translated in AFP20020329000015.

50. See, for example, Geslin, 'Diamond Connection' and Chris Zambelis, 'Radical Islam in Latin America', *Terrorism Monitor*, The Jamestown Foundation, no. 23, December 2, 2005, among many treatments.

51. His translated remarks are found in his article Malyshenko, Y. V. (1997) 'Interaction of the Police and Private Security Services in Combating Terrorism: The Experience of Other Countries', Foreign Military Studies Office, Ft. Leavenworth, Kansas, March, available at: http://fmso.leavenworth.army.mil/.

private guard enterprises, but even most Moscow schools began to hire private security personnel, mostly unarmed, after the Beslan, North Ossetia terrorist attack in September 2004.[52]

Specifically, for example, the proposal has been advanced in 2006 to protect and secure the Russian pipeline system of some 1 million kilometers of energy pipelines (oil and gas) of various types. The vulnerability of the system is underscored by the fact that criminal elements illegally divert some 10 thousand metric tons of fuel a year, not to mention committing acts of terrorism against gas pipelines in the north Caucasus. Too, as the chief of the Center for Military Forecasting at the Academy of Military Sciences indicated "just as they did 30 years ago when there was a drop in pressure in one sector of a main pipeline, staffers of the Unified Gas Supply System—which has jurisdiction over 150,000 km of gas pipelines and 256 compressor stations—dispatched a breakdown team without knowing who and what will meet them at the scene of the incident." What he proposed was the creation of special Russian private military organizations—the ChVO's noted earlier—to protect the "operational-strategic" pipeline network in a commercial-Federal-partnership.[53]

This kind of proposal, aimed at infrastructure and other metropolitan and national security protection initiatives for key assets has been advanced by a number of academic and government professionals and specialists in the West as well, particularly in the wake of the 9/11 and other major terrorist attacks over the last half decade.[54] On-going programs abound, with new initiatives in progress and on the horizon. In the US, popular and more scholarly critiques of these concepts are advanced as well, usually focusing on the uneven or poor screening, training, and competence of some security firm personnel juxtaposed with the critical homeland security functions they are being asked to perform.[55] Relative risks, benefits and overall value-added will, in the West at least, be worked out in the public policy debates centered on appropriate private security roles (and for that matter the analogous critiques and discussions of government and public institutional performance).

52. ITAR-TASS, February 2, 2005; and Abdullaev, N. (2005) 'The Lost Lessons of Beslan', *ISN Security Watch*, September 1, available at: http://www.isn.ch/ (in news archive).
53. Tsyganok, A. (2006) 'Otdat' truboprovody pod okhranu chastnykh voyennykh organizatsiy' (Put Pipelines Under the Protection of Private Military Organizations), *Nezavisimoye Voyennoye Obozreniye*, January 9, available at: http://nvo.ng.ru/ (archives).
54. See, for example, Connolly, C. P. (2003) 'The Role of Private Security in Combating Terrorism', *Journal of Homeland Security*, July; Morabito, A. & Greenberg, S. (2005) *Engaging the Private Sector to Promote Homeland Security: Law Enforcement-Private Security Partnerships*, NCJ 210678, US Department of Justice, Bureau of Justice Assistance Washington, DC, 2005, available at: http://www.ncjrs.gov/pdffiles1/bja/210678.pdf; and the forthcoming (Spring 2007) chapter by Carafano, J. & Kochems, A. (nd) "Engaging Private Security Firms and Contractors in Counterterrorism Operations', in *Countering Terrorism in the 21st Century*, ed. James J.F. Forest, to be published by Praeger.
55. These include, for example, Meeks, B. N. (2005) 'Are 'rent-a-cops' threatening security?', *MSNBC*, March 9; and Hetherington, C. J. (2004) 'Private Security as an Essential Component of Homeland Security', Master's Thesis Naval Postgraduate School, Monterey, June.

But returning to the potential for the penetration of private security firms by terrorists—an approach endorsed and recommended by Abu Bakr Naji in his *Management of Savagery (jihadist)* strategy, and underscored by many criminally corrupted private security enterprises around the world— some recent illustrations may highlight this special danger, which is especially notable when expatriate populations are involved. For example, in 2005 and continuing into 2006, Spanish security personnel charged with investigating potential Islamic terrorism became interested in a "significant" number of "Chechen Islamists" who had settled in Spain, mainly Madrid and Barcelona. They were thought to be hiding, resting, or organizing in Spain after undertaking combat action in Russia and possibly Europe as well. While the reasons for their presence in Spain were not clear, it was postulated that it could be related to funding future terrorist actions. The famous Costa del Sol and a few other Spanish areas had for some time been major organized crime centers for money laundering and other crime associated with Georgians, Russians, and other ex-Soviet citizens. The mechanisms for illegal financial activities in the wealthy tourist areas were well established. The focus of police and intelligence inquiries was on a "security" dimension of their activity, since it was suspected that the new Chechen immigrants had taken employment in the private security field. Since the Chechens did not have the requisite residency papers, this kind of employment would be illegal but by no means unusual in the experience of much of the rest of the world.[56]

Chechen militants in Chechnya itself have been most successful in infiltrating or subverting private security organizations there, even those with official sanction and close association with the pro-Moscow Chechen Ministry of the Interior. Private security officers under the Chechen Interior Ministry have been arrested for directly aiding the armed resistance groups, including providing protection for leadership. Bribery of such personnel to secure their silence or cooperation has been extremely successful, whatever role clan and ideological imperatives may play. The frequency of this kind of unreliability has made Russian military and security forces loath to use their services, even as translators.[57]

The northeast Pakistan city of Lahore—the location of thousands of Afghan immigrants and storied location of Rudyard Kipling's Great Game spy novel Kim—is the center of an effort by the Pakistani law enforcement Special Branch to compile a database of Afghan who are employed or have businesses in the city. In addition to developing a means to identify Afghan refugees involved in a number of "robberies, kidnappings for ransom, killing for money and smuggling weapons and narcotics crimes", the police effort revealed some striking information about the city's private security companies surveyed. These companies were asked to provide details about their Afghan employees, with

56. 'Chechen and Colombian rebels said settling in Spain', *El Mundo*, February 28, 2006, translated in EUP20060301950017.
57. 'Two Chechen Police Officers Arrested for Aiding Separatists' (2004) *The Caucasus Times*, August 21, translated in CEP2004082200005.

the result that Special Branch offers were able to determine that half of them were former *jihadists* who had fought in Afghanistan, albeit under unspecified circumstances.

Aside from whatever technical violations of Pakistani law such employment might mean for Afghan refugees, police concerns were mainly centered on the potential for terrorist/extremist mischief they have in the more than 5-million person city. How well-founded such concerns might be is problematic—most of the 10,000 Afghan families remaining in Lahore have simply determined to rebuild their lives there and not return to the difficulties in Afghanistan. The discovery of so many former Afghan *jihadis* in potentially sensitive jobs will no doubt result in continued police attention. In any event, it underscores the magnet that private security represents for those who possess only skills of former police, soldiers, and guerrillas, whatever their intentions.[58]

The erupting violence in France by youths and others drawn largely from the marginalized Islamic population of France's bigger cities, has preoccupied French police, security and intelligence organizations increasingly over the last year. The violence—beginning in the fall of 2005 and relieved subsequently by simmering unrest and tension among business and the populace - increased the importance of private security resources to supplement French local and national law enforcement. Months before the worst of the riots broke out, however, the discovery by French authorities in early 2005 that many of the commercial business and entertainment facilities in the Paris area were being guarded by a firm whose personnel were recruited by a notorious *jihadist*, pointed to the grave vulnerability such firms could pose. Since then security and guard service companies have been the subject of particular attention and surveillance, with several suspected of being infiltrated by Islamic extremists.[59]

The firm that created this increased awareness was established in 2004 and overseen by an individual of Algerian extraction. The company was particularly active in sub-contracting roles for larger companies. While the senior Algerian manager seemed perfectly ordinary at first, the deputy manager and personnel recruiter of the firm was readily determined to have ties to the "Salafist Group for Preaching and Combat" (GSPC) which itself was associated with al-Qaeda. He had been active in the late 20th and early 21st century in conducting Islamic-oriented

58. Khan, S. (2006) 'Police cracks down on Afghan criminals; Intelligence agencies say illegal immigrants were involved in violent February 14 riots', *Daily Times*, February 23, available at: http://www.dailytimes.com.pk/. It is worth noting that the group Jamaat-ul-Fuqra, with headquarters in Lahore and cells located primarily in North America, is reputed to have organized at least two private security firms in Brooklyn, New York to guard their communities known as *jamaats*. These firms are supposedly able to compete for commercial or even government security contracts. (Apparently appearing first in Christian M. Weber, 'Examine Gunman's Possible Ties to al Furqa', *Soldiers for Truth*, [October 30, 2002] and echoed in other media.) Jamaat-ul-Fuqra was formerly designated a terrorist organization by the US State Department in the 1990s and continues to find its way into some terrorist listings.
59. 'J.C.', 'A Security Company Employed Convicted Islamists', *Le Monde*, February 27, 2006, translated in EUP20060227029002.

training around France, and at least two of the trainees had been killed fighting in Afghanistan. Recruits for the security company included individuals tied to support networks for the Algerian terrorist organization, Armed Islamic Group (GIA). Taxes were never paid and employees were never reported, generating additional revenues (500,000 euros or US $600,000) that were evidently used to support unspecified *jihadist* agendas. While many questions remained, the Algerian and his deputy were indicted. The Paris newspaper *Le Monde* summed up the import of the case well, noting that "the affair poses the problem of infiltration of the private security sector by criminals or terrorists who find it a source of hidden revenue, an opening for secret networks and a means of access to sensitive sites."

Conclusions

Private security is absolutely essential in many areas of the world where the capacity of public law enforcement and justice agencies—whether through lack of resources, expertise, or will—are unable to meet the basic and specialized needs of public safely and national security. In many areas of the world, private security may be inequitable in application, may not be available to everyone who needs it, may be flawed in execution, and may have an almost crippling financial impact on national and local economies required to bear the costs. But, in these areas, private security is sometimes the *only* functioning security and "protection businesses" provide at least pockets of security for infrastructure, business, and individuals that would otherwise be non-existent. In one of the several countries where the police anti-kidnapping squad may actually be carrying out the kidnappings themselves, a reliable bodyguard service is worth whatever can be afforded. In short, privatized security can mean the difference between a failed state and a faltering one and a means of buying time for the maintenance and strengthening of key institutions.

Where regulation and oversight are adequate—and where there is public policy consensus on appropriate roles, missions and limits—private security can be a valuable and reliable government partner for enhancing public safety and increasingly important too in the fight against international terrorism. However, private security firms have shown themselves to be notably vulnerable to criminal and terrorist penetration when these conditions are not present, and even sometimes when they are. The sheer-numbers of these firms in many countries—licensed and unlicensed—as well as the obscurity sometimes imposed by ethnic or clan silence and impenetrability, often means that even the most egregious kind of illegality remains invisible for thinly-resourced government oversight mechanisms. Concerns are not with petty theft and traditional kinds of crime, e.g., the Japanese security guard caught stealing cash and beer coupons from the Ministry of Finance building. Rather, it is on the major kinds of on-going abuses illustrated above, which have the potential for expanding and becoming so institutionalized that they are part of the fabric of a society. Among the potential and well-understood effects of criminal penetration of private security venues are:

- Undermining citizen confidence in state institutions and the very legitimacy of the state and leadership, where robbery, extortion, kidnapping, extrajudicial murder and other crimes are perpetrated with government impotence or complicity;
- Facilitating the traffic in arms, drugs, and other contraband under legal or perceived legal cover;
- Weakening further public security organizations through corruption, coercion, and undermining dedication and morale;
- Providing powerful disincentives to local and national economic development by internal and external investors due to security concerns;
- Imposing even greater economic costs as individuals and institutions seek to overcome ineffective public and private protection venues; and
- Discouraging alliances and international support in the face of enduring corruption and unreliability in portions of the security establishment.

While these kinds of problems may be addressed—and in some cases are being slowly addressed—with focused national and international programs aimed at strengthening government institutions and oversight, the vulnerability of private security businesses to terrorist penetration may prove just as challenging, even when strong regulation and oversight is present. The stated *jihadist* intent to infiltrate such institutions—and examples that provide models for how this might happen-underscore the need for law enforcement and intelligence attention to the recruiting, affiliations, and activities of private security companies charged with sensitive tasks. For American interests, requirements in the continental United States (CONUS) are clear enough, if certainly challenging. They are more complex for foreign security companies abroad, however, as even a cursory survey of how the non-government security picture has evolved over the last decade indicates. Beyond CONUS, US facilities, deployed forces, citizens, and commercial or other interests may be compromised by foreign security regimens in which corrupted private security businesses constitute a real vulnerability. That will make understanding the "private" dimension of the operational environment all the more critical for analysts, planners, and operators.

The Use of Beheadings by Fundamentalist Islam

Lisa J. Campbell

When you're wounded and left on Afghanistan's plains,
And the women come out to cut up what remains,
Jest roll to your rifle and blow out your brains
An' go to your Gawd like a soldier.

Lisa J. Campbell, Maj, CA-ANG, is an Intelligence Officer with the 146th Airlift Wing. She attended the Air Force Officer Intelligence School at Goodfellow AFB in Texas. At her current unit of assignment she evaluates military, political and non-state threats to aircraft, personnel, and operational air bases at home and abroad. She provides unit commanders with intelligence assessments and recommendations with regard to airlift missions, force protection and base defense. She has deployed recently in support of airlift missions for Operation Iraqi Freedom, Operation Enduring Freedom, and the Horn of Africa. She has a Bachelor of Science degree in Geology from Cornell College. She is a member of the Los Angeles Terrorism Early Warning Group, and has contributed to Counter-OPFOR Program, NLECTC-West publications supporting law enforcement on Man-Portable Air Defense Systems (MANPADS), the directed energy threat, and a database on suicide bombings. She wrote "Applying Order of Battle to Al Qaeda Operations" in Networks, Terrorism and Global Insurgency (Routledge, 2004).

Go, go, go like a soldier,
Go, go, go like a soldier,
Go, go, go like a soldier,
So-oldier of the Queen!
Rudyard Kipling

The present-day use of beheadings by Islamic Fundamentalists is a tactic that has been used for thousands of years on and off the battlefield, and by both state and non-state entities. Since 2002, Islamic Fundamentalist militants have purposefully carried out highly public beheadings.[1] Subsequently, there has been much discussion as to why the militants are using beheadings, how they justify them, and how they exploit the media to accentuate the effect of the beheadings worldwide. Why and how Islamic Fundamentalists, and even some non-Islamic cultures, are using beheadings today has historical precedent, asymmetric practical usage, and could possibly help explain some aspects of Fourth Generation warfare. Today's beheadings may also be an indicator that the world is in a current state of upheaval. Although Islamic Fundamentalists will argue that beheadings have religious justification, described in the Koran or by hadith,[2] most Muslims do not agree with this way of thinking. Furthermore, Islamic Fundamentalists are purposely inconsistent in their use of beheadings and, with the assistance of various media, publicize their use of this tactic at will and on any level, global or local.

During 2004 and early 2005—the beginning of the post-Saddam era—a surge of internet broadcast beheadings brought this tactic into public view and reminded the world of its horrific nature. While the number of publicized beheadings has had a great impact, the sheer number of unpublicized beheadings is of equal or possibly greater significance. In June 2006, two militants were arrested within days of each other in Iraq. One, Ahmad Hussein Dabbash al-Battawi, it was found, had single-handedly carried out hundreds of beheadings.[3] The other, Hamza Khairi al-Ani, according to an official statement in Baghdad, was guilty of the murder and beheading of dozens of citizens.[4] Although it would be impossible to retrieve and catalog the data on each of the beheadings carried out by these two militants, this type of information might shed light on the current use and even future use of beheadings. Recent Islamist beheadings have surfaced in Thailand, Indonesia,

1. Several works on this topic have been accomplished. See 1) Jones, R. H. (2005) *Terrorist Beheadings: Cultural and Strategic Implications*, Carlisle: Strategic Studies Institute, US Army War College, June; 2) Furnish, T. (2005) 'Beheading in the Name of Islam', *Middle East Quarterly*, Spring, vol. 7, no 2, pp. 3–4; 3) *Islam and Beheading*, available at: www.muhammadism.org, (accessed 3 April 2005).

2. A narrative record of the sayings or customs of Muhammad and his companions, or, the collective body of traditions relating to Muhammad and his companions; *Mirriam-Webster Dictionary*.

3. See David Frum's Diary, *National Review Online*, June 4, 2006, reviews news stories from *AP* and *Gulf Times*.

4. Ibid.

India, Pakistan and Somalia. The questions remain on whether the use of this tactic will further spread outside of these areas, on what scale, and by whom.

Beheadings: An Historical Perspective

From as early as biblical times, beheadings have been used during war or revolution, for punishment, forewarning, and by both state and non-state entities. Leaders of nations, military personnel, and monarchs were beheaded, as were commoners—no one was exempt. Even women were commonly beheaded. Beheadings were not always carried out on individuals or small numbers. In 1086, Yusuf Ibn Tashfin, leader of the Almoravid Empire, killed 24,000 Castillians in the battle of Zallaqa. Ibn Tashfin then ordered the beheading of each of the 24,000, had them thrown into piles shaped like minarets, and let the 'muezzins' stand and sing praises to Allah on them.[5]

State-run beheadings were typically a means of capital punishment. Through the late eighteenth century, decapitated heads were spiked and displayed as a means to deter criminals. With time, this practice faded. State-run beheadings were commonly carried out with a sword or an axe, which was cheap and practical but considered by many, including the Greeks and Romans, to be humane and even honorable.

Having nearly disappeared in the late eighteenth century, beheadings suddenly made a dramatic revival. In 1792, the French introduced the guillotine, a beheading machine. Although the guillotine was a progressively civilized tool of execution, in an unusual response, the British renewed their ancient tradition of beheading with the knife and axe.[6] European and Asian countries discontinued the use of beheadings around the turn of the twentieth century. Less crime, increased humanitarianism, and an overall heightened public sensitivity to the convention may have contributed to its decline. While beheadings have surged and faded, the tools of beheadings have not had such an understandable flow. For example, why did the British not adopt the guillotine when the French did? And why did they revert to more primitive tools?

The Death of Husayn Ibn Ali

Many famous people, across many cultures, have been beheaded throughout history. From Biblical times, the most famous beheading was that of John the Baptist. Prior to that there was Goliath's beheading at the hands of David. The most numerous famous beheadings were carried out in England, followed in number by the French (during the French revolution). Famous beheadings also included Celtic Saints, Chinese, and Colonial Americans. The most famous Muslim to have been beheaded was Husayn ibn Ali, the grandson of the Prophet

5. Furnish, (2005), p. 3.
6. Regina Janes, R. (2005) *Losing Our Heads: Beheadings in Literature and Culture*, New York University Press, New York, p. 43.

Muhammad, the founder of Islam. The death of Husayn was very significant. It not only marked the split between Sunni and Shia Muslims but Muhammad himself had foreseen Husayn's martyrdom in Karbala.

Husayn ibn Ali, was killed and beheaded in the Battle of Karbala in 680. The city of Karbala was near the city of Kufa, a former stronghold of Husayn's father. The residents of Kufa largely pledged full support to Husayn. Husayn had been on a pilgrimage from Mecca to Kufa to confront Yazid ibn Muawiya, the current caliph, named by his own father, the previous caliph. Husayn's pilgrimage was in part at the behest of his followers and in part based on his own principles. Many Muslims did not support Yazid's untraditional appointment as caliph and the fact that this appointment began an unprecedented dynasty, considered the first Arab dynasty. By definition, a caliph has both temporal and spiritual power. Yazid had only temporal power, of which he was well aware, and demanded allegiance from Husayn who the Muslims regarded as their spiritual leader. Husayn refused because he believed he needed to preserve the true values of Islam. Following Husayn's refusal, Yazid had his army block Husayn, from entering Kufa, where Husayn was popular. Husayn and a very small contingent of men met their fate in Karbala and were all beheaded. Seventy-two heads at the tips of spears were taken to Kufa and then on to Damascus to where they were presented to Yazid.

Beheadings During Times of Mahdi Uprisings

Beheadings tend to surge in times of upheaval or unrest. During the French Revolution and the Guatemalan Civil War, for example, beheadings played a major role. Similar surges in beheadings occurred during Mahdi uprisings, which resulted when a leader emerged, claiming to be the Mahdi. According to Islamic tradition, the Mahdi, or *Guided One*, will emerge before the Day of Resurrection to usher in a worldwide, perfect Islamic state. Only every few generations does a leader claim to be the Mahdi. The aggression of such a claim causes a division in the Muslim world between the new Mahdists and their opponents. Each labels the other as an unbeliever, which enables them to behead one another, and call up Koranic verse 47:3 in their defense.[7] The beheadings were either an intimidation, or a show of victory, or both. In any event, Mahdist movements bring extreme controversy and militant reaction that incorporates beheadings. In 1885, during a Mahdi uprising in Sudan, even a British general, Charles Gordon, was beheaded.

The last Mahdist movement occurred in 1979 and culminated in an attempt to overthrow the government of Saudi Arabia. The uprising was led by Juhayman al-Utaybi in the name of his brother-in-law Muhammad bin Abdallah al-Qahtani whom he proclaimed as the Mahdi. The movement called for severing ties with the West, overthrowing the "illegitimate" Saudi regime and redistributing its wealth,

7. Furnish (2005), p. 4.

and expelling all foreigners from the Arabian Peninsula. Al-Utaybi and several hundred men stormed the Great Mosque in Mecca, momentarily seizing it until the Saudis retook it. The surviving attackers were all executed, many beheaded.

The Anglo-Afghan Wars

In the 1800s, the British conquered Afghanistan three times but never held it—even though they successively improved their equipment and increased their numbers. During the occupations, the British tended to underestimate the status of their welcome. In the first Anglo-Afghan war, a British deputy, Alexander Burnes, chose to live in the city of Kabul, instead of within the relative safety of the cantonment. The Afghans, who from the hills had been watching the every move of the British, found the separated deputy to be an easy target. A mob gathered at Burnes' residence and he was hacked to pieces. Sir William McNaughten, the Senior Envoy, met a similar fate when he rode to a suspicious pre-arranged meeting. His headless, limbless corpse was hung from a pole in the bazaar. This type of killing is typical for the constantly-warring Afghans. As a result, the British were often caught off guard by the Afghans, which resulted in the loss of an enormous number of troops and civilians who accompanied them. During the British retreat in the first Anglo-Afghan war, there was only one survivor out of the 17,000 who fled. In 1878, during the second Anglo-Afghan war, the Afghans again trapped the British and forced them to leave Kabul by calling for a Jihad, which rallied 100,000. In 1919, the third Anglo-Afghan war began as a Jihad when Afghanistan attacked the British across the Indian border, taking advantage of a period of unrest there.[8]

Death of a Princess

A very prominent Saudi Arabian state-sanctioned beheading was aired in a 1980 PBS documentary, *Death of a Princess*. The film was a collection of interviews conducted by journalist Antony Thomas about the public execution of a Saudi Arabian Princess and the man with whom she had committed adultery. The princess was shot, whereas her lover was beheaded. Documenting this execution caused a great deal of controversy. At the time of its release, Ted Koppel remarked that *Death of a Princess* was perhaps the most controversial film in the history of public television, one that stirred up an international hornet's nest. Much of the controversy was that the Saudis felt the film was an attack on Islam. Furthermore, Mr. Thomas' quest to get the full truth of the story was controversial in itself. During his quest, Thomas encountered a witness whose description of the Princess's lover's beheading did not conform to how state-run beheadings were typically described. What also surfaced in the documentary was

8. 'The Young British Soldier', Analysis section, www.cs.rice.edu/ ~ ssiyer/minstrels/poems/1146.html.

that the executions may not have been conducted by a government ordained executioner, but instead by one of the guards of the Saudi Royal Family. Perhaps the reason the princess and her lover were executed in such a way, and very soon after they were caught, was to make them an example to the public. The executions came at a time when women were traveling outside of Saudi Arabia more frequently and getting ideas from western societies. By executing one of their own nobility, the Saudi Royal Family's intent may have been to keep their society from getting out of Islamic control.[9]

The Samurai Warrior and Japanese Beheadings

Beheadings were a large part of the samurai warrior's way of life. Battles and seppukus (ritual suicide) of the samurai almost always ended in a beheading. It was understood that samurai battles always ended in a beheading to preserve honor. Death had to be beautiful and honorable. Samurai beheaded for two reasons: 1) to proclaim victory over the other and 2) to complete a suicide (if a samurai's self-inflicted death became prolonged, a fellow samurai would behead him). The samurai considered their opponents equal combatants and legitimate by the laws of warfare. Long after the days of the samurai ended due to modern weaponry and western domination, their legacy reemerged with the Japanese soldier. In 1931, when Japan invaded Manchuria and China, along with their guns, Japanese officers carried swords like the samurai. But they did not use the swords like the samurai. Instead, they dishonorably slaughtered and beheaded civilians and prisoners of war. Furthermore, when the Japanese began to lose WWII, they turned to suicide. Unlike the suicide of a samurai warrior, Japanese suicides in WWII were offensive. In 1943, suicide actually became a form of combat for the Japanese. Their signature form of suicidal combat was crashing planes into US warships, a highly unconventional tactic for the time.

Nazi Germany Use of Beheadings

During his reign, Hitler extensively beheaded by guillotine. Execution by beheading was German law for all condemned criminals but the practice dramatically increased under the Nazi regime, particularly between 1938 and 1945. Hitler not only had criminals executed but also those who opposed his regime. These executions were brought on through state run trials and typically carried out by hanging or guillotine. Hitler also increased the number of crimes punishable by death, lowered the criminal age limit, and had 20 guillotines built and dispersed to prisons throughout Germany and Austria. While Nazi beheadings were conducted largely within prisons, hangings were used more publicly to terrorize the local populace and entertain troops.

9. *Death of a Princess*, Frontline, PBS Video, 1983–2005, WGBH Educational Foundation.

Contemporary Beheadings

Today's beheadings reflect historical beheadings on many levels. Current beheadings are primarily carried out on foot soldiers, civilian contractors (innocents), police, and rival criminals, to name only a few.

High-Profile Targets

Although a marked escalation, beheading a state leader would not be unprecedented. In June 2006, seventeen terror suspects were arrested in Toronto. At least one of the seventeen was plotting to storm the Canadian parliament and behead officials, including the Prime Minister. Beheading the Canadian prime minister would have been the first famous person beheaded in post-modern times. While the plan did not materialize, the terrorist's intent could be an indicator of future plots against similar high profile targets.

Sunni v Shia

The split between Sunni and Shia Muslims, which has its roots in the beheading of Husayn ibn Ali, remains contentious today and is a source for current sectarian beheadings in Iraq. Today's beheadings by Islamic militants mimic the battlefield beheadings of early Islam. Tales of past Islamic battles, some of which have become hadith, inspire the militants and perpetuate and justify their actions. Furthermore, the large number beheaded on past battlefields, such as the seventy-two men of Husayn, could also be a model for the militants' current desire to behead as many of their enemies as possible, including all infidels.

A New Mahdi?

Some will argue that we are currently in the midst of another Mahdist movement. And Shia and Sunni Muslims alike accept the idea of the coming of a Mahdi. The potential claimant: Usama bin Ladin. Bin Ladin has not claimed to be the Mahdi but his physical attributes as well as his philosophy closely match those described for the Mahdi. Bin Ladin's words also echo the rhetoric used by Islamic militants in the 1979 Mahdist uprising.[10] Furthermore, enough myth surrounds the Mahdi for any dissimilarities to bin Ladin be overlooked by many Muslims. To claim bin Ladin as the Mahdi would likely not be beneficial to the Arab world, however, causing Muslim opposition and more division than unity.

10. Furnish, T. R. (2002) 'Bin Ladin: The Man Who Would Be Mahdi', *Middle East Quarterly*, Spring, p. 3.

A Fourth Anglo-Afghan War?

Bin Ladin, whose residence in Afghanistan is the cause of US and coalition presence there today, is the cause of what may be the fourth Anglo-Afghan war. What is different is that the Anglo forces are using modern warfare, while warfare in Afghanistan has hardly changed. Like past Anglo-Afghan wars, beheadings along with other forms of killing are once again taking place in Afghanistan as well as in unresolved border regions of its neighboring Pakistan. The beheadings are largely conducted by the Taliban, which is comprised of a mixture of foreign and indigenous fighters. Pro-Taliban militants, who also may be either indigenous or foreign, assist them. Thus far the victims have not been the British. They are mostly non-Anglo foreign workers such as cab drivers and Afghans, including police, soldiers and civilians. Many victims are accused of collaborating or "spying" for the US forces (see Table 1). To date, it is unproven whether any US or coalition casualty in Afghanistan has been beheaded.

Beheadings in the Afghan-Pakistan region are actually taking place on three fronts: 1) in the war against the occupiers, 2) in the Taliban's localized fight against criminals, and 3) against Afghan civilians who break the imposed Sharia laws in small Taliban-dominated towns.

As their timing would suggest, the beheadings in Afghanistan are sometimes considered to be spillover from Iraq. But the spillover is not so much a copycat scheme as one that is due to foreign fighters making their way from Iraq to assist Afghanistan.

Japanese History and Today's Islamist Beheadings: A Comparison

The circumstances that led to the use of suicide bombings and beheadings by the Japanese in WWII and by Islamists today are very similar. In both cases, they were overwhelmed by a superior, more modern enemy and became desperate. Like the Japanese WWII soldiers, Islamic militants are successfully using suicide bombings to combat a far superior enemy, (e.g. Hamas vs. Israel and 9/11). The use of beheadings is having similar success. The Japanese and Islamists also mimic their legacies—the Japanese their samurai legacy, the Muslims their legacy of Muhammad—in a parallel but adulterated manner. As their Muslim predecessors, Islamic militants are slaughtering (beheading) the civilians and soldiers they capture. And Islamic militants who behead innocents with an unorthodox sawing action are like the sword wielding WWII Japanese soldiers who beheaded civilians in a similar manner.

The Exporting of Beheadings

The Saudi-taught radical Wahhabism is blamed as the cause of much of the Islamic terrorism in the world today. Saudis and other foreign fighters are largely to blame for bringing terrorism and beheadings into Iraq. Although beheadings in Iraq are not state-run, they are in part an exported version of Saudi state-run judicial

Table 1 Non-state Islamic beheadings since 2002[a]

Date	Event	Group	Location	Remarks
Feb 22, 2002	Daniel Pearl	The National Movement for the Restoration of Pakistani Sovereignty	Pakistan	Four suspects captured later, reason stated, *to strike a blow at the US and embarrass the Pakistani government* (Videotaped)
Aug, 2002	Two Jehovah's Witnesses	Possibly Abu Sayyaf	S. Philippines	Heads found in bags, attached notes calling for jihad, and stating, *this is what will happen to those who do not believe in Allah.*
May 2004	Nick Berg	Al Qaeda in Iraq	Iraq	Possibly carried out by Zarqawi. (Videotaped)
Jun 2004	Paul Johnson	Al Qaeda linked group	Saudi Arabia	Called *The Fallujah Brigade* (Videotaped)
Jun 13, 2004	Robert Jacob	Unknown	Iraq	Shot prior to beheading (Videotaped)
Jun 21, 2004	Afghan soldier and his interpreter	Taliban	Afghanistan	Captured, beheaded after becoming separated from their patrol
Jun 22, 2004	Kim Sun-il	Jama'at al-Tawhid wa'l Jihad	Iraq	South Korea refused to meet terrorist's demands. (Videotaped)
Jun 22, 2004	Four Taliban fighters	Afghan soldiers	Afghanistan	Retaliatory beheadings for Jun 21, 2004 beheadings
Jun 27, 2004	Former deputy village chief	Local insurgents	Thailand	Just prior to Prime Minister Thaksin visit

(*continued*)

Table 1 - *Continued*

Date	Event	Group	Location	Remarks
Jul 26, 2004	55 year old man and his two children	Separatist rebels	Indian Kashmir	Suspected of being informers for security forces. Nine militants entered his house.
Jul 29, 2004	Bulgarian hostage head found	Unknown	Iraq	
Aug 2004	Nepalese workers	Ansar al Sunna Army	Iraq	One of twelve kidnapped was beheaded. (Videotaped)
Aug 8, 2004	Mohammad Mutawalli	Unknown	Unknown	(Videotaped)
Aug 9, 2004	Bulgarian hostage Georgi Lasov	Unknown	Iraq	Body found in Tigris River (Videotaped)
Aug 11, 2004	CIA Agent	Unknown	Iraq	(Videotaped)
Aug 31, 2004	Khaled Abdul Messih	Unknown		(Videotaped)
Sep 13, 2004	Turkish truck driver-Durmus Kumdereli	Tawhid and Jihad[b]	Iraq	(Videotaped)
Sep 15, 2004	Three bodies found	Unknown	Iraq	The beheaded bodies were all male, with tattoos and no documents
Sep 20, 2004	Eugene Armstrong	Tawhid and Jihad	Iraq	HostingAnime website that showed video defended "free speech" (Videotaped)
Sep 20, 2004	Three Kurds	Ansar al Sunna Army	Iraq	Beheaded for cooperating with American forces (Videotaped)
Sep 21, 2004	Jack Hensley	Tawhid and Jihad	Iraq	(Videotaped)
Oct, 2004	Three Iraqi National Guardsmen	Brigades of Abu Bakr al-Sidq	Iraq	Al Jazeera reportedly declined the part of the tape that showed the beheadings
Oct 2, 2004	Iraqi National	Ansar al Sunna Army	Iraq	

Oct 7, 2004	Kenneth Bigley	Tawhid and Jihad	Iraq	Kept for two weeks, ransom demanded (Videotaped)
Oct 11, 2004	Luqman Mohammad Kurdi Hussein	Ansar al Sunna Army	Iraq	Translator working for Titan Corp.
Oct 11, 2004	Maher Kemal	Ansar al Sunna Army	Iraq	Turkish contractor working at the al Bakr Air Base
Oct 12, 2004	Ala al-Maliki	Ansar al Sunna Army	Iraq	Described as member of Moqtada al-Sadr's movement (Videotaped)
Oct 13, 2004	Two Iraqi intelligence agents	Brigades of Abu Bakr al-Sidiq	Iraq	(Videotaped)
Oct 14, 2004	Turkish truck driver	Tawhid and Jihad	Iraq	(Videotaped)
Oct 17, 2004	Eleven Iraqi National Guardsmen	Abu Mussab al-Zarqawi Group	Iraq	
Oct 22, 2004	Seif Adnan Kanaan	Ansar al Sunna Army	Iraq	Reason given-he was employed by the US Army (Videotaped)
Oct 23, 2004	Iraqi	Unknown militant group	Iraq	Accused of collaborating with US forces, claimed pictures posted on internet
Oct 30, 2004	Shosei Koda	Unknown group linked to Zarqawi	Iraq	Japanese citizen who entered Iraq on his own. Apparently tortured. (Videotaped)
Nov 2004	Buddhist village leader	Muslims	Thailand	Avenge killing for Muslim rioters killed by government forces
Nov 2004	Major Hussein Shanoun	Ansar al Sunna Army	Iraq	Iraqi officer, "apostate" (Videotaped)
Nov 3, 2004	Three unidentified bodies found	Unknown	Iraq	Dozens of hostages were missing at the time, bodies not identified

(*continued*)

Table 1 - *Continued*

Date	Event	Group	Location	Remarks
Nov 3 2004	Three Iraqi National Guardsmen	Brigades of the Iraqi Honorables	Iraq	Previously unknown group; produced a video, part of which al Jazeera aired (omitted the beheading)
Nov 9, 2004	Buddhist plantation worker	Muslims	Thailand	
Nov 18, 2004	Iraqi contractor	"Jihadists"	Iraq	
Nov 20, 2004	Twelve Decapitated bodies found	Unknown	Iraq	Bodies found strewn about the city of Mosul
Dec 2, 2004	Christian man	Islamic militants	Iraq	Mosul
Dec 8, 2004	Iraqi soldier	Islamic militants	Iraq	
Dec 17, 2004	Westerner	Unknown	Iraq	Gunmen killed three foreigners and their driver, beheading one who tried to escape
Jan 3, 2005	Iraqi citizen	Ansar al Sunna Army	Iraq	Headless body subsequently booby-trapped with a bomb that kills a police officer
Jan 21, 2005	Iraqi worker	Islamic militants	Iraq	One of two
Jan 21, 2005	Iraqi worker	Islamic militants	Iraq	2nd of two missing
Jan 22, 2005	Two truck drivers	Islamic militants	Iraq	Kidnapped, beheaded on a public street while executioners chant "Allahu Akbar"
Mar 8, 2005	Christian pastor	Islamic militants	Bangladesh	Returning home from work
Mar 9, 2005	Bodies found	"Jihadists"	Iraq	41 bodies total, many beheaded, including several women and young children

Apr 4, 2005	Iraqi National Guardsman	Al Qaeda in Iraq	Iraq	
Apr 9, 2005	Russian soldier	Chechen rebel	Chechnya	
May 14, 2005	Three Bodies found	Unknown	Iraq	Three beheaded corpses found with evidence of torture
May 15, 2005	Bodies found	"Jihadists"	Iraq	34 bodies found dumped in three locations; some in handcuffs, many tortured and beheaded
Jun, 2005	Elderly Buddhist man, Kamol Chunetr	Muslim Insurgents	Thailand	Retired teacher, age 65, head found in a bag two km from his home
Jun, 2005	Buddhist man, Lek Pongpla	Muslim Insurgents	Thailand	Shot in the back while at a tea shop. Head placed in a fertilizer bag, found later, a mile away
Jun 2, 2005	Four civilians	Mujahideen	India	Abducted members of two families
Jun 6, 2005	Plantation worker	Muslim Insurgents	Thailand	Head left roadside with a note
Jun 7, 2005	Civilian	Mujahideen	India	Abducted from his home
Jun 9, 2005	Iraqi Shiites	Unknown	Iraq	Bodies of 17 found bound and executed, some beheaded
Jun 24, 2005	Two Lao migrant workers	Muslim Insurgents	Thailand	Young couple
Jul, 2005	Surin Somjit	Islamic militants	Thailand	Muslim dominated tip of Buddhist Thailand. No one claimed responsibility
Jul 4, 2005	Civilian	Sunni Insurgents	Iraq	Also tortured
Jul 5, 2005	Sergeant Samphan Onyala	Islamists	Thailand	Abducted, member of security forces
Jul 7, 2005	Ten Afghan soldiers	Taliban	Afghanistan	Another 15 able to escape

(*continued*)

Table 1 - *Continued*

Date	Event	Group	Location	Remarks
Jul 9, 2005	Six police	Taliban	Afghanistan	Bodies and heads found dumped
Jul 18, 2005	Farmer	Islamic Insurgents	Thailand	
Aug, 2005	Bodies dumped	Unknown	Iraq	Witnesses saw at least 11 bodies dumped from pickup truck, some blindfolded & shot, others beheaded
Aug 2, 2005	Three Afghans	Taliban	Afghanistan	Accused of spying. Abdul Latif told Reuters: *the punishment is permissible in Islam and today's beheadings should be a lesson for others who are involved in espionage activities for the Americans*
Aug 15, 2005	Christian woman	"Holy warriors"	Iraq	
Aug 29, 2005	Civilian	Likely Islamic Insurgents	Iraq	
Aug 31, 2005	Cleric	Taliban	Afghanistan	For participating in an election
Sep 5, 2005	Elderly woman	Mujahideen	India	
Sep 12, 2005	Two males	Ansar al Sunna Army	Iraq	(Videotaped)
Sep 17, 2005	Civilian	Mujahideen	India	
Oct, 2005	Three Christian schoolgirls	Muslim	Indonesia	Anti-Christian society, recent turnover of population and politics to Muslims
Oct, 2005	Five soldiers and one civilian	Islamic Insurgents	Thailand	
Oct 5, 2005	Two males	Ansar al Sunna Army	Iraq	(Videotaped)
Oct 5, 2005	Civilian	Islamic Insurgents	Thailand	

Oct 14, 2005	Buddhist cattle farmer	Islamic Insurgents	Thailand	Age 68
Oct 22, 2005	Badr Brigades member	Al Qaeda in Iraq	Iraq	(Videotaped)
Nov 2, 2005	Five police	Taliban	Afghanistan	Surprise attack on drug-fighting police unit, five captured/beheaded
Nov 6, 2005	Five beheaded bodies found	Unknown	Iraq	Five of eleven bodies found were beheaded.
Mar, 2006	30 beheaded bodies found	Islamic militants	Iraq	Village north of Baghdad
Mar 6, 2006	Two former Afghan government officials	Taliban	Afghanistan	One was pro-govt militia commander. Per Taliban: *We beheaded them because they had committed heinous atrocities*
Mar 11, 2006	Two police	Probable Taliban	Afghanistan	
Apr, 2006	Headless body found	Islamic militants	Pakistan	Waziristan area. Note attached saying the victim was an American spy, warning to others
Apr 17, 2006	Two Pakistani civilians	Islamic militants	Pakistan	Collaborators w/US
Apr 25, 2006	Cab driver	Pro-Taliban militants	Pakistan	Accused of being US informants
Apr 30, 2006	Indian engineer	Taliban	Afghanistan	Ransom demand, tried to escape
May 11, 2006	Man	Pro-Taliban militants	Pakistan	Tribal area near Afghanistan

(*continued*)

Table 1 - *Continued*

Date	Event	Group	Location	Remarks
May 14, 2006	Administration official	Baluchistan Liberation Army (BLA)-claimed	Pakistan	Note left w/body
May 16, 2006	Two Civilians	Taliban	Afghanistan	
May 17, 2006	Somali fighters	Islamist gunmen	Somalia	Overran US-backed warlord alliance outside Mogadishu, beheading several
May 28, 2006	Three Civilians	Islamic militants	Iraq	
May 28, 2006	Three policemen	Taliban	Afghanistan	Fierce battles had occurred in area
Jun 4, 2006	Eight heads found	Unknown	Iraq	Heads found stuffed into fruit boxes
Jun 6, 2006	Nine heads found	Unknown	Iraq	Wrapped in black plastic bags and shoved into fruit boxes. Some of the heads were blindfolded.
Jun 10, 2006	Three alleged Shiite death squad members	Ansar al Sunna Army	Iraq	Posted video three days after Zarqawi's death (Videotaped)
Jun 13, 2006	Afghan national	Taliban	Pakistan	Letter attached: *Anyone spying for the American and Afghan forces will meet the same fate*
Jun 20, 2006	One of two US soldiers	Al Qaeda in Iraq	Iraq	Stated that successor to Zarqawi slaughtered them. (Videotaped)

Jun 22, 2006	Four Afghans	Taliban	Afghanistan	Accused of being spies for the US and the Afghanistan govt
Jun 25, 2006	Two Russian Embassy workers	Al Qaeda in Iraq	Iraq	Statement on video: *God's verdict...revenge for torture, killing and expulsion of brothers and sisters.*

[a]From un-posted database: Beheadings in the Post-Modern Era, derived from Open Sources.
[b]One of Zarqawi's groups.

executions with different settings and methods. Sectarian violence and beheadings in Iraq exist concurrently with beheadings of foreign fighters, none of which are openly supported by any state.

Today's Use of State Beheadings

State-run beheadings are used to punish criminals and date far back into history. Today only a handful of nation-states authorize beheadings as capital punishment—Saudi Arabia, Iran, Yemen and Qatar. Saudi Arabia is the only country to actively practice public beheadings. Iran only beheads on rare occasions, and Yemen and Qatar are currently not conducting them. In March 2006, leading clerics in Afghanistan proposed beheading a man for his conversion to Christianity, leading to the question of whether the newly formed Afghan government would adopt beheadings as an official means of capital punishment. Each year the Saudi government beheads men and women for murder, rape, sodomy and drug offenses. In 2003, the Saudi government beheaded 53 people, one of whom was female; in 2004, thirty-three men and one woman were beheaded. In Iran, one man was beheaded in 2003, the first in many years. The Saudi Arabian government condemns militants who decapitate hostages or innocents. They believe that their state-run beheadings, however, are sanctioned by Islamic tradition.

A Saudi State-Run Beheading

Convicted offenders are given tranquilizers and taken by a police van to a public square after midday prayers, typically on Friday. A large audience gathers to observe the beheading(s). With hands tied behind their back and feet shackled, prisoners are led by a police officer to the center of a large blue plastic sheet, where they are made to bow to the executioner and kneel, facing Mecca. The convicted offenders are usually dressed in their own clothes, barefoot, and blindfolded. The purpose of the blindfold is so that the prisoner will not move when the sword is swung. The prisoners' names and crimes they have committed are read aloud by an Interior Ministry official. Beheadings are conducted using a huge, very sharp sword, so usually the head is severed completely on the first blow. A policeman hands the sword to the executioner, who raises it up, swings it two or three times, and then strikes the prisoner. Cries of *Allahu Akbar!* (Arabic for *God is Great!*) are heard from onlookers while the executioner beheads the prisoner. The prisoner's severed head is later brought to a doctor, who sews it back on the body, and the prisoner is buried in an unmarked grave in the prison cemetery.[11] On a related note, it is said that Saudi executioners proudly hand down their craft from generation to generation.

11. *Associated Press* (2004) Riyadh, Saudi Arabia, Sunday Jun 27. Available at: http://www.taipeitimes.com/News/world/archives/2004/06/27/2003176725.

Variations on State Beheadings

Some nation states carry out beheadings, among other atrocities, on their own people, such as rebel ethnic groups. In 1982, the Guatemalan government led a campaign against indigenous guerillas and conducted mass atrocities, including beheadings. Burma is another such country where today it is reported that government troops perform beheadings on rebels. The use of amphetamines has been suggested to play a role in this gruesome behavior.[12] Irregular state-run beheadings are carried out in other nation states that are usually poorly governed and autocratic. The use of beheadings by governments seems extreme but, like the 1982 Guatemalan state terror campaign, can aid in significantly reducing crime. Because such government atrocities often take place in rural areas, it has been difficult to prove whether 1) these beheadings have actually taken place, and 2) who has conducted them, insurgents or the government. For these reasons, human rights groups have also been unable to respond as they would like.

Saddam Hussein's regime was characterized by torture as a means of control, one form of which was beheadings. Beheadings under Saddam's rule were state-run but not part of a formal judicial process. Such deviation from traditional state-run beheading among other aberrations from the conduct of lawful nation states put Saddam Hussein's Iraq in the category of a criminal-state. After losing the Gulf War in the early 1990s, in an attempt to consolidate power Saddam Hussein reverted to both tribal and "Islamic" traditions that were even more criminal than his prior style of rule. As a means to prevent and intimidate defecting or dissident males, Saddam instituted very public beheadings of their wives. Saddam took this intimidation a step further by decreeing prostitution a crime punishable by death and accused many women of being prostitutes. The criminal allegations against these women, however, were frequently baseless and uninvestigated. Hundreds of alleged prostitutes were beheaded by the Saddam Fedayeen,[13] and many beheadings were personally conducted by Saddam's son Uday. The beheadings often took place in front of the women's family and neighbours, including their children. Saddam required that the head be displayed for several days, often posted on a fence outside the family's home. These beheadings continued into the new millennium; between June 2000 and April 2001, at least 130 Iraqi women were beheaded.

The men were beheaded in front of their families like the women, but were also privately beheaded in prisons such as Abu Ghraib. Beheadings and other torture under Saddam in the prisons were characterized by Koranic verses and chants and an unnatural furor and ecstasy. A four minute video of torture at the Abu Ghraib prison includes ancestral-style sword raising and recitations of the Koran.[14] The

12. New evidence backs claims of genocide in Burma - *BBC & London Telegraph*, Mar 06, 2006.

13. *Fedayeen Saddam* was the paramilitary organization led by Uday Hussein, Saddam's eldest son. *Fedayeen* means "those willing to die for Saddam." See Schulz, N. (2004) *Abu Ghraib on National Review Online*, June 17, and the Office of International Women's Issues, *Fact Sheet*, Washington, D.C., March 20, 2003.

14. For a complete description of the Saddam-era torture video, see Schultz, N. (2004) 'Abu Ghraib', *National Review Online*, June 17.

video is replete with all types of torture and culminates in a ritual beheading. The prisoner's arms are tied behind his back and he is shoved to the ground. A black-clad Fedayeen loosens the prisoner's shirt while another stands holding a long silver blade by its curved handle. The executor raises his arms and strikes, slicing the head from the body. He then picks up the head and ceremoniously places it on the victim's back as the camera pans in closer and closer to the face. This video provides evidence that remnants of Saddam's criminal-state may be involved in or influencing beheadings in Iraq today. Furthermore, beheadings in the recent videos in Iraq (2004–present) are strikingly similar to the description of the beheading in the Abu Ghraib video.

Today's Non-State (Criminal) Use of Beheadings

Non-state beheadings are an asset to asymmetric warfare; they are low-tech but a highly effective means of waging war against far superior enemies. As with suicide bombings, the graphic effect of non-state beheadings by terrorist groups is counter to what the civilized West can tolerate. Non-state beheadings complement such tactics as kidnappings but are also used as an alternative to suicide bombings, shootings, rocket propelled grenade (RPG) and improvised explosive device (IED) attacks, all of which are rampant in Iraq and Afghanistan.

In contrast to state-run beheadings controlled from a formal judicial process, non-state Islamic beheadings are unsanctioned by any government. Instead of being ritual executions, non-state beheadings are ritual murders that arise from an insurgency or jihad. Non-state Islamic beheadings are similar to state-sanctioned beheadings in the fact that both are steeped in Islamic tradition. Additionally, like nation-states, Islamic militant groups view their captives as criminals who deserve and require punishment. Since non-state beheadings are technically occurring on a battlefield, captives should be viewed and treated as combatants. But Islamic militants do not consider their enemies combatants, nor even close to equal opponents, as in samurai battles. Instead they are considered infidels, almost subhuman. The beheading victims can be soldiers, law enforcement, and civilians (e.g., foreign workers or local citizens). In most nations, civilians and police officers cannot legally be targeted in warfare. But the Islamic militants consider all of their enemies to be legitimate targets and that beheading them is in accordance with Allah's will. As part of a jihad, beheadings are doctrinal. Western legal, moral, religious, and political voices are largely ineffective against the actions of Islamic militants, because the militants operate under a completely different set of rules, and ignore most international laws.

While non-state beheadings are doctrinal, they are also steeped in a hatred which is as much a practice as it is an emotion. Hatred of the West is propagated by Islamic militants as well as in schools or *madrassas* in Islamic states. Recent videos of beheadings depict victims being slaughtered much like animals. Certain passages in the Koran discuss apes and swine, referring to people who had incurred Allah's wrath and were transformed into these animals.[15] Some Islamic militants view the Jews and Christians as apes and swine, respectively, due to the literalist translation of the Koran that is reportedly being taught in the madrassas of Fundamentalist Islam. It is this literal translation coupled with a fervency that could explain why militants behead in such a crude manner. Furthermore, if the militants considered their captives as equal combatants, they might kill them more skillfully, or allow them a more humane or honorable death.

Beheading Videos

Videos of beheadings among other Islamist successes are produced, distributed, and sold on DVDs in marketplaces worldwide, as well as broadcast on the internet. Each beheading video is different. Some are crudely made while others are more professional. The beheadings on the videos often appear difficult to perform. Furthermore, from the videos, there appears to be no standardized procedure for conducting a beheading ritual (and there is no Islamist handbook on how to perform a beheading). No standard sized knives are used; they range from pocket-knives to machetes. Knives are presumably used in lieu of swords, their ancient counterpart. Hamza al-Ani, a key militant beheader captured in Iraq, reportedly used a saw.[16] In the videos, a variety of unorthodox techniques are used to sever the head, many of which are messy. Many videos appear to have been edited to avoid showing a messy beheading in its entirety. The splicing or editing may also have been done to make the beheading look more professional and the killers less incompetent. In each video, the cutting approach is random, beginning from the front or the side of the neck; cutting the spinal cord is usually left until last. The cutting motion varies from slicing to hacking, from slow to rapid. In a few videos the victim is already deceased prior to the actual beheading, but most often the victim is alive. As during Saudi state-run executions, the cry of *Allahu Akbar* is heard in most of the beheading videos conducted by the Islamic militants. In the videos the cries are made by the participating militants, while during Saudi executions the cries emanate from a large crowd of spectators. In many of the videos, *Allahu Akbar* is repeatedly called prior to, during, and after the beheading. *Allahu Akbar* is similarly exclaimed in videos made by Chechen militants of their operations against the Russians.

While each video is different, they contain many commonalities, such as logos on banners and similarly performed rituals that occur before and after the beheading. The logo of the video producer is often seen in a corner of the screen. Videos are typically set indoors; three or more militants usually stand behind one or more captives. The militants completely cover their heads except for their eyes, wear military vests over their traditional clothing, and carry at least one weapon. Often a militant will read in Arabic what sounds like a sentencing. In a

15. *Koran* 2: 62–65, and 5: 59–60.
16. David Frum's Diary, *National Review Online*, June 4, 2006. Frum reviews news stories from *AP* and *Gulf Times*.

few of the videos, the reader, who is often the same as the beheader, was said to have been Zarqawi. It is unknown what rank or status is required to become the beheader. Zarqawi, was considered the leader of al Qaeda in Iraq, among other titles; and to militants, he was a Mujahed sheik. The victims initially are not blindfolded and are usually seated. In some videos, they speak or read. Following the speeches or readings, a militant dramatically pulls a knife from his vest front or side, and one or more other militants push the victim over, and while holding him still the beheader begins to cut. The victim is almost always shown with a blindfold on during the beheading. Many of the videos have music in the background at various times. The most common scene in the videos is at the end: after the beheading, the head is almost always placed on the back of the prone body. Often the head is first held up high for the camera, at which time the cries of *Allahu Akbar* are the loudest.

Symbology

Imagery is an abundant, important part of Islamic culture. In several of their videos, the Islamic militants are dressed entirely in black, including their head coverings. The color black is said to be very significant in the Islamic tradition. Black is often used to emphasize the importance, or occurrence, of a jihad and to evoke a perceived need to re-establish the Sunni caliphate.[17] The black flag, seen in the background in many of the videos and with Arabic writing on it, traces its roots to the very beginning of Islam.[18] The Prophet Muhammad carried the black flag as did the leader of the Abbasid revolution, which aimed to replace a corrupt Caliphate with a new, more proper Islamic ruling house. The contemporary Islamist movement uses the black flag to symbolize both jihad and the re-establishment of the Islamic Caliphate.[19] In the background of beheading videos, militants are often shown holding weapons, typically rifles. Weapons also have symbolic importance in Islamic culture. The sword is a pre-modern weapon which is considered noble and is associated with early Islamic heroes and their jihads. Rifles, on the other hand, represent modern weapons that illustrate the violent nature of jihadi warfare and signify a show of force. In addition to colors and weapons, many pre- and post-modern Islamic symbols are seen together in video-taped beheadings.

Jihadist Rhetoric

There has been plenty of rhetoric by Islamic militants giving us fair warning that they not only justify the beheading practice, they intend to continue to use it. In 2002, the beheading video of American journalist Daniel Pearl included text that

17. The Islamic Imagery Project (2005) *Visual Motifs in Jihadi Internet Propaganda*, West Point: The Combating Terrorism Center, Department of Social Sciences, United States Military Academy, p. 105.
18. Ibid., p. 95.
19. Ibid., p. 95.

portended future beheadings of Americans. A May 2004 statement by Islamic militants that followed the beheading of American Nicholas Berg was not only intended to encourage followers and recruits to behead but was yet another grim message to the US.

> Have you not had your fill of the war of conferences and battle of words? Is it not time for you to take the path of jihad and carry the sword of the Prophet of prophets?...The Prophet, the most merciful, ordered (his army) to strike the necks of some prisoners in Badr (Battle of) and to kill them...And he set a good example for us.. And you will get shroud after shroud and coffin after coffin slaughtered in this manner.[20]

Following the death of Abu Musaf Zarqawi in June 2006, the leader of the Shura Council in Iraq vowed to the US and its allies "as for you, the slaves of the cross, the grandsons of Ibn al-Alquami and every infidel of the Sunnis, we can't wait to sever your necks with our swords".[21]

Beheading Cells

In October 2005, a terrorist killed in Iraq, Nashwan Mijhim Muslet (aka Abu Tayir or Abu Zaid) was reportedly the leader of a beheading cell. Not only did he personally assist in at least three videotaped beheadings, he was a senior operational leader of al-Qaida in Iraq. Possibly a first of its kind, his cell was known as the primary beheading cell for two al Qaida emirs who were captured and killed in 2005. Many beheadings conducted under Nashwan's leadership were videotaped and the films were reportedly used to intimidate not only the local population of the city of Mosul but citizens throughout Iraq.[22] It is unknown whether there are other beheading cells.

Islamist Beheading Tactics

Islamic militants use a variety of beheading tactics which reflect the past, the present, or a combination of both. Beheadings may be performed 1) as a revenge killing, 2) in conjunction with kidnapping for ransom, 3) to intimidate, 4) as a public example, and 5) as a means of display for recruitment, validation (to money donors), and/or propaganda. Displays are commonly spiked heads or videotaped executions (the modern day version of the spiked head), either for global or local distribution. Furthermore, a sixth tactic might be to behead in large numbers, as evidenced by the high numbers of heads and headless bodies found in Iraq (see Table 1). In the past, large numbers of beheadings

20. Statement by militants who beheaded an American in Iraq, *The San Diego Union Tribune*, Reuters, SignOnSanDiego.com, May 11, 2004.
21. Hendawi, H. (2006) 'Insurgents post videos of three beheadings', AP, *The Washington Times*, June 11.
22. Blackanthem Military News (2005) 'Mosul terrorist cell leader killed', October 26, www.blackanthem.com.

occasionally occurred in one battle. Fortunately, with today's small-unit warfare, militants are not able to take large numbers of casualties at once and behead them.

Beheading as a Means Of Revenge

Revenge beheadings have been seen sporadically in several countries. In Thailand, the head of a village chief was found in a fertilizer bag on a road with a note that read *a revenge for the innocents of Tak Bai district*. Seven Muslim protesters were killed in Tak Bai and an additional 78 were arrested and suffocated or crushed in army trucks.[23] In Iraq, a video stamped with the logo of al Qaeda that posted the beheadings of Russians began with a voice reading, "those who aggress on you, you aggress on them".[24] When those Russians were initially abducted, demands were made for Moscow to pull out of Chechnya and release Islamic militants from its prisons. Demands were not met and the Russians were beheaded. Following the beheadings, a statement read "God's verdict has been carried out on the Russian diplomats...in revenge for the torture, killing and expulsion of brothers and sisters by the infidel Russian government".[25] A story out of Afghanistan describes tit-for-tat beheadings: Afghan soldiers beheaded four Taliban fighters who had earlier cut off the heads of a soldier and his interpreter.[26]

Beheading as a Result of Kidnapping for Ransom

Beheading may result from a ransom demand gone awry or unmet. When Islamic militants kidnap for ransom, their demands often seem intentionally impossible to meet or otherwise unreasonable. As a result, more often than not, the ransoms for such kidnappings either go unmet or the victim's country simply does not negotiate with terrorists. In any case, when the given time limit expires, the kidnapped individual(s) is(are) beheaded. When three civil engineers, Jack Hensley, Eugene Armstrong and Kenneth Bigley were kidnapped in Iraq, the ransom was the release of all Iraqi women prisoners by coalition forces. Neither the US nor Britain negotiated with the kidnappers. All three captives were beheaded. Kidnapping, as a means of extortion is a common and profitable tactic in Iraq, and elsewhere, and is used far more frequently than for beheading.

23. 'Thai Buddhist found decapitated,' Aljazeera.net, November 2, 2004.
24. Nadia Abou El-Magd, 'Qaeda Murders Four Russians, Then Posts Execution on the Web', AP, *The New York Sun*, June 26, 2006, http://www.nysun.com/article/35066.
25. 'Russian Hostages are Beheaded.' ABC, *Blue Star Chronicles*, weblog, June 25, 2006, www.bluestarchronicles.com.
26. 'Afghans behead Taliban in revenge for beheadings', *Reuters*, June 22, 2004.

Beheadings as an Intimidation Tactic

The Taliban uses intimidation in areas where they are able to overtake small towns. They have murdered and beheaded many teachers in order to keep certain schools closed. Recently, in Kandahar, a letter pinned to a mosque reportedly read "girls going to school need to be careful for their safety. If we put acid on their faces or they are murdered then the blame will be on their parents".[27] Teachers and children were thus terrorized out of going to school by the threat of beheadings and by several other methods of intimidation as well.

Beheading as Public Execution Tactic

Public beheadings are not only performed by state governments. Sunni insurgents in Iraq and the Taliban in Afghanistan also conduct public beheadings, most recently in small towns they have overtaken (or re-taken). In the Prophet Muhammad's time, it was his practice to gather as many people from the community as possible to witness executions, the carrying out of Islamic law.[28] Recent stories are circulating that public beheadings are occurring in Iraq and Afghanistan, sometimes daily; and some are required attendance, even for children. One such story stated that same-day DVDs of the beheading were available in the market,[29] ensuring an even wider audience. Additionally, watching the beheadings is appealing, even to children, making them a more desirable form of execution than others, such as hangings or assassinations, and thus likely to continue.

Non-state public beheadings assist the insurgent group with asserting control over an unoccupied or ungoverned town and imposing strict Sharia law. The insurgent group is often also backed with foreign fighters. As a result of these small town takeovers, Islamism will slowly, almost imperceptibly spread, especially if the takeovers are ignored or unstopped.[30] In contrast to the al Qaeda-affiliated groups in Iraq who mass broadcast their beheadings, the small-town operatives who conduct beheadings do not want to draw attention beyond their local audiences, *especially* media attention that might bring overwhelming opposition.

An intercepted letter from Ayman al-Zawahiri to Zarqawi, the *Sheik of the Slaughterers*, advised Zarqawi to stop the grisly beheadings. Beheadings, Zawahiri felt, were hurting al Qaeda's cause by alienating Muslims. Following Zawahiri's letter, from October 2005 through early June 2006, there were no publicized videos of beheadings. During that time, however the overall practice of beheading did not decrease. Zawahiri's letter revealed that al Qaeda responds to Muslim

27. Coghlan, T. (2006) Taliban use beheadings and beatings to keep Afghanistan's schools closed', *The Independent*, July 11, http://news.independent.co.uk.
28. Answers by Dr. Abu Ameenah Bilal Philips, 'Question on Death', Militant Islam Monitor website.
29. Ackroyd, J. (2005) 'The New Yorker town hall meeting on Iraq', *TPMCafe online*, September 24.
30. See various news stories on Somalia, where Fundamentalist Islamists have recently taken over one town at a time with fighting and immediately imposing their own Sharia laws.

opinion, and that winning hearts and minds is as important to al Qaeda as it is to any political group. Realistically, it is unlikely that winning hearts and minds by appealing to mainstream Muslims has much to do with their fight, except as a temporary tactic to buy time, keep recruits flowing in, and avoid widespread disapproval that might precipitate defeat. Understanding the media's role, Zawahiri was translated as saying: "I say to you: that we are in a battle, and that more than half of this battle is taking place in the battlefield of the media...".[31] Manipulating the media is a well-developed tactic of al Qaeda. They place beheading videos on the internet when they want to make a statement, while they do not broadcast their beheadings when pressure from the predominantly Muslim public becomes too great.

People Not Beheaded and Why

Some captives are not beheaded when a kidnapping is for extortion or purpose other than beheading. Also not all Islamic terrorist groups or insurgencies practice beheading. Hamas and Hezbollah do not use beheadings. Additionally, some groups behead selectively; Muqtada al Sadr's militia in Iraq beheads Sunnis but not coalition troops due to their political aspirations there. To behead or not may also depend on the victim and their country of origin. In 2004, at the peak of the video beheadings, two French journalists held for four months, were released without their captor's demands being met. The demand was that the French reverse their ban on head scarves in state schools. Instead the captives, with the assistance of a French negotiator, convinced their captors that they had no affiliation with the US or coalition forces in Iraq.[32] Beheading the Frenchmen might have caused political consequences to al Qaeda outweighing the benefit of releasing them. Two female Italians, who were also held captive during the peak of the video beheadings, were freed in Iraq but because the ransom was paid by the Italian government.[33] Jill Carroll, a journalist with the Christian Science Monitor, was held for three months and then released. Dozens of Arab representatives spoke out against her capture, which may have precipitated her release. Muslims likely spoke out on her behalf because Carroll's sympathy toward the Iraqi people was well known as were her fair journalistic practices. It is unknown if women have an advantage over men in not being beheaded but in the high-profile cases involving women all were released but one, who was killed but not beheaded. A male Turkish captive in a similar situation was convinced he was released due to frequent praying. He "felt that if they would see me praying, they might release me", implying that his visible display of faith as a Muslim would save him.[34] While Muslims are being beheaded as much if not more than non-Muslims, true Muslim vs non-true Muslim

31. 'Al Qaeda letter called 'chilling'', www.cnn.com, October 12, 2005.

32. Interview with French reporter Christian Chesnot, *Democracy Now* (online), June 8, 2005.

33. Villelabeitia, I. (2004) 'Chained hostage in Iraq renews appeal to Blair', Reuters, www.abcnews.com, September 29.

34. Jacinto, L. (2004) 'Death by Sword, Why Militants Prefer Beheadings - And Muslim Hostages Are No Longer Spared', www.abcnews.com, August 11.

status is an important factor weighed by captors. Furthermore, it is unknown why some captives are shot while others are beheaded but the reason could be as simple as that shooting is much easier.

Countertactics—a Challenge

It may be beneficial to identify countertactics to beheadings. Reviewing case studies of all hostages who have been released may be just as important as studying actual beheading cases. The portrayal of beheadings in videos as terrorizing rituals with theatrical overtones shows their purpose. As aptly stated by a Georgetown University professor, "It's not so much the punishing of the individual as the using of the individual".[35] The released Turkish captive described his captors as capricious and that this was the most unsettling aspect of his experience.[36] Developing a countertactic to such impulsive behavior by militants would be extremely difficult. In some cases, the release of a hostage(s) may have had an element of luck—a chance element beyond our control. An individualized countertactic by a hostage would be very challenging mid-experience, due to diminished will, extreme fear, and possible beatings or drugs. Daniel Pearl reportedly refused offered tranquilizers before he met his fate. By being fully conscious through his beheading, Daniel Pearl had a small personal victory, which may have been a type of countertactic. An Italian captive had a similar victory. Just before his beheading, which was video-taped, the Italian jumped up, tried to remove his hood and proclaimed "now I'll show you how an Italian dies!" His hands were not tied. Al Jazeera would not broadcast the video, citing it was *too gruesome*.[37] It has been suggested that the Italian hostage wrecked his beheading video. His defiance did three things, 1) it prevented the video from being aired, 2) it showed rebellion in the face of a fearsome death, and 3) it lessened the success of the militants. Furthermore, though he still died a gruesome death, the Italian died heroically. Each of these small victories again may be considered a type of countertactic.

Spread of the Tactic

Since the first video-taped beheading in 2002, more beheadings are occurring worldwide. Both Islamic and non-Islamic entities are conducting these beheadings. Global access of video-taped beheadings may be inspiring more worldwide beheadings, although in many locations beheadings are not new and already have historical and cultural precedent. While current Islamist beheadings are based on religious premises, non-Islamic beheadings are commonly related to crime.

35. Ibid.
36. Ibid.
37. 'Italian hostage 'defied killers'', *BBC News*, April 15 2004.

Table 2 Recent non-state, non-Islamic beheadings[a]

Date	Event	Group	Location	Remarks
Sep 30, 2004	Three Haitian policemen	Chimeres, a pro-Aristide gang	Haiti	Alleged campaign against the government, dubbed "Operation Baghdad."
Feb 23, 2005	One youth	Maoist Rebels	India (Ranchi)	Beheaded for attempting to vote at a polling booth. Head was displayed as a warning to others.
Feb 22, 2006	Christians behead Muslims	Christians	Nigeria	Christian mobs sought revenge for similar attacks by Muslims in the wake of the Cartoon Riots
Apr 21, 2006	Two Police	Drug Trafficking	Mexico (Acapulco)	Note found with the beheaded bodies that read: *So that you learn to respect*. Heads found in a different part of the city.
Jun 15, 2006	Rioting inmates behead five	Rival gangs	Brazil	In prison riot, inmates behead at least five, and display heads on stakes on the prison roof
Jun 16, 2006	One male	Naxalites	India	Tribal male dragged from his house, severely beaten before being beheaded with a sharp weapon
Jun 17, 2006	Civilian bus passenger	MASSOB	Nigeria	MASSOB, in their fight against Muslim dominance, took civilian passengers off a bus, and beheaded one of them.
Jun 21, 2006	Three Baja cops and one civilian	Drug Cartel	Mexico	Bodies found in Rosarito Beach, heads found hours later in Tijuana
Jun 24, 2006	One policeman	Drug Gang	Mexico (Guerrero)	Three of four policemen were kidnapped and shot, the fourth beheaded.
Jun 29, 2006	Man's head found	Drug Cartel	Mexico (Acapulco)	Severed head found on steps of City Hall, with a handwritten note
Jun 30, 2006	Two heads found	Drug Cartel	Mexico (Acapulco)	Heads were placed in front of a government office, with note that read: *One more message, dirtbags, so that you learn to respect*.

[a]From un-posted database: Beheadings in the Post-Modern Era, derived from Open Sources.

Copycat Beheadings

Beheadings are inspiring more beheadings; they are increasing in number and are surfacing in other countries, not all of which are Muslim (see Tables 1 and 2). In September 2004, Haitian gangs beheaded three police officers during a pro-Aristide campaign they dubbed "Operation Baghdad." In 2004–2005, in Muslim-dominated areas in Thailand, a rash of beheadings began that were said to be copies of those in Iraq. However, in the 1990s, Islamic militants in Chechnya, Kosovo, and Algeria had already been conducting numerous beheadings. These beheadings were not video-taped or aired in the media. Beheadings now taking place in Iraq are often aired in the media, making it appear as if they originated in Iraq, while in actuality the beheadings in Chechnya, Kosovo and Algeria were chronologically the first in recent history. Nonetheless, it is still difficult to determine who is copying whom because the militants in Iraq added a new dimension to beheadings by videotaping them. It is more likely that today's beheadings are copying ancestral battles vs beheadings taking place in any country today.

Non-state, Non-Islamic Beheadings in the Americas

Latin American gangs and drug cartels place second to Islamic militants in conducting beheadings and they are doing so in growing numbers. The most abundant and recent beheadings are taking place in Mexico (see Table 2). Beginning in April 2006, most of the beheadings taking place in Mexico are likely the result of drug cartels moving in on rivals. Previously rare in this country, the spread of beheadings is thought to be due to either the existing drug cartel enforcers adopting new tactics or the arrival of a new criminal element from Central or South America. Simultaneous to the beheadings has been the hotly contested presidential race. Beheading targets thus far have included police officers, and increasingly those of higher rank. Furthermore, in recent beheadings in Mexico, the criminals took extra effort to place the heads in different parts of the city or country than the bodies. This practice of geographically separating heads from bodies is also done in Iraq and Thailand. Although the reasons are unknown, it is certain in most cases that the criminal or militant group wants not only the bodies, but the heads to be found. Perhaps fear and intimidation are doubled or spread by placing body parts in two or more geographic areas. And the criminal or militant group may appear to have a more widespread presence.

Beheadings have not been uncommon in Central America, and have been a result of gang vs police, gang vs gang, or vigilante vs gang warfare. Vigilante groups, who have been the victims of gang extortion, drug dealing, and murder, often behave as brutally as their nemeses. Attacks by vigilantes include beheadings, single-shot executions, and routine acts of mutilation and torture.[38] A vigilante group in Guatemala City who recently beheaded a member of Mara 18, a violent Central American street gang, left a note with the body. The leaving of notes with the dead is a common tactic of vigilante groups, as it is with gangs. The vigilantes' use of notes is to intimidate rather than to claim responsibility for their actions. Islamic militants on the other hand, almost always claim responsibility for their actions. Vigilantes are more commonly using the internet to promote their cause, however, which is similar to how Islamic militants use it. Vigilante groups use the internet for the added purpose of publishing the names and addresses of gang-members, which is intended to result in more gang deaths.

In Central America, inter-gang warfare often includes beheadings and eye-gouging. Mara Salvatrucha, also called MS-13, is a gang with beginnings in Los Angeles that is known for using beheadings. MS-13 is comprised of cells and is heavily involved in drug and human trafficking. Dismembered corpses, complete with the decapitated head, are often left behind at the scene of murders conducted by MS-13. And they commonly leave a grim note attached to the body. MS-13 is growing in number and spreading throughout the United States. MS-13 is one of several mara gangs, which are estimated to have 100,000 members in Central America and fraternal links to 8,000–10,000 members in more than 30 states in the US.[39]

It is not likely that the beheadings in Central America and Mexico are copycats of the Islamic beheadings in the Middle East and Asia. It is likely, however, that they have been an inspiration to them. The Hispanic culture has its own past that includes beheadings, which they would be more likely to emulate than today's Islamic beheadings. But it is curious that the beheadings in both the Americas and the Middle East are concurrently growing in number. Furthermore, beheadings in Mexico are of concern to the US, due to their common border. Two occurrences bode ill for the US and the potential arrival of beheadings: 1) the northward migration of beheadings into Mexico, and 2) the increasing US presence of the MS-13 gang, known to behead.

Christian and Other Retaliation

In late January 2006, Muslim anger began to mount over controversial Danish cartoons reprinted in newspapers, depicting the Prophet Muhammad. Religious-based Muslim riots ensued in many countries worldwide, including Nigeria. Evidently driven to a breaking point by some of the worst Muslim attacks there, Christian mobs retaliated by attacking Muslim motorists and traders in Onitsha, Nigeria; more than thirty were killed, a number of which were beheaded. The

38. Rosenberg, M. (2006) 'Ten Dead in Suspected Guatemala Vigilante Killings', *Reuters Foundation*, Alertnet, February 10.
39. Lakshmanan, I. A. R. (2006) 'Gangs Roil Central America; Troubles Linked to US Deportees', *The Boston Globe*, www.boston.com/news/world, April 17.

attacks were the first by Christians as counterattacks to the cartoon riots worldwide. Described as being hordes of angry men, the Christians were armed with machetes, guns, and boards with nails pounded into their ends.[40] It must be considered whether retaliatory events such as this one and the ongoing anti-gang vigilante attacks in Guatemala will lead to more of the same. Will Christians and other religious groups continue to be pushed to the point where they respond to brutality with like brutality? In June 2006, two US soldiers in Iraq were ambushed and taken by militants; both captives were mutilated, one was beheaded. A grisly video of the aftermath of the attack was then placed on the internet by an al Qaeda in Iraq umbrella group. Intense anger stirred up among US troops, by events such as this one, makes it feasible that US soldiers will, counter to policy, begin to use more brutality, including retaliatory beheadings similar to that of the Christian counterattacks in Nigeria.

Modern Day Precursors

There are recent events and evidence that suggest Islamist beheadings are making their way west and will eventually arrive in the US. In Amsterdam in November 2004, Theo Van Gogh, a highly controversial Dutch film-maker, was murdered because of the uproar over his latest film, *Submission*, which offended Islam. A radical Islamist slit Van Gogh's throat (a variation of beheading). In January 2005 in the US, an entire Egyptian Coptic Christian family who was highly outspoken against Islam was murdered by Muslims, who cut their throats in a brutal attack. Voices on Jihadi websites quickly called these murders beheadings, took credit for them, and praised Allah. One Muslim board translated from Arabic read, "The heads of the family have been separated from their bodies (they have been beheaded) at their home in New Jersey";[41] another bulletin board read, "The good planting has started to yield thank Allah and soon, Allah willing, an intense Islamic revolution all across America that holds the right and bring down the falsehood that they've created".[42] Both the Van Gogh and Egyptian family murders involved those who were outspoken against Islam. Daniel Pearl's 2002 beheading was seen worldwide as an isolated incident, when in reality it was the first in a string of related beheadings that continue today. It is too risky for the West to presume that the Van Gogh and Egyptian family murders are isolated incidents.

A painting depicting the decapitated head of Oriana Fallaci, a renowned Italian journalist and author, was recently displayed in a Milan gallery. The artist, Giuseppe Veneziano depicted the head of Fallaci because she had criticized Islam to the point where fundamentalists probably wanted to see her beheaded in real life. Although the painted beheading of Fallaci was only symbolic, its display in a prominent gallery alongside a compilation of leftist anti-US artwork was like

40. Timberg, C. (2006) 'Christians Turn on Muslims In Nigeria; More Than 30 Die', *Washington Post Foreign Service*, February 23.
41. Jihad Watch, www.jihadwatch.org/archives/004772.php, January 23, 2005.
42. Ibid.

handing the Islamists a small victory in their jihad. The Fallaci painting along with the Van Gogh and Egyptian family murders all are indicators of future Islamist turmoil that includes beheadings occurring in the West. It is unsettling that being outspoken against extremist Islam can result in beheading. It is also ironic that beheading is the means to silence outspoken mouths.

Historical times of upheaval and change have been marked with beheadings. It is clear we are currently in one of those times but because we are a civilized society it is still surprising to see beheadings multiplying in location and number. Like official state-run beheadings, non-state beheadings are derived from ancient customs. But the non-state beheadings are criminal acts that may be an inspiration to others, whether in jihad or not. What differentiates criminal beheadings from one another are the ways in which the offending groups use them to achieve their goals. The short-term gains from beheadings, in combination with other hostilities, help groups conducting them achieve their long-term goals. While the well-known, videotaped Islamist beheadings in the Middle East are taking place, lesser-known beheadings are increasing in number in other areas of the world. As they appear or spread, especially in countries where previously they were rare, beheadings may be indicators of a greater turmoil or the introduction of an unknown element. Whether a beheading occurs in the form of a group's new tactic, with the arrival of a new hostile group in a region, or in conjunction with an escalation of existing hostilities, the outlook is always grim (Figure 1).

Figure 1 David Bebber, *The Times, London.*

Acknowledgements

Special thanks for the contributions of Sara Haeckel and Robert J. Bunker.

Afterward: Law Enforcement Response Strategies for Criminal-states and Criminal-soldiers

John P. Sullivan & Keith Weston

John P. Sullivan is a Lieutenant with the Los Angeles Sheriff's Department, where he serves as Director of the National TEW Resource Center. He previously served as Officer-in-Charge of the Los Angeles Terrorism Early Warning Group. He has managed intelligence, emergency operations and terrorism response activities and is a researcher specializing in terrorism, intelligence, urban operations, and police studies. He is author or co-author of four books and over 60 chapters, papers, articles or monographs on these and related topics. He is co-editor (along with Peter Katona and Michael D. Intriligator) of Countering Terrorism and WMD: Creating a Global Counter-Terrorism Network (Routledge, 2006). His recent research focus includes suicide bombings, civil-military interaction in peace operations and counterinsurgency. He holds a M.A. Urban Affairs and Policy Analysis from the New School for Social Research, New York, NY, and a B.S. in Government from the College of William and Mary in Virginia. **Keith Weston** QPM M.A., is a Senior Research Fellow in Counter Terrorism and Deputy Director of the Cranfield University Resilience Centre, based at the Defence Academy of the United Kingdom. In 2005, after 32 years service, he retired from the Metropolitan Police Service with the rank of Detective Chief Superintendent. He was a career counter-terrorist officer and served in both Special Branch and the Anti-Terrorist Branch. His last post was head of the Police International Counter Terrorism Unit. He currently leads the UK Foreign and Commonwealth Office's Counter Terrorist Crisis Management programme, in specific countries. He is a regular speaker at UK and international conferences and is on the International Board of Advisors at New York University Law School, Centre on Law and Security. In 1992 he was awarded a Master of Arts Degree by Exeter University. In 2003 he was awarded the Queen's Police Medal.

Criminal-soldiers come in many guises. They may be members of a street gang or mara, members of a mafia or organized criminal enterprise, terrorists, insurgents, pirates, or warlords. In all cases, they challenge the traditional state monopoly on violence and political control. They may co-exist within stable states, dominate ungovernable, lawless zones, slums, or 'no-go' zones, or be the *de facto* rulers of criminal enclaves or free-states. Likewise, the 'criminal state' may range from a street gang's narrow gang-controlled turf of a few blocks or segments of blighted housing estates to larger uncontested neighborhoods in a *barrio*, *favela*, *gecekondu*, *chawl*, slum or mega-slum. Alternately, they can exist as 'para-states,' 'statelets' or 'virtual states' in a combination of physical and increasingly networked terrain.

In the worst case, the destabilization of state control and growth of ungoverned areas could result in a dualistic 'Bladerunner' type scenario like that described by Mike Davis:

> Night after night, hornetlike helicopter gunships stalk enigmatic enemies in the narrow streets of the slum districts, pouring hellfire into shanties or fleeing cars. Every morning the slums reply with suicide bombers and eloquent explosions. If the empire can deploy Orwellian technologies of repression, its outcasts have the gods of chaos on their side[1].

This afterward will examine these potentials then suggest possible law enforcement and police strategies for mitigating, containing, and negotiating this social terrain, minimizing broader application of Davis' all-too-likely worst-case scenario.

Criminal-soldiers are active on a planet-wide basis. For example, in June 2006, a convoy of 40 vehicles with 70 heavily armed, masked men trawled the streets of Rosarito Beach in Baja California. These men, members of a drug cartel, were intercepted by three lightly armed police officers. The gangsters subsequently captured the unfortunate police officers. The next morning the officers' mutilated bodies were found in an empty lot, while their heads were discovered in the Tijuana River.[2] Similar instances of the barbarization of conflict and crime are found in assassinations of police, judicial officials, and journalists in Mexico and other contested zones. As John Robb observes, "We have entered the age of the faceless, agile enemy. From London to Madrid and Nigeria to Russia, stateless terrorist groups have emerged to score blow after blow against us. Driven by cultural fragmentation, schooled in the most sophisticated technologies, and fueled by transnational crime, these groups are forcing corporations and individuals to develop new ways of defending themselves."[3]

1. Davis, M. (2004) 'The Urbanization of Empire: Megacities and the Laws of Chaos', *Social Text*, no. 81, Winter as quoted in Davis, M. (2006) *Planet of Slums*, Verso, New York, p. 206.
2. Marosi, R. (2006) 'Mexico's Cartels Escalate Drug War', *Los Angeles Times*, June 23. Available at: http://www.latimes.com/news/printedition/front/la-fg-behead23jun23,1,4156759.html.
3. Robb, J. (2006) 'Security: Power To The People', *FastCompany*, iss. 103, March, p. 120. Available at: http://www.fastcompany.com/magazine/103.

The Threat to the State: Defining and Understanding the Operational Space

The first step in crafting an active defense to these threats is the recognition that criminal soldiers have altered the nature of crime and war and, in doing so, have altered the operational space that police and security services must negotiate. As Sullivan observed in his essay "Terrorism, Crime and Private Armies,"

> Terrorists, criminal actors, and private armies of many stripes have altered the ecology of both crime and armed conflict. In many cases, the two are intertwined. Several factors reinforce these links. Global organized crime, which increasingly links local actors with their transnational counterparts, coupled with chronic warfare and insurgency (which yields economic benefits to some of its participants) can propel local or regional conflicts into genocidal humanitarian disasters. These regions, which are essentially criminal free-states, provide refuge and safe haven to terrorists, warlords, and criminal enterprises.[4]

These non-state actors share a common tendency toward becoming violent, pernicious threats to global security and civil society. Those at the lower threshold (street gangs of the first and second generation) are contributors, but those at the middle to higher threshold (third generation gangs, first and second phase cartels and warlords) are particularly dangerous. As these non-state, criminal-soldiers evolve, they increasingly challenge the status of state and political organization. States are, at least in the current international political community, entities that possess a legitimate monopoly on the use of violence within a specified territory. Criminal-states—that is, criminal free states or free enclaves—essentially act as statelets or para-states, in effect, entities that challenge that monopoly. This is much the same condition as that created by warlords within failed states.[5]

Lawless zones and criminal enclaves are areas (ranging from neighborhoods, to regions, to states, to cross-border zones) where gangs, criminal enterprises, insurgents, or warlords dominate social life and erode the bonds of effective security and the rule of law.[6] Failed states are those where these bonds are totally removed from normal discourse. Failing states are those where these bonds are substantially eroded, while transitional states are those where these bonds are being reconstituted.

The second step to negotiating this operational space is developing an understanding of the dynamics of the actors occupying it. For example, John

4. See Sullivan, J. P. (2005) 'Terrorism, Crime and Private Armies', in *Networks, Terrorism and Global Insurgency*, ed. Robert J. Bunker, Routledge, London, pp. 69–83 for this observation and an expanded discussion of the privatization of violence.

5. See Bunker, R. J. & Sullivan, J. P. (1998) 'Cartel Evolution: Potentials and Consequences', *Transnational Organized Crime*, vol. 4, no. 2, Summer, pp. 55–74; and Sullivan, J. P. & Bunker, R. J. (2002) 'Drug Cartels, Street Gangs, and Warlords', *Small Wars and Insurgencies*, vol. 13, no. 2, Summer, pp. 40–53 and Bunker, R. J. (ed) (2003) *Non-State Threats and Future Wars*, Frank Cass, Portland, pp. 40–53 for a comprehensive discussion of the effects of non-state criminal actors in the deterioration of civil society and the rule of law in areas of conflict and high intensity crime.

6. Ibid.

Rapley in his *Foreign Affairs* essay "The New Middle Ages" gives an account of what he calls 'gangsters' paradise.'[7] In this account, he describes how local gangs maintain their own system of law and order, 'tax' residents and businesses, and provide rudimentary social services. Rapley describes the impact of Jamaican gangs, which he terms as fluid but cohesive organizations that dominate clearly demarcated territory but participate in global narcotics trafficking. These gangs, according to Rapley, are indicative of "the rise of private 'statelets' that coexist in a delicate, often symbiotic relationship with a larger state."[8] The glue for that relationship is frequently corruption and co-option of legitimate government actors. Rapley asserts that the "power of statelets and other new political actors will be less transitory, more significant, and more resistant to intervention than is usually assumed."[9] A poignant example of such an enclave has been documented in Ciudad del Este or the Tri-Border region at the confluence of Brazil, Paraguay, and Argentina. This region has been described as a virtual "Star Wars Bar" of criminal enterprises and terrorist entities co-locating in an area with weak structures of governance to conduct their various solo and interdependent enterprises with potential global reach.[10]

Rapley is essentially describing the impact of "third generation gangs"[11] within megaslums.[12] He notes that "Vast metropolises, growing so quickly their precise populations are unknown, are dotted with shantytowns and squatter camps that lack running water, are crisscrossed by open gutters of raw sewage, and are powered by stolen electricity. Developing states are constantly struggling to catch up. In some places they succeed, barely. In others, they are losing control of chunks of their territory."[13] Brazil is illustrative. Rapley observes that "Many of Rio de Janeiro's favelas, for example, are now so dangerous that politicians enter only with the local gang leader's permission. The gangs deliver votes in exchange for patronage. Beyond that, the politicians and the state remain largely invisible and irrelevant. The gangs do not wish to secede from Brazil, but they can compel its government to negotiate the terms of its sovereignty."[14]

7. Rapley, J. (2006) 'The New Middle Ages', *Foreign Affairs*, vol. 85, no. 3, May/June, pp. 95-103.
8. Ibid, p. 96.
9. Ibid.
10. See for example Bunker R. J. & Sullivan, J. P. 'Cartel Evolution: Potentials and Consequences' for an early and detailed description.
11. See Sullivan, J. P. (1997) 'Third Generation Street Gangs: Turf, Cartels and Netwarriors', *Transnational Organized Crime*, vol. 3, no. 3, Autumn, pp. 95-108; Sullivan, J. P. (2000) 'Urban Gangs Evolving as Criminal Netwar Actors', *Small Wars and Insurgencies*, vol. 11, no. 1, Spring, pp. 82-96; and Sullivan, J. P. (2001) 'Gangs, Hooligans., and Anarchists—The Vanguard of Netwar in the Streets', Arquilla, J. & Ronfeldt, D. (2006) *Networks and Netwars: The Future of Terror, Crime, and Militancy*, Santa Monica: RAND, pp. 99-126 for detailed discussion of the evolution of street gangs into networked actors with broad reach.
12. See in Davis, M. (2006) *Planet of Slums*, Verso, New York for a trenchant analysis of the politics of slums and political exclusion in global context.
13. Rapley, p. 100.
14. Ibid.

Essentially, third generation gangs (3 GEN Gangs) have taken on the state. In May 2006 a wave of 3 GEN Gang violence engulfed São Paulo when the state's shadowy yet premier criminal gang, the prison-based Priemeiro Comando da Capital (PCC), lashed out against state interference. In five days of PCC-initiated mayhem and retribution, 150 people (a quarter of them police) were killed, 82 buses were torched, and 17 banks attacked. Prison rebellions raged at 74 out of 140 prisons. Schools, shopping centers, transport and commerce were stalled. The PCC's fluid structure was described as "more like al-Qaeda's than a tightly run mafia."[15] Similar threats challenge much of the developing world, where "groups ranging from criminal gangs to Islamist civil-society networks have assumed many of the functions that states have abandoned, funding their operations through informal taxes as well as with proceeds from the drug trade, human trafficking, and money laundering."[16]

The third step in understanding this operational space is recognizing that gangs (and organized crime), terrorists, and warlords of various stripes have converged in a dynamic, distributed network that links local and global enterprises in new ways. Profit, corruption, and political violence are merging in several ways that challenge traditional law enforcement and security structures. Justine Rosenthal observes that "Criminal sources of financing are mixing with non-state actors of different sources to create three models of operation."[17] These are ideologically-driven terrorists who use criminal profit as a means to an end; criminal profiteers that use terrorist labels as a pretext; and hybrid organizations that blend both attributes to varying degrees over time. All of these groups engage in or maintain alliances with other criminal enterprises to fuel their operations. For example, contemporary terrorists grow opiates, mine diamonds, kidnap for ransom, and traffic in arms and drugs.

Rosenthal gives the example of the Abu Sayyaf Group (ASG) as a case of a pretextural group. ASG began as a pure terrorist group seeking an Islamic state in the Philippines. While still espousing that goal, it has become increasingly criminally motivated, in one case blowing up a passenger ferry when its extortion demands went unmet. Similar dynamics are currently at play with the Islamic Movement of Uzbekistan (IMU) that dominates drug trade in the Ferghana valley where the Uzbek, Kyrgyz and Tajik frontiers converge. The RUF (Revolutionary United Front) in Sierra Leone is another criminal-terrorist hybrid that, while espousing the need for political change, engaged in torture, terrorism and the exploitation of the diamond industry. All three of these groups flourish in lawless zones where corruption is rampant and police few. All three also demonstrate networked attributes. The IMU has reported links to al-Qaeda, Abu Sayyef, Chechen and Uigur insurgents; Abu Sayyef has been linked to both al-Qaeda and

15. The mob takes on the state' (2006) *The Economist*, May 20, p. 39.
16. Rapley. p. 102.
17. Rosenthal, J. (2006) 'Business Bombs: The Rise of Terrorism-for-Profit', *The American Interest*, vol. 1, no. 4, Summer, pp. 28-32.

Jemaah Islamiya; and the RUF has had links with Charles Taylor in Liberia, Hezbollah, HAMAS, Abu Sayyaf, and al-Qaeda at various times.[18]

Louise Shelly, Director of the Transnational Crime and Corruption Center at American University, coins this convergence of transnational crime, corruption and terrorism 'The Unholy Trinity.' Contrasting newer, networked organized crime groups with their traditional predecessors, Shelly notes that these groups thrive on the "shadow economy, the absence of an effective state, and endemic corruption."[19] These groups benefit from state instability and the profit-making opportunities offered by prolonged conflict and instability. This situation threatens not only the directly impacted contested zones, but also broader global stability. According to Shelly, "The embedded nature of network crime structures in local communities and the inability of both domestic and international militaries, as well as law enforcement agencies, to control their activities make them a growing danger."[20] Shelly continues that this emerging "terrorist-transnational crime relationship extends beyond a marriage of convenience that generates profits or provides logistics: it goes to the very heart of the relationship between crime groups and the state."[21] These groups benefit from weak state structures, the presence of ungoverned lawless zones, and the linkages between such zones, and employ privatized violence, fraud, corruption and the manipulation of political and financial systems to exist, thrive, and expand their reach in pursuit of profit, plunder, and power.

Maintaining Stability and Order

In the context of criminal-states and criminal-soldiers, police and law enforcement agencies are pivotal. The activities of criminal, non-state soldiers are based in and thrive on crime and criminal transactions. Crime control at local levels, linked into a distributed global network and supported by intelligence, diplomatic, economic, military, and civil society action, can help limit and ameliorate the threat posed by gangs, criminals, and terrorists acting both locally and globally.

Law enforcement and the police services are responsible for ensuring internal stability and social control. Police maintain order, investigate criminal activity and conspiracies, and respond to emergencies. In addition, police support judicial process and interact with intelligence and security services to balance internal and external security. Law enforcement agencies also play key roles in combating terrorism and transnational organized crime in their own jurisdictions and increasingly in co-operation with their global counterparts.

18. Ibid.
19. Shelly, L. (2005) 'The Unholy Trinity: Transnational Crime, Corruption, and Terrorism', *Brown Journal of World Affairs*, vol. 11, iss. 2, Winter/Spring, pp. 101–111.
20. Ibid, p. 102.
21. Ibid, p. 104.

Stability and order are essential elements of a functional society. In order for the organs of government to operate effectively, people must be free to conduct their daily lives without the threat of criminal and terrorist violence. Businesses must be free from disruption and extortion so they can perform their functions and support an economy. The people, government, and business must be secure from violence and corruption to engage in the many activities that constitute a thriving community and state. Criminal organizations, ranging from street gangs to indigenous and transnational organized crime groups, engage in protection, extortion, drugs, arms (potentially including in the worst case special nuclear materials or biologic agents), and human trafficking, money laundering, cigarette, alcohol, and petroleum smuggling, prostitution, and auto theft. All of these actors use the profits from their activities to co-opt and corrupt political and legal structures. All use violence as an instrument to protect and expand their turf, reach, and capacity to operate. When left unchecked, such criminal activity erodes social stability and state solvency. At all phases of conflict, but especially in the aftermath of broad conflict, criminal enterprises, gangs, insurgents, terrorists, and corrupt influences present tangible challenges to institutions of order and justice.

Typically, crime control for these issues is segmented into bureaucratic specialties, and across jurisdictional boundaries. For example, local police focus on community policing and street crime, and may have a gang enforcement unit, an organized crime unit, and participate in local, regional, or national level anti- or counter-terrorism units. National police or investigative agencies may concentrate on major crimes, organized crime, and terrorism, while intelligence or security services may concentrate on internal and external intelligence gathering. These activities are often isolated into specialized silos and frequently compete for resources, information, and organizational prestige.

International and domestic intelligence operations have commonly been separated with law enforcement and intelligence operating in separate spheres. Response to foreign failing, failed, and transitional states has generally been the province of the diplomatic and military services. Military peacebuilding, peacekeeping, and peacemaking activities, while supported by United National Civil Police (CIVPOL) contingents pulled together in an *ad hoc* manner, have rarely benefited from cohesive police-military interoperability and effective co-operation. All of these seemingly interdependent activities at various phases need to interact in order to stem the tide of criminal-states and criminal-soldiers. Stability operations, anti- and counterterrorism, counterinsurgency, genocide and war crime prevention, intervention, attribution, and prosecution all require law enforcement and police investigative skills and capabilities to be effective.

Two law enforcement approaches have utility across this spectrum of operations. These are community policing and intelligence-led policing. Both require an in-depth understanding of community activity and crime. Both recognize that community support is essential to establishing stability, public order, public peace, and the rule of law. Community police officers on patrol form the foundation of securing a community. These individual officers are then supported by intelligence analysis of broad community, societal, and criminal trends. Enforcement and investigation help ensure criminals are identified, arrested and brought to the bar of justice. Corruption eradication is an essential adjunct to these tasks. Intelligence and analytical support to investigations for all crimes is also vital.

Consider the police response to terrorism in the United Kingdom. According to Keith Weston, UK efforts rely upon a partnership between the police and security service; high visibility, targeted police operations to disrupt, detect, or deter terrorist activity; post-event investigations; and community reassurance, partnership, and consequence management efforts.[22] In the area of domestic (US) gang prevention, gang intelligence and enforcement efforts have been viewed as essential to stabilizing communities. Gang reduction activities seek to promote stable neighborhoods by collaboration among local police, sheriff, and federal law enforcement agencies; often this involves multi-agency/multi-strategy policing and social control efforts, including partnerships among police, probation officers, corrections officials, and social workers. In areas where multinational gangs (maras) operate, these are (or can be) bolstered by efforts to strengthen the rule of law in cooperating nations, by cooperation with immigration authorities to limit illegal movement of gangsters, and by cooperative, international gang intelligence and awareness activities.[23] In addition, both gang reduction and organized crime control efforts have been bolstered by antigang and organized crime legislation, including 'Racketeer Influenced Corrupt Organization (RICO)' and similar anti-conspiracy legislation. Some jurisdictions have also employed civil injunctions and process to limit gang influence over neighborhoods.

Restoring Order in Transitional States

Peacemaking and nation-building are important strategic concepts for sustaining and reconstituting civil security and justice structures in failing, failed, and transitional states. Security is foremost among the key action areas in nation-building. For example, the RAND study *Establishing Law and Order After Conflict* (2005) describes four components of security in transitional states. Similar actions are also applicable to failing or failed states. These are: 1) conduct peacekeeping and law enforcement; 2) rebuild internal security institutions, such as police and military; 3) engage in justice sector reform; and 4) demilitarize, demobilize, and re-integrate ex-combatants.[24]

22. Weston, K. (2004) 'The Terrorist Threat: The British Police Response', in *The Changing Face of Terrorism*, ed. Rohan Gunarantna, Eastern Universities Press, Singapore, pp. 74–82.
23. See for example Johnson, S. & Muhlhausen, D. B. (2005) 'North American Transnational Youth gangs: Breaking the Chain of Violence', *Backgrounde*, no. 1834, Heritage Foundation, Washington, DC, March 21.
24. Jones, S. G., Wilson, J. M., Rathmell, A. & Riley, K. J. (2006) *Establishing Law and Order After Conflict*, Santa Monica, CA: RAND, p. 11.

During conflict, stability and support operations, counterinsurgency, and post-conflict situations, police functions are vital. Yet they are frequently non-existent, often broken requiring reconstitution and, in many cases, plagued by corruption. During combat situations, military forces often fill the void; in these and other situations a mix between general military forces, military police, United Nations Civilian Police (CIVPOL), and new police organizations exists. Determining the appropriate military-police force structure, interaction, and mix of service at each stage is a central need in these contested areas.[25] Public security and crime control are essential to restoring order (as they are in preventing or reversing the onset of instability experienced in failing or failed states). For example, in post-war Iraq, public opinion surveys show that Iraqis feel more threatened from pervasive criminal violence than they do from the impact of insurgency. In fact, the inability and perceived lack of interest by the Coalition Provisional Authority (CPA) to control criminal violence at the onset of the insurgency may have fueled initial support for the insurgency. Thus, a reduction of criminal violence can be expected to advance stability in Iraq and bolster support for the government and police.[26]

Even in counterinsurgency and conflict situations, counter-crime activities are essential. Controlling crime and protecting citizens helps build the legitimacy of the police and state and contribute to effective counterinsurgency actions. Efforts to suppress gangs, organized crime, narcotics smuggling, and corruption must then be viewed not as secondary or follow-on missions to insurgency suppression, but as necessary adjuncts to counterinsurgency. As a consequence, community-oriented police can build trust and "gather intelligence at the street level that allows the arrest of terrorists before they strike."[27]

Constabulary and Gendarmerie Capabilities (EXPOL)

In states where community police and sophisticated criminal investigative capabilities are non-existent or must be rebuilt, foreign law enforcement assistance is necessary. In an immediate post-conflict setting or transitional state where insurgency and high intensity crime co-exist, constabulary or gendarmerie capabilities are likely to be needed to augment military and CIVPOL capabilities. Robust 'hybrid' police organizations that are able to transition from warfighting to high-intensity crime, from community policing to complex investigations, and from disorder and back are a potential solution to this deficiency in force structure. These specialized, formed units are able to perform diverse missions and employ highly disciplined group action when needed and provide 'close-in'

25. See Sullivan, J. P. (2006) 'Establishing the Rule of Law/CivPol', in *Countering Insurgency and Promoting Democracy*, Council for Emerging National Security Affairs (CENSA), Washington, DC.
26. Perito, R. (2006) 'Policing Iraq: Protecting Iraqis from Criminal Violence', *USIPeace Briefing*, United States Institute of Peace, June, available at: http://www.usip.org/pubs/usipeace_briefings/2006/0629_policing_iraq.html.
27. Ibid.

community policing when required. Such police units include the Italian Carabinieri, French Gendarmerie, Spain's Guardia Civil, and the Dutch Marechaussee. Traditionally these formations have been known as constabulary forces or gendarmeries. These expeditionary police services (EXPOL) are also known as stability police units (SPUs).[28] The development of such capabilities can assist in the investigation of war crimes, genocide, ethnic cleansing, and the suppression of criminal violence in the unstable, conflict-prone areas. Development of such capabilities within UN, US, NATO, and allied/coalition force structures should be a priority consideration.

These new capabilities and existing structures need to develop strategic and tactical plans that identify the problem and provide workable solutions. These plans are enhanced when contingency planning, realistic exercising, specialist training and continuous research and development provide direction and focus. The vulnerability of any strategy is the failure of governments and institutions to invest in long-term strategic planning and to reduce or withdraw funding when other issues, considered to be a higher priority, achieve primacy. This usually results in intermittent levels of resourcing. One way of countering this vulnerability is for those who provide the financial support and those entrusted to deliver the strategic strands to jointly agree on a series of project initiatives that sustain the key elements. The projects need to be strategically led, adequately funded and to have specific terms of reference, that are measurable, achievable, with realistic outcomes and subject to regular review. Examples of the types of projects:

- Legal framework
- Professional development of law enforcement staff
- Technical measures
- Surveillance capability
- Asset tracing
- Witness protection schemes
- System for handling persistent offenders
- Proactive use of informants/agents, and
- Highly developed analytical techniques

The wise management of project initiatives supported by a continuous program of review provides the opportunity to identify challenges and opportunities in the area of comparative policing. For example, in the United Kingdom, a prime example is closed circuit television. In its first generation, it provided a valuable asset in terms of prevention. In its second generation, it was deployed in greater numbers and advantages were seen with overlapping areas of camera coverage. In its third generation, CCTV has been integrated with Automatic Number Plate Readers, facial recognition technology, and enhanced image recovery. The result is that CCTV can provide prevention in its deterrent mode, pro-active assistance

28. Sullivan, J. P. 'Establishing the Rule of Law/CivPol'.

to detect movement of offenders, and post-event help with offender identification. In countries where issues of privacy are considered to outweigh the threat from terrorism, serious crime, or anti-social behavior, the use of CCTV would be less effective. Also, where the infrastructure of the country has not developed to be able to support such technology, CCTV would be less of a priority than other strategic projects.

A further example of cross fertilization of techniques relates not to the investigation of crime but to those activities broadly categorized as Emergency Planning, Disaster Management, and Disaster Recovery. The world of Emergency Planning has produced the compelling concept of an, 'All Threats, All Hazards', approach to draw together all the relevant resources to a particular challenge. This approach provides a continuum of threats and hazards supported by an integrated and cohesive structure to respond, manage the crisis, and provide for a speedy return to normality. Adopting the "all threats all hazards" approach will help to eliminate, or at least significantly reduce the 'stovepipe' or 'silo' mentality found in many law enforcement organizations. This approach will lead to senior officers and planners considering the holistic problem solving model that will lead them to address the causes of the problem together with the results of the problem rather than just trying to address the problem on its own.

Other overlaps occur in the areas of partnerships with potential victim communities. Such partnerships will include representative bodies catering to community, social, and commercial groups. This partnership activity allows synergy with respect to priority of effort. For example, in terms of insurgency or terrorist attack, official energy will concentrate on protecting life thus there is obvious scope for increased private sector effort to protect property. This process is supported by the development of an understanding of the complementary roles of the public and private sectors and assisted by communication circuits within the private sector. The business community has also recognized the need to develop in-house and mutual support in terms of Crisis Management, Disaster Recovery and Business Continuity.

Another major asset to law enforcement is the development of Forensic Science. The real benefit of Forensic Science as an investigative asset relies upon extremely detailed and meticulous scene examination. The advances in scene examination in recent years have been dramatic and represent an excellent future prospect for further development and application. The capture of incontrovertible evidence from a crime scene that leads to the identification of a suspect will lead to additional convictions, in turn leading to an increase in morale of the investigators and increased confidence from the community.

Above all, the most important foundation for an effective law enforcement strategy is the priority of an intelligence system. This is the absolutely critical investment and it should be the last element to be adjusted, which normally means reduced, according to perceptions of the threat. The absence of a system of intelligence that includes the following elements is a recipe for disaster for law enforcement agencies:

> Intelligence collection - Using both human and technical sources,
>
> A method of assessment of the raw intelligence, and
>
> A means of disseminating assessed intelligence – to those who have a *need* to know, rather than those who would *like* to know.

The reasons for this assertion are threefold. First, during times of increasing uncertainty as to the origin of the threat, it is even more important to be aware of incipient developments that may have an impact. Second, accurate intelligence provides the basis for making wise decisions about resource intensive overt operations. Third, assessed intelligence can assist contingency planning by accurately reporting whether or not insurgents, terrorists or criminals possess the capability, means, and intent to undertake specific types of attack or crime. A close working partnership between local law enforcement and national intelligence agencies is crucial to the efficient and effective management of intelligence into usable and useful evidence. A safe and secure working relationship, founded on mutual understanding of the different organizational needs and concerns, is crucial to this partnership. The absence of this understanding provides opportunities for misunderstanding, rivalry, and, at worst, enmity. The establishment of a multi-agency unit, staffed by experienced intelligence officers and police officers, who have an overarching knowledge of the roles and responsibilities of their parent organizations, engenders an atmosphere of confidence, trust, and visibility that would otherwise be absent.

Of equal importance to the collection, assessment, and dissemination of intelligence is the cohesion of the component elements of law enforcement within an integrated command and control system. The secret of cohesion is identification with the common aim: 'To protect the public and to pursue the criminal'. If the aim is clearly understood and owned, then the objective becomes more important than individual 'Formation' identity or 'Cap Badge' loyalty and there are opportunities for real achievement. The simple message is that: 'No single agency can sustain law enforcement on its own.'

Conclusion: Networking Intelligence and Law Enforcement

The traditional barriers to effective law enforcement and intelligence co-ordination and co-operation must be broken. This will require better integration of domestic and foreign intelligence. It will also demand that law enforcement agencies develop a broader understanding of intelligence and intelligence analysis. All too often, law enforcement intelligence is viewed solely as investigative support or crime analysis. Tactical case support prevails, yet operational or strategic analysis and predictive intelligence or warning intelligence is non-existent or misunderstood. This is changing and will necessarily continue to change as the threats of global organized crime and terrorism continue to morph and challenge stability. Efforts such as intelligence fusion centers, terrorism early warning groups (TEWs) in the United States, and the Criminal Intelligence Service Canada's strategic early warning system project are examples of such needed efforts at networked, distributed intelligence for serious crime and terrorism. These efforts need to be expanded and nurtured in contested regions.

Ultimately, to be effective, such intelligence efforts will need to embrace the entire range of global security threats (e.g. crime, terrorism, health risks such as pandemic, and environmental degradation) to effectively deny transnational organized crime maneuver space. Since criminal-soldiers exploit the seams between conventional structures, new and responsive structures need to link multiple crimes, across multiple jurisdictions and disciplines. This demands multilateral intelligence and law enforcement co-operation and the co-production of intelligence. The activities of transnational enterprises are dispersed and distributed among global networks, across transnational space. The formal and informal response requires similar networked structures to develop the intelligence necessary to combat such threats.[29]

Law enforcement response to criminal-states and -soldiers must build from effective policing practices for community interaction, investigation, intelligence, and enforcement. This must start locally with an eye on global trends and links. At the local level, police must actively work with the community to protect against crime and victimization. At all levels, the police must be visible, engaged community partners, actively building trust and not serving as instruments of repression and corruption. Linking professional, accountable, and democratic police and law enforcement agencies in a distributed networked fashion is also a requirement. "Because overseas criminal and terrorist support networks are beyond the territorial jurisdiction of domestic law enforcement authorities, they can evade the normal countermeasures pursued in their home countries, further contributing to international insecurity. Law enforcement is constrained by a world without borders, while international criminals and terrorists move in a borderless world."[30]

Police and law enforcement need to cooperate across and erode these borders in order to preserve the rule of law in all nations and sustain global security. Building capabilities that expand upon formal structures such as Interpol and Europol, while stimulating new multilateral connectivity and cooperation, is essential to combating these global criminal threats. These capabilities must be

29. The rationale and benefits of a distributed network to counter threats can be found in Sullivan, J. P. & Bunker, R. J. (2006) 'Multilateral Counter-Insurgency Networks', in *Networks, Terrorism and Global Insurgency*, ed. R. J. Bunker, pp. 183–198. For a detailed discussion of intelligence co-production see Sullivan, J. P. (2005) 'Terrorism Early Warning and Co-Production of Counterterrorism Intelligence', paper presented to the Canadian Association for Security and Intelligence Studies, *CASIS 20th Anniversary International Conference*, Montreal, Quebec, Canada, October 21, available at: http://www.terrorism.com/modules.php?op = modload&name = Documents&file + get&download = 432.

30. Gunaratna, R. (2006) 'The Terror Market: Networks and Enforcement in the West', *Harvard International Review*, vol. 27, no. 4, Winter, p. 69.

able to scale from local through global and back, and operate at varying stages of stability and conflict within and across boundaries. They must embrace civil society within and across normal turf and territorial divides and, to be effective, incorporate a distributed networked approach that understands cultural context and seeks cooperative approaches to operations and the co-production of intelligence to secure the emerging global security space.

Selected References

Aboul-Enein, Y. H. (2003) 'The Hezbollah Model: Using Terror and Creating a Quasi-State in Lebanon', *Marine Corps Gazette*, pp. 34-35 (June).
Adams, T. K. (1999) 'The New Mercenaries and the Privatization of Conflict', *Parameters*, vol. 24, pp. 103-116 (Summer).
Aguilar, S. (2004) 'New Security Threats in the Western Hemisphere', *USAWC Strategic Studies Institute-Florida International University Conference*, Center for Strategic and International Studies (CSIS), Washington, DC (29 June).
Ahmed, R. (2002) *Jihad: The Rise of Militant Islam in Central Asia*, Yale University Press, New Haven.
Ajami, F. (2005) 'Syria's Sopranos', Commentary', *U.S. News & World Report*, p. 57 (7 November).
bin Al-Yaman, H. (n.d.) 'The Hadiths or Sayings of the Prophet', *As-Silsilah As-Sahihah*, vol. 1, no. 5.
Arana, A. (2001) 'The New Battle for Central America', *Foreign Affairs*, pp. 88-101, (November/December).
Arana, A. (2005) 'How the Street Gangs Took Central America', *Foreign Affairs*, vol. 84, no. 3, pp. 98-110 (May/June).
Aravena, F. R. (2003) 'Nuevo contexto de seguridad internacional: nuevos desafios, nuevas oportunidades?' *La seguridad en América Latina pos 11 de Septiembre*, ed. F. R. Aravena, FLACSO-Chile, pp. 23-43.
Aristotle. (1984) *The Politics*, Lord, C. (trans), University of Chicago Press, Chicago.
Arquilla, J. & Ronfeldt, D. (eds) (1997) In *Athena's Camp: Preparing for Conflict in the Information Age*, Santa Monica, RAND.
Asher, D. L. (2005) 'The North Korean Criminal State, its Ties to Organized Crime, and the Possibility of WMD Proliferation', *Policy Forum Online*, 05-92A, [online]. Available at: www.nautilus.org (15 November).
Associated Press (2005) 'U.S. Calls North Korea 'Criminal Regime'', p. 1, [online]. Available at: www.nytimes.com (7 December).
Associated Press (2006) 'Text of Bin Laden Tape' (19 January/Released 15:43 Eastern Standard Time).
Authorization for Use of Military Force (AUMF) (2001), 115 Stat. 224.
Avant, D. D. (2005) *The Market for Force: The Consequences of Privatizing Security*, New York, Cambridge University Press.
Azzam, A. (1987) *Join the Caravan*, [online]. Available at: http:www.al-haqq.org.
Badger, A. J. (2002) *The New Deal: The Depression Years*, Ivan R. Dee, Chicago.
Baldrate, B. C. (2005) 'The Supreme Court's Role in Defining the Jurisdiction of Military Tribunals: A Study, Critique, & Proposal for *Hamdan v. Rumsfeld*', Vol. 186, pp. 1-116, [online]., Available at: http://www.loc.gov/rr/frd/Military_Law/Military_Law_Review/2005.htm (Winter).
Barnett, T. P. M. (2004) *The Pentagon's New Map: War and Peace in the Twenty-First Century*, G.P. Putnam's Sons, New York.
Barnett, T. P. M. (2005) *Blueprint for Action: A Future Worth Creating*, Putnam Adult, New York.

Bayart, J.-F., Ellis, S. & Hibou, B. (1999) *The Criminalization of the State in Africa*, eds A. de Waal & S. Ellis, African Issues Series, Indiana University Press, Bloomington.
de Becker, G. (2002) *Fear Less: Real Truth About Risk, Safety, and Security in a Time of Terrorism*, Little, Brown, New York.
Becker, J. (1984) *The PLO: The rise and fall of the Palestinian Liberation Organization*, St. Martin's Press, New York.
Bejarano, A. M. & Pizarro, E. (2003) 'Colombia: A Failing State?', *ReVista: Harvard Review of Latin America*, pp. 1-6, (Spring).
Belaunde, L. B. (1990) 'Corrupción y discomposición del Estado', *Pasta Basic de Cocaina, abuso de drogas*, eds F. R. Leon & R. C. de la Mata, CEDRO, Lima, pp. 301-321.
Bell, K. (2003) 'Hizballah fund raising in the American Heartland', *Policywatch*, no. 700, [online]. Available at: http://washingtoninstitute.org/templateC05.php?CID = 1578 (15 January).
Bell, S. (2004) *Cold Terror: How Canada nurtures and exports terrorism to the world*, John Wiley & Sons Inc., New York.
Bennett, G. (2000) *The Ministry of Internal Affairs of the Russian Federation*, CSRC, Camberley.
Bennett, J. C. (2003/2004) 'Networking Nation-States: The Coming Info-National Order', *The National Interest*, no. 74, pp. 17-30 (Winter).
Berdal, M. & Malone, D. M. (2000) *Greed & Grievance: Economic Agendas in Civil Wars*, Lynne Rienner Publishers, Boulder.
Bergen, P. L. (2006) *The Osama Bin Laden I Know: An Oral History of al Qaeda's Leader*, Free Press, New York.
Berkowitz, E. & McQuaid, K. (1988) *Creating the Welfare State: The Political Economy of Twentieth-Century Reform*, Praeger Publishers, Lawrence.
Berry, L. V. et al. (2002) *A global overview of narcotics-funded terrorist and other extremist groups*, Federal Research Division, Library of Congress, Washington, DC.
Beyerchan, A. (1992/1993) 'Clausewitz, Nonlinearity, and the Unpredictability of War', *International Security*, vol. 17, no. 3 (Winter).
Blakely, E. J. & Snyder, M. G. (1999) *Fortress America: Gated Communities in the United States*, Brookings Institution Press, Washington, DC.
Bobbitt, P. (2002) 'Get Ready for the Next Long War', *Time* (1 September).
Bobbitt, P. (2003) *The Shield of Achilles: War, Peace and the Course of History*, First Anchor Books, New York.
Bonilla, O. (2004) 'Current Situation of Gangs in El Salvador', Unpublished paper for the Consejo Nacional de Seguridad Pública, El Salvador (November).
Bowden, M. (1999) *Blackhawk Down: A Story of Modern War*, Atlantic Monthly Press, New York.
Brodie, B. (1946) *The Absolute Weapon*, Ayer Company Publishers, New Haven.
Brodie, B. (1973) *War and Politics*, The Macmillan Co, New York.
Bruce, M. (1974) *The coming of the welfare state*, Schocken, London.
Bruneau, T. C. (2005) 'The Maras and National Security in Central America', *Strategic Insights*, vol. 4, iss. 5, [online]., Available at: http://www.ccc.npps.navy.mil/si/2005/May/bruneauMay05.pdf (May).
Bundy, M. (1988) *Danger and Survival; The Political History of Nuclear Weapons*, Random House, New York.
Bunker, R. J. (1996) 'Street Gangs—Future Paramilitary Groups?', *The Police Chief*, pp. 54-59 (June).
Bunker, R. J. (1997) 'Epochal Change: War Over Social and Political Organization', *Parameters*, vol. 27, no. 2, pp. 15-25 (Summer).
Bunker, R. J. (2006) 'Combatants or Non-Combatants? Where Private Military Companies Fit in Modern, Classical and Legal Definitions', *Journal of International Peace Operations*, vol. 2, no. 1, pp. 17-18 (July/August).

Bunker, R. J. & Begert, M. (2005) 'Operational Combat Analysis of the Al Qaeda Network', in *Networks, Terrorism and Global Insurgency*, ed. R. J. Bunker, Routledge, London, pp. 146–169.
Bunker, R. J. & Sullivan, J. P. (1998) 'Cartel Evolution: Potentials and Consequences', *Transnational Organized Crime*, vol. 4, no. 2, pp. 55–74 (Summer).
Bunn, M. (2006) 'Cooperation to Secure Nuclear Stockpiles A Case of Constrained Innovation', *Innovations*, pp. 115–137 (Winter).
Bunn, M. & Wier, A. (2006) *Securing the Bomb*, Project on Managing the Atom, Belfer Center for Science and International Affairs, John F. Kennedy School of Government, Harvard University p. 27 [online]. Available at: http://www.nti.org/e_research/stb06webfull.pdf (July).
Bush, V. (1949) *Modern Arms and Free Men*, Simon and Schuster, New York.
Campbell, L. J. et al. (2005–2006) 'Beheadings in the Post-Modern Era', *Open Source Database*.
Carafano, J. & Kochems, A. (Forthcoming) 'Engaging Private Security Firms and Contractors in Counterterrorism Operations', in *Countering Terrorism in the 21st Century*, ed. J. J. F. Forest, Praeger, New York.
Cariboni, D. (2006) 'New Breed of Paramilitaries Infiltrate Urban 'Refuges'', Inter-Press Service (IPS), [online]. Available at: http://p.7.newes.re2.yahoo.com/s/oneworld/20060626/ (27 June).
Center for Nonproliferation Studies (1999) *Overview of Reported Nuclear Trafficking Incidents Involving Turkey, 1993–1999*, Monterey Institute of International Studies, Monterey, [online]. Available at: www.cns.miis.edu/research/wmdme/flow/turkey/index.htm (July).
Cilluffo, F. et al. (2006) 'Out of the Shadows: Getting Ahead of Prisoner Radicalization', *Prisoner Radicalization Task Force*, George Washington University Homeland Security Policy Institute and University of Virginia Critical Incident Analysis Group, Washington, DC.
Clapham, C. (1996) *Africa and the International System, the Politics of State Survival*, Cambridge University Press, Cambridge.
Clark, M. T. (1998) 'The Continuing Relevance of Clausewitz', *Strategic Review*, vol. 26, no. 1 (Winter).
von Clausewitz, C. (1976) *On War*, Howard, M. & Paret, P. (eds & trans), Princeton University Press, Princeton.
Cohen, K. R. (1973) *British Nationalization 1945–1973*, Macmillan, London.
Comité Central del Partido Comunista del Perú. (1986) *Desarrollar la guerra popular sirviendo a la revolución mundial*, Comité Central del Partido Comunista del Perú, Lima.
Connolly, C. P. (2003) 'The Role of Private Security in Combating Terrorism', *Journal of Homeland Security* (July).
Cornell, S. E. (2006) 'The Narcotics Threat In Greater Central Asia: From Crime-Terror Nexus to State Infiltration?', *China and Eurasia Forum Quarterly*, vol. 4, no. 1, pp. 37–67.
van Creveld, M. (1991) *The Transformation of War*, The Free Press, New York.
van Creveld, M. (1993) *Nuclear Proliferation and the Future of Conflict*, Free Press, New York.
Cuthbertson, I. (2004) 'Prisons and the Education of Terrorists', *World Policy Journal*, vol. 21, pp. 15–22 (Fall).
Daeniker, G. (1995) *The Guardian Soldier: on the Nature and Use of Future Armed Conflict*, United Nations Institute for Disarmament Research, New York.
Davies, S. (1996) *Big Brother; Britain's Web of Surveillance and the New Technological Order*, Pan Books, London.
Davis, D. E. & Kohn, W. S. G. (1977) 'Lenin's 'Notebook on Clausewitz', in *Soviet Armed Forces Review Annual*, ed. D. R. Jones, vol. 1, Academic International Press, Gulf Breeze.

Davis, M. (2004) 'The Urbanization of Empire: Megacities and the Laws of Chaos', *Social Text*, no. 81 (Winter).

Davis, M. (2006) *Planet of Slums*, Verso, New York.

Diaz, T. & Newman, B. (2005) *Lightning out of Lebanon: Hezbollah terrorists on American soil*, Ballantine Books, New York.

Dixon, R. (2006) 'Cape Town Gangs Seek Out Children', *Los Angeles Times*, [online]. Available at: http://www.latimes.com/news/nationworld/world/la-fg-gangs25sep25,1,186603.story?coll = la-headlines-world (September 25).

Dorff, R. H. (2003) 'Strategy, Grand Strategy, and the Search for Strategy', in *The Search for Security: A U.S. Grand Strategy for the Twenty-First Century*, eds. M. G. Manwaring, et al. Praeger, Westport, pp. 127–240.

Dowdney, L. (2003) *Children of the Drug Trade: A Case Study of Organized Armed Violence in Rio de Janeiro*, Viva Rio/ISER, Rio de Janeiro (7 Letras).

Dowdney, L. (2005) *neither War nor Peace: international comparisons of children and youth in organised armed violence*, COAV, Rio de Janeiro, [online]. Available at: http://www.coav.org.br.

Downie, A. (2006) 'Brazil gang takes on state', *Christian Science Monitor*, [online]. Available at: http://www.csmonitor.com/2006/0516/p06s01-woam.html (May 16).

Doyle, C. (2006) *Material Support of Terrorists and Foreign Terrorist Organizations: Sunset Amendments in Brief*, CRS Report for Congress, Order Code RS22222, [online]. Available at: http://www.fas.org/sgp/crs/terror/RS22222.pdf (Updated March 17).

Drake, R. (1995) *The Aldo Moro Murder Case*, Harvard University Press, Cambridge, MA.

Drucker, P. F. (2005) 'Trading Places', *The National Interest*, no. 79, pp. 101–107 (Spring).

East-Asia-Intel (2005) ''Soprano state': N. Korean economy called dependent on organized crime' (November 30)

The Economist (2006) 'The mob takes on the state' (20 May).

The Economist (2006) 'Nasrallah wins the war', p. 9 (19 August).

The Economist (2006) 'The revenge of the bell curve', pp. 20, 22 (7 October).

The Economist (2006) 'Meritocracy and its discontents' pp. 23–24, (7 October).

Engels, F. (1991 [1844]) *The Condition of the Working Class in England*, Electric Book Company, London.

Esty, D. C. et al. (1998) 'The State Failure Project: Early Warning Research for U.S. Foreign Policy Planning', in *Preventive Measures: Building Risk Assessment and Crisis Early Warning Systems*, eds J. L. Davies & T. R. Gurr, Rowman & Littlefield, New York.

Executive Order 9066: The Internment of 110,000 Japanese Americans (1942), [online]. Available at: http://www.sscnet.ucla.edu/aasc/ex9066/.

Farah, D. (2001) 'Al Qaeda cash tied to diamond trade: Sale of gems from Sierra Leone rebels raised millions, sources say', *Washington Post*, [online]. Available at: http://www.washingtonpost.com/ac2/wpdyn?pagename=article&node=&contentId=-A27281-2001Nov1 (2 November).

Farah, D. (2001) 'Digging up Congo's dirty gems', *Washington Post*, [online]. Available at: http://www.globalpolicy.org/security/issues/diamond/2001/1230hezbol.htm (30 December).

Farah, D. (2004) *Blood from stones: The secret financial network of terror*, Broadway Books, New York.

Fenzi, E. (1987) *Armi e bagagli: un diario dalle Brigate Rosse*, Costa & Nolan, Genoa.

Finckenauer, J. & Voronin, Y. (2001) *The Threat of Russian Organized Crime*, US Department of Justice, National Institute of Justice, Washington, DC.

Fishel, J. T. & Grizzard, M. (2005) 'Countering Ideological Support to Terrorism in the Circum-Caribbean', *CSRC Discussion Paper 05/52* (September).

Fishel, J. T. & Manwaring, M. G. (2006) 'The Central Political Challenge in the Global Security Environment: Governance and Legitimacy', *Uncomfortable Wars Revisited*, University of Oklahoma Press, Norman, pp. 55–70.

Fisher, M. (2005) *Military Tribunals & Presidential Power*, University of Kansas Press, Lawrence.
Flora, P. et al. (eds) (1983) *State, Economy and Society in Western Europe, 1875-1975*, St. James Press, London.
Flora, P. & Heidenheimer, A. J. (eds) (1981) *The Development of Welfare States in Europe and America*, Transaction Publishers, New Brunswick.
Flynn, S. E. (1993) *The Transnational Drug Challenge and the New World Order*, Center for Strategic and International Studies, Washington, DC.
Frank, S. (1999) *Crime, Cultural Conflict, and Justice in Rural Russia, 1856-1914*, University of California Press, Berkeley.
Freeman, R. A. (1975) *The Growth of American Government; A Morphology of the Welfare State*, Hoover Institute Press, Stanford.
Friedman, L. (1981) *The Evolution of Nuclear Strategy*, St. Martin's Press, New York.
Frierson, C. (1987) 'Crime and punishment in the Russian village', *Slavic Review*, vol. 46, no. 1.
Fukuyama, F. (1991) *The End of History*, Avon Books, New York.
Furnish, T. (2002) 'Bin Laden: The Man Who Would be Mahdi', *The Middle East Quarterly*, [online]. Available at: http://www.meforum.org (Spring).
Furnish, T. (2005) 'Beheading in the Name of Islam', *Middle East Quarterly*, vol. 7, no. 2, pp. 3-4 (Spring).
Galeotti, M. (2001) ''Who's the boss, us or the law?' The corrupt art of governing Russia', in *Bribery and Blat in Russia*, eds. S. Lovell et al., Macmillan, Basingstoke.
Galeotti, M. (2001) 'The challenge of "soft security": crime, corruption and chaos', in *Securing Europe's East: new security challenges in postcommunist Europe*, eds D. Averre & A. Cottey, Manchester University Press, Manchester.
Galeotti, M. (ed.) (2001) *Russian and Post-Soviet Organised Crime*, Ashgate, London.
Galeotti, M. (2002) 'Kaliningrad at the Crossroads', *Jane's Intelligence Review*, vol. 14, no. 8.
Galeotti, M. (2002) 'Underworld and Upperworld: Transnational Organized Crime and Global Society', in *Non-State Actors in World Politics*, eds W. Wallace & D. Josselin, Palgave Macmillan, New York.
Galeotti, M. (2003) 'Russian police reform: centralisation, modernisation and Paramilitarisation', *Crime & Justice International*, no. 70.
Gellner, E. (1983) *Nations and Nationalism*, Cornell University Press, Ithaca, *Geneva Convention (III) Relative to the Treatment of Prisoners of War* (12 August, 1949 [1955]) 6 U.S.T. 3316, T.I.A.S. No. 3364 (Third Geneva Convention).
Giap, Gen. V. N. (1961) *People's War, People's Army: The Viet Cong Insurrection Manual for Underdeveloped Countries*, Foreign Languages Publishing House, Hanoi [Frederick A. Praeger, New York, 1962].
Gilbert, N. & Gilbert, B. (1989) *The Enabling State; Modern Welfare Capitalism in America*, Oxford University Press, New York.
Glazier, D. (2005) 'Precedents Lost: The Neglected History of the Military Commission', in 'The Laws of War: Past, Present, and Future' *Virginia Journal of International Law*, vol. 46, no. 1 (Fall).
Global Witness (2003) *For a few dollars more: How al Qaeda moved into the diamond trade*, [online]. Available at: http://www.globalwitness.org/reports/show.php/en.00041.html
Goldberg, J. (2000) 'Inside Jihad U.; The Education of a Holy Warrior', *New York Times Magazine* (25 June).
Golunov, S. (n.d.) *Transngranichnaia prestupnost' v zone iuzhnykh postsovetskikh rubezhei rossii: Sotsialnye i politicheskie aspekty problemy*, Transnational Crime and Corruption Center (TraCCC) at American University pp. 1-95, [online]. Available at: http://www.american.edu/traccc/resources/publications/goluno02.pdf

Greenfield, A. (2003) *The minimal compact: A minifesto for virtual states*, [online]. Available at: www.v-2.org (25 February).
Griffith, I. L. (1997) *Drugs and Security in the Caribbean: Sovereignty Under Siege*, Pennsylvania State University Press, University Park.
Grossman, Lt. Col. D. (2004) *On Combat*, with Christensen, L.W., PPCT Research Publications, Belleville.
Guevara, C. (1961) *Guerrilla Warfare*, Monthly Review Press, New York.
Gunaratna, R. (2002) *Inside Al-Qaeda*, Columbia University Press, New York.
Guzmán, A. (1985) 'El Discurso del Dr. Guzmán', in *Los partidos políticos en el Perú*, ed. R. Mercado, Ediciones Latinoamericanos, Lima.
Haas, E. B. (1968) *The Uniting of Europe: Political, Social and Economic Forces, 1950-1957*, Stanford University Press, Stanford.
Hagedorn, J. M. (2005) 'The Global Impact of Gangs', *Journal of Contemporary Criminal Justice*, vol. 21, no. 2 (May).
Hajjar, S. G. (2002) *Hizballah: Terrorism, national liberation, or menace?*, Strategic Studies Institute, US Army War College, Carlisle [online]. Available at: http://www.carlisle.army.mil/ssi/pubs/2002/hizbala/hizbala.htm (August).
Hammond, J. D. (ed.) (1999) *The Legacy of Milton Friedman*, Edward Elgar Publishing, Cheltenham.
Hamzeh, A. H. (2004) *In the path of Hizbullah*, Syracuse University Press, Syracuse.
Handel, M. I. (1986) *Clausewitz and Modern Strategy*, Frank Cass, London.
Harik, J. P. (2004) *Hezbollah: The changing face of terrorism*, I.B. Tauris & Co Ltd., New York.
Hart, B. H. L. (1967) *Strategy*, 2nd ed, Frederick A. Praeger, New York.
Hazim, H. (2005) *American Realism Revisited, Lethal Minds & Latent Threats*, Iuniverse, Lincoln (October).
Hendawi, H. (2006) 'Insurgents post videos of three beheadings', *The Washington Times* (11 June).
Henriksen, T. H. (2001) 'The Rise and Decline of Rogue States', *Journal of International Affairs*, 2001, vol. 54, no. 2, pp. 349-373 (Spring).
Hetherington, C. J. (2004) *Private Security as an Essential Component of Homeland Security*, Master's Thesis, Naval Postgraduate School, Monterey (June).
Hobsbawm, E. J. (1969) *Bandits*, Weidenfeld & Nicolson, London.
Horgan, J. & Taylor, M. (1999) *Playing the Green Card: Financing the Provisional IRA, Part 1. Terrorism and Political Violence*, vol. 11, no. 2, pp. 1-36 (Summer).
Howard, M. (1981) 'The Forgotten Dimensions of Strategy', *The Causes of War*, Temple-Smith, London.
Hudson, R. (2003) *Terrorist and organized crime groups in the Tri-Border Area (TBA) of South America*, Federal Research Division, Library of Congress, Washington, DC.
Human Rights Watch (2004) *The Wrongs of Passage: Inhuman and Degrading Treatment of New Recruits in the Russian Armed Forces*, [online]. Available at: http://hrw.org/reports/2004/russia1004/index.htm
Huntington, S. (1996) *The Clash of Civilizations and the Remaking of World Order*, Simon & Schuster, New York.
International Crime Threat Assessment (2000) 'Chapter V: The Future of International Crime', US Government Printing Office, Washington, DC (December).
Irish, J. (1999) *Policing for Profit: The future of South Africa's Private Security Industry*, ed. M. Schönteich, Monograph no. 39, Institute for Security Studies, [online]. Available at: http://www.iss.co.za/Pubs/Monographs/No39/Contents.html (August).
Islam and Beheading (2005), [online]. Available at: www.muhammadism.org (April).
Jackson, P. (2004) 'Legacy of Bitterness: Insurgency in North West Rwanda', *Small Wars & Insurgencies*, pp. 19-37 (Spring).

Jaffa, H. V. (2000) 'What is Politics? An Interpretation of Aristotle's *Politics*', *The Conditions of Freedom: Essays in Political Philosophy*, The Claremont Institute, Claremont.
Janes, R. (2005) *Losing Our Heads: Beheadings in Literature and Culture*, New York University Press, New York.
Johnson, S. & Muhlhausen, D. B. (2005) 'North American Transnational Youth gangs: Breaking the Chain of Violence', *Backgrounder*, no. 1834, Heritage Foundation, Washington, DC (21 March).
Jones, R. H. (2005) *Terrorist Beheadings: Cultural and Strategic Implications*, Strategic Studies Institute, US Army War College, Carlisle (June).
Jones, S. G. et al. (2001) *Establishing Law and Order After Conflict*, RAND, Santa Monica.
Jordan, Amb. D. C. (1999) *Drug Politics: Dirty Money and Democracies*, University of Oklahoma Press, Norman.
Kaplan, D. E. (2003) 'Homegrown terrorists: How a Hezbollah cell made millions in sleepy Charlotte, N.C', *U.S. News and World Report*, [online]. Available at: http://www.usnews.com?usnews/news/articles/030310/10hez.htm (10 March).
Kaplan, R. D. (2000) *The Coming Anarchy*, Random House, New York.
Kazmias, A. M. (1966) *Politics, Society and Secondary Education in England*, University of Pennsylvania Press, Philadelphia.
Keegan, J. (1994) *A History of Warfare*, Alfred A. Knopf, New York.
Kennedy, P. (1987) *The Rise and Fall of the Great Powers*, Vintage, New York.
Kennedy-Boudali, L. et al. (2006) *The Islamic Imagery Project: Visual Motifs in Jihadi Internet Propaganda*, Combating Terrorism Center, United States Military Academy, West Point.
Khinshteyn, A. (1991) '15, 000,000 $ dlya Basayeva' ($15,000,000 for Basayev), *Moskovskiy Komsomolets* (20 November).
Khomeini, R. (2001) *Velayate Faqeeh* (Governance of the Jurist), Algar, H. (trans), Institute for Compilation and Publication of Imam Khomeini's Works, International Affairs Division, Iran.
King, L. (2006) 'Much Soul-Searching Ahead for Israeli Army', *Los Angeles Times*, p. A9 (Sunday, 27 August).
Klein, M. W. (1995) *The American Street Gang*, Oxford University Press, New York.
Kukhianidze, A. et al. (2004) *Smuggling Through Abkhazia and Tskinvali Region of Georgia*, TraCCC, American University, Georgia: Polygraph, Ltd., Tbilsi, [online]. Available at: http://www.traccc.cdn.ge/publications/index.html
Kupatadze, A. et al. (2007) 'Policing and Police Reform in Georgia', in *Organised Crime and Corruption in Georgia*, eds. L. I. Shelley, Routledge, London.
bin Laden, O. (1996) 'Declaration of War Against the Americans Who Occupy the Land of the Two Holy Mosques', [online]. Available at: www.Islamic-news.co.uk (23 August).
bin Laden, U. (1996) 'The New Powder Keg in the Middle East', *Nida'ul Islam*, iss. 15 (October/November).
bin Laden, O. (1998) 'International Islamic Front for Jihad Against the Jews and Crusaders', [online]. Available at: www.pbs.org (22 February).
bin Laden, U. (1998) 'Jihad against Jews and Crusaders', World Islamic Front Statement (23 February).
bin Laden, O. (2002) 'Feast of the Sacrifice', *Middle East Media Research Institute*, no. 476 [online]. Available at: www.memri.org (5 March).
bin Laden, O. (2002) 'Will', *Al-Majallah*, London, [online]. Available at: www.fas.org (2 November).
bin Laden, O. (2002) 'bin Laden's "letter to America"', *The Observer*, [online]. Available at: www.observer.co.uk (24 November).

Lahneman, W. J. (2000) 'Summary of Proceedings', *Conference on the Evolution of the Nation-State Through 2015*, University of Maryland, College Park [online]. Available at: www.cissm.und.edu (18 April).

Lake, A. (1994) 'Confronting Backlash States', *Foreign Affairs*, vol. 73, no. 2, pp. 45-55 (Spring).

Laqueur, W. (1999) *The New Terrorism*, Oxford University Press, Oxford.

Lee III, R. W. (1990) *The White Labyrinth*, Transaction, New Brunswick.

Lee, R. W. (1998) *Smuggling Armageddon: The Nuclear Black Market in the Former Soviet Union and Europe*, St. Martin's Press, New York.

Lee, R. (2006) 'Nuclear Smuggling, Rogue States and Terrorists', *The China and Eurasia Forum Quarterly*, vol. 4, no. 2 (May).

Lee, R. (2006) *Reappraising Nuclear Security Strategy, Policy Analysis*, Cato Institute, no. 571, [online]. Available at: htttp://www.cato.org/pubs/pas/pa571.pdf (14 June).

Lincoln, A. (1861) *Suspension of the Writ of Habeas Corpus Relating to the Events in Baltimore, 1861*, With Winfield Scott. Headquarters of the Army, Washington [online]. Available at: http://www.civilwarhome.com/Writ.htm (27 April).

Litwak, R. S. (2000) 'A Look at Rogue States: A Handy Label but a Lousy Policy', *The Washington Post* (20 February).

Litwak, R. S. (2001) 'What's in a Name? The Changing Foreign Policy Lexicon', *Journal of International Affairs*, vol. 54, no. 2, pp. 375-392 (Spring).

Logan, S. (2006) 'Brazil's P.C.C.: True Power Behind the Violence', *PINR: Power and Internet Report*, [online]. Available at: http://www.pinr.com/report.php?ac ± view_printable&report_id=495&language_id=1 (24 May).

Logan, S. & Bain, B. (2006) 'Street gangs, a transnational security threat', *ISN Security Watch*, [online]. Available at: http://www.isn.ethz.ch/news/sw/details.cfm?id=14715 (8 February).

Logan, S. & Bain, B. (2006) 'Recruitment, redemption in the MS-13', *ISN Security Watch*, [online]. Available at: http://www.isn.ethz.ch/news/sw/details.cfm?id = 14778 (14 February).

Lopez, R. J., Connell, R. & Kraul, C. (2005) 'MS-13: An International Franchise: Gang Uses Deportation to its Advantage to Flourish in U.S', *Los Angeles Times*, [online]. Available at: http://www.latimes.com/news/local/la-me-gang/30Oct30,0,6717943.story?coll = la-home-headlines (October 30).

Londono, J. & Guerrero, R. (1999) 'Violencia en América Latina: epidemiología y costos', IADB Working Paper, no. R-375, [online]. Available at: http://www.iadb.org/res/publications/pubfiles/pubR-375.pdf (August).

Luk'yanov, I. & Kazanskaya, O. (1999) 'Kakiye lyudi bez okhrany' (What Kind of People Are Without Protection?), *Profile*, vol. 45, no. 167 [online]. Available at: http://www.profile.ru (November).

Luttwak, E. N. (1995) 'Towards Post-heroic Warfare', *Foreign Affairs* (May/June).

Machiavelli, N. (1965) *The Art of War*, DaCapo Press, New York.

Mackinlay, J. (2002) *Globalisation and Insurgency*, The International Institute for Strategic Studies, London.

Madani, B. (2002) 'Hezbollah's global finance network: The triple frontier', *Middle East Intelligence Bulletin*, vol. 4, no. 1 [online]. Available at: http://www.meib.org/articles/0201_12.htm.

Maguire, K. (1993) 'Fraud, Extortion and Racketeering: the Black Economy in Northern Ireland', *Crime, Law and Social Change*, vol. 20, no. 4, pp. 273-292 (November).

Mansbach, R. W., Ferguson, Y. H. & Lampert, D. E. (1976) *The Web of World Politics, Nonstate Actors in the Global System*, Prentice Hall, Englewood Cliffs.

Mantle, P. J. (2004) *The Missile Defense Equation*, AIAA, Washington, DC.

Manwaring, M. G. (1998) 'Italian Terrorism, 1968-1982: Strategic Lessons That Should Have Been Learned', *Low Intensity Conflict & Law Enforcement*, pp. 121-135 (Summer).

Manwaring, M. G. (2005) *Street Gangs: The New Urban Insurgency*, US Army War College, Strategic Studies Institute, Carlisle (March).
Manwaring, M. G. & Fishel, J. T. (1992) 'Insurgency and Counterinsurgency: Toward a New Analytical Approach', *Small Wars & Insurgencies*, pp. 272–305 (Winter).
Maritain, J. (1951) *Man and the State*, University of Chicago Press, Chicago.
Marks, T. A. (2003) 'Urban Insurgency', *Small Wars & Insurgencies* (Autumn).
McCarthy, D. (2003) *Narco-terrorism: International drug trafficking and terrorism-A dangerous mix*, Hearing before the Committee on the Judiciary United States Senate, 108th cong, 1st sess, Government Printing Office, Washington, DC, [online]. Available at: http://www.state.gov/p/inl/rls/rm/21129.htm (23 May).
Mead, G. H. (1934) *Mind, Self, and Society*, University of Chicago Press, Chicago.
Menahem, M. (2004) 'Reform vs. Islamism in the Arab World Today', *The Middle East Research Institute*, Special Report, no. 34, [online]. Available at: http:www.memri.org (15 September).
Miller, M. M. (ed.) (1907) *Life and Works of Abraham Lincoln (centenary edition)*, [online]. Available at: http://ehistory.osu.edu/uscw/library/books/lincoln/index.cfm.
Milward, A. S. (1984) *The Reconstruction of Western Europe, 1945–1951*, Methuen, London.
Minnero, P. (2002) 'Rogue States—State Sponsors of Terrorism?', *German Law Journal*, pp. 1–8, [online]. Available at: www.germanlawjournal.com (September).
Morabito, A. & Greenberg, S. (2005) *Engaging the Private Sector to Promote Homeland Security: Law Enforcement-Private Security Partnerships*, NCJ 210678, US Department of Justice, Bureau of Justice Assistance, Washington, DC, [online]. Available at: http://www.ncjrs.gov/pdffiles1/bja/210678.pdf(September).
Moran, S. E. (ed.) (1986) *A Rand Note: Court Depositions of Three Red Brigadists*, RAND, Santa Monica (February).
Mosse, G. L. (1975) *The Nationalization of the Masses*, Howard Fertig, New York.
Naim, N. (2005) *Illicit: How Smugglers, Traffickers and Copycats are Hijacking the Global Economy*, Doubleday, New York.
Naji, A. B. (2006) *Management of Savagery: The Most Critical Stage Through Which the Umma Must Pass*, McCants, W. (trans), John M. Olin, Institute for Strategic Studies, Harvard University (23 May).
Nasr, V. (2006) 'When the Shiites Rise', *Foreign Affairs*, [online]. Available at: http://www.foreign affairs.org (July/August).
Nasser, G. (1955) *Egypt's Liberation: The Philosophy of the Revolution*, Public Affairs Press, Washington.
National Memorial Institute for the Prevention of Terrorism (2006) 'Legal case profiles: 00-CR-147', *Terrorism Knowledge Base*, [online]. Available at: http://www.tkb.org/CaseHome.jsp?caseid=615 (11 July).
Naylor, R. T. (1993) 'The Insurgent Economy: Black Market Operations of Guerrilla Organizations', *Crime, Law and Social Change*, vol. 20, no. 1, pp. 13–51 (July).
Nemeth, C. P. (2004) *Private Security and the Law*, Butterworth-Heinemann, Boston.
News24 (2004) 'Haiti 'could be criminal state'', (US Senate), [online]. Available at: www.haiti-info.com (September 26).
Noble, R. K. (2003) *The Links Between Intellectual Property Crime and Terrorist Financing*, Hearing before the Committee on International Relations, House of Representatives, 108th cong, 1st sess, [online]. Available at: http://wwwc.house.gov/international_relations/108/nob0716.htm (16 July).
Office of the Press Secretary, The White House (2002) 'President Delivers State of the Union Address', [online]. Available at: www.whitehouse.gov(29 January).
Office of the Press Secretary, The White House (2006) 'President's Address to the Nation', [online]. Available at: www.whitehouse.gov (11 September).

Olson, W. J. (1997) 'International Organized Crime: The Silent Threat to Sovereignty', *The Fletcher Forum* (Summer-Fall).
'Opening Statement by Secretary General Lord Robertson at the Informal Meeting of the North Atlantic Council at the Level of Defence Ministers' (2002) *NATO Speeches*, p. 1, [online]. Available at: www.NATO.int (24 September).
Orbach, B. (2001) 'Usama bin Laden and al-Qa'ida: Origins and Doctrines', *Middle East Review of International Affairs*, vol. 5, no. 4, [online]. Available at: http://meria.idc.ac.il (December).
Orlando, F. (ed.) (1980) *Siamo en Guerra*, Armando, Rome.
'Draft Declaration on Security in the Americas' (2003) Approved by the Permanent Council of the Organization of American States at its regular session, Mexico City (22 October).
'Para-States - Scope Note' (n.d.), [online]. Available at: www.fas.org.
Paret, P. (ed.) (1986) *Makers of Modern Strategy: From Machiavelli to the Nuclear Age*, Princeton University Press, Princeton.
Pellet, A. (1999) 'Can a State Commit a Crime? Definitely, Yes!', *European Journal of International Law*, vol. 10, no. 2, [online]. Available at: www.ejil.org.
Perito, R. (2006) 'Policing Iraq: Protecting Iraqis from Criminal Violence', *USIPeace Briefing*, United States Institute of Peace, p. 0, [online]. Available at: http://www.usip.org/pubs/usipeace_briefings/2006/0629_policing_iraq.html (June).
Perry, T. (2005) 'Fallouja Insurgents Fought under Influence of Drugs, Marines Say', *Los Angeles Times*, p. A6 (Thursday, 13 January).
Peters, R. (2006) 'Survival strategy: Middle Eastern Islam, Darwin and terrorism', *Armed Forces Journal International*, vol. 143, no. 7, pp. 42-44 (February).
Petrov, N. (2005) 'Siloviki in Russian Regions: new dogs, old tricks', *The Journal of Power Institutions in Post-Soviet Societies* (February).
Pisano, V. S. (1982) 'Libya's Foothold in Italy', *The Washington Quarterly*, pp. 179-182 (Spring).
Pisano, V. S. (1987) *The Dynamics of Subversion and Violence in Contemporary Italy*, Stanford University, Hoover Institution Press, Stanford.
Polgatti, A. C. (2004) *Conflicto y Guerra en la Post Modernidad*, Mago Editores, Santiago.
Pollard, N. A. (2002) 'Globalization's Bastards: Illegitimate Non-State Actors in International Law', in *Low Intensity Conflict & Law Enforcement*, vol. 11, no. 2/3 (Winter), ed. R. J. Bunker, Special issue on 'Networks, Terrorism and Global Insurgency'.
della Porta, D. (1995) 'Left-Wing Terrorism in Italy', in *Terrorism in Context*, ed. M. Crenshaw, Pennsylvania State University Press, University Park.
Porter, B. D. (1994) *War and the Rise of the State*, Free Press, New York.
Providing Appropriate Tools Required to Intercept and Obstruct Terrorism (PATRIOT) Act of 2001 (2001) Pub. L. 107-56, 115 Stat. 272 (26 October).
Pyadushkin, M. with Haug M. & Matveeva, A. (2003) *Beyond the Kalashnikov: small arms production, exports and stockpiles in the Russian Federation*, CAST/SaferWorld, Geneva.
Radu, M. (2005) 'Europe, Fall 2005: Gangs in Search of an Ideology', *Watch on the West*, Foreign Policy Research Institute, vol. 6, no. 7 [online]. Available at: http://www.fpri.org/ww/0607.200511.radu.eurpopegangs.html (August).
Rapley, J. (2006) 'The New Middle Ages', *Foreign Affairs*, vol. 85, no. 3, pp. 95-103 (May/June).
'Le due anime delle Br' (Declaration of Red Brigades). (1987) Sent to *L'Expresso* (1 March).
Replogle, J. (2005) 'In Guatemala, a rise in vigilante justice', *Christian Science Monitor* (6 October).
Richardson, J. (2005) *Paradise Poisoned: Learning about Conflict, Terrorism and Development from Sri Lanka's Civil Wars*, International Centre for Ethnic Studies, Colombo.

Robb, J. (2006) 'Security: Power To The People', *FastCompany*, iss. 103, [online]. Available at: http://www.fastcompany.com/magazine/103 (March).
Robb, J. (2007) *Brave New War*, Wiley, New York (Spring).
Rosenthal, J. (2006) 'Business Bombs: The Rise of Terrorism-for-Profit', *The American Interest*, vol. 1, no. 4, pp. 28–32 (Summer).
Rotella, S. (1997) *Twilight on the Line: Underworlds and Politics at the U.S.-Mexico Border*, W.W. Norton & Company, New York.
Saad-Ghorayeb, A. (2002) *Hizbu'llah: Politics and religion*, Pluto Press, Sterling.
Salmi, R. H., Majul, C. A. & Tanham, G. K. (eds) (1998) *Islam and Conflict Resolution*, University Press of America, Lanham.
Sassen, S. (2005) 'The Global City: Introducing a Concept', *Brown Journal of World Affairs*, vol. 9, iss. 2 (Winter/Spring).
Sassen, S. (2005) *Denationalization: Territory, Authority and Rights in a Global Digital Age*, Princeton University Press, Princeton.
Satter, A. (2003) *Darkness at Dawn: The Rise of the Russian Criminal State*, Yale University Press, New Haven.
Scammell, W. M. (1983) *The International Economy Since 1945*, Macmillan, London.
Schluenes, K. A. (1989) *Schooling and Society; The Politics of Education in Prussia and Bavaria, 1750–1900*, Berg Publishers, Oxford.
Shelley, L. (2005) 'Unraveling the New Criminal Nexus', *Georgetown Journal of International Affairs*, pp. 5–13 (Winter/Spring).
Shelley, L. (2005) 'The Unholy Trinity: Transnational Crime, Corruption and Terrorism', *Brown Journal of International Affairs*, vol. 11, no. 2, pp. 101–111 (Winter-Spring).
Shelley, L. et al. (2005) *Methods and Motives: Exploring Links Between Transnational Crime and International Terrorism*, National Institute of Justice, US Department of Justice (23 June).
Singer, P. W. (2004) *Corporate Warriors: The Rise of the Privatized Military Industry*, Cornell University Press, Ithaca.
Singer, P. W. (2005) *Children at War*, Pantheon Books, New York.
Smith, S. B. (1983) 'Hegel's Views on War, the State and International Relations', *American Political Science Review*, vol. 77 (September).
Spencer, D. (2001) *Colombia's Paramilitaries: Criminals or Political Force?*, US Army War College, Strategic Studies Institute, Carlisle (December).
Staar, R. (1998) 'Russia's military: corruption in the higher ranks', *Perspective*, vol. 9, no. 2.
Stedman, J. C. (2005) *Counterfeit goods: Easy cash for criminals and terrorists*, Hearing before the Committee on Homeland Security and Governmental Affairs, United States Senate, 109th cong, 1st sess, Government Printing Office, Washington, DC, [online]. Available at: http://hsgac.senate.gov/_files/TestimonyStedman.pdf (25 May).
Stephenson, N. (1992) *Snow Crash*, Bantam Books, New York.
Stirk, P. M. R. (1996) *A History of European Integration since 1914*, Pinter, London.
Sullivan, J. P. (1997) 'Third Generation Street Gangs: Turf, Cartels, and NetWarriors', *Crime & Justice International*, vol. 13, no. 10, Article 688, 8 pp, [online]. Available at: http://158.135.23.21/cjcweb/college/cji/index.cfm?ID=688 (October/November) .
Sullivan, J. P. (1997) 'Third Generation Street Gangs: Turf, Cartels, and Net Warriors', *Transnational Organized Crime*, vol. 3, no. 3, pp. 95–108 (Autumn).
Sullivan, J. P. (2000) 'Urban Gangs Evolving as Criminal Netwar Actors', *Small Wars and Insurgencies*, vol. 11, no. 1, pp. 82–96 (Spring).
Sullivan, J. P. (2001) 'Gangs, Hooligans, and Anarchists—The Vanguard of Netwar in the Streets', in *Networks and Netwars: The Future of Terror, Crime, and Militancy*, eds J. Arquilla & D. Ronfeldt, RAND, Santa Monica, pp. 99–126.

Sullivan, J. P. (2002) 'Terrorism, Crime and Private Armies', in *Low Intensity Conflict & Law Enforcement*, vol. 11, no. 2/3 ed. R. J. Bunker, Special issue on 'Networks, Terrorism and Global Insurgency', pp. 239–253, (Winter).

Sullivan, J. P. (2005) 'Terrorism Early Warning and Co-Production of Counterterrorism Intelligence', paper presented to the Canadian Association for Security and Intelligence Studies, *CASIS 20th Anniversary International Conference*, Montreal, [online]. Available at: http://www.terrorism.com/modules.php?op=modload&name=Documents&file ± get&download=432 (21 October).

Sullivan, J. P. (2005) 'Child Soldiers: Warriors of Despair', *Small Wars Journal*, vol. 2, [online]. Available at: http://www.smallwarsjournal.com/documents/swjmag/v2/sullivan.htm (July).

Sullivan, J. P. (2006) 'Establishing the Rule of Law/CivPol', *Countering Insurgency and Promoting Democracy*, Council for Emerging National Security Affairs (CENSA), Washington, DC (Forthcoming).

Sullivan, J. P. & Bunker, R. J. (2002) 'Drug Cartels, Street Gangs, and Warlords', in *Small Wars and Insurgencies*, vol. 13, no. 2, ed. R. J. Bunker, Special issue on 'Non-State Threats and Future Wars', pp. 40–53 (Summer).

Sullivan, J. P. & Bunker, R. J. (2002) 'Multilateral Counter-Insurgency Networks', in *Low Intensity Conflict & Law Enforcement*, vol. 11, no. 2/3, ed. R. J. Bunker, Special issue on 'Networks, Terrorism and Global Insurgency', pp. 353–368 (Winter).

Testrake, J. (1987) *Triumph over terror on Flight 847*, Fleming H. Revell Company, Old Tappan.

Thompson, J. (2002) 'Is There Such a Thing as a Rogue State?', *The Centre for Applied Philosophy and Public Ethics Working Paper*, no. 8, University of Melbourne, Melbourne, [online]. Available at: www.cappe.edu.au.

Tilly, C. (1992) *Coercion, Capital and European States, AD 990–1992*, Blackwell, Oxford.

Trac Reports (2006) *Criminal Terrorism Enforcement in the United States During the Five years Since the 9/11/01 Attacks*, Transactional Records Access Clearinghouse, Syracuse.

Trial of the Major War Criminals Before the International Military Tribunal (IMT) (1945–1946) Nuremberg, [online]. Available at: http://www.archives.gov/iwg/research-papers/trial-of-war-criminals-before-imt.html (14 November–1 October).

Tse-tung, M. (1961) *On Guerrilla Warfare*, Griffith, S.B. (trans) Frederick A. Praeger, New York.

Tstung, M. (1972) *Six Essays on Military Affairs*, Foreign Language Press, Peking.

Turbiville, G. (1995) 'Organized crime and the Russian armed forces', *Transnational Organized Crime*, vol. 1, no. 4.

Tzu, S. (1977) *The Art of War*, Griffith, S.B. (trans), Oxford University Press, London.

UN General Assembly (2000) *Crime prevention and criminal justice*, [online]. Available at: http://www.uncjin.org/Documents/Conventions/dcatoc/final_documents/383e.pdf,(2 November).

Uniform Code of Military Justice (UCMJ) (1951) 10 U.S.C. § 801 et seq.

US Agency for International Development (2006) *Central America and Mexico Gang Assessment*, Bureau for Latin American and Caribbean Affairs, Office of Regional Sustainable Development, Washington, DC (April).

US Department of Justice, United States Attorney, Eastern District of Michigan (2006) 'Nineteen charged with racketeering to support terrorist organization', Press Release, [online]. Available at: http://www.usdoj.gov/usao/mie/press/mar_2006.pdf (29 March).

US Department of Justice, United States Attorney, Eastern District of Michigan (2006) 'Two men plead guilty to racketeering', Press Release, [online]. Available at: http://www.usdoj.gov/usao/mie/press/2006/2006-07-10_ihamadeh.pdf (7 July).

US Department of State (2005) *Trafficking in Persons Report 2004*, Washington, DC.

US Department of State (2005) *Country reports on terrorism 2005*, Washington, DC, [online]. Available at: http://www.state.gov/s/ct/rls/crt/c17689.htm.

US Department of State (2006) *Honduras: Country Reports on Human Rights Practices-2005*, Bureau of Democracy, Human Rights, and Labor, Washington, DC (8 March).

US Department of State (2006) *Guadalajara, Mexico: 2006 Crime and Safety Report*. Overseas Advisory Council, Washington, DC, [online]. Available at: http://www.osac.gov/Reports/report.cfm?contentID=45279 (20 April).

US Department of the Treasury (2004) 'Treasury designates Islamic Extremist, two companies supporting Hizballah in Tri-Border Area', Press Release, [online]. Available at: http://www.treas.gov/press/releases/js1720.htm (June 10).

US Drug Enforcement Administration (2002) 'More than 100 arrested in nationwide methamphetamine investigation', News Release, [online]. Available at: http://www.dea.gov/pubs/pressrel/pr011002.html (10 January).

US Drug Enforcement Administration (2002) *DEA Update, 1 (01)*, [online]. Available at: http://www.Usdoj.gov/dea/pubs/update/012302.html (23 January).

US Federal Bureau of Investigation (n.d.) *Operation "Smokescreen"* FBI dismantles terrorist financial support cell, Press Release, Washington, DC, [online]. Available at: http://www.fbi.gov/page2/smokescreen2.htm.

US Government Accounting Office (2003) 'Terrorist financing: U.S. agencies should systematically assess terrorists' use of alternative financing mechanisms', Washington, DC, [online]. Available at: http://www.gao.gov/new.items/d04163.pdf.

US Library of Congress Federal Research Division (2002) *Involvement of Russian Organized Crime Syndicates, Criminal Elements in the Russian Military, and Regional Terrorist Groups in Narcotics Trafficking in Central Asia, the Caucasus, and Chechnya*, Washington, DC.

US Library of Congress Federal Research Division (2003) *Nations Hospitable to Organized Crime and Terrorism*, Washington, DC.

US National Intelligence Council (2006) *Trends in Global Terrorism: Implications for the United States (U)*, National Intelligence Estimate (NIE 20006-02D), Washington, DC, [online]. Available at: www.dni.gov/press_releases/cover.pdf (April).

Vardalis, J. J. (1992) 'Privatization of Public Police', *Security Journal*, vol. 3, no. 4, pp. 210-214.

Varese, F. (2001) *The Russian Mafia*, OUP, Oxford.

Vartabedian, R. et al. (2006) 'Rise in Bribery Tests Integrity of U.S. Border', *Los Angeles Times*, Monday, pp. A1, A16-A17 (23 October).

Waszink, C. (2000) *Security and Development Brief: Guatemala*. Program on Security and Development, Monterey, [online]. Available at: http://sand.miis.edu/research/2000/may2000/guatebrief.pdf.

Watkin, K. (2005) *Warriors without Rights? Combatants, Unprivileged Belligerents, and the Struggle over Legitimacy*, No. 2, Program on Humanitarian Policy and Conflict Research, Harvard University, Cambridge (Winter).

Weber, E. (1976) *Peasants into Frenchmen*, Stanford University Press, Stanford.

Weber, M. (ed.) (1976 [1923]) *Economy and Society*, G. Roth, New York.

Webster, W. et al. (1997) *Russian Organized Crime*, CSIS, Washington, DC.

Weston, K. (2004) 'The Terrorist Threat: the British Police Response', in *The Changing Face of Terrorism*, ed. R. Gunarantna, Eastern Universities Press, Singapore, pp. 74-82.

Winthrop, W. (1920) *Military Law and Precedents*, rev. 2nd ed., War Department, Washington, DC.

Wolffe, R. & Bailey, H. (2006) 'The 'Islamofascists'', *Newsweek*, pp. 24-25 (11 September).

World Bank (1992) *World Development*, Baltimore.

World Customs Organization (2006) 'The first review: Customs and Counterfeiting 2004', Press Release, [online]. Available at: http://www.wcoomd.org/ie/En/en.html (18 August).

Wriston, W. (1992) *The Twilight of Sovereignty: How the Information Revolution is Transforming our World*, Scribner, New York.

Zacher, M. W. (1995) *Governing Global Networks: International Regimes for Transportation and Communication*, Cambridge University Press, London.

Zaitseva, L. (2002) 'Illicit Trafficking in the Southern Tier and Southern Turkey Since 1999: A Shift from Europe?', *The Nonproliferation Review*, [online]. Available at: http://cns.miis.edu/pubs/npr/vol09/93/93zait.pdf (Fall/Winter).

Zaitseva, L. & Hand, K. (2003) 'Nuclear Smuggling Chains Suppliers, Intermediaries, and End Users', *American Behavioral Scientist*, vol. 46, no. 6, pp. 822–844 (6 February).

ZarQawi, A. M. (2004) 'Pledge of Allegiance to Al Qaeda', *Mu'asker al-Battar*, iss. 21, [online]. Available at: jihadi websites (17 October).

Zawahiri (2005) *Zawahiri letter to Zarqawi*, Released and declassified by the Director for National Intelligence 25 October 2005, [online]. Available at: http://www.dni.gov/release_letter_101105.html (9 July).

Zawahiri (2005) *Al-Zawahiri urges Pakistan quake aid*, [online]. Available at: http://www.Al-Jazeera.net, the English Al-Jazeera website (23 October).

Zawahiri (2006) *Al-Qaeda Deputy Ayman Al-Zawahiri's Latest Video on Al-Jazeera TV*, Aired on Al-Jazeera TV, The Middle East Media Research Institute (trans) (30 January).

INDEX

For Product Safety Concerns and Information please contact our EU representative GPSR@taylorandfrancis.com Taylor & Francis Verlag GmbH, Kaufingerstraße 24, 80331 München, Germany

Batch number: 10726410

Printed by Printforce, the Netherlands